Receive One

Metropolitan of Pergamon
JOHN D. ZIZIOULAS

Receive One Another

– 101 Sermons –

Edited by
Bishop Maxim Vasiljević of Western America

Translated by
Rev. Fr. Gregory Edwards, Ph.D.

Sebastian Press 2023

Published by
St. Sebastian Press
Western American Diocese

Originally published in Greek
Μητροπολίτης Περγάμου Ἰωάννης Ζηζιούλας,
Ἑκατὸ κηρύγματα (Athens: Ἄρτος Ζωῆς, 2023),
Published with permission of *The John Zizioulas Foundation*

Edited by
Bishop Maxim (Vasiljević)

Prepress & printing
Interklima-grafika, Vrnjci, Serbia

Contemporary Christian Thought Series, number 82

Address all correspondence to:
Sebastian Press
1621 West Garvey Avenue ∴ Alhambra, California 91803
Email: info@sebastianpress.org ∴ Website: www.sebastianpress.org

---

Publishers Cataloging in Publication

Names:	Zizioulas, Jean, 1931- author. | Vasiljević, Maksim, 1968- editor. | Edwards, Gregory, Father, translator.
Title:	Receive one another : 101 sermons / Metropolitan of Pergamon John D. Zizioulas ; edited by Bishop Maxim Vasiljević ; translated by Rev. Fr. Gregory Edwards.
Other titles:	Ekató kirýgmata. English
Description:	Alhambra, California : Sebastian Press, 2023. | Series: Contemporary Christian thought series ; no. 82. | "Originally published in Greek: Ekató kirýgmata (Athens: Ártos Zoís, 2023)"--Title page verso.
Identifiers:	ISBN: 978-1-936773-92-3
Subjects:	LCSH: Zizioulas, Jean, 1931- Sermons. | Orthodox Eastern Church--Sermons. | Orthodox Eastern Church--Doctrines.
Classification:	LCC: BX330 .Z597 2023 | DDC: 252/.019--dc23

To the Holy Patriarchal
and Stavropegic Monastery of
St. John the Baptist in Essex, United Kingdom
μὲ εὐγνωμοσύνη

Contents

Prologue

The sermon is a "ministry" or "priestly service" (Rom 15:16). The word of God differs from every kind of human word, because it aims at transmitting the will of God to man, to revealing and transmitting to man the message of God's love, the assurance that "God is with us" throughout our lives. This is particularly true when the word of God is heard and offered in the context of the Divine Liturgy, in which the Word "takes flesh" and is offered to man for communion. In this context, the sermon must be offered with awe and care to not disturb the worship atmosphere created by the Divine Liturgy.

The sermon is interpretation. The goal of the sermon is to translate the message of the Gospel into the language and concepts of each particular era, centering it on the cultural context of a particular time and place. The foundation of the sermon must always remain the Scripture readings, both on Sundays as well as on the feasts of the saints. This is why the sermon is placed in the Divine Liturgy after the holy readings, as it has been throughout the Church's history from the first centuries, when the catechumens would be dismissed after the readings, just as it is still done today in the Ecumenical Patriarchate as well as among the Roman Catholics and Protestants. Moving the sermon to directly before Holy Communion is an innovation within the Church of Greece, which was introduced only in the 20th century out of zeal for the sermon, which sacrifices the structure of the Eucharist for the teaching and missionary work of the Church. The Divine Liturgy, according to Saint Maximus, is the journey from history to the eschaton, and the sermon brings us again back to history. Thus it constitutes an overturning of the whole concept of the Divine Liturgy and should be corrected as quickly as possible.

The sermon is the "Word of exhortation and consolation" (cf. Heb. 13:22 and 1 Cor 14:3). The censorious sermon, which we hear from many preachers today, has no place in the Divine Liturgy; it disturbs the faithful's peace of soul and focuses primarily on those who do not participate in the Liturgy or to society in general. The Holy Eucharist transmits and "incarnates" God's love and mercy to all, even sinners. It is no accident that, in the eucharistic assemblies, the Apostle Paul says that "prophesying" contributes to "edification and exhortation and comfort to men." The censorious sermon neither "builds up" nor comforts, nor does it transmit "peace," which the celebrant continually calls for. (Saint John Chrysostom's sermons, which are cited as a prototype of the censorious sermon, were delivered outside the Divine Liturgy.)

Finally, *the sermon should focus on man's existential concerns*, and not the constantly changing news cycle. Life, death, love, freedom, and other similar questions which have occupied man for centuries must constitute the core of the sermon's subject matter. The Gospel comes to answer these kinds of questions, and this represents the core of the Holy Eucharist, which according to Saint Ignatius is the "medicine of immortality, the antidote we take in order not to die."

This volume contains one hundred sermons of the one thousand or more that I have preached over 35 years of hierarchical ministry. Some of these were preached at churches in Greece and others at the Holy Monastery of Saint John the Baptist in Essex, England. They all represent the spoken word that was recorded—none of them were in written form. The Artos Zois publishers' initiative to publish these sermons in the current volume was due to the publications manager Stavros Zoumboulakis, to whom I express my warmest gratitude. The fact that an intellectual and author of Stavros Zoumboulakis' stature was interested in my humble offering to the ministry of the Church should constitute another opportunity to be grateful to him. For the not insignificant work of recording, my gratitude turns to Andreas Goulas, an invaluable friend in my life. May God richly bless him with His grace.

This volume is dedicated with gratitude to the Holy Patriarchal and Stavropegic Monastery of St. John the Baptist in Essex, England, where many of these sermons were preached. The love of the sainted founder, of the fathers and sisters of this lively spiritual beehive were for me an invaluable support and a gift from God.

Athens, October 2022
Metropolitan John of Pergamon

Greek Publisher's Preface

The sermon was not at the center of Metropolitan John of Pergamon's theological thought and ecclesiastical praxis. His focus was elsewhere. He saw the sermon as expressing a missionary understanding of the Church, of Protestant origin, which emphasizes attracting followers or creating intentional Christians. According to this understanding, the weight of meaning falls on the pulpit or the lecture hall, to the detriment of the Holy Eucharist. This "pulpit-centric" understanding—as he called it—disturbs the Divine Liturgy and lessens its eschatological intensity. This understanding was brought to Greece by the pietistic organizations and cultivated with zeal. The movement of the sermon to the time right before Holy Communion, on the grounds that that's when the most people are in the church—constitutes, according to Zizioulas, a brazen overturning of the structure and spirit of the Liturgy. He has expressed these views several times in his texts (and even more in discussions). I cite:

> *The sermon is not in view in the liturgical manuscripts. There was, of course, a tradition of giving sermons, but it was not considered obligatory in the ancient Church. Even the sermon must adapt to the eschatological atmosphere and not transpose us from the Kingdom of God to here on earth. Nor must we concern ourselves with the problems of the day, forgetting our real homeland and the real faith of the Church, the Kingdom of God. Personally, I consider the sermon to be very difficult and it scares me like little else. For if obstinacy can destroy the eschatological experience that the Divine Liturgy wants to give us, how much more so when the sermons are given as they are today right before Holy Communion, according to this new tradition introduced by the organizations. In my humble opinion,*

> *giving the sermon right before Holy Communion is an outrage, even though everyone has accepted it. It does violence to the structure of the Divine Liturgy, overturning it. For the Church is doing something else at that time; it is not teaching.*[1]

I discussed this issue with him many times and there can be no doubt that His Eminence was not only upset with having the sermon right before Holy Communion, but more generally he was skeptical of the sermon. I agree that the sermon's correct place is after the Scripture readings, although I don't consider it an "outrage" to move it to another time. However, I believe, *contra* Zizioulas, that the sermon is extremely important and I even told him that the sermon is a mystery, the sacrament of the Word of God, and that its place *par excellence* is within the Divine Liturgy. Outside the Liturgy, it is a lecture or Bible study. Inasmuch as His Eminence attributed great significance—always or only recently?—to the post-Resurrectional appearances of Christ, I resorted to citing His appearance to the disciples on the road to Emmaus (Lk 24:13-35), where He explained what the Scriptures said about Him, "starting from Moses and all the prophets." The disciples recognized Him in the breaking of the bread because they had previously heard Him open the Scriptures to them and their hearts burned within them. The Word and the Eucharist are inextricably bound, the one not being understandable without the other. His Eminence was unmoved by my argument. He did not want to see the essence of the argument, focusing instead on the content and quality of the sermons heard in the various churches and the time during the Liturgy in which they were preached. Who can disagree that the overwhelming majority are unacceptable? Nevertheless, whatever His Eminence's views on the sermon, he did not refuse to preach. He was not a systematic preacher and despite his unique episcopal ministry—without a see or flock—he nonetheless preached. During his years as a bishop, His Eminence estimated that he had given over 1000 sermons!

[1] Metropolitan John of Pergamon, *Εὐχαριστίας ἐξεμπλάριον* (Megara, Mazi: Holy Monastery of St. Paraskevi, 2006), pp. 126–127 [in Greek]. See also pp. 26–27, 85, 137, 220 (n. 58).

We met regularly at the house of his doctor and close friend Georgios Papageorgiou, where we openly discussed different topics. His Eminence relished the discussion and would get annoyed at those who had no objections to anything. He needed interlocutors rather than followers. One evening I proposed to him (without much hope) that we publish some of his sermons at Artos Zois in the "Sermon Library" series. After initially voicing a few reservations, he accepted immediately out of love for the subject, although he felt it would not win the proper attention. He gave me more than a hundred sermons, after which he began to kindly pressure me to publish as quickly as possible, without understanding how much work was needed to transform these rough drafts into a book. I selected the title "One Hundred Sermons" myself (which is why I rounded off the number), which he accepted without hesitation. I asked him to write a prologue, which he sent me on October 21, 2022, and which expresses his appreciation for the sermon to a greater extent than one would expect from Zizioulas. He accepted that the word of the sermon was a ministry that assured people of God's love, particularly when "it is heard and offered in the context of the Divine Liturgy, in which the Word 'takes flesh' and is offered to man for communion." He added that its purpose was to "translate the message of the Gospel into the language and concepts of each particular era, centering it on the cultural context of a particular time and place." This prologue brought me great joy and I let him know that. Nevertheless, it would be a misunderstanding of my comments above to suggest that his positive evaluation of the sermon in the prologue was somehow due to my discussions with him. I don't believe any such thing. I do believe, however, that it was due to the very fact of publishing his sermons. Publishing by itself was a recognition of the sermon and the prologue expressed exactly this appreciation.

We believe in a God Whom we speak to and Who speaks to us; He addresses us and we address Him. In the Liturgy, we hear the Word of God—or better—we hear the dialogue between God and man that exists in the Scriptures. The Scripture readings are located at a certain point in the Liturgy, and this alone means that the sermon has a liturgical place and value. This was believed by the early Church, to whom we owe the prayer that is read to this day before the reading of the Gospel—but which unfortunately is read silently in most churches—which asks God to "open the eyes of our mind that we may comprehend the proclamations of your Gospel." The sermon comes precisely to aid this understanding. In one of the oldest liturgical books, the *Sacramentary of Serapion* (middle 4th c.), there is a prayer before the Scripture readings and another prayer "after rising up from the sermon." I quote here an excerpt from the former (according to F. E. Brightman's 1900 edition):

> *I pray you to send the Holy Spirit into our minds and grant us to learn the Holy Scriptures from the Holy Spirit and interpret them purely and properly, for the benefit of all the people here present.*[2]

The Metropolitan of Pergamon, who himself attended to the Word of God because the Word held meaning first of all in his own life, interpreted it in his sermons "purely and properly" for us all, for the common benefit of the people of God. We are grateful to him!

Stavros Zoumboulakis

Postscript

The Metropolitan Elder John of Pergamon departed in peace on February 2, 2023, on the feast of the Presentation. He was not able to hold this book in his hands. His prologue has thus become a farewell. May his memory be eternal!

[2] Panteleimon E. Rodopoulos, *The Sacramentary of Serapion*, Thessaloniki, 1967, p. 116.

1.
1st SUNDAY OF LUKE
"They left everything and followed Him" (Lk 5:1–11)

The passage we just heard, my dear brothers and sisters, is shocking. Beside the Lake of Gennesaret, the Lord calls his first disciples, Peter, James, and John, who will form the nucleus of the twelve disciples. They will be the ones around him throughout his earthly life, as well as in the Kingdom of God. And He calls these disciples in a miraculous way.

The disciples were fishermen, and all night long they tried to fish, but they couldn't catch anything. Then the Lord said to them: "Try again, go further out to catch fish." And Peter replied: "We've been trying all night and nothing is happening, but because you say so, we'll do it." Miraculously, they caught so many fish that they couldn't fit them all in the boat, so they had to fill other boats as well. Then Peter, dazzled, shocked, fell at Christ's feet and said to him: "Depart from me, for I am a sinful man, O Lord!" The Apostle Peter's shock, which is also the first miracle of the Lord's earthly life, is followed by another shock—our own. And I would like to pursue this thought, my beloved brothers and sisters, because it is quite instructive for us. The other shock of which I am speaking is that, after all this, after this miracle, the Lord calls these three men to follow Him. And "they left everything and followed Him." This, if we think about it, is truly shocking.

When it says "they left everything," it means that they first left the boat and the nets. In other words, they abandoned the means by which they lived. It is like saying that they left the factory they worked in or the tools they used for a living. They also left their families. In his recounting of this story, the evangelist Matthew provides more detail into what happened and says that "they immediately left their nets [...] and their father" (Mt 4:20). They left their families! And the Apostle Peter was married. He left his family and followed Christ. Imagine leaving your profession, your job, your family and following someone into the unknown. Where is he going, what awaits him? But the text also indicates something more. They leave behind their logic, because, it tells us, they "immediately" left everything. They didn't say "Let's think about it. Let's sleep on it and decide tomorrow," as any reasonable person would say. No! Without a second thought they left everything to follow Jesus. Therefore, they even sacrifice their logic. And ultimately, as their lives prove, they sacrificed themselves with a martyr's death.

One wonders, my beloved brothers and sisters, why the Lord asked all these hard things from his disciples. Did it have to be so difficult? Isn't this inhumane and cruel, to ask another to leave his profession, his family, his logic, and to surrender to the will of another and, ultimately, to surrender his life as well?

These questions arise in the mind of every reasonable person. However, there is nothing in what the Lord does and in what He allows to happen that does not have its own logic, its own reason. Why, then, must the Lord's disciples abandon everything?

First, my beloved brothers and sisters, Christ Himself left everything. He emptied himself of the glory of His divinity. He became a man, humbled Himself, sacrificed Himself. He sacrificed His own will for his Father's will. It is, therefore, something that he did not ask of others without having done it Himself.

But why should he undergo all this humiliation and self-denial? Here, then, my beloved brothers and sisters, we enter into a deep theological interpretation of this event. With this abandonment of everything, both Christ Himself and those who followed Him reversed the course and attitude of the first man, who abandoned God and relied on himself, on his logic, on his strength, and in this way he lost communion with God, and the tragic event of our Fall occurred. Man would never be able to overcome this, would never be able to redeem himself from this, unless this course were reversed. And instead of man relying on himself and his own strength, instead of placing his security in earthly and perishable things, in money, in profession, in anything else, he now had to abandon all these and turn with absolute trust to God. It was, therefore, necessary for man to go through this reversal of his way of life. To give up his selfishness, to give up this attachment to what is transitory in this life, to trust God again so that, if God calls him to take a leap of faith into the void, he will have no doubt that God will protect him. This is the essence of faith. Faith is not a simple thing, it is not easy, it is not simply declaring that God exists. Even the demons know this and confess it, says Saint James. It is faith to take this leap simply because God is asking you to. It is faith to reach the point of abandoning yourself and everything you have, and placing your security in the God Who calls you.

My beloved brothers and sisters, this must sound not only excessive but also absurd. Think about it! To leave one's family, to leave one's profession, to leave everything one has and to leave oneself to God. We have found a thousand ways to avoid this. And those of us who consider ourselves good Christians never get there. Some of us even use logic to find various ways to justify avoiding this self-denial. However, it is not possible to explain what we see the Lord's disciples do other than to say that it involved a total commitment and abandonment of the self, what our Elder Sophrony called abandoning ourselves to the point of self-hatred. This, of course, sounds not only extreme but also completely antithetical to our contemporary culture, to our daily lives. Today, far from abandoning everything, our culture calls each of us to live by continually adding to what we already have. And so man accumulates goods, and he goes to find his happiness but doesn't, so he accumulates more things… And while in fact he enjoys a life of real wealth, he does not find his happiness and his satisfaction. Nevertheless, this is the ideal of our time. And for this reason, this message in today's Gospel passage is illogical for modern man; it is unacceptable. So why does the Church promote this? Why does the Gospel continue to be preached by the Church in this original form without modifying it to make it more acceptable?

First, my beloved brothers and sisters, because, as excessive and impossible as this may seem for man, there were and are people, apart from the disciples of the Lord, who make it happen in their lives. They are all the saints of our Church. The saints of our Church reached the point of self-abandonment, and the martyrs the point of giving their lives. And the righteous, through a struggle of abandoning their will, reached a state of self-crucifixion, from which they found the way to follow God and His will. And, therefore, the Church gives us examples of people who made this unimaginable sacrifice of abandoning everything. These the saints of our Church, therefore, are the measure by which we are called to be measured. And this makes us feel humiliated. When we think that we are so far behind them and not capable of reaching the point of giving up everything, then we understand not only that we are sinners but also that we are the worst sinners of all, and we do not judge or criticize anyone, because we understand that we are far from this measure. When we compare ourselves with this measure of the saints, then we try, to the extent we can, to approach it. We may not reach the absolute level where they are, but in our daily life, in every detail of our life, we can bring before us their example. When, within a family, there is a conflict of wills, "will it be mine or yours?", let us think of the saints. And we may not reach the point of completely abandoning our own will, but let's make an effort. And by abandoning our own will for the sake of the other, we will keep love and peace and unity in the family. If divorces are on the rise today, this is precisely because the two wills collide, and neither of them gives way to the other. And this applies to our daily life. So if we do not reach the point of abandoning everything, like the disciples of the Lord and the saints, let us try every time to leave something of ourselves, in order to draw closer to the other. Whatever it is, whether it is a material good that we relinquish to give to someone else, whether it is our opinion—which is man's greatest problem, which we do not want to give up—or anything else within this spirit of self-sacrifice, let us be sure, my beloved brothers and sisters, that our world becomes better, and our lives become more blessed. Therefore, even if we do not reach the level of the saints, we will still experience a taste of this holiness. With this, we place our hope in God's mercy, that He will draw us near Him even though we have not achieved perfection.

These, my friends, are shocking things the gospel passage tells us.

I repeat that it is very difficult to accept it, but let us be absolutely certain that this and only this path is what man needs, today and always, to be able to rid himself of everything that the Fall of man has accumulated in our lives—enmity, hatred, conflicts, selfishness, and even death itself. Because death is also a manifestation of our distance from God.

So, my beloved brothers and sisters, let us look at the saints of the Church with these two dispositions: First, let us ask for their intercession, their grace, so that we can follow their example. And secondly, let us make every effort to avoid the temptation to promote ourselves and rely on ourselves and on the goods of this world. Following this path, this way of existence, the mercy of the Lord will accompany us all the days of our lives, until we are accounted worthy through the intercessions of the saints to reach the Kingdom of God. This I pray for all of us. Amen.

At the Holy Monastery of Saint John the Baptist, Essex, England
September 25, 2016

2.
3rd SUNDAY OF LUKE
The victory over death (Lk 7:11–16)

The Gospel passage we just heard, my dear brothers and sisters, describes a scene full of cruelty, pain and tragedy.

It is about the death of a young man, an only son, whose mother was accompanying to his final resting place. A mother who was herself a widow, which means that she had already tasted the bitter cup of death. And there was "a large crowd." And there the Lord appears and performs the miracle we just heard about, the miracle of resurrecting the dead.

This simple narration contains, my beloved brothers and sisters, the entire meaning of the Gospel. The whole meaning and purpose for which the Lord came into the world. Because the Lord did not come into the world to be a great teacher; many teachers have passed through history. He did not come to be an example of virtue. He came to save man from the last enemy, which is death. Because man, my brothers and sisters, man has not received anything more precious than deliverance from death, and this is the thing that God alone (and no one else) can give him.

Death is inherent within our createdness. It is something we cannot avoid, because we were born mortal, God made us mortal, he did not make us immortal. Only God is immortal, "who alone has immortality" (1 Tim 6:16), as the Apostle Paul says.

But, while he created us mortals, he wanted us to remain immortal. And he wanted to give us the same immortality that He Himself has. And for this reason He created man free, so that he could bring this whole world that was subject to death into communion with God, the immortal God, and so that God's creation could in this way be freed from death and live eternally.

However, man decided with his freedom to declare himself god and in this way to bring the whole creation, together with himself, before death.

For it was not possible for a mortal creature, such as man, to bestow immortality. Thus was born in the hearts of men a nostalgia for immortality, a nostalgia for eternity, a desire for immortality, and indignation against death.

And that is why the Lord came in today's passage and, it says, "had compassion on her." He shared man's pain and indignation against death. God does not want death. God does not want man to suffer from death. He wants man to be immortal. And this is why the Lord came with this ultimate goal: to give man his immortality.

And today's passage, this miracle of the resurrection of the young man of Nain, is precisely an indication, a model of the victory over death. The Lord wants to declare this victory over death to us with today's miracle. Let us observe, then, how the victory over death is achieved.

First, as the passage we heard demonstrates, the Lord has power over death. With one word—by giving a command to the dead young man—he gives life. But that's not all. "He touched," it says, "the bier."[1] Why? Did his word not suffice? It wasn't enough to demonstrate that it is impossible for a dead body to receive life, if it doesn't come into contact, physical contact, with God Himself.

The Lord thus established the condition for defeating death. The first prerequisite is our belief that the Lord can defeat death and, second, our communion with Him—even, I would say, physical communion with Him. This physical communion infuses life. And it is this physical communion that left us the mystery of the Eucharist. This is the way to defeat death. Communion with the very body of Christ, to allow it to touch us, for us to touch Him, to touch his body, to embrace his body. To become one with his body. In this way, my brothers and sisters, the Lord demonstrates that a resurrection that does not include the body is not a resurrection. And a resurrection that includes the body must assuredly have physical communication with God. As strange as this may sound, the dominant view that the body is bad, that we don't need a body to communicate with God, is an enormous mistake.

[1] Lk 7:14.

The Lord touches the dead young man. His body touches the body of the dead. And in this way He gives it life. And he gives this life to him in the name of the Resurrection of His own body. If the body of the Lord is not resurrected, death cannot be defeated. And if the body of Christ does not overcome death, the human body cannot achieve immortality.

And there's something even more important. The Lord has no need for the Resurrection of His own body. If He resurrects His own body, it is because His ultimate purpose is to resurrect our bodies. And that is why a human body is resurrected, so that in this way He can demonstrate to us that his own Resurrection is nothing but our own resurrection. And it is a resurrection, my brothers and sisters, of bodies, not a resurrection of souls. It is necessary, therefore, to see the Resurrection of Christ as a prerequisite for our own resurrection. And as the Apostle Paul also says, "But if there is no resurrection of the dead, then Christ is not risen" (1 Cor 15:13). It makes no sense for Christ to rise if our own death is not defeated. The Resurrection of Christ is prefigured in this miracle that we saw today.

And this miracle, my brothers and sisters, contains in its narration a detail that is very touching. As soon as the Lord resurrected the young man, says the evangelist, "he gave him to his mother."

What do you do with resurrection, what do you do with immortality, if you do not share it with others? The resurrection of a body, as an individual, has no meaning. The resurrection takes place in order for him to enjoy the presence and life of others who love him, like his mother above all, but also all those who live in his love. Resurrection and immortality without love, therefore, have no meaning. It is an individual resurrection, which means another death.

"And he gave him to his mother."

And in this way the Lord reveals that in our resurrection, no matter how much immortality God grants us, we will not be isolated individuals. We will be a communion of persons; we will be bound by love. Because death aims precisely not only at the dissolution of the body but also at the dissolution of relationships of love. That's where it hits; that's where it wants to do damage. And it is precisely there that the Lord comes to heal, to heal man from death, giving him love.

Now we can understand, my brothers and sisters, why it is so important to be in communion with the Church, in order to gain victory over death. No matter how holy we are as individuals, no matter how many individual virtues we may have, it is not possible to defeat death on our own. To defeat death, we must be placed in a communion of love with others. In other words, we must go through the communion of love that is the Church in order to defeat death.

It is very important, my brothers and sisters, to remember what the holy fathers formulated, namely that outside the Church, there is no salvation. There is no salvation from death.

There may be salvation from our individual sins, there may be salvation from anything that concerns us as individuals, but victory over death is not an individual matter. All humanity will be resurrected, death will be defeated for all people, and indeed for all creation, and thus we will enjoy the presence of the other eternally.

This is precisely what the Church offers us. And it offers us this, my brothers and sisters, first and foremost in the Divine Liturgy.

And what is the Divine Liturgy? It is the space in which the separation brought about by death is overcome, and the dead and the living are united, communing with each other in the body of Christ.

Anyone who believes that God has defeated death knows that in the Divine Liturgy we celebrate the feast of our immortality. We perform the sacrament of the victory over death. And we cannot do it as individuals. We cannot attain immortality as individuals. We celebrate it only as a community, as a Church. That is why we do not attend the Divine Liturgy as individuals; we go to meet each other, as we will meet each other in the Kingdom of God, when death will have been defeated.

So these are the profound meanings of today's otherwise simple gospel passage. It is the message that death is intolerable; it is man's last enemy. Death is only tolerable in one case: when our life is given freely and out of love for someone else. Then love conquers death. He who gives his life for another does not remain dead. He lives eternally, like the martyrs whom our Church celebrates. And this is why he who sacrifices his life for the sake of God and for the sake of others wins his life.

In no other case, however, is death tolerable. When the Lord said to the widow in today's passage, "Do not weep," he did not say it in the sense that death is nothing and therefore not worth crying about. Instead, he says "Don't cry because I will resurrect your child," because death does not have the last word, because there is victory over death, and I will give you back your child.

In the face of death, our only consolation is that we will take our loved ones back again and see them again. And the Church, my beloved, has nothing more valuable to give than the sure knowledge that death will be defeated and that, just as the living and the dead enjoy communion in the Church, so will it be in the Kingdom of God, when the last enemy will have been defeated. Amen!

Holy Church of Saint George, Karykis
October 6, 2002

3.
3rd SUNDAY OF LUKE
The resurrection of the young man in Nain (Lk 7:11–16)

As we heard, my beloved brothers and sisters, the Lord comes face to face today with man's most tragic problem, death. And not simply with death, which we would somehow call normal, but with an irrational death. He sees, as soon as he enters the city of Nain, that a young man is being buried by his mother. It would be normal the other way around, to bury the young man's mother, but this passage wants to particularly emphasize the absurdity of death.

Death is absurd. Absurd, whether in its normal form or the tragic form presented to us in today's Gospel (Lk 7:11–16), because it is in fact unnatural. God created man for eternity, for immortality; he was not created for death. Death was a derailment from man's natural course, because man, in moving away from God and proclaiming himself god, was cut off from the only source of immortality, which is God. Only God is immortal by nature.

In his love, however, God wanted man to also become immortal by grace, by uniting with God and acquiring immortality through this communion. But man preferred to proclaim himself god, and to disobey God's will, which resulted in death. That is, to be cut off from the only source of immortality which is God. Thus, man wound a crooked path, thinking that what he was doing was natural, while in reality going against his true nature, against his true desire and inclination, which was immortality.

Death, therefore, entered man's life because of his disobedience, his proclamation that he was god. Man then became unfulfilled. Within him lived this inclination towards immortality, which God gave him by forming him in his image and likeness. However, he could not experience this immortality, because he had been cut off from its only source, which is God. And thus man became a tragic being, who cannot divest himself of his desire for immortality, but also cannot realize it alone. So, this creature that God created for such glory and honor entered this tragic situation, death. But God did not leave man in the situation he was in; he was watching him and wanted to free him from it.

We heard today in the gospel passage that when the Lord saw this funeral of the young man and his mother grieving and suffering, "he had compassion on her" (Lk 7:13). In this way, he demonstrates God's mercy towards man. He does not want to leave man in this situation. He wants to save him, to redeem him, and for this purpose he sent prophets, and gave his Law in the Old Testament to bring man back to Himself, and thus to give him immortality.

Finally, God sent his own Son, because this was the only way to reverse the first man's course away from God. And man, incorporated into the Son of God and united again with God, can now attain his immortality.

Thus, the Lord, face to face with death, exercised his power over death. And with boldness and strength, he addressed the dead man and said to him: "Young man, I say to you, arise" (Lk 7:14). Get up, it is my command that death be defeated. And with this miracle, my beloved brothers and sisters, the Lord did not want to simply demonstrate His power, that He is God and can defeat death. He wanted, first, to demonstrate His love and His mercy, because He does not want to see man tyrannized by this last enemy, as the Apostle Paul calls death. And secondly, the Lord wanted to foreshadow his Resurrection, and the resurrection of all people.

My beloved brothers and sisters, today's passage with the resurrection of the young man delivers a great message about the Resurrection of Christ, the message that death will be defeated. It will be defeated by the Resurrected Lord, who, through His Resurrection, will not only defeat his own human death, but will also resurrect all men on the last day.

There is one more detail, my dear brothers and sisters, in this passage, which I think has special significance. The evangelist writes that when the Lord resurrected the child, "He presented him to his mother" (Lk 7:15). Death is not something that concerns this person who is dying. Death is something that damages love, the bonds between people, and this is perhaps the most tragic. That is why death is actually synonymous with the interruption of love and communion; it is synonymous with hate. A person who does not love has already chosen death. Because death aims at this, at cutting the thread of communion with others. It wants to tear down love.

So, when we ourselves impede love, when we ourselves break communion with others, we choose death. Love is the other side of immortality. Immortality, my beloved brothers and sisters, without love is torture; it is suffering. If the young man was not given back to his mother, if the relationship of love that was wounded by death was not restored, then his resurrection would have no meaning.

The resurrection of all people, my beloved brothers and sisters, when God determines it, will not simply be the resurrection of isolated individuals, but will be the restoration of the communion of people with each other and with God. It will be what we call the "Kingdom of God." The Kingdom of God is the communion of all with God in one body. This, my beloved brothers and sisters, is the answer to the problem of death for us who believe in Christ.

In the gospel passage today, the Lord addressed the young man's mother and said to her: "Don't cry." Of course, it is difficult not to cry when faced with the death of a loved one. We may cry in the face of death, we may be sad, because, as I said, death damages love, but we will never believe that death has the last word and can destroy the bond that love creates.

Love, true love, between people cannot be defeated by death; rather, it will defeat death. This is the message of the Resurrection of Christ. So we can cry in death and be sad, but not "as others do, who have no hope" (1Thess. 4:13). We, brothers and sisters, do not believe that death will be defeated either by science or by knowledge, nor by any of the various other means by which man tries to defeat death. For us, death will be defeated by the Risen Christ. As it was defeated in His person, so it will be defeated in all of us, because, as I said, love will have the last word.

So, until our dead are resurrected and reunited with us, we experience this victory over death in the Church, in the communion of the saints, where we are united with our loved ones, even if they have left this world. What we do at every Divine Liturgy, my beloved brothers and sisters, is a celebration of the Resurrection, which will reunite us with our loved ones again, something we get a foretaste of even now, as we share communion with them in the body of Christ.

With Holy Communion, therefore, with the Holy Eucharist, with the entire Divine Liturgy, which we celebrate with such splendor, we declare victory over death with the Resurrection. And in all these ways we declare our faith that our bond with our loved ones was not broken because of death, and that we continue to be united with them until the resurrection of all takes place, and God makes us worthy to live together in His Kingdom. Amen.

September 10, 2010

4.
4th SUNDAY OF LUKE
(The Fathers of the 7th Ecumenical Council)
The fruition of the word of God (Lk 8:5–15)

Today's Sunday is dedicated to the memory of the holy fathers who convened the Seventh Ecumenical Council in Nicaea to declare that the icons we venerate in Church are sacred and holy. In this way, they refuted those who preached against icons in the Church.

And on the occasion of this feast of the fathers, the Church chose the gospel reading that we have just heard, which speaks of the Lord as the good sower, who sows the word everywhere. This word, however, does not bear fruit everywhere. And just as the Lord sowed the word when he was in this life, in this world, so also the fathers of the Church sow the word of God. But in this case also, the word of God does not always bear fruit.

And the question that arises is under what conditions can the word of God bear fruit? Why doesn't it bear fruit everywhere? The Lord, in the Gospel passage we heard, when his disciples asked him what the meaning of the parable was, answered this question: under what conditions can the word of God bear fruit?

The first and basic condition, says the Lord, is that the seed falls on good ground. Human choice, human freedom is assuredly needed. God does not force us to accept what He tells us. He leaves it to our freedom to accept or reject not only what He tells us, but also His very existence. And there are many people who do not want to hear the word of God. They reject Him in advance. They are the ones who are completely indifferent to what God wants from us. And the Lord likens them to those who are under the influence of Satan. Because Satan is the one who constantly denies the recognition of God and His will. Those who reject Him don't question whether God's will or God's word is good or not. The fact that it comes from God is reason to reject it. And there are many people who do not want to hear anything that has to do with God. We find such people among us all the time. If the word of God falls on these people, it will be lost. The earth is such that it cannot receive the seed and the word cannot bear fruit. Despite this, the Lord and His Church, the holy fathers, continue to sow this word, even spreading it onto this land where it will not grow. Because, in order to grow, it needs our free consent.

Another reason why the seed of the word of God does not grow, the Lord tells us, is because, in order for it to grow, we must not be absorbed by the cares of this life. When we are absorbed by how we will increase our wealth, and how we will overcome the difficulties of this life, then the word of God cannot bear fruit, because what preoccupies us is ourselves, our own problems, and we do not want to hear what God wants and what God says.

And another category in which the word of God does not grow is, says the Lord, those people who accept the word of God temporarily, but when temptations and difficulties appear, then they lose their faith. Thus, the word of God cannot grow where there is little faith, where people doubt whether God can really, in the problems and difficulties they face, be present to help them and not only that, but even turn those difficulties into blessings in their lives. Because the temptations and difficulties of life can become an occasion for our salvation. When man accepts these temptations and difficulties with trust in God, then the word of God bears fruit in him.

And yet another condition for the word of God to bear fruit, the gospel passage tells us today, is our patience. It bears fruit in patience. The word of God does not immediately show its results. The seed of the word of God falls into the earth, in history, and we do not see any results. And we think that His words will never bear fruit. Yet we need patience! Patience because, just as every tree needs time to grow, so the word of God, with the measures that God Himself uses, may not immediately show us its results. However, this does not mean that it will not bear fruit somehow.

Thus, in this world, throughout the ages, the seed of the word of God falls and sometimes it bears fruit, and sometimes it does not bear fruit. However, there will always be some fruit that we don't see. Because the word of God does not like noise, it does not like publicity. It is a peaceful word; it is often even a word of silence. And in this hum, in this noise that we all make today, with all of us trying to speak and say something, to impose our views, the word of God often comes silently, without publicity. And if sometimes the Church itself falls into the temptation of publicity, it is not consistent with the nature of the word of God; the word of God needs patience, peace in the hearts of people. The word does not come to upset the world; it comes to bring a message of peace and love.

So, my brothers and sisters, in today's noisy world, this gospel passage comes to tell us that our hearts must always be ready to receive the word of God. May we accept Him even in the difficult moments of our lives—always trusting that God directs our lives, and that whatever happens to us always comes with God's blessing. God can bless any adversity in our life and turn it into good.

The word of God as a seed is not just words, it is the presence of the very face of God in our lives, the face of Christ; it is a seed that bears fruit when it falls into history and dies and rises and gives food for the world to live.

The Church has preserved this word of God throughout the centuries and it tries to preach this word to the hearts of the people. "He who has ears to hear, let him hear," said the Lord at the end of the parable. Because we may have ears but that doesn't mean that we hear. We may have closed them in a thousand ways, like those I mentioned earlier. So let's open our ears and our hearts to the word of God and let's allow this word to bear fruit, because this word is that which will save us and the whole world. Amen!

October 16, 2005

5.
4th SUNDAY OF LUKE
(Fathers of the 7th Ecumenical Council) Lk 8:5–15

In an age in which human speech is over-produced, in which people are competing to see who can speak the loudest, whose opinion will prevail, into this age comes today's gospel passage, my beloved brothers and sisters, speaking to us of another word, the word of God.

From the time God became man and His word was expressed with a human voice, from the time the Lord, before His ascension, commanded his disciples to preach the Gospel to the whole world, the divine word—the word of God—and the human speech have been so interwoven that often an important question arises: what is the real word of God? Does the word or logic of man overlap with the word of God? Do we, who preach the word of God, often preach nothing but our own word, human logic? The Church must be constantly vigilant against this, my beloved brothers and sisters, and we always need to be careful lest the human word, man's logic, overshadow the word of God. Of course, it is true that the word of God must always be expressed through human speech.

What is the difference between man's word and God's word? The first and great difference, my dear brothers and sisters, is that the Word of God is not words, it is a person. One of the most important points that the Gospel emphasizes is that the Word, about which the ancient world talked so much, became man, took flesh, and is identified with one person, the second person of the Holy Trinity. Thus we can no longer speak about the Word without referring to a person. A word that is not personal is a word that addresses our logic, a word that leads to meanings of our mind. The word as a person, however, always leads us to a relationship with the other. It refers us to someone else. And so the word of God as a person creates personal relationships. Only then is God's word confirmed as God's word and not human, when it creates real, true, personal relationships. That is why the word of God is, my beloved brothers and sisters, inextricably intertwined with love. We cannot speak of truth without love, and we cannot speak of a word of God which does not lead us to love. And this means more specifically, for us Orthodox, that the word of God leads us to the Church. It is there that we will meet the other. There that we will unite with the other. Where we will find God through our communion with others. The word of God therefore creates a gathering of people, creates communion, creates a Church. Outside the Church there is no word of God. It is simply a human word, human reason. So, when the word of God passes through love and reaches the Church, then it becomes and proves to be a real seed, as we heard in the Gospel passage. It is sown like a seed. And what is the characteristic of the seed? That it dies and in its place another existence bears fruit. So the seed, the word of God as a seed, creates in the Church what we call a "body," the body of Christ. This body now nourishes us with the word of God as the Holy Eucharist. So our faith, as Saint Irenaeus says, and the Eucharist are identical. It is one and the same. What we believe is what we experience in the Divine Liturgy; it is the person of Christ which becomes a seed, so that the world may be fed by this seed and live.

And there is another difference, my beloved brothers and sisters, between the human word or logic and the word of God. And that is that, while the human word is comprehended by the human mind, the word of God is not comprehended, but only sketched as an icon. Today our Church honors the memory of the fathers of the Seventh Ecumenical Council, who met in Nicaea to declare that the Church cannot live without icons, without the iconography of the word of God. When the word becomes an image, then many things happen. The most important thing is that now the word does not refer to itself, but beyond itself. The word as an image is referential, pointing in fact to a person. That is why Basil the Great and the fathers of the Seventh Ecumenical Council emphasized the well-known dictum that "the honor given to the icon passes over to the prototype." It passes over! When we venerate an icon, the honor we give it and our relationship to it goes beyond the icon to the person it depicts. Thus the icon becomes a word and the word becomes an icon. This is what our Orthodox Church has experienced throughout the centuries. Because in our churches, my beloved brothers and sisters, the word of God is depicted in the persons of the saints and is sung and hymned. Something happens that goes beyond human logic, the human word. It is something that tries to express the unspeakable, that which human speech cannot express. This is how our Church lived throughout the centuries even when it did not have preachers, as it does today. Most of our ancestors encountered the word of God in the faces of holy icons. With icons they spoke to God and with icons God spoke to them. Through hymnody they spoke to God and God spoke to them through hymnody. They didn't need the words of a preacher, they didn't need the word of God to be mingled with the word of man, human logic. And that, dear brothers and sisters, is how we preserved our Orthodox faith, through the worship of the Church and not through the so-called wisdom and rhetorical skill of the Church's preachers.

My beloved brothers and sisters, in this noisy society in which we live, in which noise pollution, in every form, has polluted our hearing and the air we breathe, in this society we are called to focus on the word of God, we are called to convey in our daily life the ethos of the holy icons, which is an ethos of referring us to the other, an ethos that often leads to silence in order to hear the other's words. Let the voice of the other be heard. It is an ethos that leads us to connect with others, to create what is happening in our Church, a communion of love. This is the word of God. Unfortunately, even today, my dear brothers and sisters, our Orthodoxy tends many times to become an ideology. Yes! We defend the doctrines of our faith, but if we defend them simply as words, it is useless. The doctrines of our faith, of our Church, my dear brothers and sisters, are meant to be experienced by us, and in order to be experienced they must be ecclesiasticized, Churchified, they must become a way of being, like the Church's way of being. Only in this way can we say that we are truly Orthodox. And today, my dear brothers and sisters, we especially need this understanding of the word of God, to understand that Orthodoxy is the Church and not an ideology. Orthodoxy is a gathering of people for the Divine Eucharist; this is Orthodoxy.

And this is precisely what we must experience, my dear brothers and sisters, as much as we can, because it is something that is not limited only to the church. It is something that can be extended outside, to our daily life. An ethos fitting to the word of God, the word of love, the word of personal communion. Let us follow this path, my beloved brothers and sisters, and then the word of God will not fall on stone, it will not fall among thorns, but it will bear fruit and save the world and all of us. Amen!

Holy Church of Saint Irene
Aiolou Street
October 11, 2009

6.
5th SUNDAY OF LUKE
The rich man and Lazarus (Lk 16:19-31)

And besides all this, between us and you a great chasm has been fixed (Lk 16:26)

The greatest tragedy in today's Gospel passage about the rich man,[1] even more painful and more severe than the torments of his hell, was the chasm that he felt between him and God, and also between him and Lazarus, whom he had scorned in this life. Because, my dear brothers and sisters, this chasm, which was opened by man's fall into sin, is man's greatest and most serious problem, the greatest and most serious problem for all of God's creation. God created the world in order for it to be in communion with Him; God wanted His creation to enter into His very life, to deify it, to glorify it. But this had to be done freely, because it is not possible for the beatification, glorification, and deification of creation to take place through force. And this voluntary decision was entrusted to man, a microcosm who includes within himself all of creation and who unites the material and the noetic worlds, who unites creation with God. But man decided not to realize this communion, and the chasm between God and man deepened. The world's greatest tragedy is this chasm between God and the world. This chasm brought with it death. Because death is nothing more than a chasm. A chasm between one man and another, because death separates people; in fact, it even separates the components that make up man, that is, his soul and his body. This chasm of death reigned over the whole of creation and the entire life of man.

But, my dear brethren, the Lord came to bridge this chasm, and to unite, in His Incarnation, that which had been separated.

[1] This sermon was not part of the original Greek edition of this book.

He brought about this union of the created and the uncreated, and bridged the chasm created by man's sin. While the Lord bridged this chasm, man's freedom, which has always continued to exist, maintains this chasm. In our lives, dear brothers and sisters, there is always a great chasm between us and God, and between one another. The rich man in today's parable lived his whole life with a great chasm between him and poor Lazarus. Lazarus was next to him, but a great, unbridgeable chasm separated them. The rich man was unmoved by the plight of this poor man, Lazarus, who was right next to him, and thus he maintained the chasm that distances man from God. Preserving this chasm, he finally found himself face to face with death. Then, my dear brethren, he took this chasm with him, and this chasm eternally condemned him. He wanted a reprieve. He begged Abraham to communicate with him, to at least send someone to his relatives, to relay the message that the chasm in this life leads to an eternal chasm, to never-ending torment, but it was too late; it was not possible to bridge this chasm after his death.

And why was it not possible? Because we must use our freedom to bridge this chasm, to reject it, to want to rectify it, and to fill it in. While we are living in this life, we can bridge these chasms, for as long as we have our bodies, our freedom, and time to repent, we can fill in these chasms that we have created in our lives. This ability, however, does not exist after death. From then on, everything is irreversible. The chasm separating the rich man from Lazarus became, with their deaths, eternal, forever unbridgeable. This is the greatest tragedy for the rich man in the parable.

In the *Sayings of the Desert Fathers*, which are the stories of the ascetics of the desert, there is, my brothers and sisters, a story regarding Saint Makarios of Egypt, who found a skull while walking along a path one day. Tapping it with his staff, he asked it: "Who are you?" And the skull answered: "I am a priest of idols, and I have been condemned to hell." "And how are things down there?" "I will tell you only one thing," said the skull. "We are all bound with our backs to one another, such that we cannot see one another's faces. This is our greatest punishment, that we cannot see each other's faces." In this life, however, my dear brethren, we can see each other's faces, except when we turn our faces away from each other, in which case this state will follow us into eternity, because this is our choice. And God respects our choices, He respects our freedom.

My dear brothers and sisters, we live in a world in which individualism has become the ideal. Everyone looks to see how he can live comfortably in this life, how he can increase his own happiness while being indifferent to the misfortunes of others. Is it possible, my dear brethren, that the current economic crisis that we are experiencing here is the result of this chasm that exists not only between the rich and the poor but between all of us? A chasm that we make no effort to bridge, as we did previous chasms in difficult times. We of the older generation passed through great hardships, but we bridged those chasms by caring for one another, sharing whatever food we had with someone who had none. Our tragedy today, my dear brethren, is not the economic crisis; our tragedy is the chasm, the chasm that separates one from the other to the point that we do not even know the person living right next door to us in our apartment building, whether he is in need of something. I'm not talking about those who live in some far-off place, in countries where they are starving and suffering from thousands of illnesses. I'm simply talking about taking a look around us, at our next-door neighbor. The chasm, my dear brothers and sisters, has grown considerably, and this means that we are already experiencing a foretaste of hell; this is hell. It isn't poverty. Lazarus was poor, but this did not follow him into eternity. He was able to overcome it, after his death; he was able to solve his economic problem, so to speak. Even if we could solve our economic problem, how would it benefit us, when the chasm between us all will condemn us all eternally?

My dear brethren, the Church is the communion of the saints, the community of people, our gathering. Do you see what is happening right now? We have all gathered in the same place. We want, even if only for a moment, briefly, for two or three hours, to bridge the chasm that separates us. This is the Church. And this is why our only consolation in this life is the Church. And especially the Divine Liturgy, which brings us together in the same place in order to share the same food, which is the food God gives us with the body and blood of His very Son. So that we can share the bread, the antidoron, our faces, our joy. This is the world's only hope.

Let us glorify God, my dear brothers and sisters, for the existence of the Church, and for the fact that it helps and will always help people, not to fill their bellies, but to bridge their chasms. Let us, each one of us, make this effort. Let us at least make a beginning with the small chasms that we have with our neighbors, then with our enemies, with those who hurt us, with those who speak ill of us. Let us bridge the chasm, let us be reconciled, let us empathize with those who have not, and share with them whatever we have. If, my dear brothers and sisters, we thus begin, in this life, to bridge the chasms to the best of our ability, then we will find ourselves in the Kingdom of God, where there are no more chasms, where all are united in God. My dear brethren, I pray that the Lord finds all of us worthy of this Kingdom.

Church of the Ascension, Volos
October 30, 2011

7.

6th SUNDAY OF LUKE

Saint Gerasimos of Cephalonia (Lk 8:27–39)

Now doth Cephalonia, with sacred songs of thanksgiving, call upon the multitudes of all the Orthodox Christians to extol the boast and glory of Orthodoxy, the divine and great Gerasimus, who is truly her deliverer and champion, who doth preserve her from all the harm of her foes.[1]

Reverend clergy, honorable leaders, esteemed president of the Association of Cephalonians and Ithacians of Kifissia and the Northern Suburbs, pious Christians—with these words today the holy hymnographer praises the greatest treasure of the island of Cephalonia, he praises the bright star and firm foundation of the mind of the Church, the blessed and great ascetic Gerasimos.

Cephalonia, that historic island, is shining today, drawing like a magnet crowds of believers and pilgrims to receive the grace of Saint Gerasimos, who chose this island over other parts of Greece as the resting place for his body, as well as his blessings and grace.

And Cephalonians from all over the land are celebrating, especially those who live in the northern suburbs of Attica, who today celebrate the memory of Saint Gerasimos with such festive splendor.

I am deeply moved, because at the kind invitation and canonical permission and blessing of your most reverend Archpastor, whom I thank profusely, I am presiding today over this feast and I rejoice together with you, especially with my Cephalonian and Ithacian brothers and sisters, on this joyous festival.

I am especially moved and pleased because today is also the name day of our beloved brother, the Right Reverend Archiman-

[1] Kontakion of Saint Gerasimos of Cephalonia. HTM.

drite Gerasimos, who for many years now with his faithful ministry in the Church and especially in this holy cathedral, has served as an exemplary clergyman and deserves our congratulations and best wishes on today's feast. May Saint Gerasimos intercede for him, and through his prayers, may the Lord give him length of days, health, and strength to continue his valuable contribution to the Church from an even higher position.

The saint whose memory we honor today, my dear brothers and sisters, does not only radiate grace, healing, and intercession for all of us. But he also delivers some very important messages, which we should receive with great care.

The first and most important message is that out of all the treasures that our country and our people have, the treasures that are our saints stand out.

Cephalonia was blessed by God with a history very rich in culture. It has been mentioned since the time of Homer and has many reasons to be proud of its history and culture.

However, perhaps nothing occupies as much attention as the blessing of having the incorruptible body of Saint Gerasimos.

And this proves that weakness, worldly weakness, is much stronger than worldly strength.

An ascetic—a weak man, one who many perhaps would accuse of abandoning the struggle of life and society—comes to offer to the world, to society, more perhaps than anyone else who actively works for the good of the world.

This does not mean, of course, that social activism or any other kind of activism in the world must cease or is of no importance. It means, however, that next to this activism there exists an invaluable offering, which at first glance looks like a departure from the world and history. For man needs to see history and life from a distance.

Only mixed in with the flow of history is not enough. Because history is not formed only from the inside. It is formed when we see it in its entirety and when we even want to transcend it.

And the saints of the Church, and Saint Gerasimos in particular, did exactly this: they withdrew from the world, not to abandon the world, not to despise the world, but to see calmly, outside the constant turmoil in which those of us who live in the world find ourselves. With calmness and an overall perspective.

The saints are therefore necessary within the Church. They are our strength and boast as well as our guides.

And they are necessary, because in this way the space in which we live and the time in which we live are sanctified. And Saint Gerasimos sanctifies the place where his incorruptible body is located, but also the whole world. And he sanctifies time, because even if all the ages pass, he remains a constant star in the darkness of our lives.

In today's Gospel we heard, my brothers and sisters, the miracle of the Lord's healing of the demon-possessed man.

And we all remembered this special gift that God gave to Saint Gerasimos: to heal the demon-possessed. And this prompts us to wonder, why was this gift given to such a saint, to an ascetic?

The answer, my brothers and sisters, is that evil, the demonic in man's life, cannot be defeated by man himself. Evil exists, and it exceeds man's powers. It is a delusion for man to think that in his own way he will exorcise evil and make it disappear from the world. He tries, and he does well, but he constantly finds that the power of evil cannot be stopped by our own efforts.

Problems are solved and new ones are created. The optimism that once prevailed, that man will be able to change this world into a paradise, has already been proven in the last century, with two world wars, to be an unfounded optimism.

There will always be evil and our own powers will never be enough to eradicate it. And consequently the mediation of saints like Saint Gerasimos is needed, the intervention of God is needed, so that we can be freed from the hold of evil in the world.

So, my brothers and sisters, we are receiving many messages from the island of Cephalonia today. And these messages come to a world that has believed too much in its own powers, has almost forgotten that in this noisy world in which we live, we cannot find the right direction for our life and we need to stand up once in a while and reflect. And let us see the saints as models and guides.

The people of Cephalonia are worthy of praise, because they have obviously grasped these messages from Saint Gerasimos.

They have truly appreciated them, because there is no other way to explain their devotion to the person of Saint Gerasimos. Wherever they are, they invoke his help, and they consider nothing more precious on their island than the incorrupt body of Saint Gerasimos. Today, all Cephalonians honor their saint. May the Cephalonians' behavior and attitude be an example to the modern world.

I pray that Saint Gerasimos protect and direct first the island on which he was pleased to lay his incorrupt body, and second the whole world, which is in need of his intercessions.

Congratulations, therefore, to the board of directors, its president, and the members of the Association of Cephalonians and Ithacians of Kifissia and the Northern Suburbs, and I pray that they celebrate this great feast in good health for many years to come.

Holy Metropolitan Church of Saint Demetrius of Kifissia
October 20, 2002

8.
7th SUNDAY OF LUKE
The tragedy of death (Lk 8:40–56)

In today's gospel passage, my beloved brothers and sisters, the Lord works a miracle by healing an ill woman, who suffered for many years since no doctor could heal her. The Lord, however, was not satisfied with only healing, releasing the person from disease, but he proceeded with another miracle to release someone from death.

Death, as the Apostle Paul says, is our last enemy. It is the greatest enemy of man and of all creation. And the Lord came to this world to free man from the bonds of sin, but with the ultimate purpose of freeing him from death.

Why is death so tragic? Why is it so intolerable that God Himself comes into the world to defeat it?

Death is indeed intolerable because it dissolves man's very existence. Man was created by God to be body and soul together—a psychosomatic being. God did not make man only a soul, nor only a body, but he made him a composite of these two elements so that when we say "person" we mean both the soul and the body. Not just the body as biology teaches us. And not only the soul, as unfortunately many people believe, even some Christians. The soul and the body are components of the human being and death strikes precisely at this human existence and dissolves it.

Death is also intolerable, because, my brothers and sisters, it keeps man a slave, a prisoner. It keeps him captive to all the passions we know. All human passions come from the fear of death. From here proceeds our self-love, our struggle to survive. This is where our greed comes from—what we have is not enough for us, we want more because we are insecure, we subconsciously fear death. From here proceeds hatred against others, envy of our brothers, because we feel that their own advancement and their own existence diminish us, threaten us. That is where avarice and the collection of many goods come from—we are afraid that we will not have enough to secure our life. From here proceeds the love of pleasure, because man uses this to enjoy life as much as he can, without understanding that life slips right out of his hands when death, lurking nearby, finally wins.

This is why death is intolerable and why the Lord comes to destroy it, as can be seen in today's Resurrectional Dismissal Hymn (*apolytikion*): "the joyful message of the Resurrection."[1] Because death is destroyed by God with the Resurrection of the Lord. See here how the Lord's Resurrection acquires meaning through our faith and through the Gospel.

Death is further intolerable, I would say, for a much more important reason. It damages and dissolves—or tries to dissolve—love. Death separates people and is intertwined with individuality. Death does not tolerate communion between people and through the ages these two things—death and love—have been in conflict. The Holy Scriptures say that love is "as strong as death" (Song 8:6). Our brothers in the West have emphasized rather more the Cross of the Lord. Of course, the Cross of the Lord, as we will see in a moment, is also intertwined with the victory of death, but they gave the interpretation more that God sent his Son not so much to defeat death as to redeem us from our sins, to free us from the guilt of our sins. However, the tradition of the fathers of the Church puts all the emphasis on God's ultimate purpose in the Incarnation and the victory over death. Athanasios the Great says that God could not bear to see the human race tyrannized by death and that is exactly why we celebrate the Resurrection more than anything else. Ultimately, for us, the Resurrection of the Lord is what redeems us. Because if we are redeemed from everything else and death is not defeated, we do not have real redemption and real salvation.

But how is death defeated? The Lord explains it to us. Here, of course, applies the response recorded today by the Evangelist Luke, that "they laughed at him" (Lk 8:53).

[1] Tone 4.

Who accepts the Resurrection of the Lord? Perhaps many will accept it, but regarding our bodily resurrection, as the Apostle Paul preached in the Pnyx, the sages of Greece chuckled.

Today in the Gospel we heard "they laughed at him" when the Lord told them that Jairus' daughter was not dead but sleeping. However, faith in the Resurrection, my brothers and sisters, is a basic presupposition for defeating death. The Lord trampled upon death and promised us that, with His Resurrection, we won't die but rather sleep, awaiting the final resurrection. Death is defeated when we follow the way in which it was defeated by the Lord. The more one willingly suffers death, the more one conquers death. The Lord's Cross was a victory over death because it was a voluntary death for the sake of others.

The Apostle Paul says that we are called daily to put to death our self and our members. Christ is the path to victory over death. This is precisely what we sing in our "Christ is risen" hymn: "trampling down death by death." We must traverse the path of death, putting to death ourselves and above all our self-love and passions, in order to love and no longer fear death. Otherwise, death wins by cultivating fear of death. When these things happen, death is defeated within us—the death that we take up. As all the saints, martyrs, and righteous attest, death is defeated with the death of our passions and primarily our self-love, with our sacrifice for others unto death, giving ourselves to God unto death.

Death is also defeated in one more way. I told you before that death aims at love. It wants to damage love and communion between people.

Here then, the Lord, wanting to grant us the power to defeat death, offers us the Church. The Church—primarily through the Holy Eucharist and the Divine Liturgy, which we now celebrate—is the communion in which death is defeated.

Here, then, is where the Lord, wanting to give us the possibility to defeat death, offers us the Church. The Church is the communion in which death is defeated—above all with the Eucharist in the Divine Liturgy, as we celebrate at this time. When death thinks that it has managed to separate us from our loved ones, the Church comes with the grace of the Lord and the Holy Spirit and unites us again. Therefore, outside the Church, outside the Eucharist and the Divine Liturgy, there is no victory over death. Death is defeated only in the Church.

My brothers and sisters, man fears death, he abhors it. If he simply disapproved of death, or if he was simply pained by death, it would be within the context of our faith and our Gospel. Just as the Lord in Gethsemane was pained before he drank the cup of death. Death isn't something that we should accept as correct or even natural, as biologists tell us. For yes, life continues when one man dies. Nevertheless, the unique person is lost or, rather, is in danger of annihilation.

At that time when death comes and separates us and dissolves our psychosomatic existence, we cannot but say with Saint John the Damascene what we sing during the funeral service: "I mourn and ache when I think of death and I see the image of God disintegrating in this way and suffering decay." However, it is one thing to be in pain and even resentful of death, and another to despair.

The Apostle Paul says precisely as much: "you will not grieve as indeed the rest of mankind do, who have no hope."[2] Not that you should not be sad, but that you should not despair, as those who have no hope. That is the crux of the matter. We have hope; we have faith in the Resurrection. This is what the Lord today, with the resurrection of Jairus' daughter, wanted to convey to us, to emphasize to us what seemed so funny to them that they laughed.

Death is now, after the Resurrection of the Lord, a sleep, an expectation of resurrection, which we receive a foretaste of in the Church and especially in the Divine Liturgy, where we are all united together, living and dead, and we commemorate them all, and then "we become one body," partaking of the Lord's Body and Blood. These things, my brothers and sisters, are not secondary, but we must rather make them the center of our faith, since one cannot be a Christian if he has not fully accepted them.

[2] 1Thess. 4:13.

May the message of today's Gospel give us, my brothers and sisters, the answer and the solution to the biggest problem, namely the problem of death, which, whether we recognize it or not, subconsciously dominates within us. Let us replace this problem with the faith and hope of the Resurrection. Amen.

September 28, 2001

9.
9th SUNDAY OF LUKE
Concerning foolishness (Lk 12:16–21)

Foolishness is the subject of today's gospel passage, a very simple passage that is well known to all of us, but whose meaning is profound and concerns us all. The Lord presents in today's parable a rich man, who had increased his crops and his property so much that he had lost his peace, not being able to find a way to store all this and use it. And finally he found the solution by increasing his storehouses and filling them with all these goods so that he could say to himself: "Soul, you have many goods laid up for many years; take your ease; eat, drink, and be merry." At that moment, however, God intervenes to remind him of a truth he had forgotten, that his death was imminent. His death would come even faster than he expected, and therefore all this effort and his thinking turned out to be foolishness. So the rich man of the parable was a fool. But why was he a fool? To what is his foolishness due?

It is necessary, my brothers and sisters, to delve deeper into this question, because in this way we will also be able to place ourselves in the position of the foolish rich man, since nothing in the Gospel concerns only certain people, but concerns all of us. It is a mistake to think that today's parable only applies to the rich and therefore not to those of us who are poor. In fact, the Gospel is for everyone. So to what is the foolishness of the rich man due?

Since man was cut off from God, since he freely decided to consider himself god and therefore to base all his powers on himself, he lost his security. Being a creature himself, i.e., a creature subject to decay and death, he could not really support himself, and because he had nowhere else to support himself, he developed two ways to be able to survive: one is to develop his intellectual powers and all his other powers, while the other is to use the nature that exists around him so that he can acquire goods on which he will now base his security.

Thus, man entered into an endless effort to accumulate goods, to develop his intellectual powers, to develop all these economic systems that we know, so that in this way he could exploit nature more and more and thus feel safe. So, the foolishness of the rich man in today's parable has deep roots in our existence, because we all participate in this decision of the first man, to turn away from God and to declare himself god.

In this way, we all participate in this agonizing effort; how will we acquire more and more goods so that we can feel safe. So the deepest cause of the rich man's foolishness is the insecurity he feels from the moment he has cut himself off from God and has placed all his strength and hopes on himself. This is how greed also developed, because the more goods one accumulates, the more secure one feels. However, this greed has no end, because complete security never comes and one feels that if he does not increase what he has, he will lose it. And there is an axiom, known to all of us, in the economic life of people, that "if you don't increase the money you have, you will lose the little you do have." So you have to increase your goods, and to increase them you have to enter into a constant struggle and thus lose your peace.

Here, then, is how foolishness emerges from the insecurity created by our separation from God and by proclaiming ourselves gods. But this insecurity also created something else, a new logic: the logic that the fool is the one who does not accumulate property, and this is now common sense. To be rational in our culture, you must be a fool, in the sense of the fool in today's parable—that is, to amass goods, to amass for tomorrow, for your children, for your grandchildren, and if you do not do that, then it means you are a fool. The logic of the Gospel has been turned upside down. While the Lord calls the one who amasses foolish, our common sense calls the one who does not amass foolish.

This is how this new logic entered our thinking, a logic we live with every day and upon which we build our culture. It requires a great deal of bravery to overturn and reject this logic; if one rejects it, he will be at risk. Not only will his life be at risk, but he will also be considered irrational and, I would say, even immoral, because the correct ethics now is the ethics of accumulating goods for the future.

The first man's insecurity leads us to direct all our effort, all our struggle, and all our energy toward ourselves, fearing that perhaps we will lose our existence. We cling to our existence and, when we cling to ourselves, we forget that there are other people, too. Then the Lord's words today about the foolish rich man apply: "So is he who lays up treasure for himself." We acquire wealth for ourselves and not for others. We don't think of others and, if we do, we think about them only secondarily. This means that we provide well for ourselves, our children, and our family and, if there is anything left over, we give it to others. So the priority is ourselves and this is how life and our culture become individualistic. We all become self-centered because we fear that we will lose ourselves if we don't hold on.

This insecurity, my brothers and sisters, has another consequence, a very tragic one, which we see especially in our days. It is about the harm we bring to nature. We try to amass goods and multiply them, attempting in our insecurity to always have more, and exploiting nature to such an extent that we reduce it to raw material for the production of goods. This is the root of today's so-called ecological problem. This is why man destroys nature, because his insecurity has now increased to such an extent that, if he does not multiply his goods, he feels that he is lost. And in order to multiply them, he has to use nature, and he uses it without thinking that nature has its limits and that it can at some point rebel against him, as is happening now. And what they call today the ecological problem proceeds from the same cause, from the same root of evil, insecurity.

Ultimately, the most tragic consequence of all this insecurity is that, paradoxically, while we want to protect ourselves from death, we actually cause it. We provoke death with our struggle to avoid it, and death's challenge manifests itself in various ways: it comes in the way I told you, with ecological destruction, it comes with social injustice, which ultimately turns against those who commit it, and thus a world of loneliness and death is created, in which lives the foolish rich man and all of us. We all live this foolishness, and the most tragic part is that we call it wisdom and prudence. This prudence, then, is what keeps us from becoming truly wise and prudent. We need to overturn this logic, my brothers and sisters. This is what the Gospel reading today wants us to understand.

To face this problem created by insecurity, and the consequences I described to you, the ancient sages proposed the solution of moderation and temperance. They said "acquire goods but in moderation," and our whole ethics was based on this. A true, wise man is he who acquires goods, who has enough for himself and his children to live on, but does not exceed this measure. This sounds good, but the problem is: where is the line? It has been proven that man cannot find the measure. The rich man also has a measure and, according to his logic, he cannot exceed it.

We have established this logic of moderation as our conventional morality and thus we take comfort in thinking that the Gospel's words do not apply to us. After all, we do not have as many goods as the rich man. But the Gospel does not propose any measure. This may be unsatisfying, we may not like it, but the Gospel proposes that we be ready to risk and lose everything, to give ourselves and even our very lives.

This is what God Himself did when He became man, emptying Himself with His kenosis. He kept nothing for Himself, not even His biological life; He gave it as well. And this highlights a path that seems foolish, that really sounds like madness, but that turns out to be the only way for man to be free and to live with another logic, the logic that says that death is a reality and negates everything that we try to create with our wisdom. And only if we are brave enough to deny those things with which we try to avoid death, only then will we really be able to avoid it.

The Church presents us this model with its saints. The saints, my brothers and sisters, are essentially those who are foolish according to the world, who rejected the wisdom of the world, who took seriously what the Lord said to the rich man and wanted to become wise, really wise and prudent within their foolishness, which the world cannot understand—saints "of whom the world was not worthy" (Heb 11:38). The world with its common wisdom is not worthy to understand a saint, to understand why he was martyred, to understand why the holy ascetic left the comforts of the world and lives in a cave, to understand why someone does not have to ground his security in anything in this world and rather expects to survive through prayer. The world cannot understand this, because foolishness has become wisdom and wisdom has become foolishness.

Everything has been turned upside down. And the Gospel calls us to this reversal of our logic. However, someone will say: "And what will the world become if we all imitate the saints?" I do not know what will happen, my brothers and sisters. It is certain that not all of us will imitate the saints, and this is how we will continue to struggle until the Kingdom of God comes. The foolish and the wise will find themselves unable to understand each other. Our society will always have the foolish of today's parable. The Gospel cannot change society morally. The Gospel comes in order to give us a yardstick so that we can measure ourselves. For those who are able to measure themselves, all is well and good. The rest will continue their lives without any criterion.

The conclusion from today's Gospel parable is that all of us participate in the foolishness of the foolish rich man, to the extent that we feel secure only when we have goods, and we feel insecure when our goods dwindle. And prudent indeed are those who adopt another logic, the logic of the saints. This, my brothers and sisters, we too are called to adopt, to the extent we can, placing our hope in God more than in people and in ourselves, and only in this way will we really be able to avoid the foolishness of the rich man in today's parable and follow the path that leads to the Kingdom of God, of which I pray we all become partakers. Amen.

November 17, 2002

10.

11th SUNDAY OF LUKE

(of the Forefathers)

The Banquet of the Kingdom of God (Lk 14:16–24)

The Gospel passage that we have just heard, my dear brothers and sisters, includes a parable in which the Lord uses various images taken from daily life to lead us to deeper meanings, meanings that have to do with our salvation.

Today, the Lord used a parable of a man who invited many to a supper, and those who first received the invitation rejected it for various reasons. Finally, and contrary to all expectation, the man's servants gathered guests from the streets. Let's delve as much as we can into this parable, brothers and sisters.

The Lord is speaking about a supper. What is this "supper" that God prepared and offers to people? First, it is the entire creation, the entire world.

The whole world, which God created, is like a big table where he invites us to enjoy the food, but also to enjoy communion with each other, as happens at every supper. But, more than this world that God created, the supper that He prepared for all of us is His Kingdom, where the will of God will prevail, where death and separation and every form of evil will be abolished, and where people will enjoy love and will be fed by the sight of God, by the word of God, by this food which does not perish or rot.

One of the fathers of our Church, Saint Cyril of Alexandria, asks: "Why does the parable say that this man gave a supper and not a meal?", and he tries to provide an answer. First, he says, because the supper comes at the end of the day, and this is a symbolism of the coming of the Kingdom of God at the end of history. Moreover, there's another reason: he wants to refer to the Lord's Last Supper, that is, the Eucharist. The great supper that God presents is not only the world he created, it is not only His Kingdom, which will come and settle in history one day, but it also already exists in our lives: it is the Eucharist, the supper that the Lord shared with His disciples shortly before His Passion. This is the supper He gives to us and invites us every time to participate in. This, then, is the supper.

What are the common characteristics of all these images: of the Kingdom of God, of creation, of the Eucharist? It is that man needs food and he draws this food from the gifts of God. It is not something that he can create alone—food is the gift and grace of God. Additionally, as I said before, the other characteristic is that man shares this food, he communes, because in a supper, my dear brothers and sisters, no one eats alone, we all share the same table, the same food, and so in this world where God has given us all the goods of creation we are called to share them as if at a great supper.

And the Eucharist is nothing other than sharing the food that God gives us—the body and blood of the Lord. Because in the Eucharist we are not simply united with God, we are also united with each other, and this sharing that happens in the Eucharist is what forces us to always be, when we participate in the Eucharist, reconciled and loved by everyone.

We cannot go to a supper and sit next to someone we hate, for whom we have a burden in our soul. We must certainly have good relations with our supper companions. That is why in the Eucharist, in this great supper, love is imposed so that this supper is a real communion between us.

But he says that at the supper that the Lord is preparing, God invites people as a host invites his guests to supper. The supper—whether we see it, as I said, as the creation of the world, the whole world, the Kingdom of God, or the Eucharist—is something that is offered to us; we do not make it ourselves, we are invited, in this world, in the Kingdom of God, and in the Divine Eucharist. However, many times we reject this invitation, just as the Lord's guests in the parable we heard rejected the invitation.

It is important, my beloved brothers and sisters, that God leaves it to man's freedom to accept or not to accept his invitation. He does not force. And as we heard in the parable, the Lord says at some point: "Go out to the highways and hedges, and compel people to come in, that my house may be filled" (Lk 14:23). This does not mean that he compels them by force. He gives them various stimuli, various opportunities to exercise their freedom, to accept or not accept the invitation. Thus, it often happens that the Lord gives us a hardship, a disease, a temptation, and He gives it to us in a way to compel us, without being obligatory. It is an invitation to exercise, as I said, our freedom. That's why, many times in our lives, we experience trials and difficulties. But these things are ways in which God gives us the opportunity to accept the invitation He has sent us.

The invitation, as we heard, was rejected by the first guests. And these people, whom the Lord had in mind in this Gospel passage, were originally his fellow countrymen, the Jews. The Jews rejected Christ. They rejected God's invitation and thus God was forced to invite idolaters, the Gentiles, people who were despised by the Jews, sinners, and the blind, and the lame from the streets in order to fill his house. But the Lord is not referring only to the Jews. What he says also applies to all of us, since God's invitation is rejected not only by the Jews but also by all people throughout the ages.

And why is the invitation of God rejected? Basically, the Gospel passage records two excuses. The first is man's worldly cares for his survival. One says, "I bought a field," and another says, "I bought five pairs of oxen. So I have to take care of my property, attend to my worldly cares," and thus reject the invitation. Many people do not find time to come to the Divine Liturgy because they are so occupied, they have so much to do. Our worldly cares, today especially, my dear brothers and sisters, alienate us from God, and it is truly a great struggle for man in this life, which has become so difficult, to find time to pray, to go to the church, to think about God, and to respond to God's invitation.

And the other category is comprised of those who respond "I have married a wife." "I have just gotten married and I cannot come." The first category makes us slaves to our worldly cares in our daily lives. The second category makes us slaves to our nature. Our nature, which leads us to reproduce humankind, can often cause us to not respond to God's invitation. It is noteworthy, my brothers and sisters, that the Church's saints, those who said "yes" to God's invitation, abandoned their worldly concerns and even abandoned their married life.

That is why our Church has monasticism as its model, because the monk is the one who, in order to say "yes" to God's invitation, has abandoned his worldly concerns and even married life in order to live only for God. But it is not possible for everyone. So what is needed is to liberate ourselves, to the extent that we are able, from both our worldly concerns and our attachment to physical needs.

So, today's Gospel passage gives us—as does every word of the Lord—the measure by which we should measure our lives, the measure to which we must try to adapt. Having before us as our model the saints of the Church, let us try to respond "yes" to the Lord's invitation, to respond not only with our will, but with our whole life since, as the Lord said in today's parable, God's attitude toward those who reject His invitation will be austere. The householder said "none of those men who were invited shall taste my supper."

So, my dear brothers and sisters, we have a great supper before us—the supper of the Kingdom of God, which we experience a foretaste of in the Holy Eucharist—to which we are called continually to respond. Responding as invited guests, with our will and our disposition as well as our efforts, let us be those who respond completely to the will of God and become supper companions in the Kingdom of God. Amen.

December 17, 2006

11.

SUNDAY BEFORE THE NATIVITY OF CHRIST

The commandments of God and communion with God

And all these, though well attested by their faith, did not receive what was promised, since God had foreseen something better for us, that apart from us they should not be made perfect (Heb 11:39–40)

Today, the Sunday before the Nativity of the Lord, is dedicated, my beloved brothers and sisters, to the memory of all those who pleased God, from Adam to Joseph. Let us devote a few thoughts to this feast of our Church today.

When Adam, in his freedom, decided to break communion with God and to declare himself god, something tragic happened in the history of humanity. "No to God" came into man's consciousness. The idea entered man's consciousness that he is free when he says "no." And this freedom, this negative freedom, had already been introduced by the angels, many of whom chose to say "no" to God. Since then, Satan, the demons, and all the fallen angels have exercised their freedom to "deny the will of God." This, however, now entered through Adam into the whole of humanity, and into the psychology of man.

This general denial of God's will by man that captured almost all of humanity had a few exceptions. These exceptions, who consented to say "yes" to God, were the people of Israel, to whom, through the call of Abraham, He entrusted his Law and His commandments. This people accepted the Law and the commandments for God for only one purpose—for man to keep the Law, thereby providing him the opportunity, after Adam's Fall, to say "yes" to the will of God, because the Law and the commandments of God were precisely God's will.

Many people in the Old Testament observed the Law and God's commandments, and these people are called "Righteous." They kept God's commandments throughout history, ever since Abraham first obeyed God's command to sacrifice his child—a difficult and even impossible commandment for man, which Abraham nevertheless accepted. Since then, the ability to say "yes" to God instead of "no" entered into humanity. And the Righteous of the Old Testament proved this.

The "yes" of the Righteous of the Old Testament, my beloved brothers and sisters, overturned Adam's "no" as regards God's commandments, but it could not overturn the consequences of Adam's "no." These consequences were not, as we say, moral—that is, consequences that man could correct. They were deep, ontological consequences in human existence. Because when man cut off his communion with God and turned to nature, then death entered man's life. Death could not be overturned with the "yes" of the Righteous.

Man cannot be redeemed by saying "yes" to God's commandments. Something more radical was needed to overturn the terrible consequence of man's Fall, which is death, separation from God. Man could not be saved from death by his own power; man needed to be re-united with God in order to restore communion, man's union with God, and this is precisely why Christ came.

Christ did not bring a new teaching or an example of keeping God's commandments; He brought us salvation from death. He brought us reunion with God, communion, human nature's union with God. That is, He accomplished God's will for man when He created him: for man to unite with God, and with him all of creation, so that we could be saved from the destruction that Adam's "no" brought. And the Righteous, therefore, of the Old Testament needed to be saved by Christ. Even though they kept God's commandments, they could only be saved if they too were incorporated into Christ, in the union, that is, of man with God, which Christ accomplished by becoming man.

Therefore, the purpose of the Incarnation of God's Word was to unite man with God, as was God's original plan when He created man, and from which man deviated by saying "no" to God's will. And for this reason, only by looking forward to the Incarnation of the Son and Word of God, the Righteous of the Old Testament were saved.

This, my dear brothers and sisters, is surprising, and it teaches us many things. The first thing it teaches us is that we who live after Christ have a huge privilege that the saints of the Old Testament did not have. They believed in Christ and kept God's commandments with the hope that one day they would be united with God, when the Messiah, the Christ, whom they were expecting, would come. For them, it was only a hope, which they could not prove. For us, who live after Christ, it is a proven reality.

We are called to keep God's commandments, not simply hoping and waiting to enjoy the fruits of this observance of the commandments, but now knowing that these fruits exist and that we can enjoy them. We know that many have enjoyed them and that we can rely on the experience of the saints, who not only kept the commandments, as in the Old Testament, but also enjoyed the fruits of this keeping of the commandments—that is, union with God.

Therefore, we have this enormous privilege, which the Righteous of the Old Testament did not have. However, this also creates a huge responsibility for us. If they kept God's commandments simply by looking to the future and hoping, how will we justify ourselves who have behind us all this experience of the saints and our Church? How can we be justified when we do not keep God's commandments? It is a great responsibility for all of us who have the privilege of living in the age of the Church, in the age of the saints after the Incarnation of the Lord.

The other lesson we can take from today is that the observance of God's commandments is absolutely necessary; it is the gate through which one passes to reach God—as the Righteous of the Old Testament passed—but it is not enough. If keeping the commandments were enough, the Righteous of the Old Testament would have saved themselves and there would have been no need for Christ to come to save them. If keeping the commandments were enough, then the Jews who kept the Law, those of them who kept the Law, would have been saved even without

Christ. If keeping the commandments were enough, then the Pharisee, who said that he kept all the Law—which was true—he too would have been saved.

The fact that the Righteous of the Old Testament could not be saved only by observing the Law of God, but needed their incorporation into Christ, means that simply observing the commandments is not enough for us either. What saves us is our union with God, within the body of Christ.

We are saved by our communion with God in the sacraments or mysteries of the Church and especially in the mystery of the Eucharist. What the Righteous of the Old Testament longed for became a reality for us, because we can now in this mystery transcend death, and live eternally. It is a medicine of immortality, as Saint Ignatius the God-bearer says. The Eucharist, therefore, is offered to us in the Church and this is the final gift that God gives us for our salvation. And so it proves that our salvation can never be our own achievement, it cannot be the achievement of our efforts, it cannot be the result of our virtues. Our salvation, after all, is grace, it is a gift from God—He does not owe it to us, He gives it to us.

What He seeks from us is this attitude of "yes." He asks us to expel from ourselves this attitude of Adam, who said "no" to God. Of course, this "yes" implies many sacrifices and is not easy, as we heard in the apostolic passage. All these saints of the Old Testament suffered because they wanted to say "yes" to God. And if we are unable to say "yes" to God, which may even be true, we are failing because of our self-love, which has at its root this "no" to God. This is why our every effort to keep the commandments impinges on our self-love, is difficult, and requires sacrifice.

God asks us for this "yes" in order to attract His grace, and for Him to come with His gift to give us salvation. How? By incorporating us into the body of His Son, into this new creation, the new humanity that Christ brought about by becoming man and offering us His body in the Church, with the mysteries and especially with the Divine Eucharist.

My brothers and sisters, as we approach Christmas, many of us are justifiably depressed because they see man whirling around in a tumult whose meaning he does not understand. You only have to look at what is happening in the cities with this consumption of goods. And if we ask people, "What is the meaning of all this? What does all this have to do with Christmas?", they will find it difficult to give us an answer. We tend to lose the meaning of Christmas.

The Church humbly—because the Church can only change the world with its own example, with its own humble and modest word—comes today to tell us "the meaning of Christmas," which is nothing other than what Athanasios the Great wrote: God became man so that we might become god-like. This is why Christ came into the world, and this is why we celebrate. We celebrate the possibility that God gives us with His grace, by offering Him our good will with a "yes" to His commandments, uniting with Him, in the body of Christ, and becoming partakers of God's life, becoming gods too.

This great message is brought to us by Christmas. Wisely, the Church today presents us with the Righteous of the Old Testament as a model, so that we can see that the gate through which one passes into Christmas is the observance of God's commandments, but we also need our union with God, which was brought about by the birth of the God-man Christ.

I pray, my beloved brothers and sisters, that we all spend the Christmas holidays with this spirit, which the celebrated Righteous of the Old Testament give us today. This is the spirit that I pray God accounts us worthy of, to taste His salvation and His gift that the Righteous of the Old Testament were waiting for, which we have at our disposal. Amen.

December 19, 2004

12.

12th SUNDAY OF LUKE

(Ten Lepers)

"Were not ten cleansed? Where are the nine?" (Lk 17:12–19)

Ingratitude, my dear brothers and sisters, is the problem that today's Gospel passage sets before us. The Lord is marching towards Jerusalem and passes through Samaria and Galilee. On the way, he finds himself in a village where the lepers had been isolated. As you know, at that time and until recently, leprosy was considered a contagious and incurable disease and all lepers were isolated from other people. The lepers, therefore, these ten lepers, seeing that the Lord was coming, that the Lord was passing by, call out to him from afar: "Lord Jesus, have mercy on us, heal us!" And the Lord says to them: "Go to the priests so they can give you," as we would say today, a "certificate of health." Because according to the Jewish law, the priests confirmed in these cases that a leper had been cured. And as they went to the priests, on the way they were healed, they were cleansed.

However, the shocking thing, my dear brothers and sisters, is that, of these ten, only one went back to thank Christ. And the Lord looks at him with great sadness and melancholy and says: "Were not ten cleansed? Where are the nine?"

My beloved brothers and sisters, a question is posed to us with this gospel passage. Why is ingratitude so widespread? Think of the percentage! Out of ten, only one is grateful. The majority are ungrateful. It is an important question, so we have to examine why it is so difficult to be grateful.

Ingratitude, my beloved brothers and sisters, is rooted in the nature of man, ever since man—the first man, our forefather Adam—abandoned God and proclaimed himself god; from that moment ingratitude entered into man's existence. Because Adam's attitude was nothing but proof that he did not recognize that his existence was a gift from someone else, a gift from God. Therefore, selfishness entered into human nature—that is, the exaltation of our self—and selfishness is, my beloved brothers and sisters, the cause of ingratitude. Because every benefaction of the other towards us implies that we are obliged to someone else. And by being obliged to someone else, we feel humiliated. Perhaps you heard the famous and very true saying: "No one is a greater enemy than the one you have benefited." Why? Because the other's beneficence to us, subconsciously, creates in us the feeling of humiliation, of obligation to the other. It pricks our selfishness, and selfishness is the cause of ingratitude. This is why ingratitude is so widespread. Because human selfishness is widespread.

And let it not seem strange to you, my dear brothers and sisters, if someone tells us that we too, almost all of us, are not as grateful as we should be. We wake up every morning and take it for granted that we exist, we take it for granted that the sun will rise, that we will gaze at the sea, the mountain, all this creation in front of us, that we will get up and go to work. We take all this for granted. All these are gifts! We didn't earn them; they were given to us. And when we start in the morning and our soul is not filled with gratitude, with thanksgiving, then we are ungrateful. And when we fail to realize that we would not have what we have if it weren't for others working and offering them to us.

If we do not realize how much we owe to others, we are ungrateful. Every person we see next to us should be considered our benefactor, because he contributes to us being able to exist, live, and act. Human life is not individual; human life is social. We all owe others what we are. We owe our life, our biological life, to our parents, to our forefathers; we owe the fact that we have a job and live and survive to the fact that other people work too. And yet we forget this!

And we are ungrateful, too, when we believe that the abilities we have are our own, when we extol our abilities, that we are great, we have this gift or the other gift. But the word "gift" means exactly that it was given to us. There are no gifts that we can acquire by ourselves. We can work and increase them, but basically, what we have is a gift, a gift from others and, above all, a gift from God, because the others wouldn't exist either, if God didn't create us and if God didn't make give us others.

My beloved brothers and sisters, we live in an age, especially today, where people only talk about rights. They talk as if everyone owes them. And even the young children are starting to think that it is the duty of the adults to give them what they have. This insanity, which has now entered our way of thinking, is precisely this ingratitude. When the child cannot understand what he owes to his parents, when the younger cannot realize that without the elder he would not be what he is—when he does not understand that he too must give and cannot only take—our life, my beloved brothers and sisters, will be a kind of hell. And let's not be surprised when we see phenomena that we cannot explain, because people today are so demanding. Every day we hear people say "people are deprived." We, the older ones, however, know what deprivation means. We know that if we had even one hundredth of what people have today, we would be grateful.

But today, when they have so much, people are not grateful. And this, my dear brothers and sisters, has an impact on our happiness, on these very people. When you are not happy with the little you have and you are not grateful for the little you have, how will you be happy? You are an unhappy person, you will always want more, you will always complain, you will always demand. And in this way the years of your life will pass and in the end you will find yourself an unhappy person. However, if you are grateful even with the little you have, you will be happy in this life. You will spend it happily, as people used to spend it in the past who had much less and yet had a lot of happiness, and they shared this little among themselves and were truly happy.

My beloved brethren, we all hate ingratitude. We hate it especially when someone is ungrateful to us. But do we think that maybe we are ungrateful towards others and above all towards God?

Gratitude, my dear brothers and sisters, gratitude, is something that has no end; it is endless, it is like a sea that must flood our heart every moment. When our hearts are filled with gratitude, then we will truly become what the Church wants: Eucharistic people. And notice, my beloved brothers and sisters, that the Church uses the term "*eucharistia*," thankfulness, for the Holy Eucharist, the preeminent mystery of the Church, which is the Divine Liturgy. It is not by chance that we call the Divine Liturgy "*Eucharistia*." Because in the Divine Liturgy, my beloved brothers and sisters, we gather together and, instead of demanding, we give thanks, instead of complaining, we express heartfelt gratitude toward God. Because He brought us into this world, because He saved us from the devil, because He gave us eternal life, He gave us Himself, His love, by sacrificing His only Son. We do this at every Divine Liturgy.

Unfortunately, many times, my dear brothers and sisters, we come to the Divine Liturgy to ask for something from God. Let's put our hand on our heart. When we go to Church, don't we go to ask for something? Why should we only ask for things? Shouldn't we go to Church to give thanks? To praise God? The One Who gave us our very existence, the whole world that we have next to us, this wonderful creation that we are destroying. He gave us other people, He even gave us difficulties and illnesses and sorrows, for our good. So let us say together with Saint John Chrysostom, "Glory to God for all things," whatever happens to us, good and bad. Mainly, however, for all the goods we enjoy. And then, my beloved brothers and sisters, we will belong to the one leper out of the ten. And this Church, my dear brothers and sisters, is a minority. Do not look now when a crowd has gathered. Real Christians are a minority, and the Church is the place in which we practice and express our gratitude and thanksgiving.

Let us take these things into account, my beloved brothers and sisters, and let us try to be grateful to God and to all others. Then we will enjoy, from now on, the joy of the Kingdom of God, which I wish for all of you. Amen!

Holy Church of Saint George, Kamateros Attica
January 18, 2009

13.
13th SUNDAY OF LUKE
The mystery of salvation (Lk 18:18–27)

Who then can be saved?

Salvation, my beloved brothers and sisters, is a struggle with the impossible. A struggle with the humanly impossible. There are two pitfalls on the road to salvation. One is self-confidence, which is based on ethics. Ethics are rules that people set among themselves, in order to have a peaceful and harmonious coexistence. But it is also based on commandments that God Himself gives through His Law. And He calls people to observe these commandments.

And today's young man in the Gospel passage we heard had kept all the commandments. And so he was now certain that he could inherit the Kingdom of God. And he went to the Lord with this conviction, that since "All these things I have kept from my youth," he lacked nothing, and he could receive the prize of the Kingdom of God and be saved.

The Lord comes to shake this self-confidence, which was based on his moral perfection. And He says to him: "Yes, you have kept all these things from your youth, but you still lack one." And this one thing, which he lacked, was related to the second trap that exists on our path to salvation: the trap of our belief about the goods we have, about the power we have—social, moral, economic, military power, whatever you can imagine.

The young man of today's passage "was very rich." So he based his confidence on his goods and this constituted a trap, a trap for his salvation. And the Lord comes to take him out of this trap. How? By asking him for something that is humanly impossible. To sell everything he has, to give up everything he has and to follow Him. Many times we think that what the Lord said to the young man in the Gospel passage only applies to the rich. However, the Gospel does not only concern one category of people. The Gospel concerns everyone. No one is excluded from the message of the Gospel.

And the meaning of this exhortation to the rich young man, to sell everything, is something that concerns us all, poor and rich. Because the deeper meaning of this exhortation is how we must be ready not to sell a certain portion of our wealth, but be ready to lose it "all," as the Gospel passage says. To give it all away. And who among us is so poor that they don't have something? So, then, this exhortation of the Lord applies to all of us. Are we ready to lose it "all"? Everything?

Why does the Lord have this terrible—excessive, one might say—requirement for someone to be saved? The reasons, my beloved, are very deep. The first reason is that man, when he distanced himself from God, when he proclaimed himself god, then based his security on the goods he could collect, on objects. And in this way he not only declared himself god but also reduced things, objects, to a kind of god. And thus he introduced idolatry, idols; the idols of worldly power, of economic power. And then he began to worship these idols. Therefore, if man cannot abandon these idols, he cannot be worthy of the Kingdom of God.

And another reason, also deep, is that when one is attached to these idols, then one is not free. Then he is led and carried by the idols. People who have a lot—how much they struggle! To increase what they have and to not lose what they have. This is how man develops a permanent and obsessive preoccupation with how to preserve goods, and in this way he loses his freedom. And while God created him free, free from every need, he develops his needs, thinking that he can satisfy them. And it is characteristic of our culture today, my brothers and sisters—if we pay attention to it and study it more deeply—that it creates needs for us. We didn't used to have the needs we have today. So today we have more needs than ever, which are constantly increasing. And having more needs, we want to have more goods to satisfy them. And trying to have more goods, we become slaves to things.

This is why whatever we have—and everything is a gift from God—we must be ready to give up and lose at any moment. To be free internally, so that he does not depend on what he has. Instead, let him depend on what he is, because there is an enormous difference between *having* and *being*. Having doesn't give you your true self. Being genuine, regardless of what you have, is your real, true being. So, my brothers and sisters, what the Lord asks of the rich young man has a very deep meaning. And it is something, as I said, that he asks of all of us. It is not only for the rich, as one would like to think in order to excuse himself from this.

"Who then can be saved?" Who can leave everything and be saved? First, my brothers and sisters, there were the apostles of the Lord, the disciples. We know this from the way in which the Lord called them and how they responded: "they left everything and followed him" (Lk 5:11). Their profession, their boat which helped them survive—they left it! They had families. They left them. And they followed someone who was almost unknown to them, Who however liberated them from all they had in order to give them power to be free and to give themselves and even their very lives to gain the Kingdom of God. The martyrs of the Church did the same thing, giving their lives. The saints left everything. These are the ones who are the models for our Church, the power of the Church, the strength of the "weakness" of the Church.

But who else can be saved? Of course, we cannot all be apostles of the Lord, nor martyrs and saints, but we can all, to a certain extent, be ready to detach ourselves from our possessions. To be ready to give, and not only to receive. And to the degree that each one gives and does not only take, he approaches the standard that the Lord set with today's Gospel passage, of what is "impossible with men."

And the Lord comes to answer this question—who can be saved?—with this shocking phrase: "Yes, I recognize that this is impossible with men, but it is possible with God." "What is impossible with men is possible with God." This means, my brothers and sisters, that no matter what we do, no matter how many virtues we acquire, in the end God's mercy is what will save us. The awareness of our failure will save us. Saint Anthony held this key in his hands. As his *vita* says, he went to church on a Sunday like today, heard this Gospel and immediately—he was very rich—

sold everything, gave it to the poor, went to the desert and always said: "Everyone will go to heaven except me." But even that didn't save him; he never believed that what he did made him worthy of salvation. Because in the end salvation is given by God to the humble, to those who do not judge others but judge only themselves, to those who are always ready to measure their stature by this stature, by this standard that the Lord gave us in today's Gospel passage. And, measuring by this standard, they always find themselves lacking.

This, my brothers and sisters, is the Gospel. It is not a code of conduct that if you satisfy it, if you carry it out, you're all done. It is a constant struggle to reach the impossible, and the Lord calls us to this struggle. And He promises us that when we try to achieve but cannot, the grace of God comes and makes up for it—the grace of God, "which always heals that which is infirm and completes that which is lacking," as our Church says when it orders its clergy.

I wanted to share these thoughts with you, my beloved brothers and sisters—thoughts that concern all of us, thoughts that inspire fear and awe at the mystery of our salvation, but at the same time hope, hope that God does not abandon those who struggle for their salvation and ultimately grants them entry into the Kingdom of God, which I pray for all of us. Amen!

Holy Church of the Transfiguration of the Savior, Kefalari, Kifissia
November 24, 2002

14.
15th SUNDAY OF LUKE
(Zacchaeus)
The salvation of sinners

My beloved brothers and sisters, there are saints who became saints from the womb of their mothers and there are saints who became saints because they were first very sinful. The Gospel seems to have a preference for the latter. It constantly shows us cases of people who became saints after being very sinful at first. And today both the apostolic and the evangelical reading present us with exactly this case (1 Tim 1:15–17 / Lk 19:1–10).

In this Epistle reading, the Apostle Paul says that which strikes us as amazing and many times incomprehensible and inconceivable, that: Christ Jesus came into the world to save sinners, of whom I am the first. "Christ Jesus came into the world to save sinners, of whom I am chief." In the Gospel reading, we observe the case of a very sinful man named Zacchaeus, so sinful that he was known to the whole society for his sinfulness, and even provoked the comment of those present when the Lord told him he had to come to his house. How, they began to grumble, how can he stay in the house of such a sinner?

Zacchaeus was very sinful, and we are reminded what the Lord elsewhere said about rich people like Zacchaeus, that it is difficult for them to enter the Kingdom of God. When he said this, he provoked his hearers to wonder: "Who then can be saved?" And see how even Zacchaeus can be saved, and even he can become a saint. One could say that the Lord demonstrated in this passage His preference for sinners.

There were people who kept the Law. There were people who were not stigmatized in society as sinners, but he preferred to deal with sinners. Why? The answer to this question is given by both the Epistle lesson and the gospel passage that we have just heard.

In the Epistle reading, the Apostle Paul tells us that "Christ Jesus came into the world to save sinners, of whom I am chief," primarily for two reasons: to demonstrate the magnitude of His mercy and longsuffering. In other words, to show that we are not saved by our virtues, but by the mercy of God. When someone is a sinner and is saved, then it is more clearly seen that he was not saved because of his virtues, but only because of God's mercy. And Paul says: The Lord wants to demonstrate in me all His long-suffering. To demonstrate how great his long-suffering is, since He surrounded a man like me, a persecutor, with His grace and saved me.

So this is the first reason, to show that God is long-suffering, that His mercy is great and embraces even the most sinful. And the Apostle Paul says this "as an example for those who would" be saved. That they might know in this way that no sin—absolutely no sin—is unforgivable. Our sinfulness is not a dead-end; the mercy of God is so great that it can even turn a persecutor into a saint.

This preference of the Lord for sinners is also explained through the Gospel passage, which ends with the Lord's words: "for the Son of Man has come to seek and to save that which was lost." This is why He prefers sinners, because He did not come into this world for any other purpose. He did not come for the righteous, He did not come for those who think they are righteous—He came for sinners, for the lost sheep.

The word "lost" [ἀπολωλὸς] is striking here, my brothers and sisters. What does ἀπολωλὸς mean? It means the one who lost his way, who ran away from home, who doesn't know where he is, who tries to find his way and doesn't succeed. He is lost. He searches here and there and does not find a way out. And this is reminiscent of man through the ages, and especially in our modern age; a man who searches as if lost in the dark and cannot find his way.

So he is lost, he is lost. And the Lord characterizes these people as "the lost sheep of the house of Israel" (Mt 15:24). What makes an impression on us is that both the Apostle Paul and Zacchaeus were faithful Israelites. They were religious people and not unconnected, because the Lord also says about Zacchaeus: "he, too, is a son of Abraham" (Lk 19:9). And despite all this, the Lord characterizes them as "lost."

The Apostle Paul had lost his way, he was searching in the dark and could not find it due to excessive religious zeal. He says of himself that he was "exceedingly zealous for the traditions of my fathers" (Gal 1:14). So we see that one can lose his way through extreme zeal and become "lost."

Zacchaeus became lost through his greed—his desire and his effort to increase his goods—even if it meant injustice towards others. Thus, he was also lost, despite being a child of Abraham—that is, he grew up in Israel, in which it was assumed that there were no lost sheep. It was assumed that they knew the true God, and yet Paul and Zacchaeus had lost their way.

My brothers and sisters, this teaches us that there are lost sheep in the Church, in our faith, and I would say that we are all lost. All of us, more or less, have lost our way and there is no other way out than the Lord. And how will the Lord save us? How will He seek and find the lost? He seeks them and calls them Himself.

In the Gospel passage, it is no coincidence that the Lord called Zacchaeus and said to him: "Zacchaeus, come down," and his salvation came because he willingly responded to this call. He also called Paul, and he too was saved because he responded to this call. And the response to the call was followed by a change of life, by real repentance, both in Paul and in Zacchaeus. Because Zacchaeus was not satisfied with simply responding to the Lord's call, but immediately proceeded to change his life and said: "to those whom I have wronged, I now repay fourfold. I no longer follow the same way and the same path of life that I had until now." This is how the lost find their way again.

However, this call of the Lord, this search for the lost, aims not only at a response to the call, but the Lord goes further and said to Zacchaeus: "Zacchaeus, make haste and come down, for today I must stay at your house." He wants to stay at a sinner's house. He wants to dwell in him, and only then can the lost find their way. It is not by simply changing his life and willingly responding to God's call, but by offering himself as God's abode.

That is when man is truly sanctified, when a sinner becomes a saint. Holiness is not an achievement of our efforts and our virtues, it is a gift that God gives us when He accepts to dwell in us with his Holy Spirit and we offer ourselves to him as a dwelling place for Him to stay.

My brothers and sisters, this is exactly what the Church does with all of us. It is not enough for the Church to speak to us, to preach the word of God, to call people to repentance, but it goes further and offers us the Eucharist, the Divine Liturgy, as an opportunity to become God's abode—for the Lord Himself to dwell in us.

The prayer we read before Holy Communion is very characteristic. It is one of the most moving prayers, which reminds us of the case of Zacchaeus: "I am not worthy, O Lord and Master, that You should enter under the roof of my soul; but since You, in Your love for men, do will to dwell in me, I take courage and I draw near."[1]

This is the completion of man's salvation. The fact that the Lord stayed in the house of Zacchaeus is more important than the fact that Zacchaeus repented. The blessing of God's presence in a person's life and God's desire to dwell in us, as is the case with the Eucharist, is the most exalted thing He can give us. And for this reason, my brothers and sisters, it is not enough to be good people, it is not enough to be worldly and from a moral point of view not sinful, it is not enough to be respectable in society; we are all deep down and to some extent sinners. And even our repentance is not enough, it is not enough to change our life—what is needed is our union with Christ.

We need to become dwelling places for Christ and for this reason we cleanse our souls through repentance. Not to show how beautiful and good we have become, but for God Himself to dwell in us. And this is how sinners are sanctified. All of us who are sinners encounter the grace of God within us in the same way, and we then recognize and confess that what saved us is the mercy of God and not our merit and our virtue.

[1] Fourth Prayer of Saint John Chrysostom.

These are my thoughts today, my brothers and sisters, on both the Epistle and Gospel readings. They are not theoretical but relate to our lives. They are thoughts that can and should lead us to the right path, because, as I said, we can be lost and not have the right path even if we are members of the Church. It is the duty of the Church, with the light of the Gospel, to guide all of us on the right path.

I pray that these thoughts be for all of us, my beloved brothers and sisters, a guide in our lives so that despite our sinfulness we too are accounted worthy to become the abode of the Holy Spirit, and to live eternally in the Kingdom of God with the only Holy One, the Lord Jesus Christ. Amen.

15.
16th SUNDAY OF LUKE
(The Publican and the Pharisee)
Humiliation (Lk 18:10–14)

Atheism is not a phenomenon that concerns only those who reject God. It happens that this also applies to those who profess faith in God. Atheism is when man relies on his own strength and his own worth. When he has self-sufficiency and autonomy before God and believes that now he can save himself through his own power.

Man was created by God to be in constant communion with him, and the tragedy of humanity begins when the first man believed that he could exist without communion with God. From the moment he proclaimed himself god. From the moment that man declared independence, gained his self-sufficiency, and effectively said to God: "I don't need you, I can move forward and succeed on my own power." And in this tragic history of humanity, God responds by choosing a people, a people who promise faith in Him, who promise that they will obey His will, which is to be expressed through true obedience to His Law. And obedience to His Law meant that man would observe everything in God's Law. And look what happened! Satan manages to distance man once again from God. This is the technique that Satan uses quite successfully. He manages—through observance of the Law—to guide man to atheism. In other words, man no longer has any need for God but is instead buoyed by his own powers, by the very fact that he observes the Law, by his own virtues.

How strange! But so true! And this is demonstrated, my brothers and sisters, by today's parable, which we have just heard. What is a Pharisee? A faithful Jew. We usually associate him with hypocrisy. And, of course, there was hypocrisy, because when someone wants to rely on his own strength and his own virtues and does not succeed, as the Law of God is beyond him, then he finds various ways to escape from observing God's commandments while at the same time giving the impression that he observes them.

However, the Pharisee of today's parable was not lying when he said what he said. Indeed he kept the Law, indeed he gave one tenth of his property to the poor, indeed he did not wrong anyone, he did not embezzle; he kept the Law completely and, therefore, one would expect that he would be saved. And the Lord comes and overturns this whole situation. And He comes and proclaims in the most official way that the virtue of the Pharisee was not only not enough to be saved, but was even an obstacle to his salvation. What a tragic irony! From where salvation should come, ultimately eternal damnation comes.

And on the other hand, the parable presents another man who did not keep the Law, who had no virtue to display and who, for this very reason, believed that he was not self-sufficient and autonomous. God's mercy was definitely needed. And thus he was justified and not the Pharisee. So, a sinner is justified and a righteous man is condemned! Why? Because the righteous man, through his virtue, considered himself worthy of salvation and the reward of his virtue, while the other, through his sinfulness, sought God. And he believed that without God he cannot exist, that it is not possible to be independent from God, that his entire existence depends on God's mercy. And so the Lord comes today to reward the one who humbled himself so that he could find God, and to condemn the one who, through his virtues, moved away from God.

Why is this humility of the publican the way to salvation? It is a question that we must ask ourselves because the Lord does not decide things—just as He did not decide in today's parable—without some deeper meaning. I think that this question has two main answers. One is that humility is not just a moral virtue, but the truth of ourselves, our reality. The Pharisee fell short not because he broke a moral commandment; indeed, he didn't break any of the moral commandments. He fell short in terms of his assessment of reality, of the truth. And what is the reality that only the publican discovered? That all of us, whatever we do, are sinners! Because all of us—no matter how many virtues we have—all need God's mercy. And this truth is discovered and accepted only by those who draw near to God and know Him. Whoever is far from God does not know what holiness is. And he thinks that his own virtues are capable of making him a saint. He, however, who approaches the holiness of God understands that all his virtues are rubbish. They have absolutely no value, because only God's holiness is true holiness. Thus the humble person is close to the truth and the proud one is far from the truth of himself. And all the saints of our Church, those who really, with their valiant struggle, managed to get close to God, it is not by chance that all of them, every single one, first of all the Apostle Paul, believed and confessed that they are the chief among sinners. Because they are more sinful than all the others. In this way, they overturned the attitude of the Pharisee, who proclaimed that he was "not like this tax collector."

Thus, holiness, real holiness, leads to humility. Not, I repeat, as a moral virtue, but as a truth of our existence. Because we are not holy compared to the holiness of God, no matter what we do! Consequently, all the saints—and I recall at this moment the words of Saint Anthony, that great ascetic—believed that all the rest would go to heaven and they themselves would go to hell. The one who fought with the demons, the one who knew what holiness meant, was the one who believed that he was more sinful than all the others.

This, then, is the first reason that humility is the only way to our salvation. It is the recognition of the reality of ourselves. It is our sinfulness, because nothing, absolutely nothing, no matter what we do, can remove our sinfulness as a defining factor of our existence.

And the second reason is, my brothers and sisters, that this same God, in the person of our Lord, in order to demonstrate His love, humbled Himself to the point of Hades, visited places where only the most sinful people went, and ate with sinners. His association with sinners provoked the comments and anger of the Pharisees. If, therefore, God Himself through His love comes down and attaches value to the sinner, who are we to look down on others and condemn others in order to exalt ourselves? So this is also a basic reason why, if we do not travel via this road of humility, we will never reach God.

My brothers and sisters, today we enter the period of the Triodion. And this period is, as we know, a period of spiritual struggles, a period for practicing virtue. However, it is not by chance that the Church today presents before us this parable of the Lord. To tell us that no matter how many virtues you cultivate, no matter how much spiritual struggle you engage in, never think that you have conquered holiness and, above all, never look down on others. Do not believe that you are superior to others, do not believe that others are condemned and you are saved. The way to be saved is truly through our spiritual struggle and the virtues that we cultivate, but we must believe that we have achieved nothing, absolutely nothing, that has made us worthy of salvation. Only God's mercy can make us worthy of salvation. My beloved brothers and sisters, let us adopt this mindset, because nothing is so common in the life of Christians as—in one way or another, directly or indirectly, and often with great skill—we judge others, criticize others, in order to project our own virtue. And this is the path of destruction, it is the path of the Pharisee. On the contrary, the road of the publican, as I said, the road of recognition that nothing makes us worthy of salvation, is the road that will bring God's mercy upon us, and in this way we demonstrate that without God we cannot exist, we cannot be saved. It is not our virtues that will save us. It is the mercy of God alone, which I wish for all of us, my beloved brothers and sisters, as we enter the period of the Triodion. Amen.

Church of the Holy Belt, Kypseli
February 24, 2002

16.
MEATFARE SUNDAY
The judgment (Mt 25:31–46)

The Gospel passage that we have just heard, my dear brothers and sisters, brings us face to face with certain truths that we usually forget in our lives, perhaps because it is more convenient to forget.

One of these truths is that there will be an end to the history of this world and to our own personal history, and that this end is not determined by us but by the One Who gave us life, time, and history. And this end will be accompanied by the Judgment.

What do we mean by the word "judgment" [κρίσις]? Judgment indicates separating good from evil, and truth from lies. These things are very intertwined in our lives. Often we think that something is true, when in reality it is not true. Often we think we love others, when in reality we love ourselves. Often we think we are telling the truth to others, while in reality we are hiding something from ourselves. These things—good and evil, truth and lies, life and death— are always intertwined because we say we live, while in reality we are constantly dying.

And, therefore, this life and this world and this history of ours need a judgment. They need cleaning. There must be light. Light must be shed on everything that we construct—often cunningly and hypocritically—in our lives. Light must be shed so that ultimately we can know what is true. Let us not deceive ourselves. It is not by chance that the devil is called in the Bible the "father of lies" (John 8:44). He is the one who manages to present evil as good, falsehood as truth, death as life. He is the one who sets up idols in our lives and, not fully understanding what we are doing, we think that we are worshiping the truth and God when in fact we are worshiping those idols. And so there must be light. And the light is difficult. We need light to live, but when there is too much light, it is not always pleasant. We always want to keep secret compartments inside our hearts. We always want to appear different than what we really are. And this has to end sometime. The light must shine, the truth must be revealed, "the judgment of the world" must take place, as today's Gospel passage said.

And how will the judgment of the world take place? By what criterion will God judge the world? This light that will shine, what will it be in the end? If we pay attention to the Gospel passage, there is only one answer: love! God's love and man's love. The love of God! It is not by chance, my brothers and sisters, that God gave the judgment of the world to Christ. He will judge the world. "And He has given Him authority to execute judgment, because He is the Son of man" (Jn 5:27). He will judge the world and all people precisely because He became man. The love of God became incarnate and, consequently, He can judge us from within our very existence. And God will judge the world with our love. Precisely because Christ became man, He identified with people and indeed, as we heard in the Gospel passage, with the most humble and most insignificant people, with those we despise, with those we marginalize, with those we do not even consider worthy of our love and attention; He identified with these "least among us." And, consequently, one can no longer say that he loves God if he does not love man. One cannot set man out of the way and connect with God directly. We reach God through man. Because God also reached us with His love through man. Thus, our life will be judged based on this truth. This light will shine on us and the measure of our love will be seen: the measure of our love for our fellow human beings and through them our love for God, and not directly to God alone.

The commandment to love the Lord your God with all your heart and with all your soul and with all your mind can only be practiced in conjunction with the second commandment to "love your neighbor as yourself" (Mk 12:30–31). John says: "If we do not love the person whom we see, how can we say that we love God whom we do not see?" (cf. 1 John 4:20). Consequently, the criterion for judgment will be our love for our fellow human beings. And there the love of God—the love that became flesh in the person of Christ—will be present and will accept this love of ours.

"Inasmuch as you did it to one of the least of these My brethren, you did it to Me." The love you demonstrate to your brothers, to people, is addressed to me and ultimately reaches me. And vice versa, if you think that you can love God without loving people, then you are deceived, and the light that will shine on the Day of Judgment will reveal exactly this to you. It will reveal to you that you made a big mistake when you believed that you could approach God without going through man, through the love of man.

And the other truth is also very important: that the love we demonstrate to people will have less to do with whether we have harmed them, and more to do with whether we have failed to love them. If we omitted something, that will judge us. An omission is the reversal of ethics, because ethics tells us: "If you do this or this and that, you are okay." But omission tells you that no matter what you do, something is still missing, there is something more you should do, something more you should give, and this is the difficult part. Ethics tells us "don't steal" and Basil the Great tells us that "what you have legally and ethically, since no one else has them, you have stolen them." So what is the ethical criterion? Love transcends ethics, love always wants to give more and never reaches the point of saying that it has given everything. It gives, and something is always missing. And this means, my brothers and sisters, that our judgment will not be an easy matter; the question is how many of us will be in a position to satisfy these criteria.

So we are left with the effort, we are left to love and to owe love, as Paul says, "Owe no one anything except to love one another" (Rom 13:8), a love that is never paid off. And in this case, God's mercy is our only hope. This mercy that the publican sought two weeks ago, this mercy that the prodigal son sought last Sunday, this mercy of that love which has no end and which will judge us by comparison with our own love. And this is ultimately the only thing we can hope for and not in our own virtues, not in our own achievements, not in our own moral achievements. And this will make us humble and make us feel that we cannot judge anyone. "Judge not, that you be not judged" (Mt 7:1). Because by judging, we forget our own judgment, which will be based, as I said, on quite serious and difficult criteria.

My beloved brothers and sisters, God has given us two great gifts and He will judge us by the use we make of these gifts. The one gift is our time. Time is so precious that if it slips out of our hands without conveying love, then we are lost. The gift will be gone and we will not be able to recover it, because time is not recovered, unless within that time we have instilled elements that will survive eternally, so that with these elements of eternity we can regain the lost time.

And the other gift is our body. As long as we have time and the body, let's not neglect them, let's implant love in them. Because the body, like time, can leave our hands and then we will no longer convey with us elements of eternity to regain this body, which was given to us to be given and not to keep for ourselves us.

You see, my brothers and sisters, how this Gospel passage brings us face to face with great and difficult truths. It judges us, and this is what the Church announces to us today. The Church wants to make us feel how responsible we must be towards the time that God gave us and the body that God gave us, to give it for the love of others and not to keep it for ourselves. And thus we will be able to stand at the right hand of the One Who did exactly this, who gave His entire life on earth—as well as His body itself—to love, to his love for us. We cannot be found "in Christ" eternally if we do not have this common point with Him. So let us turn our attention there, my brothers and sisters.

With these thoughts, let us enter into Great Lent with the light continually shining into our lives and into our hearts, so that we can, when the light shines profusely at the judgment of the world, also have the courage to face this light and find ourselves together with the One who will judge the world. Amen.

Metropolitan Church of Saint Nicholas, Kaisariani
March 10, 2002

17.
MEATFARE SUNDAY
The parable of the Last Judgment (Mt 25:31–46)

There is a great truth revealed to us by the Gospel passage today, and by this Sunday in general, which our Church dedicates to the memory of the second, impartial, and final judgment of the world by the Lord.

This truth is not pleasing to people, because in one way or another they try to settle all their issues within history, within this life of ours. They forget that within this historical life of ours, our historical course, it is not easy—one might even say it's impossible—to distinguish absolutely between good and bad, truth and falsehood.

A lot of light needs to fall on our lives to distinguish the will of God from the will of men, to distinguish truth from falsehood, even love from our selfishness. And many times we think we love, but we love ourselves more and we love those who love us, because with the love we show them, we also receive their love and the benefits that arise from this love. It is very difficult in our actions to distinguish where our real love and self-love begin and end. There is also a confusion as to what is right and what is wrong, what is just and what is unjust.

You see how much confusion there is in the world, even as we speak, as to certain actions and decisions of the worldly authorities regarding what is right and what is wrong. Is it right to wage war? Is it right not to wage war?

There are so many discussions, because good and bad are so mixed in our lives that everyone can come up with arguments for their position, whatever choice they make. And there is difficulty in distinguishing the good from the bad even within our own behavior, because many times we convince ourselves that what we do and what we believe is right, while in reality we are mistaken. In fact, many times we deceive ourselves completely consciously—that is, we act hypocritically and give others the impression of good, while in reality the opposite is true. Our life in the world as we live it today is so difficult and so confusing that someday, finally, light must shine on it to definitively show what is right and what is wrong, what is good and what is evil. And when this light shines, there will no longer be any doubt where the truth is, where the will of God is, where God is. That is why the final judgment is necessary.

The final judgment is the light that will fall on our existence to definitively and clearly distinguish good from evil. And when this light shines, we will no longer be able to keep anything hidden and secret. "Books will be opened and hidden works made public," our Church sings today.[1] We will not be able to hide behind our hypocrisy, we will no longer have access to the dark compartments of our soul in which we can take refuge so as not to be perceived by others. The light brings with it the truth, and the truth is what sets us free and saves us. That is precisely why the final judgment is a judgment of truth.

This final judgment, however, will take place in such a way, as we heard in the Gospel passage, that the main criterion will not simply be truth, it will be love. With love we will be judged and the Lord, Jesus Christ, will judge us. To Him was given the power to judge the world, "and has given Him authority to execute judgment also, because He is the Son of Man" (Jn 5:27)—precisely because He is the incarnate love of God. God will not judge us the way people judge—that is, with justice—but with love. His love is our judgment. When His love appears, we are automatically judged and that is exactly why God gave the Judgment to Jesus Christ, love incarnate, to Him who is human like us, and therefore we can never pretend that God is judging us from the outside, outside of our existence. He judges us by our existence, taking our existence upon Himself and making it His own.

And when the Lord judges us, he will judge us with love and then a problem will appear before us, a question, which we heard in today's gospel passage. Where shall we demonstrate the kind

[1] Praises of Orthros.

of love that He demonstrated? To His person, of course. But those who were asked by the Lord say: "When did we see you, Lord, to demonstrate our love to you?" And the answer is: "You may not have seen me, but you saw my brothers, you saw the other people, you saw those you despise, the humble, the least, and if you demonstrated love to them, you demonstrated it to me."

So, my beloved brothers and sisters, a great question arises: How can love for Christ be manifested as love for other people? And how can love for others be manifested as love for Christ?

Many people say it is not necessary to love God if we love other people. But when you don't love God, neither can you truly love others. And the opposite is not correct: "I love God, but I don't love people." Saint John the Theologian says that this is a great lie, since "If you say that you love God, whom you don't see, but you don't love his image, the man whom you say, how can you be speaking the truth?" (cf. 1Jn 4:20).

The judgment, therefore, will turn on the first two great commandments: Love the Lord your God with all your heart and all your soul and all your mind, and love your neighbor as yourself" (Mt 22:37–39). It is not possible to keep one commandment without the other. These are the two great commandments, says the Lord, on which hang all the Law and the Prophets. The ascetic fathers had a wise saying: "If you have seen your fellow human being, you have seen God." We are called to strive for this combination of love toward God and our neighbor throughout our lives—since ultimately this love will judge us.

This effort, my brothers and sisters, will not be easy, since in the gospel passage we heard today the Lord will not judge only on the basis of what we did to others, but also what we failed to do for others, and our omissions, brothers and sisters, are many. We can compile a list of our good works and considers ourselves worthy to sit at the right hand of God, just as the Pharisee enumerated his works in the passage we heard two weeks ago. But if we write down our omissions, then our claims to the Kingdom of God collapse, because none of us has the right to sit at the right hand of God.

St. Basil the Great says somewhere: "You say that you don't steal, and of course you can prove that, but what you have as your property, the bread that you have to eat and someone else doesn't, that you have stolen from another." It is impossible, brothers and sisters, to be justified by our works. It is impossible to be saved by our virtues. We will be saved only by the grace of God. And this road to salvation is not only love, but love measured by our omissions, which means that the road includes repentance. Only repentance can save us; only the grace of God can save us.

Thus, today's gospel passage is not intended to inspire us to a social activism—that is, to simply start doing some good works—because no matter how much we do, there will always be omissions. It aims, therefore, to inspire us to repentance. Repentance is the road to salvation, and the grace of God is the only thing that can save us.

The judgment of the world, my beloved brothers and sisters, begins right now—it is already a reality. All human beings live this judgment, especially those who surrender themselves to this judgment in order not to endure it in a cruel way on the Day of Judgment. The saints of the Church let abundant light shine into their lives. And they call all of us to let light shine abundantly on our soul, to make us see the reality of ourselves—that is, our sinfulness. To make us humble and to lead us to repentance and confession, where everything is exposed to the light, and in this way the final judgment will not be so harsh for us.

When in this world we let the light shine freely into our being and we don't block it with efforts to project our virtues, with efforts to devalue others who are supposedly more sinful than us, when we let this light shine into our hearts and into our souls from now on, then the final judgment will be full of love for mankind.

In this state are all the saints, who allowed themselves to be bathed in the light of God's truth and grace, and in this way many of them acquire, according to God's judgment, the gift of discernment, that is, the ability and the gift to judge, to distinguish. To go to them and be told that this is right or that is wrong, to go with a confused mind, not knowing what to do, and to get the answer through them. Because the light has shined into their existence and now they see clearly in our confused world, they see clearly the will of God, the truth.

That is why, my brothers and sisters, it is within the Church alone that we can hope for God's mercy and wait for a loving and merciful judgment, to the extent that we too will allow ourselves already in this life to bathe in the light of the truth. Let us surrender ourselves to the judgment of the saints, those who can distinguish right from wrong, good from evil, and in this way within the Church we too await the final judgment with awe, with fear, but with hope and expectation of God's mercy, which I pray, my beloved brothers and sisters, that the Lord will give abundantly to all of us starting now in this life and on the day of judgment. Amen.

March 2, 2003

18.
MEATFARE SUNDAY
On Judgment and Love (Mt 25:31–46)

After the humility of the publican and the repentance of the prodigal son, the Church brings before us today—the third Sunday of the Triodion—the image of the final judgment of the world. A judgment that concerns each of us personally. Yet also a judgment that we easily forget, busy as we are with so many problems and interests in our daily lives. But the Church comes to recall for us the most important things in our lives, those things that last not only for the duration of this temporary earthly life, but which have eternal implications for us.

From this shocking description of the final judgment of the world that we heard in today's Gospel passage, I would like, my dear brothers and sisters, to dwell on one main point. How will the judgment of the world, the judgment of all of us take place? At this point, the following observations are very important.

First, it is important that it is not God the Father who judges the world, but Christ. But why does God give the judgment of the world to Christ, the Son of man, and does not come Himself to judge the world? This question is very important, because the answer is also very important.

Christ is the incarnate love of God. It is the way in which God demonstrates His love for the world. He created the world in Christ and He saves the world in Christ. Christ, the Son of God, the only-begotten and beloved Son of God, is the very love of God. God offers this love to the world, and He offers it in the flesh, that is, through a human being. And this is of great importance for the judgment, because it means that what will ultimately judge us is not God's justice, but God's love. God loves us and this will either be our eternal happiness or our eternal misery, because whoever judges us with His love judges us more harshly, and it is more difficult to endure the judgment of the one who loves us than the judgment of the one who doesn't love us.

Love judges simply by its own presence. Love itself constitutes a judgment, because it causes us to take a stand—either to accept it or to reject it. It demonstrates that it is superior to us, and makes us feel—as when someone loves us very much—humbled before this love. So love by itself judges the world, but the same love, which judges people so harshly, by its very nature is forgiving, shows understanding. God's love is strict and hard but also merciful. Christ looks at us sternly with one eye and sympathetically with the other. We see this in the icon of the Pantokrator in the Holy Monastery of Daphni, near Athens—an amazing creation of the 11th century. We see exactly how this dual quality of love is emitted: to be strict and at the same time to be merciful.

This love is embodied in Christ and that is why the judgment of the world has been given to Him. He will judge the world with this incarnate love of his. It is fitting that Christ should be the one to judge the world, because He took upon Himself and experienced all our temptations. We can no longer say "I could not resist, because the temptation was too great." This is an excuse that some of us put forward, but Christ Himself was tempted as much as any of us and even more. And the fact that He took these temptations upon Himself and resisted them is now a criterion for us. Therefore, we cannot say that it is not possible for man to resist temptations, since Christ as a man also faced and defeated temptations.

So Christ is the yardstick by which we are called to be measured. It is a bar so high that, when we measure ourselves with it—if we measure ourselves with it—then we understand how far we fall short, and this constitutes a judgment. We are judged by the incarnate love of God because this Love took part in all our temptations. He took part in all the difficulties of our life, in our pain and in death itself. And in this way the love of God in the person of Christ judges us. We are judged by God in Christ, because Christ is the love of God, who completely identified Himself with all people, even with the least, the most despised, even the most sinful. Christ identified Himself with these "least among us" and now shows us the way to God, which passes through our brothers and sisters.

He ultimately judges us for the attitude we maintain towards other people, our brothers and sisters. The Gospel passage that we have just heard insists on this criterion so much that one wonders: "How is it possible that God judges us not for actions that we have done or omitted before Him, but to our fellow human beings?" The reason is that God Himself in the person of Christ identified Himself with our fellow human beings. Listen to the Lord speaking in the passage today, saying: "I was hungry and you did not give me food, I was thirsty and you did not give me water, I was in prison and you did not visit Me." And those to whom He spoke marveled and said: "But how? We never saw you." Christ identifies Himself with the person of our neighbor, and it is precisely for this reason that Christ's judgment of the world will be a judgment that passes through our love for other people and not only for God.

Thus, my brothers and sisters, the final judgment will be rendered by Christ, as the incarnate love of God, and will essentially include the two commandments, the first and great commandments: You shall love the Lord your God with all your heart, and with all your soul, and with all your mind" and "you shall love your neighbor as yourself" (Mt 22:37–39). In the passage we heard today, Christ identifies himself with others and asks for love for our fellow human beings as love for Himself. He thus shows us that we cannot love God without loving our fellow human beings, but neither can we truly love our fellow human beings without loving God. Whoever loves God without loving his fellow man, says Saint John the evangelist, is a liar: "for he who does not love his brother whom he has seen, cannot love God whom he has not seen" (1Jn 4:20).

But there are also people who say they love others and claim that this kind of love suffices, without any need for God or love for Him. But they are also lying. Because true love for man must also include love for Him Who created us, for Him Who holds all people in existence. We cannot love the gifts without loving the One Who gave us the gifts; we cannot love our fellow human beings without loving God. It is this dual love that will judge the world. It will judge through the person of Christ, Who is love, this dual love, love for God and Father of the Lord and love toward our fellow human beings, for whom Christ gave His life and blood.

This kind of love, my brothers and sisters, is very difficult. As we heard in the Gospel passage today, it is difficult to say that one has reached the measure of this love, since we know that we will not be judged only by the actions we do take, but mainly by the actions we fail to take. And these are too many to count. How many people have we fed when they were hungry? How many people have we visited in prison? How can we fulfill this love towards others? We will always fall short. Love for God is, as the Lord says, the love that is fulfilled when God's commandments are obeyed. How can we claim that we have kept all the commandments and that we really love God? It is, therefore, difficult to say that people will be able to meet the criteria that the Lord sets forth in the final judgment that we heard today.

That is why even the saints constantly ask for God's mercy. What is necessary in the final judgment is God's mercy. The saint is the one who lives in constant repentance, and the saint is the one who constantly depends on the mercy of God. By constantly repeating "Lord, have mercy," the Church wants to remind us of this truth, that we cannot rely on our virtue to ensure eternal life. We can only rely on God's mercy, and God's mercy comes when we repent, when we realize our weakness, when we do not rely on our own virtues and our own strengths; only then does God's mercy visit us.

So, my brothers and sisters, let today's passage, about which there is so much to say, be a reminder for all of us that this world and this time that God has given us, this short life on earth, is temporary, yes, but it is also the foundation on which we will build eternity. It is our springboard into the search for eternity, since God wants us to live eternally and to be eternally blessed near Him. God does not want us to perish; God does not want us to waste this eternal life by thinking it is something that is defined by time here in this world.

Let us see this life, my brothers and sisters, as an opportunity to redeem eternal life, to find ourselves, through the prayers of the saints, at the right hand of God in His Kingdom. Amen.

February 15, 2004

19.
CHEESEFARE SUNDAY
Paradise (Mt 6:14–21)

Adam sat opposite Paradise.[1]

With these words, the hymnist of the Church introduces us, my dear brothers and sisters, to the meaning of this Sunday. This Sunday is dedicated to the memory of Adam's expulsion from Paradise. And the significance of this day is so great that it strikes the deepest chords of our being. Because nothing, my beloved brothers and sisters, is so deeply rooted in the human soul as the memory of Paradise. Nothing colors our actions, our thoughts, our efforts as much as the lost Paradise, the Paradise for which we were made.

We only have to look carefully at our lives and we will see that in all of creation only we humans feel that our existence is tragic, that what we are and what we have and what we do is not what we would like and what we desire to have and to do. There are many events in our life that testify to this.

Every time we raise a voice of protest about the injustice that exists in the world, every time we see the strong suppressing the weak, every time we see our enemies stronger than us and suffocating our rights, every time we face war, slander, the evil of others, every time our friends betray us, every time we are indignant about all this, we are yearning for Paradise.

And we yearn for it, above all, when we are indignant and protest against death and decay. In all of creation, man is the only being that cannot reconcile with death. He does not accept a natural and biological event such as death. He protests, and his protest is not simply negative. But with his protest, he creates the belief in himself that death is not so strong as to suffocate and

[1] Oikos of Orthros.

make the people we love disappear; that the people we love survive even after death.

This yearning for immortality is the cry for the lost Paradise. Because we were created for immortality. We are created for eternity. We are called to eternity. But, unfortunately, we refused this call and preferred to be deprived of this Paradise, to be deprived of this future for which God had called us, and to fall into an existence oppressed by death, decay, and injustice. And this yearning for Paradise manifests itself in all our endeavors, which turn out to be tragic. Despite this, however, they demonstrate our nostalgia for Paradise.

Look at what is happening in our culture, in every culture. What does man want to express with culture, with art, with each of his creations? He wants to declare that the world as it is does not satisfy him. He wants to fight death and decay through art, through culture, through the history he writes. But he doesn't succeed! And it is tragic when he finds that his efforts have failed. How does it happen that civilized people and nations become victims of evil and servants of evil? We saw it in the world wars we lived through in the previous century. Civilized people were the ones who took the lead in the destruction of humanity. Civilization and culture, therefore, does not ensure us Paradise.

And we think that knowledge, science, and our efforts to expand our knowledge ensures it. And today, especially in our time, we live this delusion: that science is what will solve all our problems. And the rapid progress of science testifies to nothing other than the tragic impasse in which we find ourselves. Because every advance in science entails new problems and new difficulties and new impasses. And in this way it becomes clear that even science will not be able to satisfy our desire for Paradise.

Not even education, the education in which we place so much hope, can ensure us that we will satisfy our yearning for Paradise. Because education is often connected with actions that manifest evil and that lead to hell instead of Paradise. And so, my brothers and sisters, we remain nostalgic for Paradise. And we wonder how we can find Paradise again. We will find the answer to this question if we think about how Paradise was lost. And, if we reverse the way in which Paradise was lost, we may find the way to its recovery.

Paradise was lost because man believed that he could make Paradise by himself. Because he declared himself independent of God, because he believed that he is god and took into his hands the fate of all people, his own fate, and—as we can see today with the destruction of the natural environment—even the fate of the physical world. He took all this into his hands, declared himself god, and now look at the paradise he has created. Man tried—with various political, social and economic systems—to demonstrate that he could transform the earth into paradise on his own. But the results of all these efforts have left a bitter taste in our mouths.

Therefore, in order to regain Paradise, man needs to understand his limits, his weakness—in other words, to repent. He must understand that he is not a god, that he was called to be a god but only in communion and relationship with the one and true God. And every disconnection from God, every time man declares his independence from God, is the loss of Paradise. Therefore, the way for man to regain Paradise is—as a first step—his repentance. To understand his insufficiency. To understand that he needs to be in communion with God, the true God, and that he cannot make heaven on earth by himself.

The second reason Paradise was lost is that when Adam rejected God, man—that is, all of us, because Adam is our progenitor, he is our symbol—rejected the other, every other. He elevated himself, his individual self, to god. In other words, the virus of individualism entered into human life. And if this virus is not expelled from their midst, they cannot regain Paradise.

We heard in the Gospel passage today:

For if you forgive men their trespasses, your heavenly Father will also forgive you. But if you do not forgive men their trespasses, neither will your Father forgive your trespasses (Mt 6:14–15).

Why is the forgiveness of our brothers and sisters so important? And why does the Lord connect it with the Kingdom of God, as a precondition of the Kingdom of God, that is, as a precondition of Paradise? Because, my brothers and sisters, Paradise is where our brother is, where the other is. Paradise is found in love. Paradise is the place with room enough for all of us. And the moment each of us tries to claim it for ourselves, we have lost it!

So what is forgiveness? It is not simply not harboring ill will for the other. It means, if we analyze the etymology of the word, to fit together with the other in the same space, to "co-fit," to "co-exist." So it is not enough not to harbor ill will in my soul for the other person. I must feel the need for his presence in my life all the time. I must feel the need for the other, the love expressed as the presence of the other.

Paradise is what the Church tries to give us in the Divine Liturgy. It is our coexistence with others in love. And only when this happens, then death will be defeated. Because death is nothing but our cutting off, the breaking of our relationship with others. It is the cutting off of communion with others. And "co-fitting [forgiveness]", to "co-exist" in the same space with the other, is our Paradise.

A modern existentialist philosopher, known to all of us, declared that "the other is my hell." And indeed this expresses the condition of man after his fall. But the reverse is true: the other is my Paradise. Only when we love, then we feel what Paradise is about. And we could define Paradise with just a few words: it is love without death! The love that defeats death! The love that brings us into constant coexistence with our brother.

My brothers and sisters, we are now entering Great Lent and the Church, in its wisdom, calls us today to forgive each other. This is not a formalistic moral obligation, it is not a pietistic act, it is not just a formula. We have to do here with the memory of Paradise, and with that call which God directed to Adam and which Adam rejected. It is that call which the Church directs to us now—to reverse Adam's attitude. To recognize through repentance our inadequacy, to recognize through repentance that only in communion with God can we find Paradise again and to recognize with love and forgiveness the existence of the other, as a necessary condition for our happiness, for our existence.

With these thoughts, my beloved brothers and sisters, let us enter the period of Great Lent and let us always keep in mind that we are called to Paradise. And Paradise starts already in this life; it starts already from our attitude towards God and towards our fellow man. It starts already with the reversal we will make of the attitude of our first-created progenitor Adam.

I pray that Holy and Great Lent will pass for all of us with this spirit, the spirit of repentance and love of our brother, so that we can, cleansed of our individualism and selfishness—cleansed of our self-confidence that we can create paradises in this world—see where the real Paradise is and be made worthy to live it. Amen!

Church of Saint Catherine of Ampelokipi,
Metochion of the Holy Monastery of Mt. Sinai
March 9, 2003

20.
CHEESEFARE SUNDAY
Concerning forgiveness (Mt 6:14–21)

By the Lord's grace, my beloved brothers and sisters, we have been accounted worthy to enter into the period of Great and Holy Lent. And during the preliminary period of the Triodion, on the first Sunday, the Church set before us the example of the publican, an example of repentance and confession—that is, confession of our ultimate sinfulness. Then the Church gave us the Parable of the Prodigal Son to show us that our sinfulness is not a dead end, that there is a love waiting with its open arms to welcome us and say to us: "I no longer think or want you to tell me your sinfulness; it is enough for me that you return to me." And God arranges a whole feast to celebrate the return of every sinner. After this repentance, the Church brings us the following Sunday face to face with the final judgment, to show us once more that no matter how much we strive for virtue, no matter how many efforts we make, in the end it is only God's mercy that will save us and not our virtue. And on this Sunday, the Church brings us, my brothers and sisters, face to face with one of the most difficult things, the most difficult door through which we must pass, and this is the forgiveness of our brother. Forgiveness is a difficult thing. Why is it so difficult? First of all, because we don't know what forgiveness means and we think it's very easy. But if we think about what this word means, we will see that it is indeed not just one of the difficult things, but the most difficult thing in human life.

We think, my brothers and sisters, that forgiveness is simply not wanting to harm our enemy. "I don't hold grudges," we say, and we reassure ourselves "I don't want the other person's harm. I forgive him." And how many times, in fact, do we say: "I forgive. I don't forget of course, but I forgive." We do not forget but we forgive—this is a contradiction. You cannot truly forgive if you remember the harm that the other person does to you. But how can you forget the harm that the other person did to you? How can you erase it from your memory?

True forgiveness is not that which simply withholds vengeance on our enemy, but it is that which makes us love our enemy, to embrace him, to consider him as beloved as ourselves and those closest to us, and to give him space in our existence. The word "forgive" [συγχωρῶ] means exactly this: I make space [χωρῶ], I share the same space with the other [συν-χωρῶ], I take him into my space, the space of my existence, the space of my heart, the space of my world. And it is truly a mystery, my brothers and sisters, that this space we occupy called the world, called existence, does not contain us. Everyone makes his own space and sets his boundaries—whether they are called families, states, or tribes—and he says: "This is my space and no one else can enter here."

This is what animal behaviorists observe in animals, which instinctively protect their space and attack anyone who invades it. And man "was compared to the senseless cattle, and became like them"[1] after the fall. And man too has his own space and wants to defend it. And he raises whole armies to make sure the space remains his own and no one else enters. But where did we find this space? Is it not a gift from God? Isn't this the world God created and placed us in? Did we make it? Nevertheless, we claim it as our own and leave little room for other people. We displace them from their space, we kick them out of the synagogue, we remove them from our lives. But then comes today God's demand that we forgive others—that is, that we take them into our space, we make them partakers of all the goods God has given us, participants in our very existence, participants in our hearts.

That's why I said, my brothers and sisters, that forgiveness is a difficult thing, because you can forget the harm that the other person did to you, you can perhaps not hold a grudge against him. But to take him into your home, to make him a roommate—this bad person, this criminal, this sinner? Forgiveness is a difficult thing.

[1] Ps 48:13 LXX.

But in the gospel passage we heard today, my brothers and sisters, the Lord told us in a stern tone: "You will never be forgiven if you do not forgive," and God will not accept you into His own space. Because this is how God forgives; He does not forgive emotionally or psychologically. God forgives by embracing in His existence the whole world, even His enemies, as Christ did on the Cross. In His space, then, God embraces all, and if we find ourselves in the situation of not accepting one of our brothers in our space, then we automatically exclude ourselves from God's space, because our brother is already in God's space through His love and forgiveness.

So, why can't we be forgiven by God if we can't forgive our brother? Because the space in which God will put us also contains our brother. What will we do? How will we fit in there? Therefore, if we do not accept and love our brother, we cannot fit into God's space. And thus, we will not be able to be forgiven by God. We will be apart from God.

There are, my beloved brothers and sisters, many reasons why the key to Paradise lies in the forgiveness of our brother. First of all, the fact is that our brother's sins against us, no matter how bad they are, do not compare in seriousness with our own sins against God. We have racked up a debt in the millions, and God forgives it all. But we, when our brother owes us five dollars, do not forgive him. So, this is a very significant reason. We cannot expect God to forgive the huge amount of our sins, if we do not forgive the few sins of others.

Also, my brothers and sisters, another very important reason: Who are we to judge our brother? In the Epistle reading that we heard this morning in Church, the Apostle Paul says to the Romans: "Who are you to judge another's servant?" (Rom 14:4). Who are you to say if the other is sinful? He has his own judge and his own master, and he can hold him accountable or he can forgive him. But when we take the decision into our own hands, it is like taking the decision out of God's hands, to decide for ourselves who can be close to us in our life and who cannot.

And forgiveness is further necessary, my brothers and sisters, because none of us, fortunately, depend ultimately on our past;

we depend on our future. And if we are judged based on our past, we are all doomed. However, God, who forgives us in Christ, gives us a new future, and therefore we have no right to judge our brother based on his past. Because God has given him his future. And we don't know that the one we exclude from our space will not tomorrow become a great saint, someone who will have repented, someone who will have finally found himself in the Kingdom of God. Therefore, we do not have the right to determine who we will accept and who we will reject. We cannot reject anyone. We have no right to reject anyone.

Thus, in his Kingdom, God, because he is so rich in mercy and forgiveness, will forgive sins and take many of our enemies to himself. And what will happen then, my brothers? How will we live with them forever? What shall we say then? Ah, since my neighbor is here who did me harm, I am not sitting in heaven, I want to leave. And how will we sit next to God eternally, when God forgives our brother and we have not forgiven him?

It is not possible, my beloved brothers and sisters, to be saved, or even to begin—as now with Great Lent—the first step of our effort and our repentance, if we do not forgive our brother completely, not only emotionally but also to take him into our existence. Just as in the Church, during the Liturgy, God brings us all together and makes us stand next to each other, whether someone has harmed the other or not, so in all our lives we must open the space of our soul and the space of our existence to accommodate everyone, especially our enemies.

I was impressed, my brothers and sisters, by something I read in one of our saints, Saint Anastasios of Sinai, who writes on this subject and says to the brothers:

I beseech you, turn away from the most unforgivable sin, holding grudges, and if you want to know that the darkening of the soul by holding grudges is the worst sin, listen: Every other sin takes a little time to commit and then it is over, but holding grudges is a passion that never stops burning. Where grudges have taken root, nothing avails: neither fasting, nor prayer, nor tears, nor confession, nor supplication, nor virginity, nor charity, nor any other good thing, for holding grudges towards a brother destroys everything.

I often hear many, says Saint Anastasios, saying: "Alas, how shall I be saved?" I don't have the strength to fast, I don't know how to stay awake to keep vigil, I can't live in virginity, I can't leave the world—how can I be saved?"

I will tell you how you can be saved: Forgive and you will be forgiven. This is a quick way to salvation, and I will show you another. What is it? Don't judge so that you won't be judged. He who judges before the coming of Christ is an antichrist, because he takes the position that belongs to Christ.

I said, my brothers and sisters, at the beginning that forgiveness is a very difficult thing. And Saint Silouan, under whose roof we are standing at this moment, characterized forgiveness of the brother and love of the enemy as the greatest miracle. It is a miracle. This is the miracle that God Himself has done first, accepting us sinners into His embrace, and this miracle calls us all to imitate it, no matter how hard it may be. So, my brothers and sisters, in the end what will judge us is love, especially the love of enemies, because loving the one who loves you is easy, and it can ultimately be selfish; loving the one who benefits you is logical, it is not a miracle. To love the one who hates you, that is the miracle.

So, my brothers and sisters, the Church, which is a space in which we all fit, an open space—like here at our Monastery, in which all nations, all nationalities, all tribes, all languages—fit. Let there be a space in our heart so that our brother can fit in there, so that every person can fit in there, even our enemy. And in this way, my brothers and sisters, we will indeed be able to fit into God's space, in the embrace that accepts all sinners and all enemies. In this embrace, I pray, my brothers and sisters, that we may all find ourselves eternally with God's grace. Amen.

February 22, 2004

21.
CHEESEFARE SUNDAY
Paradise and forgiveness (Mt 6:14–21)

Adam sat opposite Paradise.[1]

With these words, my beloved brothers and sisters, the hymnist introduces us to today's Sunday, which is dedicated to the memory of Adam's exit and exile from Paradise. Adam, this symbol and person who comprises all of humanity throughout the ages, is deprived of Paradise, and being outside of Paradise he cries and mourns.

Nothing, my beloved brothers and sisters, is so deeply rooted in the consciousness of human beings, nothing is so permanent in the course of the history of the human race as the memory of, desire for, and the expectation of Paradise. Underneath all our actions, under all our pains and our pursuits and our labors, this search for Paradise is hidden. Man looks for Paradise in different ways. He seeks it every time he raises a voice of protest about the injustice that exists in the world, every time he raises a voice of protest about everything that man is unjustly subjected to in this life, wishing to eliminate all of this, to maintain justice and peace and love between people. When man desires and strives for all these, he seeks Paradise. He seeks it, however, especially when he refuses to accept decay and death. Because decay and death are precisely the result of the loss of Paradise. And every time we raise within us sobs, pain, and voices of protest for the death of our loved ones, we are actually looking for Paradise. Man cannot find peace in this world; he tries to build a paradise by himself. He seeks it through the efforts of education, making—so he thinks—better people for a better society. But this does not work, because Paradise cannot be regained by educating people and

[1] Oikos of Orthros.

increasing their knowledge. And the more people's knowledge advances, the more problems arise. This is how new problems are created and instead of being happy, man increases his unhappiness. How many have promised us paradise! How many promise us paradise either with their various ideologies or with their various political and economic systems, and all of them prove in the end that they are frauds. No one can give us the Paradise we ask for! In vain do we look for it in history and in this life! But we can't help but look for it. Man, restless, seeks Paradise in every possible way—through art, through culture, through everything he creates.

Paradise, my beloved brothers and sisters, is not where we look for it, because the Paradise that was lost, the Paradise that we seek, is the Paradise that God made for us. Paradise was lost from the moment that man said to God "I will build paradise. I don't want your Paradise. I want to be the ruler of history, the ruler of the world!" And ever since man took this effort into his own hands, to make his own paradise, it has been a failure. There is only one way for man to find Paradise again: to recognize that he cannot create Paradise. In this way, he will be led to repentance, he will recognize that man is a creation of God and that Paradise is a gift from God and not the result of his own efforts. And man lost Paradise when he began to base all his hopes not only on his own efforts but also on the goods of the world. And when he accumulates goods and thinks that in this way he is creating his paradise, he is again disappointed, because it turns out that the happiness he is looking for is not offered by material goods.

Paradise was also lost, my beloved brothers and sisters, the moment that our heart became so constricted that it could not contain our fellow man. A modern philosopher told us that the other is our hell. The truth is, my brothers and sisters, that the other is our Paradise. Only if we can fit the other into our being, only then are we truly happy. Paradise is love. Paradise is love without death. Paradise is the place that holds everyone else, even our enemies. That is why the Lord in today's gospel passage spoke to us about forgiveness. That is why tonight, as we enter Holy and Great Lent, the Church invites us to Forgiveness Vespers. Forgiveness is very important, my brothers and sisters, in order to find the lost Paradise. Because this forgiveness, this love, opens the way for our life, our existence to be a big embrace, in which everyone will fit, all the "others," those who love us and those who hate us. Both our friends and our enemies. This is the true Paradise. It is love, which embraces everyone and everything.

We are now called, my beloved brothers and sisters, to enter Holy and Great Lent, this period of fasting, which means that we realize that material goods will not give us Paradise. During this period, let us give special importance to forgiveness and love. The word "forgiveness" means, precisely, to share the same space with others. To leave space in my existence so that others can exist as well.

Forgiveness is not a simple feeling. It is not simply to say "I don't hate someone," "I forgive them emotionally, psychologically." Forgiveness is to move beyond these feelings and to actually show the other that he has a place in my own space, in the space of my being.

So, my brothers and sisters, let us open our hearts wide, let us forgive everyone, and then the lost Paradise will be found again. This is the only way, my brothers and sisters, to find the Paradise we long for, which we seek through all the efforts we make in our lives. I pray that the Lord will grant us this Paradise, which begins already in this life, when we love and embrace others, both now and in eternity, when He comes to establish His Kingdom in the world. Amen!

Holy Church of St Panteleimon, Acharnion Street
March 9, 2008

22.
SUNDAY OF ORTHODOXY
Faith as a personal experience (John 1:44–52)

The Gospel passage that we have just heard, my dear brothers and sisters, describes the call of the disciples by the Lord. And the Evangelist John in particular describes this passage in a theological way, as he usually does when he presents events from the life of Christ. The other evangelists limit themselves to simply describing the events, but John also gives us their theological interpretation, their deepest theological meaning. So let's follow this passage as John describes it to us in the Gospel.

The previous day, the Lord had already called Andrew and Peter, from the city of Bethsaida in Galilee. The next day, walking there in Galilee, He also called the compatriot of these two brothers, Philip. And Philip follows him. Overjoyed as he was because he found the Messiah, whom every Israelite had been eagerly anticipating for generations, he ran to meet Nathanael and told him with joy: "We have found the Messiah—it is Jesus of Nazareth." But Nathanael is incredulous and says: "Is it possible for something good to come out of Nazareth?" How is it possible for the Messiah to come from this humble city? Then Philip, instead of trying to prove to him with words that indeed Jesus is the Messiah they are waiting for, simply tells him "Come and see."

We can never prove the truth of our faith, that is, what we believe, except through our personal experience, through personal encounter. And if we do not meet Christ personally, we can never truly believe.

Philip says, therefore, to Nathanael: "Come to meet the Messiah and, when you meet him, then you will believe." And indeed Nathanael goes to meet the Lord, and at that moment the evangelist notes a small detail that is important. When Christ saw him approaching, he said to him: "Behold a true Israelite, in whom there is no guile"—who has no guile in his heart. And in this way, the Evangelist John gives us the other condition for true faith, which is a pure heart. The other Israelites, such as the Pharisees, they too had met Christ, but their hearts were not pure, they were not obedient, and therefore they could not believe. Therefore, it is not enough to meet Christ, we must meet him with a pure heart. If our heart is full of passions, we will never recognize Christ. The purity of our heart is a condition for our faith, and not the other way around. And as the Lord says in one of the "Beatitudes" that we all know: "Blessed are the pure in heart for they will see God" (Mt 5:8). In order to recognize Christ, you must have cleansed your heart of passions, to be guileless like Nathanael.

The Lord, therefore, pointed out this characteristic of Nathanael, and in this way showed us one more condition for knowing the true God in the person of Christ. Let's meet him personally, but let's meet him with an obedient and pure heart. And the evangelist proceeds to describe to us what happened next.

And the Lord says to Nathanael: "Before Philip called you, I saw you sitting under the fig tree." Nathanael was amazed. "How did this man know I was there? How did he see me?" And this miracle prompted him to exclaimed: "You are the Messiah. Indeed, I recognize now that you are the Messiah." So the miracle made him recognize Christ, but the Lord goes ahead and says to him: "Did you believe because you saw this miracle? You shall see greater things than these." In other words, you will see greater miracles that will have much more significance than this miracle you just saw.

If we know Christ and recognize Him and believe in Him because of a miracle, it is not enough.

This kind of faith is not enough. Our encounter with Christ is not complete. And then Christ said to Nathanael: "You will see something much greater than the miracle you just saw: you will see heaven opened, and the angels of God ascending and descending, and you will see the glory of the Son of man, the glory of the Messiah." Thus, the most important thing—much more important than the miracle—is for one to know God and to approach Him; it is to see His glory, and to participate in the glory of His Kingdom.

When once the disciples of the Lord rejoiced because a miracle had happened, the Lord said to them: "Do not rejoice over this thing; rejoice more that your names are written in heaven" (Lk 10:20)—written in the Kingdom of God. Only there is our meeting with Christ truly complete, Who is our true knowledge and the object of our faith. Here, then, is the whole journey that the Gospel passage today describes: the personal encounter with Christ; the encounter with a guileless heart; the readiness to accept the miracle, but not to depend on the miracle for our faith. Even more, it is look forward to our eternal relationship as well as to the glory of God, with our participation in this glory, if He so wills.

Today, my beloved brothers and sisters, the Church dedicates this Sunday to Orthodoxy, to the honor of Orthodoxy. And the Church did not appoint this passage in the readings today without a reason, because what is Orthodoxy? Orthodoxy, the true and genuine Orthodoxy—because there are also some versions of Orthodoxy which are not completely genuine—does not proselytize, it does not rush to convince people of the truth it believes in, to convince them logically, to convince them with logical arguments. Orthodoxy invites people to come and see. The sermon of the Orthodox Church begins and ends in the church temple, where the Eucharist is celebrated, and in the life of the Church. "Come and see, I don't logically oblige you to believe. And only after you come and see, if you believe, you are welcome. However, if you don't want to believe, you are free to do so."

What is happening with the monastery here is a good example. It exists in an environment in which it could proselytize, go around and try to make everyone Orthodox. But it doesn't. It is simply here and anyone who wants to can "come and see." And whoever sees, let him believe, if he wants to believe. This is the Orthodox way to preach Christ.

And when someone comes to the Orthodox Church, what will they see? He will certainly see all of us sinners and, alas, many times he will be affected by this and will turn his back and leave. But we will not show him our own sinfulness, we will show him the saints of our Church. We will show him those who not only met Christ with a pure heart but were also glorified by Him. They participated in the glory of God, and they are, my beloved brothers and sisters, our face that we will show to others—our saints and martyrs, who were glorified by God because they knew him in a personal relationship after they purified theirs hearts and made them truly guileless.

That is why, within our Orthodox Church, my dear brothers and sisters, we represent the martyrs and the saints, as well as Christ Himself, and show them to the world, with glory and splendor, with light—with our icons. It is not by chance, my dear brothers and sisters, that today, as we celebrate the Sunday of Orthodoxy and hear this shocking gospel passage, we also honor and display the holy icons. For the holy icons there was a great struggle, as you know from history. The controversy lasted for over a hundred years, and many even had to give their blood defending the holy icons.

Many could not understand why there was so much debate about icons and why our Church attaches so much importance to icons. It is precisely because we want to depict this glory of God that the Lord speaks of in today's gospel passage, to show it as a reality in the faces of our saints. Our saints are the reflection of the glory of Christ, the glory that we will see in the Kingdom of God, when we will now see God face to face and, those of us who deserve it, we will have before us the whole scene that the Lord describes today speaking to Nathanael: The heavens will be opened, the angels will ascend and descend and the glory of God will be appear before us.

This glory, therefore, is shown to us by the holy icons and that is why the Orthodox Church gives so much importance to the icons. And in fact, today we hold them up, we honor them, we venerate them, because this is what we have to show the world. Next to our own sinfulness stands the holiness of Christ and the saints. And because the Lord accepts to have us in this body of saints, in the body of the Church, even though we are sinners, we can only preach and show one thing, and that is our saints, it is the glory of Christ as depicted in our saints. This, my dear brothers and sisters, is the boast of Orthodoxy.

It often seems, my dear brothers and sisters, that the Orthodox are triumphalist and say: "We have the truth, and no one else." Yes, but what does "we have the truth" mean? Do we have it in our mind? Do we have it in the arguments we can present to the world? Will our logical arguments convince anyone that we have the truth? Or do we have it because God has called us to be stewards of this tradition of the saints, stewards of the tradition of icons, the tradition of our divine worship—which we must keep undefiled as our most precious good—and this is our boast. Our boast, my beloved brothers and sisters, is the tears of the saints and the blood of the martyrs.

And it is no coincidence that, when our Church refers to the saints, it speaks of brilliance. It is said that the Church wears the blood of the martyrs as purple. And the Cross of Christ is for the Apostle Paul the only boast: "But God forbid that I should boast except in the cross of our Lord Jesus Christ."[1] That is the pride of the Orthodox Church.

Within the Orthodox Church, in the course of our history from ancient times but also in our modern era, there is the Cross. In general, our Church raises the Cross of Christ, and this Cross is its glory. And by lifting the Cross of Christ in this life, we open the door to see what the Lord said to Nathanael: The angels of God ascending and descending upon the Son of man. This glory, the glory of the last days, the glory of the Kingdom of God, I pray, my beloved brothers and sisters, that the Lord bestow on all of us. Amen.

March 16, 2008

[1] Gal 6:14.

23.
3rd SUNDAY OF LENT
(Veneration of the Holy Cross)
The Cross of Christ and the struggle against evil (Mk 8:34–9:1)

Today, my beloved brothers and sisters, the Church calls us to venerate the Holy Cross.

We are called to venerate the Holy Cross at this particular moment in time primarily because the Church wants to give us a source of strength to continue the struggle of fasting and the spiritual struggle against the passions. And one wonders: Why is the Cross a source of strength and empowerment? The Cross is a source of power and strength because evil was defeated on it with the death of our Lord, and the greatest struggle with evil in history took place there. Up there, on the Cross, the entire power of evil was manifested, which primarily aims to war against God Himself and everything God created.

This war against God and against God's will is evil itself. This is what the devil has tried to do since the very beginning. When God manifested Himself to the world and in history, He provoked evil to its full extent and power. And when evil wanted to kill God Himself on the Cross, then what else can it do? When evil exhausted its power over God Himself and killed Him, then there was nothing else it could do. And that is why from that moment the Cross became the most effective means of fighting evil.

It is no coincidence that the pious Byzantine emperors, from the time of Constantine the Great, used the cross to defeat evil. The famous "Ἐν τούτῳ νίκα"[1] which Constantine the Great saw written in the sky, put an end to the wrath of evil in the form of persecutions against Christians. The Cross put an end to these persecutions and since then every battle against barbarians, as the hymns we hear today say, is fought in the name of the Holy Cross.

[1] *In hoc signo vinces.* "In this sign, you shall conquer."

The Church always fights evil with the cross. It is not by chance that we make the sign of the cross over the sick in order to be freed from the disease. It is not by chance that the cross makes the demons go away. Evil and the devil cannot tolerate the cross. But why, my beloved brothers and sisters, was the Cross needed to defeat evil? Couldn't God, with the power He has, annihilate evil? Why did He have to be crucified to redeem us from evil? Surely we cannot explore the depth of the wisdom of God who chose this way, but we can humbly, my beloved brothers and sisters, point out two things.

First, that the Cross was the requirement of God's love. God, of course, could do anything with His power, but He wanted to destroy evil by entering into our own existence and sharing the consequences of evil. If evil strikes us and we suffer and die, God does not see these events from afar, as Aristotle imagined his immovable and unmoved god. Our God, my brothers and sisters, entered into our very existence and sought to take upon Himself the consequences of evil. And He teaches us in this way that we cannot, my brothers and sisters, demonstrate our love for others without sharing their pain. And God many times allows us to suffer, to be tortured, to be wronged, to be slandered, because otherwise we will not understand within our own existence what it means to withstand all these evil attacks. In order to say that we truly love others, we must share in their pain.

With the Cross, Christ demonstrated something else besides His love, which I mentioned in yesterday's sermon—His respect for freedom. If God annihilated evil by force, then our freedom would be lost. And let us not forget that evil came precisely from our freedom; there would be no evil if God had not made free beings.

God, then, made free beings in order to keep them free forever. And, in order to eliminate the evil, there was nothing else He could do that would respect our freedom other than to allow Himself to be struck by our freedom. And this is precisely what happened on the Cross. All the power of the freedom of evil, the negative aspect of freedom, was exhausted. And this is why a person who respects the freedom of others, following the example of the Cross and the Crucified Lord, will never force another into becoming his friend or subjugate him; he would prefer to become a victim himself of the other's negative freedom rather than deprive him of his freedom.

Thus, the Cross was only the only solution. The Cross of love and freedom had before it to defeat evil, and that is why we now believe that love and kindness defeats evil. It seems weak at first sight, but our love has great power. The Apostle Paul says: Do good to your enemy, "for by so doing you will heap burning coals upon his head" (Rom 12:20). He burns, he cannot bear them. Evil seems, for a moment, to be stronger than good, but good wins in the end, and this is the great message that the Cross of Christ brings to our lives.

The Church, my brothers and sisters, calls us today to venerate the Cross, not only to draw strength from the power it has to defeat evil—against which we struggle daily, against temptations, passions and all evil—but also to take up our own cross, as we heard in the gospel passage a little while ago. Yes, when we see the Cross and worship it, we can get strength from it, but that's not all. We too must lift up the Cross of Christ. And here one can observe two forms of the cross which the Cross of Christ calls us to lift.

First of all, there are the imposed crosses of life, and of course our life is full of such crosses: illnesses, sorrows, betrayals of friends, slander, so many evils that befall us throughout our lives, without wanting it, and all of these we are called to bear with patience, whatever happened. Many times we think that the other person's cross is lighter than ours, but even if it is, let us accept the cross that God grants us, because with every cross that God grants, He aims at our good and our salvation. And this is obviously the cross for us—this is our personal, imposed cross.

However, my brothers and sisters, if we look at the Cross of Christ, we will see that the cross that we are called to lift is not an imposed cross, but a voluntary cross. Christ was not obliged to be crucified, to take up His Cross. He could have defeated His enemies even at the last moment, as He explained to his enthusiastic disciple, Peter, shortly before the Crucifixion, saying that He could call twelve legions of angels and avoid crucifixion. He also could have avoided the Cross because he was not only innocent, but sinless.

Our own crosses, on the other hand, most of them anyway, are due to our own sins and our own mistakes. "He had done no violence, nor was there any deceit in His mouth" (Is 53:9), yet He took up the Cross willingly. And He calls us, too, in this way, to take up not only our imposed crosses with patience, but also to take up voluntary crosses as well, crosses that we are not obliged to take up. And here, my brothers and sisters, is the measure of the saints, where things become very difficult but also magnificent, blessed, and full of grace. Every small cross that we willingly take up brings abundant grace from God.

The Church offers us such voluntary crosses, but leaves it to us whether we will take them up. If we don't want to, the Church doesn't force us to. The Church advises us, for example, to fast, but it's not obligatory. It is a cross of sacrifice, a renunciation of something that we feel the need for—food—so that we too can take up a voluntary cross. To give alms—not from our abundance but from our lack—is to deprive ourselves in order to help others. It is not an imposed cross; it is a cross that we are called to bear voluntarily. The same is true for many other things.

We could, for example, take an enemy of ours to court and put him in prison—this is what justice demands, because he has wronged us and harmed us. It is a voluntary cross for someone to say that I will not strike my enemy even if I am in the right. One could enumerate many such crosses. What I want to emphasize is that all the saints of the Church took up crosses willingly, and the martyrs of the Church could have avoided martyrdom, but they lifted their cross voluntarily. Who forced the saints to go to the desert? Who forced them to go through these deprivations and tears? This decision was entirely voluntary—their own, free decision—as were the actions they took.

Therefore, my brothers and sisters, today when we venerate the Cross of Christ, let us take it not only as a source of strength—because indeed it is a source of strength—but also as a measure by which we will measure ourselves. I am sure that we will all be found lacking, incomplete, if we are measured by the Cross of

Christ. But God is merciful, and knows and measures our intention more. Do we want to follow and take up the Cross of Christ? As difficult as it is, He will give His grace, He will give His blessing. What we must never do is turn our face away from the Cross of Christ or use it only to get benefit from it. The Cross of Christ is meant to be lifted up by all of us, and that is why today the Church presents it to us for veneration.

With this spirit, my beloved brothers and sisters, let us also move forward into the rest of Holy and Great Lent, so that we may be worthy, with the grace of the Lord and with the power of the Cross, to lift up voluntary and involuntary crosses, and thus participate in the Cross of Christ, to worship His Honorable Passion and His Holy Resurrection, which always passes through the Cross of Christ. Amen.

24.
4th SUNDAY OF LENT
The demonic, fasting, prayer (Mk 9:17–31)

This kind can come out by nothing but prayer and fasting.

As we journey, my beloved brothers and sisters, through the wilderness of Great Lent, the period of fasting and spiritual struggles, the Church brings before us today, through the gospel passage we have just heard, the great mystery, the horrible and awesome mystery of the demonic.

What we heard in the Gospel passage is truly shocking, because an innocent creature, from his childhood, through no fault of his own, is tormented by a demonic power. And it is also shocking that his disciples tried and failed to expel the demon before the Lord came and healed him.

But what, my brothers and sisters, is the demonic? How does it come about? How does it manifest itself? How is it treated? If you'll indulge me, these are some of the questions I would like to explore at this time. The demonic is every tendency and force for destruction, even self-destruction. The demonic is a force that man cannot control; he tries in vain to expel it from his existence. The demoniac introduces sin into the world via man's freedom. The demonic keeps man captive to sin. The demonic manifests itself in many forms, especially those that are not amenable to human control. These include not just the more extreme forms of demon possession, such as today's Gospel described, but any form that holds man prisoner—prisoner to his passions, to the point that he wants to change but cannot overcome the passions' strength.

One does not have to search very far for examples. Let's each look at ourselves, let's look to see how many passions man finds it difficult to stop, in order to be freed from them. Simple things, like smoking; it's really impossible for many people. And let us not enumerate many other passions which control man's life and which man cannot overcome. The demonic entered the world first through the freedom of angels, then of men, the freedom which includes not only the ability to say "yes" but also "no." The demonic entered as a rebellion against God and this is precisely its essence. The demonic wants to destroy everything created by God, because in the face of creation it sees God Himself, and this is what it ultimately wants to destroy, but it cannot. Therefore, the demons' struggle is not essentially a struggle against people; it is a struggle against God Himself. But because the same demons and the same people who are under the influence of demons are also God's creations, the result of this demonic tendency, of demonic power, is self-destruction. They are not content with destroying others, but, because they themselves are creations of God, they want to insult the Creator in this way and to destroy themselves.

The demonic is a reality, my brothers and sisters, which no matter how much one wants to question it with his logic, he cannot, because indeed there are forces in our lives that we cannot control, the forces of evil, which escape our control. And that is why man, faced with this power of evil, tried to find different ways to banish evil from his life. However, none of these methods have worked. One such way is to think that, when you teach people what is good and what is evil, they will themselves prefer the good and banish evil. How false this is, my brothers! Because man usually knows what is good and what is evil. But his will does not allow him to follow the good.

Many thought that education would be able to make people good in order to expel the demonic from their lives. But even this turned out to be false. Those of us who lived through the Second World War have to remember, my brothers and sisters, that a people of great education, and indeed humanistic education, was so taken over by the power of the demonic that it nearly destroyed the world. So education does not solve the problem of evil. Does our virtue, our effort to become better, solve it? This, too my brothers and sisters, proves to be insufficient to deliver us from evil. Let us remember the case of the Pharisee, who indeed kept the commandments but somehow became a prisoner of evil.

It is not up to us to get rid of evil. That's why the Church presents us today with some surprising words from the Lord. When His disciples asked Him why they could not cast out the demon, He answered them that this generation—that is, the generation of the demons—cannot be driven out by anything other than prayer and fasting. One naturally wonders why these two things are powerful enough to defeat the demonic, which neither our education, nor our virtue, nor our knowledge, nor science, which often deceives us, is in a position to defeat. They hold out the promise that they will defeat evil, disease, even death itself, and it turns out that every problem they solve ends up creating new problems.

So why prayer and fasting? Because, my brothers and sisters, the demonic entered the world, as I told you before, through the rebellion of free beings—both angels and men—against God. And this rebellion, as it was manifest in Adam, the first man, was nothing less than the dethronement of God, man proclaiming himself god. So people's autonomy became the vehicle for the demonic in our lives. And prayer is the one thing that negates this individualization. It is the one that recognizes that the only Sovereign against evil, the only One who can defeat evil, is God Himself. And, in this way, prayer makes man humble before God. It makes man ask for God's mercy—that is, it makes man understand that he is not God. He is not capable of facing evil except in God and through God, through the power of God Himself.

Fasting is also the reversal of what happened during man's fall. Because man, when he fell, broke the commandment of fasting. God said to him: "You shall not eat from this tree." And he thought: "So what if God said no? I am going to eat from this tree." And in this way he fell and became a prisoner of evil and the demonic. Fasting is actually so blessed that it can turn a person's attitude towards God upside down, and actually allow him to attract God's mercy, in order to secure victory against evil in this way.

My brothers and sisters, we live in a culture that believes, and makes us believe, that man alone, with his powers, can turn this life into a paradise and banish evil from the world. And the

Church—at this time when her children are struggling spiritually against evil—comes today and proclaims to this culture and this world that it is a great mistake to believe that we can defeat evil by our own power. And the Church calls us to turn in prayer and fasting toward the mercy of God, since He—and only He—can defeat evil. He defeated it with the intervention into history of His Son and Word. He defeated it with the Resurrection of the Lord, which demonstrated that evil does not have the last word in the world. Ultimately, the world will be transformed into the Kingdom of God, but only with the Second Coming of Christ. And then, those of us who are close to Christ, those of us who are faithful to Him alone—not by our own power or any power of this world, or on the strength of our science, knowledge, and virtue—only then will we become worthy of the Kingdom of God, which will be the final victory against evil. Amen.

Church of the Holy Trinity, Piraeus
April 6, 1997

25.
4th SUNDAY OF LENT
Epistemology—Church

Your Eminence Metropolitan of Piraeus,[1] Mr. President of the Dental Association, dear fathers, and brothers and sisters, once again the Church of Piraeus, thanks to its enlightened shepherd and his distinguished associates, opens its embrace, spreads its wings to cover with affection and to enlighten today's man in his greatest problems. It is truly a blessing from God, because in these difficult times, a shepherd like the Metropolitan of Piraeus and churches like this local parish stand out. Today's commemoration of the holy martyr Antipas the Wonderworker by the association of dentists is, I think, an event of great importance. First, because it testifies that in our days, science and the Church work together harmoniously and recognize that not only is there no opposition between them, but they need each other in their common ministry to man. Gone are the days when these two were in opposition to each other. Today, medicine understands that the human organism is a psychosomatic entity and that no treatment is effective without the appropriate spiritual infrastructure, which the Church offers. And the Church, for its part, understands today more than ever that its work is essential in offering solutions to contemporary problems, as well as in human life as a whole. Today's celebration is also significant because a saint of our martyric Asia Minor is being honored by an elite branch of science. As the humble hierarch of the martyric city of Pergamum, whose first bishop was Saint Antipas, I feel deeply moved, because in his person my metropolis—may the Lord have mercy—its flock, and its pastor are all honored today. However, today's inaugural celebration is important because its organizers

[1] This talk was given in the parish hall of the Church of the Holy Trinity, Piraeus, in the context of the feast of the holy martyr Antipas the Wonderworker, patron of dentists, and an event in honor of the professor of dentistry Orestes Louridis.

took the laudable initiative to honor an outstanding representative of dental science, a brilliant child of our Church, an Archon of the Ecumenical Throne and a benefactor of the Greek nation, Professor Orestis Lourides. And rightly so, because Professor Lourides combines in his person the healer of dental science and the one who more than anyone else appreciated and promoted Saint Antipas in our days. The only church in Attica bearing the name of Saint Antipas is entirely a gift of his chosen child of the Church. It adorns the premises of the Dentistry School of the University of Athens and stands as an example of the marriage of science and the Church, according to the model of the glorious history of the benefactors of our nation. I congratulate from the bottom of my heart both the association of dentists of Piraeus and the esteemed professor for this just distinction.

In this speech on the inaugural of the Piraeus dentists' association, I would like to focus on certain concerns, of a more general nature, common between medical science and the Church in our days. As I mentioned a little while ago, the era of the opposition between science and the Church is over. Today the problems are common and it is recognized by both sides that without the cooperation of these two—the Church and science—modern man will be faced with terrible impasses. The 21st century will be the starting point of great possibilities for science, but also of terrible dangers for man, precisely because of scientific progress. These dangers will not be avoided without the substantial assistance of the Church. What are these dangers? I will mention them just briefly.

First is the danger of the destruction of the natural environment. This danger is not unrelated to the progress of science. The use of atomic energy, radioactivity, chemistry, etc. in medicine is readily available and certainly beneficial. But the negative possibilities behind all this are also serious. The contamination of the environment by radioactivity, the use of chemistry in the preservation of food, etc., to mention only a few, constitute dangers for the natural environment which also extend to human health. Where will the golden ratio be fixed so that the advances of science do not prove harmful to man? It is clear that science first needs enough humility to admit that each of its advances is simultaneously the cause of great dangers. And secondly, science needs to recognize that any such progress automatically poses crucial ethical dilemmas, which demand the cooperation of science and the Church. After all, the more general problem of pollution of the natural environment is in essence nothing but a spiritual problem. Facing it is impossible without man's repentance and conversion—that is, without man realizing that he is not the owner and master of creation but its steward and priest, designed to offer it up as thanksgiving to the Lord and its Creator; man is to abstain from its rape and the satisfaction of his own desires and instead use it with ascetic frugality. Only the Church—not science or politics—can teach us this and embed it in people's consciences.

The second great danger that awaits man from the progress of science in the coming century is the danger of the destruction of the human person. This danger comes from the rapid development of technology and genetic engineering. Already the first signs of this enormous danger have emerged. The concept of the person will now be the most important concept at this critical juncture for our civilization. What is the person? The person is a unique, irreplaceable, unrepeatable identity that stems from a relationship of love. This identity does not depend on its physical properties, but on its uniqueness that is freely recognized by someone else. As in the existence of the Holy Trinity, the Father, the Son and the Spirit are Persons because each of them constitutes a unique and unrepeatable, and irreplaceable identity due to the loving relationship that connects them—the Father cannot be Son and Spirit and vice versa. In the same way, every person, as belonging to God, is unique, unrepeatable, and irreplaceable. Any attempt to remove or degrade his uniqueness is a destruction of the human person; it is the end of the very meaning of man. Both technology and genetics, which offer tempting advantages to social and economic life as well as to human health, simultaneously threaten to annihilate the human person. Just a few days ago on a television show, a professor of genetics, supporting the cloning of even humans, gave as an example the hypothetical case of a mother who lost her ten-year-old child, saying that this mother would be happy to have an identical copy of her lost child. This is a complete breakdown of the concept of the person as a unique and irreplaceable being. Man would be nothing more than an animal if he reacted to the death of a loved one by replacing them with an identical copy. There are many more examples of dangers to the person, both from technology, with its potential to catalyze the freedom of the person, and from biology, which will soon be able to invade the individuality of each person after or even before his birth.

So what is there to do about this situation? It would be futile to expect that legal means or moral imperatives could stop scientific research in its tracks. When it offers—as it does—the possibility of truly great benefits, it proves too alluring and, once begun, it is almost impossible to check its development. No one knows where this road will take us. Man's intervention into nature can only remain benign for the human person as well as material creation if our human consciences remain vigilant, and we see God behind every being. In other words, our culture must recapture the concept of sanctity. Only the Church can offer this because the Church is the only sacred space left.

We've homogenized everything. We scrutinize everything with our rational minds. We have brutally invaded material creation and turned it into a profit—anything that is useful and beneficial, that is. Only the Church reminds us of the sanctity of the world and the human person and, if it weren't for the Church, surely the end of the world would come.

Your Eminence, beloved brothers and sisters, the Church often gives the impression that it is either "worried and troubled about many things" or that it is indifferent to everything. Neither is correct. The Church knows, or should know, that it is the guardian of the sanctity of the world and of the human person. The Church's head gave it this mission and woe to us if we neglect it. With spiritual discernment, the Church is called upon to raise its voice every time scientific developments threaten this sanctity. However, more than an attitude of protest, the Church is called to develop an attitude of cooperation with science, "so that what is lame may not be dislocated, but rather be healed" (Heb 12:13). We can already see examples of this cooperation between science and the Church in this metropolis, including today's festal gathering. May others follow this example and may it lead to a deeper and more fruitful relationship between them, so that the lost concept of the sacred can become embedded in the consciousness of us, including the scientists. Thus, the blood of our dentists' patron saint will prove beneficial to modern man, who lives in apocalyptic times, comparable to those of the saint's time. I pray that the Lord, through the intercessions of His saint and first bishop of martyric Pergamum, will bless this beginning of the beautiful effort that is being launched today, for the glory of the Triune God and man's salvation.

These are the thoughts I wanted to share with you on this great feast. Although humble, I think they are timely and necessary, and of some significance for the future, the present, and the past. Thank you again for this opportunity.

April 6, 1997

26.
4th SUNDAY OF LENT
The demonic and man (Mk 9:17–31)

This kind can come out by nothing but prayer and fasting.

Today's gospel passage, my dear brothers and sisters, is about the demonic. We all heard the shocking description of the condition of this man who was possessed by demons from his childhood. And we heard how powerless the Lord's disciples were to help, how unable they were to cast out the demon. So the Lord casts out the demon and then answers the disciples' question why they were unable, with the words I just quoted.

What is the demonic? The demonic is mania, the tendency to completely destroy everything. It is a rebellion against existence. It's a rebellion against God and everything God created and loves. It is the tendency toward nihilism, toward absolute nothingness. It is hostility toward existence. Since existence is a gift of God, the will of God, the demonic element not only turns against God, but also against every being that exists.

The demonic is a mania of self-destruction, uncontrollable by human effort. It exceeds man's powers. Man cannot control it. It comes from without. Man's freedom is not capable of controlling it. And in this way it becomes obvious that the fall of man happened because the angels—the first of God's creations—fell first and became demons who were turned against God and against His creation. Thus, the demonic comes into existence as a rebellion against God, a rebellion against God's own creation. And it takes various forms. It takes the form of physical evil, that which we humans cannot control, no matter how hard we try: sickness, decay, death. It takes the form of so-called moral evil, man's tendency to harm other human beings and God's creation. And it also takes the form of those passions that man cannot control. How often does someone want to get rid of certain passions but can't? We look with compassion, for example, at a simple case:

someone who wants to quit smoking. How difficult it turns out to be! How many other passions prove to be so strong that man cannot by his own strength free himself from them.

Man, faced with these evil forces that overwhelm him, often—if not almost always—ends up succumbing to them and turning them into something like divine forces. Then it becomes the idolization of the demonic. Man sees evil, the demonic, as something that not only cannot be overcome, but is also useful and convenient for life. And this is how idols appear in human life. The idolization of his passions begin to manifest. The idolizations of those forces appear, which have so much power that they seem truly divine and insurmountable, such as political, economic, or military power; forces that man cultivates and ultimately turns into idols, which he then worships! Will he say "I worship idols"? He will say that he turns them into absolute values, which he commits to serve. "I am obedient to these." And thus man becomes a slave to these powers. And the demonic reaches to the point of becoming divine within the life of man, such that it is no longer easy for one to distinguish between what is demonic and what is divine. Because, many times in our lives, forces of evil become invested with divine qualities that seduce man into thinking that he should devote his whole life, to give his whole self to them.

However, man never ceases to feel that he wants to get rid of evil. And he tries in various ways and fails. He tries to fight evil with education, by educating people, to make them know what is good and evil, so that by knowing good they turn away from evil. But how futile is this effort! We only need to take a look at the history of just the last century, which we all lived through, to see how evil forces, truly demonic, sprung from peoples who had the highest level of education. It is no use knowing what is good and what is bad. This does not mean that this is how you necessarily choose the good. For the same reason, man's other attempt to get rid of evil, through ethics, also fails. It's the same thing. We think that if we teach people and tell them what is good and what is bad, if we make these distinctions and compile a list of good and bad things, then we will solve the problem of evil. But it cannot be solved, thus proving that man's will is stronger than the knowledge of good and evil.

Yet another effort that man makes, and he makes it especially in our days, is to get rid of evil with the help of science. We hope, with the progress of science, that diseases will be defeated, death and decay will be defeated, and that at least the form of cosmic evil will be defeated. Thus we invest all our hopes in the progress of science. But to see how futile this effort is, one needs only to consider that every step of progress in science means at the same time the appearance of new problems. There is no progress in science that does not bring new problems to the surface and does not create, especially in our days, enormous problems of a moral nature—problems for the very existence of man.

Well, then, because the effort is futile, the effort of man to get rid of the demonic is futile. This is why the Lord's disciples could not cast out the demons. And why did the Lord answer them the way He did? To this I would now like to turn our attention.

"This kind can come out by nothing but prayer and fasting." This may sound somewhat formulaic. In other words, if I pray and if I fast, then the demonic will leave. If, however, we look what hides behind these words of the Lord, we will understand that it is not a formality, not simply about following a formula, but rather something very essential.

What is prayer? Prayer is man's orientation towards God, the Giver of his existence, and therefore it is the recognition that he cannot be god in any way. And he cannot really rule the world. This is precisely the first step that is needed for man to move in the right direction in dealing with evil. Evil, no matter how hard man tries, cannot be eradicated from the world unless God intervenes—that is, if man does not recognize that his existence is dependent on God. From someone else. If he does not recognize the Other, the One from whom he comes, he will never be able to overcome evil. That is precisely why the Lord speaks about prayer. Not simply to repeat certain prayers, but to orient ourselves towards God Himself, towards the Other, who gave us existence, and who can, and proves how he can, be Lord even over demonic forces.

And fasting? Fasting is precisely the reversal of the tendency that led to the demonic, the tendency of demons, and subsequently of humans, to conquer and dominate existence; to use it for themselves. Selfishness is what created evil during the very first entry of evil into existence. Man's self-proclamation as god, this turning, which man caused, of all things towards himself. And fasting is exactly the reversal of this trend. It is the best way, I would say, to free man from selfishness, from the deification of himself.

The Church has no other way to confront evil. Let's not let certain representatives of the Church waste our time. Evil is not dealt with by the methods of this world. It has these forgotten methods of prayer and fasting, by which man cleanses himself of the passion of self-love and turns to the other, to God, the Other par excellence, and to others, with love, without considering himself a superior, for whom everyone and everything must work.

Today, my brothers and sisters, the grace of God has brought us to this beautiful church, which I will not cease to proclaim with due gratitude that we owe it to an excellent son of our nation, Professor Lourides. This church, under the spiritual ministry of a brilliant cleric, Fr. Georgios, has become a center of worship and spiritual life. So we have gathered here in this church dedicated to Saint Antipas to honor the memory of this martyr and miracle worker. And it brings to mind the words of the book of Revelation about this saint. Addressing the bishop of Pergamum, the Holy Spirit refers to the faithful witness, who was martyred in Pergamum, "where," Revelation says, "Satan's throne is" (Rev 2:13). In the place, then, where Saint Antipas was martyred, the demonic was enthroned in all its majesty and power. Commentators on this book of the Holy Bible see in this phrase an indirect reference to Roman authority and the Roman emperor, who had indeed established his worship there in a special way and was worshiped there. And so the martyrdom of Saint Antipas comes to show us that the only way to destroy the idols, the only way to defeat the demonic, is martyrdom, which is another form—the highest form, I would say—of asceticism, of prayer, of fasting, to which the Lord referred.

If one does not give his life, the world cannot be liberated from evil. It cannot be liberated from evil when life itself is the highest good, to such an extent that we are not ready to sacrifice it. The world cannot be liberated from evil when we, for example, sacrifice our own life while at the same time dragging the lives of others into sacrifice as well. When, however, we sacrifice ourselves without sacrificing others, then it appears externally that evil prevails, that it is stronger, but the example of saints such as Saint Antipas, and of all the martyrs of our Church and the ascetics and the faithful, testify that it may appear from the outside that the martyrs and the faithful and the ascetics are weak, but in reality they are the ones who transform history. They are the ones who introduce the good into our existence and displace evil in this way.

So, my brothers and sisters, today honoring the memory of Saint Antipas, honoring his martyrdom, and listening to these words of the Holy Gospel, let us be especially careful to the extent that each of us can and is called to do so, to free ourselves from self-love, from this root of all evils and all passions, and to use the means that the Church offers us for this, the means of prayer and fasting. And in this way let's invoke the power of God, who is the only One who can defeat evil. And, as it happened with the holy martyrs, who also perform miracles, because evil no longer dominates them, in this way let us also go towards the worship of the Resurrection of the Lord, which is nothing over than the victory over death through the Cross, that is, through the mortification of ourselves.

With these wishes, I congratulate you all because today you have come here to honor the memory of the bishop of Pergamum, of our martyric Pergamum, of that blessed land, which was watered by the blood of Saint Antipas and which, due to sins known only God, can no longer honor his memory. But we are sure that evil does not have the last word. God does. Therefore, may God account us worthy again to pray in those blessed lands and to honor the saint. Amen.

Holy Church of Saint Antipas
School of Dentistry, University of Athens
April 14, 2002

27.
4th SUNDAY OF LENT
On prayer and fasting (Mk 9:17–31)

This kind can come out by nothing but prayer and fasting.

With these words, the Lord responded to His disciples' query: Why couldn't they cast out the demon from the sick child? Why couldn't this whole tragic situation be solved with human power? Why did it require Christ's intervention to liberate the demon-possessed child from this demon? And the Lord responds: This evil cannot be cast out from man by anything but prayer and fasting.

Allow me, my beloved brothers and sisters, to devote a few thoughts to the Lord's words here. How is it that these two things—prayer and fasting—have such power, the power to defeat evil, which cannot be defeated any other way? Let's first examine prayer.

What is prayer? It is not simply words we say to God; it is, rather, an "orientation of our existence." Our whole existence is oriented toward God. Just as a plant orients its whole existence toward the sun in order to live, so man, through prayer, orients his existence toward God. And how is this connected with the problem of evil?

Evil entered the world precisely because man turned away from God. Instead of turning toward God, man turned to himself, to the created world, and naturally he was no longer able to avoid evil since man was now trapped in the limits of his created existence. He could not overcome corruption and death, which is the ultimate evil, because the cycle of corruption and death exists within our very nature. We cannot control evil because we began from the presumption that we could, by ourselves and through our own power, liberate our very nature from evil. And this is exactly what has happened to man throughout history, and what continues to happen today.

Man believed that, with his own power, he could defeat evil. The ancient Greek philosophers said that, if man can recognize good and evil, he will always prefer the good—in other words, our subjugation to evil proceeds from our ignorance. This is why an effort began to improve man, to liberate him from evil *through education and formation*. And man thought that he would thus defeat evil, but we have enough history behind us to evaluate if this in fact happened.

Even in our own era, in the previous century, humanity suffered the most awful forms of evil from peoples who were greatly educated. Education and knowledge cannot solve the problem of evil, nor can ethics. We attempt to teach humans to distinguish between good and evil, ethical and unethical. In reality, though, these two things are so intertwined that, when we commit an ethical act, this same ethical act includes the opposite. This is what we are experiencing in our days.

How can we be sure that the act we commit, a political act or decision, contains only the good? Perhaps we don't see that the major decisions made today by the people who rule the world, despite the effort to take ethical actions, also contain within them evil? How can man, by himself, with his ethics, defeat evil? I would even go a step further to suggest that we cannot defeat evil even with asceticism. The great ascetics of the Church knew that their own effort, their own struggle, could reach the point of shedding blood, but they could not defeat the demons and evil. It was impossible for the saints' efforts to defeat evil, and that is why they took refuge in prayer.

Only through God's intervention could evil really be checked. Our own efforts are not enough. This is why prayer is the only way, because we are deluded when we think that we can defeat evil by turning to ourselves. It is well known, my dear brothers and sisters, that evil entered the world through food. God gave one commandment to man—to not eat one type of food. Man's disobedience allowed evil to enter into his existence.

This may appear to be simply a coincidence, an accident. But it is not as simple as it appears, my dear brothers and sisters, because food gives us simultaneously both life and death. Food contains everything that we need to metabolize in order for our body to live, but at the same time we acquire corruption and death from the same material that we use to live. This antinomy, this contrast—we take life together with death—resides within our very existence. We don't die at a certain moment of our life; rather, we are dying as we live.

So food, which is a basic way of sustaining life, must be cleansed from the evil it brings within us—and this is the deeper meaning of fasting. Because with food we take the world as a way to survive—that is, we make it a selfish act which some other *being* in the world has to pay for. We feed ourselves with the death of others. It's a selfish act, and this self-love constitutes the source of all evil.

We need food to live, but the Lord comes with His words today and the Church comes with fasting to say: Be careful, this act which allows you to survive runs the risk of simply satisfying our self-love to the detriment of others. Fasting, then, is the way for us to understand and live this danger that lies within our taking of nature.

Often, we deprive others of that which we take. We need, then, to realize that we must deprive ourselves of food in order to cleanse ourselves of our self-love. The deprivation of fasting, then, is a deprivation of our self-love. It is a way for us to realize that we are not the center of the world, that the world doesn't exist because of us. We can humble ourselves by understanding that, yes we need food, but we will not make food a means to serve our self-love.

Evil, my beloved brothers and sisters, will depart from the world only when man understands that *his ego* is not the center of the world, that the world does not exist to serve our ego, our selves. The source of all evil is self-love. We have to do either with individual self-love, or collective, national, social, or class-based self-love. Self-love drives conflicts, war, evil, hate, enmity, and death, and ultimately results in our own death.

It is no accident that the Church during Great Lent, which we are passing through now, calls us to precisely these two things—prayer and fasting. And it is no accident that the Church abandons fasting when we celebrate the Holy Eucharist, the Divine

Liturgy. The Church has decreed that we cannot celebrate the Holy Eucharist, as we do today, on a fasting day. Why? Because, with the Divine Liturgy, we celebrate the victory over evil, we celebrate the Kingdom of God, which will not be subject to evil. But we need fasting, we need abstinence, to be able to enjoy this victory over evil.

Let us—at least those of us in the Church, who try to pray and fast—take these things into serious consideration. As you see, and as I tried to tell you, these are not simply empty forms. They have depth, a depth which touches our very existence. They are matters of life and death.

A person who doesn't pray, who doesn't fast, is already dead, since he has turned the whole world toward himself, and this turn toward himself is his death.

I pray that these words of the Lord enter deeply into our hearts, and that we use them—to the best of our abilities—to confront evil, which is inevitable in our lives. And that we confront evil not with the weapons of self-love, but with the weapons of prayer and fasting, which means the weapons of love and mercy. Amen.

April 10, 2005

28.
5th SUNDAY OF LENT

Sacrifice as the path to the Kingdom (Mk 10:32–45)

For even the Son of Man did not come to be served, but to serve, and to give His life a ransom for many.

Today's Gospel passage, which we just heard, my dear brothers and sisters, is read just before we enter Holy Week, to remind us of the importance of the Lord's sacrifice. To remind us that the glory that Christ's disciples sought to obtain is only obtained through sacrifice. And that one cannot reach the Resurrection, nor the Kingdom of Heaven, nor the glory of the Kingdom of God, if one does not go through the sacrifice of the cross. Because this is the path that the Lord Himself carved; the path of sacrifice is the path to glory.

But the Lord's sacrifice, my beloved brothers and sisters, is unique. It has characteristics that cannot be compared to any other sacrifice. There are many sacrifices in the world. Many people sacrifice themselves, for many different reasons, but the Lord's sacrifice is unique. Because it includes three elements, to which I would like, my brothers and sisters, to devote our attention.

First, it is a voluntary sacrifice. Secondly, it is a sacrifice for others. Thirdly, it is a sacrifice "instead of others." The first makes the Lord's sacrifice a matter of freedom. It is an absolutely free sacrifice. The second makes it a sacrifice of love. And the third makes it representative, "a ransom for many." Let there be one sacrifice instead of making the others suffer.

The Lord's sacrifice is voluntary. Because he could have avoided this sacrifice. The Cross was not imposed on him by any force. It may appear superficially that the world power of that time, the political and military power, imposed their will on Jesus. However, when his enthusiastic disciple wanted to prevent this sacrifice, telling the Lord to allow him to use his power, the sword, the Lord answered him: "If I wanted, at this moment I could call twelve legions of angels,"—that is, as much as the entire military power of the Roman Empire was—"and I could avoid this Cross and this sacrifice. But I do not." The Lord really could have avoided the Cross, but He chose it freely. And every sacrifice, my brothers and sisters, which is voluntary has a special weight and holds a great significance, because we all undergo involuntary sacrifices, we all take up crosses that are imposed on us, but only the voluntary crosses and voluntary sacrifices have any value.

And it is a sacrifice for others, because the Lord Himself did not derive any benefit from the Cross and this sacrifice. It was not done to benefit Himself; He had no need of this sacrifice. It was a sacrifice purely of love; it was an offering for others. And this is also of great importance, because it does not make much sense to sacrifice oneself in order to benefit oneself. We make many such sacrifices, and in the end we get a return. Even, I would say, sacrifices made by parents for their children, or friends for their friends, are ultimately sacrifices that yield a return to us, with something that we essentially need, and that is why we submit to these sacrifices. However, the Lord's sacrifice did not come from any need; He did not look to any benefit of His own.

And it was a representative sacrifice, it was a ransom for many, because this sacrifice would have to be paid by us. We are the ones who owe God, because we left communion with Him, we insulted His love, and it would be fair, really, for us to suffer the consequences as well as the punishment for our apostasy. He is "a ransom for many" because we are hostages from the moment of our fall, hostages of the devil, hostages of satanic forces, hostages of decay, hostages of death, and just as, in order for a hostage to be freed, someone must pay the ransom, the ransom for our own liberation is paid for by Christ himself, and in this way he becomes the one who takes our place, the place in which we should be. We should have been on the cross and not Him. But in order to free us from this sacrifice, He paid the ransom. What greatness, my beloved brothers and sisters, lies behind the Lord's sacrifice. It is not really possible to find such a sacrifice anywhere else, because in every sacrifice at least one of the elements I mentioned is absent.

The Church did not limit this sacrifice to the person of Christ. It continues it. The martyrs and the faithful, the saints of our Church took it upon themselves. The saints of the Church are nothing but the continuation of this sacrifice of the Lord. And on the sacrifice of the saints, the martyrs, and the faithful, the body of the Church is built. Because they subject themselves to sacrifices, without being obliged to undergo them. They suffer voluntarily, they suffer for the sake of others and instead of others. Because they truly take upon themselves responsibility for others.

One such witness is the one whose memory we have gathered here today to honor. He is the witness Antipas, "the faithful one," as the Lord calls him in Revelation (2:13). He who watered with his blood the blessed land of Asia Minor, the land that holds in its bowels the blood of the martyrs and the tears of the faithful. It holds in its bowels the pain and sorrow of people who were forcibly uprooted, people who left the land of their fathers. And Saint Antipas could have avoided the sacrifice, but he did not avoid it. He could also worship "the throne of Satan," as Revelation calls the Pergamum of that time. He could, that is, be reconciled with the secular power of that time. Let him worship the emperor and save his life. But he didn't, and by giving his life, by giving himself, by giving his blood, he did what many others could not do. In other words, he overthrew the throne of the emperor, the throne of the idols. He tore down the idols. At that time, when the power of Rome was truly invincible, who could have imagined that the world power would collapse? And it would collapse from the sacrifices of humble people, like Saint Antipas. Because it wasn't a war or any worldly power that caused the Roman Empire to collapse, and the idols to fall. They fell through the blood of the martyrs. And so Saint Antipas became like the Lord Himself, a sacrifice, a ransom that freed people from the worship of idols, from the power of Satan. And in the same way, one could say, this blood that was lost will again be the ransom that will free us, in that land where it was shed. Only the power of faith, the sacrifice of the martyrs, only this, my brothers and sisters, will free us from all forms of violence.

My brothers and sisters, it is difficult to love voluntarily. It is difficult to take the place of the other. It is difficult in a trial for someone to go and say "judge me" without being at fault. Love upends this sense of justice. Love does not know justice; it transcends it.

The Lord, being innocent, sacrifices Himself. He sacrifices himself to show us that we must take upon ourselves the sins of others. And this was done by all the saints and all the martyrs of the Church. And they still do. They are the ones who—instead of judging and criticizing others, instead of administering so-called justice while exempting themselves from all responsibility—take upon themselves the responsibility for the misdeeds of others. And they walk precisely in the footsteps of the Lord. This is the great sacrifice which is set before us, my brothers and sisters, as an example difficult for anyone to follow. But this is the Gospel—a very high standard by which we are called to be measured. And only those who manage to somewhat reach this measure, only they can say that they follow the Lord and are His faithful disciples.

But even if we cannot do it, at least we are all called to try. In light of this magnificent sacrifice of the Lord, we are called to adapt our own lives as well. Now that the Week of His Passion is approaching and we will soon find ourselves in front of His voluntary sacrifice, let us worship it truly understanding its great importance and with the disposition to imitate it ourselves. Amen.

Holy Trinity Cathedral, Piraeus
April 21, 2002

29.
PALM SUNDAY

Let love prevail over reason. (John 12:1–18)

Why was this myrrh poured out rather than being sold?

Today's gospel passage paints two scenes, my dear brothers and sisters. One takes place in Bethany and the other in Jerusalem. Both take place a few days before Easter. And they are, precisely for this reason, very important, because they reveal to us truths and meanings that we must keep in our thoughts and in our hearts during Holy Week, which we enter tonight.

The first scene is of Jesus' visit to Lazarus' house, shortly after his resurrection, where Lazarus' sisters serve Him a supper of thanksgiving. And Lazarus is there eating with them. It is a supper after the resurrection, truly a foreshadowing of the great supper of the Kingdom of God, which will follow the resurrection of all, the General Resurrection. In every Holy Eucharist, this follows the Resurrection of our older brother, the first among men, Jesus Christ.

During this dinner, a shocking scene occurs. Lazarus' sister, Mary, approaches Jesus and anoints His feet with valuable myrrh, and then wipes them with her hair. And in this way, she shows her gratitude for what the Lord did for her brother and for them with his resurrection. Gratitude is shown in no other way than through love. And love is not shown in any other way than through gratitude, thanksgiving for love itself. The Lord did not simply raise Lazarus like an ordinary man. He resurrected him, says the Gospel, as the beloved. When he first saw him dead, He cried, and this may be the only time that Jesus cries in the Gospels. This so impressed the onlookers that they exclaimed: "See how He loved him!" (John 11:36). "He resurrected Lazarus because he loves him!" He did not raise him simply to demonstrate a miracle, to show His power. And He will resurrect us too, all of us, because He loves us. Love forces resurrection; it forces eternal life. It does not accept death.

And it is for precisely this reason that Mary's actions scandalized Judas. And I would say that it was quite logical for him to be scandalized, ethically as well. He sees this valuable myrrh being poured on the Lord's feet and he rightly asks: "Why was this myrrh poured out rather than being sold for 300 denarii"—an enormous sum—"and given to the poor?" What is more logical than that? What is more ethical?

But the Lord's answer comes to really shock us! "Let this woman," he says, "express her love and her gratitude. Because she is doing this symbolically, for the day of My burial." Let love prevail over reason. Let the heart, which sees better than the mind, express its feelings. Let her go, because there is nothing more important than these two things: love and death. These are the two extreme limits of our existence and these are the two criteria by which everything will be judged.

Not everything is judged by logic or ethics. They are judged in love! They are judged in this manifestation of the heart which does not calculate what is beneficial, what is practical, what is rational.

This, then, is the Lord's answer. Because he came precisely to defeat death with His love. He did not come, as we usually perceive it, to become a great teacher. There have been many great teachers, both before Him and after Him, and there will be probably be more in the future. But no one sacrificed himself for the love of others. And no one fought with death to defeat it with love. This is precisely why this scene unfolding in Lazarus' house is very important. It's really shocking!

This scandal to Judas, my beloved brothers and sisters, has been repeated throughout the centuries. Surely, when you hear these words of mine, you will ask yourself: "But do people sometimes ask the question that Judas asked? Are we sometimes scandalized by expressions of love that are excessive? Are we not scandalized because people dedicate precious things to the churches, because our churches are loaded with gifts of love, of the gratitude of people, of the faithful, because the Church has this, for many, unacceptable luxury? Why do our priests have these vestments, which scandalize some? Why are there gilded and silver icons? Imagine how much money we could make if we sold all of this, to give to the poor!"

This is the logic of Judas! Because this is not an exceptional and rare case. And the evangelist intervenes here to make a comment. "This he said," John writes, "not that he cared for the poor, but because he was a thief, and had the money box; and he used to take what was put in it." And this is often—I would even say always—what happens, my brothers and sisters, when people invoke logic and ethics in caring for the poor with other people's money. Usually, when we care for the poor and shout and are scandalized, we do this because we want an equal distribution of wealth and not to actually give ourselves, to deprive ourselves of something. This view of social justice is well known. At its root lies the same attitude that the Evangelist John pointed out about Judas. When we acquire authority to distribute common funds to the poor, we hold something back for ourselves. And we are those who do not sacrifice. Love, however, sacrifices everything. This love, which is "absurd" when it spends three hundred denarii to express itself, this love is the one that will at some point give all of itself for the poor, for others. Because it is the heart—the heart and not the mind, not logic, not equality, not justice—that really loves and distributes goods to the poor.

And the second scene, my dear ones, which takes place in Jerusalem, is also worthy of attention. Jesus comes to Jerusalem triumphantly and the people welcome him with chants of devotion and praise. This is the side of the enthusiastic reception. However, there is also a different side which the Gospel notes and which I would like us to pay attention to. "They came," it says, "not for Jesus' sake only, but that they might also see Lazarus, whom He had raised from the dead." They did not come only to accept Christ with love and devotion. They came because a miracle had happened and they wanted to make sure of the miracle. They had this curiosity and at the same time they were looking for proof of the miracle. And only on this basis, only on the fact of the miracle, did they offer the Lord this enthusiastic reception.

And what would happen, my brothers and sisters, if Christ did not perform the miracle, what would happen if they did not see Lazarus resurrected?

Well, simply put, what happened during Holy Week. We will see in a few days that the same people who cried "Hosanna!" will later exclaim "Crucify Him!" Why? Because this powerful figure, Who performed miracles, will now be so humiliated and appear so weak as to not be worthy of our devotion; we can no longer rely on Him to help us. Why? Because what we expect is some benefit to us. The Jews of that time expected the Messiah to provide some benefit to them, to win them political independence. In other words, He will satisfy our needs: our daily needs, our historical and social needs. And when these are not satisfied, when He appears weak, then we turn our face away from Him. Not only do we no longer cheer for Him, but we condemn Him to the Cross.

In these coming days, my dear brothers and sisters, we will all be filling the churches, watching with reverence the holy services, which are absolutely unique. We will recall and see shocking events. And the most shocking is to see a weak God facing the world's evil—a God given over to be crucified, a God that appears to be completely useless to us, since He can't do anything for us and cannot offer us anything.

And there exactly our faith will be tested. Do we want a God who will be useful to us? Do we believe because God is useful to us? This will be the big question of Holy Week. A question addressed to all of us: Why do we believe? Do we believe because we expect something from God and, if He does not give it to us, then we also turn our face away from Him? Do we believe because He is, as we say, a "Higher Power"? Because He performs miracles? Is it because He loves us and we love Him? We will be called to answer these questions during Holy Week, throughout our lives, every day, at every opportunity. We have these questions before us.

We believe in God not because He is powerful and useful, not because we can turn to Him and ask Him to satisfy our requests, but because He showed us in the person of His Son and His sacrifice that He loves us. And He calls our heart, like the heart of

Mary, to express its love for God. Without passing it through the logic and reasoning that I mentioned before. Only in this way, my beloved brothers and sisters, will we be able to understand why God was crucified. He was crucified because love had to defeat death, and precisely for this reason, the Resurrection, which will follow the Crucifixion, will be the proof that this is the only way that can death be defeated. And God wants to give us, my brothers and sisters, in the person of Christ, nothing less than victory over death.

All our requests, all our pursuits, everything is ephemeral, everything is without importance! What is important is victory over death! And that's why in today's apolytikion hymn we sang: "we cry out to You the Victor over death: Hosanna in the highest! Blessed are You, the One, who comes in the name of the Lord."

April 28, 2002

30.

THOMAS SUNDAY AND SAINT JOHN THE THEOLOGIAN

Two different paths. (John 20:19–31)

Two apostles are presented today by our Church, my beloved brothers and sisters, as confessors of the Lord's divinity.

One is the apostle Thomas, who, seeing the resurrected Lord, confessed and said: "My Lord and my God." The other is the disciple whose memory our Church is commemorating today: John the Theologian, who, as we heard in the epistle reading, also confesses the Lord's divinity, writing these very important words: "That which was from the beginning, which we have heard, which we have seen with our eyes, which we have looked upon, and our hands have handled, concerning the Word of life" (1 John 1:1).

Both of these disciples confess the Lord's divinity, but each one arrives at it from a different path.

The Apostle Thomas, in order to come to confess the Lord's divinity, first goes through doubt. He cannot believe unless he has evidence in his hands. He cannot believe and confess the Lord's divinity and His Resurrection if he does not see him personally and does not put his finger on the "print of the nails"—that is, to establish that this is the crucified Lord, the One who was resurrected, he is his Lord and his God.

"Unless I see in His hands the print of the nails, and put my finger into the print of the nails, and put my hand into His side, I will not believe."

He believes, therefore, after passing through doubt, passing through research, and satisfying his logic.

John follows a different path. John confesses the Lord's divinity by going through the path of love. He never doubted the Lord's divinity, because he was completely dedicated to him. He was bound to him by the bond of love. And John kept this love faithfully, and there was never any doubt in his mind. He was always the one who considered him the Son of God, his Lord and God. He had never loved any other person as much as he loved Christ. He had not given his love to anyone else and no one had received God's love so powerfully and tangibly that he too could say that "our hands have handled" the love of God, because he leaned upon the Lord's chest at the Last Supper. He was the one who never left Him; he followed Him to the Cross, even when all the other disciples had abandoned Him. He took the Lord's mother, Panagia, to his home and remained faithful to Him until the end. That is why the Church called him "the beloved disciple." He held this title in the Holy Gospel itself. And the Church added the title of "virgin" to him, because the betrayal and denial of the Lord never crossed his mind. Virginity is not only a matter of physical cleanliness and chastity. It is the purity and stability of our thoughts, of our heart, towards a person to whom we are fully devoted. So the temptation of betraying the Lord and doubt did not exist for John, and that is why he was called a virgin—a virgin from every temptation to turn away from the Lord. Moreover, the Church gave him another very important title. It called him Theologian, a title not given to the other disciples of the Lord, despite the fact that they also confessed His divinity. The Apostle Peter confessed it on the way to Caesarea Philippi, saying "You are the Christ, the Son of the living God" (Mt 16:16). And the Apostle Paul also reached the third heaven and "heard inexpressible words, which it is not lawful for a man to utter" (2 Cor 12:4).

They, and the other disciples, knew God and confessed Him, but none except John spoke to us about the very being of God, about how God is, His very existence. John did this, using his experience and his relationship with Him, and that is why he was able to say that God in His very nature, in His very personal existence, is love: "God is love" (1 John 4:8). This was not a revelation that came to him suddenly, without going through the experience, because his whole life was an acquaintance with God's love. The other disciples knew God's love after they first went through the road of repentance, the road of tears, like the Apostle Peter, because they had moved away from this love, they had betrayed it. John never betrayed that love. And he was accounted worthy to be the Theologian and to show us what true theology has to say. And for this reason, my dear brothers and sisters, we must lean a little on this great disciple of the Lord, who is and must be our teacher, our Theologian, the only one of the apostles to whom the Church bestowed this title.

John, therefore, knows from his personal relationship with God that God is the Holy Trinity, the three persons of the Holy Trinity, who are bound together by the love between Them. And this love was poured out on the world with the sending and incarnation of one of these persons, the Son and Word of God. And so John shows us what real theology is. And he also shows us the source from which theology draws and must always draw. And this source is love itself.

One does not reach God with the mind, with thought, with arguments. But with love he can reach God. Because God is love itself.

And when John speaks of love, as a source of theology, he has in mind a love which is not simply a feeling, as we usually understand it in our everyday language. Love, according to John, is the faithful surrender to the will of the Beloved, of the other, of God—surrender to such an extent that his will is identified with the will of God. That is why the Lord says in the Gospel according to John: "If you love me, you will keep my commandments" (John 14:15). "You cannot say you love me and not keep my commandments. What I want is for your will to match mine." And this is exactly what the Lord demonstrated in Gethsemane, when He identified His will with the will of His Father even to the point of the Cross.

Observance of God's commandments, my dear brothers and sisters, is a prerequisite for theology. One cannot theologize if one does not pass through this road. And this path also leads to the other manifestation of John's love for the Lord: his participation in the Cross of Christ. As I told you, the other disciples had abandoned Christ on the Cross; John, however, remained by His side. He participated in the suffering of the cross, he lived it, he experienced it. And for this reason one can say that he truly loved the Lord and that from this love he came to know true theology.

True theology, then, also goes through the Cross. It goes through the difficult path of renouncing our own will, of crucifying our will, as happened to the Lord Himself, and that is exactly why John is the Theologian, because he travelled this path.

There's something else that strikes us, brothers and sisters. John's privilege of being a theologian must be related to the fact that he took the Virgin Mary into his home. At first glance, it's difficult to see the connection, but the more we think about it, the more we will see that the person of the Lord is so interwoven and bound up with the Virgin Mary that one cannot love the Lord without simultaneously loving the Virgin Mary and being dedicated to her. That is why our theology, my beloved brothers and sisters, also goes through this road of love, respect, and devotion to the Virgin Mary and to all the saints whom the Lord Himself loved. That is why, my beloved brothers and sisters, John is the Theologian, the great Theologian of our Church.

So, my beloved brothers and sisters, the paths that lie before us to reach the recognition and confession of the Lord as God are different. They are not the same for all people. For the Apostle Thomas, the way was research, logical research. God does not deny this path to man. If he wants to follow Him, he can, but the Lord does not bless him. He said to the Apostle Thomas, "Okay, now you are satisfied, your curiosity is satisfied, your logic is satisfied, but blessed are those who do not go through this road: Blessed are those who have not seen and have believed." Not because this road is forbidden. The Lord does not forbid scientific research. What is heard many times, "Just believe and do not think too much," is not what the Church actually believes. Research is also a way. And the fathers of the Church were real scientists in theology, they were able to reach the confession of faith through the path of research, but this is not the only path.

The other path, followed by the other apostles, such as Peter and Paul, is the path of repentance, the path of tears. The passage from the denial of God, the Lord, through repentance, to a firm confession of faith in the Lord's divinity. This is also a path, which I would say is perhaps the most common for all of us. Because all of us, more or less, have fallen and are falling into the betrayal of

God's love. And we all need to go through the path of repentance, of tears, and then confess: "My Lord and my God." So this is the path for most of us.

Saint John the Theologian's path is a rare one. It is a path that goes through complete surrender to the Lord without doubt and without betrayal and abandonment. And these are truly the blessed, they are blessed by the Lord in today's gospel passage.

All these roads, my brothers and sisters, are before us. In order to arrive at the confession of the Lord as our God, as the God of our existence, we can follow any path, as long as we desire it and strive towards this confession.

But we must start with love. Let us not approach the Lord as a scientific object that we simply want to know with our mind. We must approach Him as someone we love, who we want to be our God. And after we start with this, then He will reveal Himself to us and we will say with the Apostle Thomas: "My Lord and my God, glory to you!"

At the Holy Monastery of Saint John the Baptist, Essex, England
May 8, 2016

31.
SUNDAY OF THE MYRRHBEARERS
Concerning the body and resurrection (Mk 15:43–16:8)

Today's Sunday is dedicated, my beloved brothers and sisters, to the myrrh-bearing women and the myrrh-bearing men who cared for the Lord's body with tenderness and love, both after His Crucifixion and during His burial. It is a very touching day because it shows how important the human body is. The Lord's body was a human body, like our own bodies, and that is why it is of great importance to approach the treatment of the human body, the body of the Lord, with myrrh.

The Lord, shortly before His Passion and death, was in the house of Lazarus after raising him from the dead, when Mary, Lazarus' sister, as a sign of gratitude, anointed the His feet with a precious myrrh. Then, as we all remember, Judas was scandalized and said: "This myrrh is very expensive. We could sell it and distribute the money to the poor." Then the Lord replied: "Leave the woman alone, in this way she is preparing me for burial" (cf. Jn 12:4–7). Why is myrrh so connected to the entombment of the Lord and in general to the entombment of the body?

First, because in this way we demonstrate the sanctity of the human body. Man, my brothers and sisters, is made by God not only as a soul but also as a body. A great theologian of our time, the late Georges Florovsky, wrote that man without a soul is a corpse, but also that man without a body is a ghost. It is not possible to have a complete person without also having a body.

The body is a creation of God. Man is both a soul and a body, which is given by God so that God may be glorified through it, as the Apostle Paul says: "Therefore glorify God in your body and in your spirit, which are God's" (1 Cor 6:20). And we were given this body to communicate with the rest of the material world, because man is the crown of all creation; so that we can unite this material world—all animals, all that is inferior to us in nature—

and bring it into communication with God. And also God gave us the body to communicate with each other in space and time. Therefore, the human body is sacred, and that is why God will resurrect it, as He resurrected the body of the Lord, so that all the bodies of people who believe in him will be resurrected.

But man either despises his body or cares about it so much that he makes it the center of his individuality and not a means to communicate with God and with others. Thus, not only does our body unite us with others, but it can also separate us from others. When the body is a means for our selfishness, to receive pleasures, it separates us from others, it separates us from God. But our body is given to communicate with others, to offer it in a spirit of self-sacrifice to others, and ultimately to God himself.

Thus people don't know what to do with their bodies. Sometimes they take care of it excessively and in this way the human body loses its meaning, sometimes they despise it and give it over to abuse, to wear and tear, and sometimes people in today's era even go so far as to burn it after the person's death.

But the Resurrection of Christ declares that the body is destined to be resurrected, that it is sacred. The myrrh-bearing women and myrrh-bearing men, such as Joseph and Nicodemus, who immediately after the Crucifixion of the Lord, after His death on the Cross, rushed to care for His body, show us how sacred the human body is. And with myrrh, man wants to show that he does not tolerate the decay of the body, because death is the result of decay and expresses the decay of the body, the decomposition—and this, man does not accept. He reacts to death, he reacts to decay, and he wants to show how careful he is so that the body does not wear out. He wants to express how much he believes that the final purpose of the body is not its decay but life. Fragrance, like that which is exuded by the holy relics of the saints, points us toward the final destination of the human body.

Ultimately, this treatment of the Lord's body with myrrh shows us that love and tenderness is the only way to face death. Death does not aim simply at the dissolution of the human body, but also at the interruption of communication and love between people. Death cuts off communion and thus wounds love; and love reacts and does not accept death, because it wants to have eternal communion between people, persons who love one another.

We see man's reaction to death, his response with love, with the tenderness of the myrrhbearers. Death wounds love, and love reacts in this way. Thus it seems that, in the end, with the resurrection, love will win and not separation, which death seeks. And man will conquer death only with love and in no other way.

My brothers and sisters, as we heard in the Gospel passage, as the myrrh-bearing women were going to the Lord's tomb, they were preoccupied with a question: "Who will move the stone for us so that we can anoint the Lord's body with myrrh?" And the evangelist says that they found the stone rolled away—"for it was very large"—and no human could have moved it. In this way, the evangelist shows us that death cannot be moved, that no human power can overcome it; it requires an intervention from on high. Only God can defeat death, not man. And while we try in various ways to defeat death, prolonging life either through science or in other ways, in the end it turns out that no one but God can defeat it.

Because the stone at the tomb "was very large." Somehow, however, they found it removed. Here is where the stone had moved. What does this tell us? It tells us that death does not have the final word in history, in the life of the world, but life does, God does—this is the great message of the Lord's Resurrection. The Lord, my brothers and sisters, did not come to give us some great teaching, He did not come to save us only from our sins, He came for something much more important: to give us life to defeat death. Because man wants nothing else in this world than to defeat death. Don't think this strange, because we may not all consciously realize it, but everything we do is a result of our fear of death.

Our efforts to hoard wealth are a reaction to death. Our efforts to gain fame and visibility are an attempt to preserve our memory forever. We strive in various way to overcome death. This is the great problem for man—his mortality. Unfortunately, the meaning of the Gospel has been lost on those Christians who do not put all the emphasis on Christ's Resurrection—as we Orthodox do—but instead on other salvific actions of the Lord. Christ came to redeem us from death; this is the message of the Gospel. That is why, my brothers and sisters, our Orthodox celebration of the Lord's Resurrection expresses the conviction and the certainty that death has already been defeated in the person of the Lord.

Therefore, death does not dominate us, and we proclaim and experience this truth in the Church, especially in the Divine Liturgy—that the death of our loved ones is not their annihilation. They exist, they live in the body of the resurrected Lord, and we all—united in this body, in the Eucharist, in the Divine Liturgy—experience this transcendence of death.

So, my beloved brothers and sisters, today's feast is not only moving but also instructive. It teaches us that the greatest gift that God has given us is our resurrection—the victory over death. And this holy body that He gave us, we must guard it in such a way that it is worthy to participate in the resurrected body of the Lord, that it too will be resurrected one day, and then death will be, as the Apostle Paul says, man's "last enemy" (1 Cor 15:26) to be defeated.

So, my brothers and sisters, let us draw this faith from today's celebration and walk with the joy of our certainty in the Resurrection during these holy days of celebration that have been given to us in the Church. I pray that the resurrected Lord will strengthen us in this faith and grant us all the resurrection of our own bodies, the eternal Kingdom and blessedness near Him.

April 25, 2004

32.
SUNDAY OF THE SAMARITAN WOMAN
God and woman. (John 4:5–42)

There are a plethora of lessons in today's gospel passage, my dear brothers and sisters. The Lord goes to Samaria and there, next to Jacob's well, He enters into a conversation with a Samaritan woman. We can learn a great deal from this conversation and what followed. If you'll allow me, I would like to highlight some of these rich lessons from today's gospel.

First, it is truly amazing that the Lord would converse with a Samaritan woman, being Himself a Jew. His disciples also wondered how this thing happened, since it was well known, as the Gospel tells us, that "Jews have no dealings with Samaritans." They had no contact at all; in fact, they hated each other. And the Lord, by engaging the woman in conversation, wanted to demonstrate that differences between people—which are many times religious in nature, as in this case—are condemned before God. And the differences in this case, which were also ethnic, had to do with the fact that the Samaritans believed that God should be worshiped on Mount Gerizim, while the Jews believed that God should be worshiped in Jerusalem.

We often think, my beloved brothers and sisters, that what we believe fanatically is truly the right thing. However, people with a type of zealotism often close their eyes completely to any communication with others in order to defend their faith. This was the case with the Jews and the Samaritans, where this difference over the place of God's worship had led them to hate each other. A religious difference, then, leads to hatred, leads to a lack of communion, and this is exactly what the Lord is coming today not simply to condemn, but to transcend. And how does He transcend it? By telling the Samaritan woman that God is not worshiped in a certain place; God is worshiped everywhere and in the Holy Spirit because He Himself is Spirit. The Holy Spirit is that which causes people to unite, to love one another and not to hate one another. Therefore, it is not possible in the Holy Spirit for people to hate each other, even for religious reasons.

The Lord thus taught the Samaritan woman that worship should now be spiritual and that man should not be attached to certain forms, which can also create division. Of course, forms are necessary in the worship of God, but they should never lead to division and hatred between people. Another prejudice that the Lord removes with this conversation is the fact that the woman was despised; she was considered a second-class person. The Lord causes the disciples to marvel that "He was talking with a woman." Indeed, this division is not only religious but also cultural, which must be overcome, and is overcome with the grace of God and the Holy Spirit.

This woman is not simply accepted by the Lord in conversation with Him, but also becomes an apostle, an equal to the apostles. She doesn't just save herself, she isn't saved by herself, but she also saves others. And just think that, as the Gospel passage told us, this woman was a sinner. Thus we see that the Lord removes even this prejudice of people; He transcends and overcomes it. He talks to a Samaritan woman, who was not only hated by the Jews, not only was she considered inferior in society as a woman, but she was also a sinner, a known sinner who had taken five husbands, while the one with whom she was living at the time was not her husband; and she the woman, my brothers and sisters, is transformed into an apostle! How easy it is to condemn people, how easy it is to say that there is no salvation for someone, and the Lord comes to teach us the opposite, that there is salvation for everyone.

No one is definitively condemned by God unless he himself refuses to open his heart to receive God's grace, and the Samaritan woman opened her heart. The fact that the Lord exposed the secrets of her life did not make her hate the messenger, as we usually do when someone tells us the truth about ourselves; it made her love Him, recognize Him as the Messiah, and preach Him everywhere.

Another important point from today's Gospel passage, my brothers and sisters, is that the Lord points out to the apostles that their apostolic work is essentially nothing but harvesting, because the seed had been sown by God from before. How many times do we think that we are doing something, that we are offering something, when in reality we forget the words of the Lord, that "others have labored, and you have entered into their labors." We always reap the labor of others. And that is why it is very important first to recognize the contribution of others, those who preceded us, because none of us, my brothers and sisters, is self-made in the spiritual life. We all owe something to someone else, to someone else's effort, and we must always have this recognition, this gratitude in our hearts, and honor our fathers, especially our spiritual fathers, thanks to whom we met Christ, and thanks to whom we have come to know the truth.

Finally, it is characteristic of today's passage, my brothers and sisters, that the Samaritans who believed in Christ, believed first based on the preaching of Saint Photini, but then they say to this Samaritan woman, after the Lord stayed with them for two days: "Now we believe, not because of what you said, for we ourselves have heard Him and we know that this is indeed the Christ, the Savior of the world." How important it is, my brothers and sisters, to take this step from the information that others give us about Christ to our own personal acquaintance with Him. Because then and only then is our salvation complete.

Thus, it should never suffice for people to simply listen to a missionary or anyone who speaks about Christ to others, as is the case with many Protestant preachers, who are content to convey the message of the Gospel to people. What happens after that? They leave them, they leave them alone. But for us Orthodox, the place where the message of the Gospel really bears fruit is inside the Church. There one knows Christ personally, there one comes into personal communion with Him, through prayer and the sacraments of the Church, and above all through the Eucharist, where one is now united with Christ and no longer believes simply because someone told him that Christ is the savior, but because he himself lives and experiences Him as the savior. Therefore, preaching that does not lead to the Church is not preaching, it is not salvation. Here, in the Church, there is salvation, because here there is personal acquaintance with the Lord.

My brothers and sisters, today, by decision of the Holy Synod of the Ecumenical Patriarchate, the memory of the holy Archbishops and Patriarchs of Constantinople is celebrated. It was a decision that the current Ecumenical Patriarch, who had just been elected, introduced to the Synod. It is truly significant that on this day, the Sunday of the Samaritan woman, the Church remembers the spiritual labor of those who came before us and who led the world of the Orthodox Church. These holy Archbishops and Patriarchs of Constantinople sowed the seed for us to reap today. And God blessed a rich harvest in the form of our monastery, which by the grace of God bears fruit. But I am sure that it does not forget that it owes this fruition to the labor of others, and above all to the labor and martyrdom of the martyred Church of Constantinople.

My beloved brothers and sisters, may the prayers of the holy Archbishops and Patriarchs of Constantinople be with us as well as the prayers of the Samaritan woman, Saint Photini, so that our lives may be fruitful, that the labors of the spiritual fathers from whom we inherited may not go to waste, and that we too bear fruit, above all, in our personal relationship with the Lord within His Church. Amen.

33.
SUNDAY OF THE BLIND MAN
Light, baptism, rebirth, repentance (John 9:1–38)

The main person in today's gospel passage, my brothers and sisters, the blind man, is a model for all of us. The man was born blind and needed God's intervention to open his eyes and be healed.

We are born blind, because we only see our immediate environment and yet we think our environment is the whole world. As newborn children, we see our mother, on whom our food depends, like the whole world, and little by little our circle widens slightly and includes our father (who again takes care of food), our family and friends, but we can't see further than that. Our myopic vision narrows our heart.

We are only able to love those who love us. We can only love our environment and our own people, and we don't see that there is another world that is waiting for our love, that needs our love. We cannot see beyond our own environment. We are born blind, also, because we only see the material world; we do not see the immaterial spiritual world. We cannot see beyond the senses, beyond what our senses confirm to us as real. We cannot see God.

We were born and created by God to see God, yet our disability prevents us from seeing Him. We are born blind because, despite wanting light, we tend to seek darkness, to hide the dark sides of our souls, our dark actions, our dark thoughts. We are like moles looking for darkness to hide something. We are also born blind because we tend to see the sins of others and cannot see our own. This tendency is implanted in our very being, and it is a terrible disability.

When the man born blind appeared and asked for the Lord's mercy, his disciples spontaneously asked Christ: "Rabbi, who sinned, this man or his parents, that he was born blind?" That is, they immediately wanted to find someone else's sin. The Pharisees went one step further, certain that his illness was due to his sins, and because of this they were so blinded that they could not recognize a truth that was confirmed by so many people: the truth of the healing of the blind man. So they say to him: "You were completely born in sins, and are you teaching us?" Here the gaze turns to the sins of others, which makes us unable to see our own sins—this is true blindness. It is a blindness that we inherited at birth. We are born blind.

This gospel passage, like the others of the previous Sundays following Easter—the paralytic and the Samaritan woman—in the ancient Church was read precisely during this period. This period was connected with the baptism of the newly enlightened, which took place at Easter. At that time, group baptisms took place, initially on the evening of Holy Saturday just before Easter Sunday, and so during this post-Easter period, the Church refers to neophytes' recent baptism. That is why the passages of the paralytic, the Samaritan woman, and today's, of the blind man, all have a reference to water, such as the pool of Bethesda, the well of Jacob, the pool of Siloam. Why?

Because baptism, my brothers and sisters, is precisely man's healing from his blindness from birth, from those sins that we inherit, that we have within our very nature, as the psalmist says: "For behold, I was conceived in transgressions, and in sins my mother bore me." (Ps 50:7 LXX). We are thus born sinners and baptism is what removes this blindness from us and gives us light. That is why the baptized were called, and we even call them in our liturgical texts, "illumined."

Baptism is the remission of our innate sins and our innate blindness. Because with baptism we are now reborn and see another world. We see beyond our immediate family, our relatives, and our friends.

Incorporated into Christ Himself, we now embrace all people with the same love that He demonstrated, even to our enemies, and then we really see the truth, that the world is not only our immediate environment; the world is much bigger. This whole world belongs to God and we are called to embrace and love it. We see truths that go beyond the limits of our senses. We see that this mystical cycle of life and death is not the final cycle of human life, but that there is life even beyond that. There is eternal life, which is not determined by the laws of biology.

We see all this from the moment we are baptized and join the body of the Church. However, in most cases, this happens when we are babies, and that is why we need a constant renewal of our baptism. We need rebirth. We need light. And we need this light to shine on our being, to penetrate to the dark sides of ourselves, to the things we hide, to the things we are ashamed to say. Let light shine on all this so that we can see the truth, the truth of ourselves first, which we constantly avoid. Avoiding the truth of ourselves, we are blind and look to examine our neighbor as much as we can, in order to forget ourselves. In this way, my brothers and sisters, we prolong this blindness throughout our lives and, when the time comes for this truth to appear before us—whether we want it to or not—then we will find ourselves in a very unpleasant position.

Blessed are those who now let the light shine into their lives, into their existence, so that when the light comes to the whole world and shines with Christ's Second Coming they can see that their whole life belongs there in the light and not in the land of darkness.

Thus, my brothers and sisters, the Church established the sacrament of confession and repentance so that we can be born again. This renewal of ourselves, this opening of our eyes, to the truth of ourselves first, will make us know the truth, the real truth of the world, to see God Himself. Because this is what the man born blind in today's gospel passage did. Otherwise, he would not have seen the truth, he would not have been cured of his blindness. But from the moment he said, "I believe, Lord" and worshiped Him, from that moment he saw the truth of God, he saw God Himself. Then his healing was complete, and in this way the Lord confirms what he said in the gospel passage. This light—the light that shines forth from Christ, the light that shines abundantly into the whole world—reveals the truth.

This light, my brothers and sisters, let us seek it constantly and limit, as much as we can, the dark compartments of our souls, so that we can move from the truth about ourselves to the truth about all things, and above all to see the true God. Otherwise, trapped in darkness, we create false gods.

May today's blind man be a guide for us so that we too can see the light and live eternally with God. Amen.

At the Holy Monastery of Saint John the Baptist, Essex, England
May 20, 2001

34.
7th SUNDAY AFTER PASCHA
The 318 Holy Fathers of the Ecumenical Council of Nicaea (325 AD) (John 17:1–13)

Today's Sunday, my beloved brothers and sisters, is dedicated to the memory of the holy fathers who convened the First Ecumenical Council in 325 AD in Nicaea of Bithynia, which, as you all know, confirmed that the Person of our Lord Jesus Christ is the Second Person of the Holy Trinity, that is, God Himself.

And as the Church today honors these fathers, it calls us to pay attention to the gospel passage we just heard, which is one of the most shocking passages in the Bible. One, at the same time, of the most theological and most deeply meaningful passages. It is about the priestly prayer of the Lord, as it is called, the prayer that the Lord addressed to His Father shortly before His Passion. Of course, it would take too much time even to just mention all the jewels contained in this passage. So we will limit ourselves, my brothers and sisters, to the beginning and the end of the passage.

At the beginning of today's Gospel passage, the Lord says to His Father: "[T]he hour has come. Glorify Your Son." The time has come for your Son to be glorified. It's strange that Christ says this just before His Passion, shortly before the Cross. And one wonders how it is possible to speak of glory at the moment when the Lord is about to undergo the worst treatment and the greatest humiliation of his life? How is it possible to speak of glory when it comes to the Cross?

There are, my brothers and sisters, two kinds of glory: the glory that rests on power and the glory that rests on love. The glory that rests on power is forced; it is a glory that one gets by imposing that power in one way or another on others; it is a glory that one gets, almost always, by sacrificing others. And the second kind of glory is that which is obtained by our self-sacrifice, by our free and voluntary self-sacrifice. There is glory in this! But this world cannot understand this. Because the world knows only the glory of power. Don't we all see how man strives to gain power and be glorified through his power? Don't we all see the struggles happening—politically, economically, and militarily—a struggle to dominate in order to gain glory! The world does not understand how someone can be glorified while being humiliated. By loving, and sacrificing Himself!

This is precisely what is revealed by the Cross of the Lord! And it is not by chance that the Lord calls the Cross His "Glory." It is a fundamental concept in the Gospel of John. A concept by which the Church—as strange as it may seem—has lived and lives throughout the centuries. Because the glory of the Church is not the glory of power. And if many times the leaders of the Church are led astray and seek worldly power, this is not the spirit and ethos of our Church. The spirit and ethos of the power of the Church are found in its saints, in the martyrs, in those who humbled themselves, in those who sacrificed themselves for others—that is, its power is found in the Cross of the Lord.

The Cross of the Lord is, my brothers and sisters, the glory of the Church. The Church has no other glory. And if sometimes its history draws its privileges and glories, these are not of the Church's essence, nor should it strive for them. The Church has glory in its humiliation, in the sacrifice of its saints.

And at the end of the priestly prayer there is something else that the Church is especially called to pay attention to. But which Church? All of us! We are all Church!

At the end of His prayer, the Lord expresses His anguish for the unity of the Church in particular. "That they may be one, even as We are one." Just as the Father is united in an unbreakable unity with the Son, as are all three Persons of the Holy Trinity, so the Lord begs His Father that His disciples and His Church and ultimately the whole world would be united. Because the Lord came to this world to unite it.

Unity is also—as I said about glory—multifaceted, my brothers and sisters. Many times people seek unity, but they do not seek it according to the model of the unity of the Holy Trinity, "even as We are one," as the Lord said. They seek it in other ways, uniting people once again in order to gain strength, in order to impose, if possible, their power on a global scale. This kind of human power is based on coercion and not on freedom. It has nothing to do with the love that unites the Father with the Son. It has nothing to do with the unity that the Church of Christ must express.

The unity based on the model of the Holy Trinity is the one that demands the Church be united. To be united and, whenever schisms and divisions appear, to hasten to heal them, to cure them, not to neglect the restoration of unity.

Unfortunately, my brothers and sisters, we have gotten comfortable with the division. We are so used to it that it is truly tragic; and when efforts are made to restore unity, they disturb us. We say that it is better to remain divided than to try to unite.

This, however, my brothers and sisters, is not God's will. God's will is unity. The unity, however, that is based on the model of the Holy Trinity—that is, based on the truth, the truth that the Church expresses through its traditions and its fathers, whom we honor today. Consequently, it is a unity in truth, but at the same time also in love, because without love there is no truth and without truth there is no love. It is false love that is not based on truth, while the truth that is not based on love is hatred, it is fanaticism, it is "a zeal for God, but not according to knowledge" (Rom 10:2). It is, unfortunately, a departure from God's will.

Thus, the Church, my brothers and sisters, is called to maintain its unity by combining truth with love, by combining correct faith with love for one another. And this combination appears difficult many times. But it is the only way for there to be unity in the Church.

Unity in the Church is shaken when everyone exalts themselves and becomes exponents and defenders of the truth. Then, we have many "popes" in our Church. We accuse another Church, which has entrusted its authority and infallibility to one person, but unfortunately we often find ourselves in the same situation, where various people express the truth by their own authority. And so we have an essential division within the Church.

But the Church has a way to unite its believers in the truth. And it is precisely the way that was used at the First Ecumenical Council, as even then there were doubts about what is true. When a great heretic of that time, Arius, questioned the divinity of the Lord and found many followers, the Church had to decide what the truth is. But look how it did it! It did it by convening a Council. The Council of Bishops is the one that finally decides on the truth. The Council is the only way for us to find out what the truth is—not everyone's individual opinion, nor the opinion of different groups.

Today, my brothers and sisters, as we honor the Fathers of the Church who formed the First Ecumenical Council, let us acquire a humble mind and attitude, which does not seek the truth in the opinion of individuals but in the agreement of the members of the Church, which is expressed through its Council of Bishops.

Only in this way, dear brothers and sisters, does the Church depict the unity that exists between the persons of the Holy Trinity. Because in the persons of the Holy Trinity there is a lasting and eternal and permanent council, a union, an unbreakable communion, a communion first of all of love, from which also springs the truth—about the reality of the world and our very existence.

My brothers and sisters, today the world seeks its unity in ways that are far from both truth and love. And this pursuit will bring us to difficult days. Because it is a pursuit based on compulsion and necessity, it is a pursuit that has nothing to do with love. Only by experiencing love, each one at the level in which he lives, in the space in which he lives, only in this way will we be able to truly unite. Because love is that which respects the difference and the otherness of the other. And in this way we have a unity in our differences and distinctions, and not a homogenizing unity, which some try to impose from above.

That is why, my brothers and sisters, the Gospel passage that we heard and the feast we are observing today in honor of Fathers of the Church are very relevant. They're relevant, because we must do everything we can to preserve—both in our daily relationships, as well as in our culture—the correct unity: the unity of love, which respects the difference and distinction of others.

With these thoughts, my brothers and sisters, let us truly honor the Fathers of the Church, who taught us what "unity" means and who truly fulfilled what the Lord said in His high priestly prayer: "That they may be one, even as We are one." Amen!

Metochion (Dependency) of the Holy Monastery of
Asomaton-Petraki of Saint Nicholas Rigillis
June 16, 2002

35.
1st SUNDAY OF MATTHEW
(All Saints)
(Mt 10:32–33, 37–38, 19:27–30)

Today's Sunday, my beloved brothers and sisters, is dedicated by the Church to the memory and honor of all the saints.

It is the culmination of the entire cycle of Pentecost. It is the end of the descent and visitation of the Holy Spirit. It is the glory and the honor of the Church.

That is why today's Sunday is one of the most moving feasts of our Church. At the same time, it is an occasion to think more deeply, as deeply as we can, about what holiness means for the Church, what holiness means for our lives, and what honor for all the saints means.

The first point we must underline is that this feast reveals to all of us that holiness has a wide variety of gifts. It is not "monolithic," as we usually perceive it. There is not only one kind of holiness in the Church. There are many forms of holiness, because there are many gifts of the Holy Spirit and holiness is not our achievement; it is not the result of our moral or other efforts. It is not a matter of virtue; it is a matter of the gift of the Holy Spirit. Holiness is given to us by the holy God. We do not achieve it ourselves, no matter how hard we try.

And the holy God, through the Holy Spirit, offers holiness in many forms. It is characteristic that the choir of saints includes prophets, apostles, hierarchs, martyrs, unmercenary healers, ascetics, righteous, neo-martyrs; a wide range of forms of holiness. Because the Holy Spirit distributes the gifts and gives to each the gift that it wants, the gift that according to the will of the holy God will build up the Church. Because the purpose of holiness is not to save only a certain person and "to sanctify," as we say, but to build up the Church. And the Church is built up by a variety of gifts; each one offers something different, and by offering something different he participates in the holiness of God. And by participating in the holiness of God, he becomes a saint. And the Church has a need for prophets, for apostles, as well as administrators, and not only for those gifts that most impress us.

Often, my brothers and sisters, we perceive holiness in only one specific form, mainly in the ascetic form. But I repeat, as the Apostle Paul emphasizes in his first epistle to the Corinthians, the Church is like a body that has many members and each member serves it in its own way. And for this reason we cannot say that a certain gift, a certain form of holiness, is more important than another. All forms of holiness are important.

The second point that should be underlined on the occasion of today's feast is what we could call the anonymity of holiness. Yes, dear brothers and sisters! Our Church has the names of saints. According to the will of God, certain persons in the Church stand out in its consciousness as saints. They are honored and placed before us as an example, but also as intercessors for God's grace. However, today's feast tells us that there are not only named saints, but there are also anonymous saints, those who did not emerge with names in the consciousness of the Church.

How many saints does the Church have? The Bible speaks of a cloud of witnesses, of a cloud of saints. They are truly innumerable! And this makes us think, to think very seriously: Is it possible that many of the people whom we despise, whom we even condemn and criticize as sinners, are actually hidden saints?

Because the real saint, my brothers and sisters, seeks anonymity, he does not seek his prominence, he does not seek his fame. On the contrary, when he hears that some rumor is spreading about him, he tries in every way to prevent it. And we know from the history of the Church a certain type of saint who came to be called a "fool for Christ"—who was, one might say, the pinnacle of avoiding fame and good repute. They were ones who sought infamy, who tried in every possible way to demonstrate that they were *not* saints.

Often, Church members know very well and practice the art of sanctification, they practice that which will make people aware of their holiness. Be assured, my brothers and sisters, that they are far from holiness: real holiness consists in our self-reproach and not in our self-promotion. There are, therefore, brothers and sisters around us who are saints, hidden saints, anonymous saints, and that is why we cannot criticize anyone, judge anyone, condemn and despise anyone.

We must treat them all as potential saints, as hidden and anonymous saints, because no one knows, my brothers and sisters, if a sinner, at his moment of truth, will not one day become a saint. No one knows if the one standing next to us, who seems to all of us sinful and condemned—does not in fact burn with love for God, burn with desire for holiness.

Indeed, we do not know what each person hides next to us and what can become a reality in his life. Thus, the feast of All Saints invites us to think of the anonymous saints and through the anonymous saints to think of each person as potentially holy—even the greatest sinner as potentially holy. And this will give us a feeling of humility, a feeling of love for everyone. This is the only way for us to approach holiness.

Another very important point, which we heard in the epistle reading, is that the saints are not sanctified as individuals; they are sanctified as members of the Church. We heard in the epistle reading that all the saints that were mentioned "did not receive what was promised, since God had foreseen something better for us, that apart from us they should not be made perfect" (Heb 11:39–40).

All these saints—who suffered as we heard and were truly sanctified—were not finished, that is, they did not become perfect saints, without us. They were waiting for us in order to be complete. In other words, they were waiting for the communion of the Church and within the communion of the Church they were truly sanctified. And every holy figure in the Old Testament, as well as every saint, my brothers and sisters, is only sanctified within the body of the Church. Only as a member of the Church is he a saint for us Christians, and indeed the Orthodox. He can have ascetic achievements, which one finds in other religions as well. He can have great virtues, which one can also find outside the Church, but he does not become a saint in this way. Because, in order to become a saint, he must become a member of the body of Christ. Because the saint, I repeat, derives his holiness from the only Holy One, who is Christ. And in a little while we will hear in the Divine Liturgy what we must always pay attention to: when the moment comes to receive communion and the priest says "The holy things for the holy people of God," the moment has now come to offer the "holy"—that is, the body of Christ and His blood—to the saints. And the response we will hear from the chanters is telling: "One is Holy, one is Lord, Jesus Christ." Let us not think that we are holy and therefore worthy to be recognized as holy, because there is only one truly Holy One, and it is by our participation in His body and blood that we are also sanctified.

Thus, my brothers and sisters, this feast of All Saints, whom we honor today, shows us that the path of holiness passes through the Church, it passes through the only Holy One and above all through our communion in the body and blood of the Lord. From this communion we also draw our communion with all the saints, and thus we hope and pray and expect that we too can be saved somewhere deep in the body of Christ, in the body of the saints. Woe to us if we believe that we can be saved by our virtues, that we can be saved by our individual holiness.

My brothers and sisters, the world in which we live takes a very strange position towards holiness. On the one hand, the world admires holiness and extols it, and on the other hand no one would want their child to become a saint. Others are the heroes to emulate today. Television mainly offers them to us, it offers them to us in the form of singers, football players, financially successful people, and all parents would like their children to become something like that. They admire holiness, but no one wants it! It is strange, but at the same time easy to explain. Because holiness requires, as the Lord said in the Gospel passage, a denial of ourselves, a transcendence of our individuality, a cutting off of our own will, an abandonment of everything.

We heard harsh words in the Gospel passage. Whoever is not ready to leave father, mother, siblings, parents, children, "is not worthy of Me." Holiness, therefore, in all the forms I mentioned has one common characteristic: that with it we overcome our individualism; our interest in our own benefit. And in this way, holiness becomes a difficult thing, unattainable. And while we admire it, we don't want to apply it to ourselves and our children.

This is how the Church, my brothers and sisters, sojourns through the ages in a world that constantly wants the Church to adjust its measure of holiness to our own measure. The Church would be well liked by doing this. Unfortunately, sadly, this often happens, but this is a betrayal and abandonment of holiness. The saints will always have a problem, in one way or another, with public opinion and the common sentiment, with what the Gospel calls "this world."

And the biggest problem for the Church will always be how to keep holiness genuine, without adulterating it to meet the demands of the world. It will always be a problem, because the saints appear in history as weak beings and that is why the Church often looks to adapt things in order to gain power in the world. But the strength of the Church is its saints, these weak saints, and we need only, my brothers and sisters, to look at history to see that all the saints in their weakness were in fact so strong that they transformed history, and not only do they work miracles with their grace, but they support the Church on its journey through history. And they support all of us.

This, my brothers and sisters, is the meaning of holiness that the feast of All Saints shows us today. The Church is called to preserve and proclaim this spirit and message of holiness, even if the world finds it difficult to accept. We will always live in this division, in this dialectic between the saints and the world. And at the end of this journey, we will one day be able to reach the Kingdom of God, in which holiness will be revealed—the holiness of the anonymous saints will be revealed—and it will be proven that the holy God is the one who directs history, the only one true and omnipotent ruler of history.

Let us, my brothers and sisters, apprehend these messages—let us love our saints, let us love holiness, let us strive for it in ourselves, cutting off our own will, overcoming our individualism, being sanctified within the body of the Church and the communion of saints and never believing that we are saints. May we be accounted worthy of God's mercy and find ourselves next to the saints. Amen!

Holy Monastery of Saint Paraskevi of Mazios, Megaron
June 22, 2020

36.
2nd SUNDAY OF MATTHEW
The Calling of God (Mt 4:18–23)

They immediately left their nets and followed Him.

At the heart of the Gospel, my beloved brothers and sisters, there is a paradox: He who, in His love, gives us everything, calls us to give it up, to let it go. It is a paradox that challenges our logic and we need to delve into it, with the grace of God and the Holy Spirit, and understand it. Why is there this paradox at the heart of the Gospel?

Today's Gospel passage is short but moving. The Lord walks "by the Sea of Galilee" and there He addresses his call, his invitation, initially to two brothers, Peter and Andrew, and then to another set of brothers, John and James. And He calls them to follow Him, leaving everything behind. He addresses them with a call that is not based on any logic, on any justification. He does not rely on the qualifications of the people He calls. What qualifications could they have? They were illiterate fishermen. The call is not based on any of their moral values. He does not examine the conditions under which He calls them. It is a completely free call, because if He called them because of the qualifications they had, then these qualifications would definitely bind the call and the One who issued it. But God's call is free. It does not depend on any conditions on our part. And it is free to the extent that we can never explain why He directs it to certain persons and not to others.

This is the great mystery. Surely, these disciples would have asked themselves during their lives: "Why us? There are so many people around. Why did God choose to call us?" There is no answer to this, because there is no answer to the mystery of freedom, to the mystery of love. So God addresses the call as a gift of love, as a gift of grace and freedom.

However, this call is also difficult, because it implies two things. First, the answer, the response must be immediate. "They immediately left their nets and followed Him." "Immediately" means without any thought process, without saying "let us think, let us see, let us study the matter, let us finally see who you are that directs this call to us." "Immediately," because the response that is postponed, because thought intervenes, is the response of our mind, and God wants the response of our heart. The response of the heart is an immediate answer, without calculations, without deliberation.

And the other difficult thing is that not only must one immediately give a response, but one must also leave everything. And one wonders: Why? Couldn't the disciples respond to the Lord's call without leaving their father, their nets, their profession, and everything? Couldn't they find a way to reconcile them, as we try to reconcile everything? No, they had to leave everything, and they did leave everything. Why?

Man's fall, my brothers and sisters, contains a great tragedy. Forsaking God, man had nothing to cling to, nowhere to stand, nowhere to find his security, which until then was in the hands of God. And he sought his security in the things around him, in nature and in himself. After all, since he proclaimed himself god, where else should he look for security? He himself was the only one who could give him his security. But it turned out that neither nature nor himself could give it to him. They were both created, and both were subject to death. And so man entered into a terrible state, trying to avoid death through things that contain death; trying to be safe in constant insecurity. So how is it possible, my brothers and sisters, to overcome this tragedy, which—if man remains hooked on these things that do not truly give him security and do not offer him the solution to his great problem—is decay and death?

In order to overcome these things, he needs to abandon them, to put the basis of his security again in God himself, and not in these things. So it is necessary to make this move away from things, away from nature, and to move toward God. Let's go to the One who calls us, leaving those things that until now we thought would secure us eternity.

It is therefore necessary, my brothers and sisters, to evaluate all those things that give us the impression that they are means for us to survive, such as family, children, profession. We must evaluate all these in the light of this truth that they do not they ensure eternity. Only God has eternity, and only if we shift the basis of our existence from these things to Him, only then will we overcome this tragedy and find our true security.

But the important thing is that we are not only called to let go of the things we have around us, the various relationships we have developed—which are gifts from God—but we are called to abandon ourselves in everything. Our own self is the one that gives us the greatest illusion of our existence. It gives us the illusion that we exist alone, as individuals, and that which in the language of patristic neptic theology, in the language of Saint Maximus the Confessor, is called self-love [φιλαυτία], this is the most difficult thing that one must give up.

There are people, my brothers and sisters, who have left their families, left their professions, maybe even reached the point of becoming monks and ascetics, but how great was the struggle to abandon themselves? It is not easy, but it is very possible to give up one's possessions, all one's belongings, and ultimately have a self-love that keeps one stuck to oneself. The most difficult spiritual struggle is the struggle against pride. The struggle that calls us not to rely on ourselves.

Look, my brothers and sisters, what happened to the disciples themselves, those whom the Lord called. These disciples responded directly, and "immediately" left everything, but let's look at their lives. Shortly before the Passion of the Lord, at that awful moment, those who have left everything approach Him and say to Him: "Lord, now that you will establish your Kingdom, won't you give us a place of honor next to you, to be among the first?" (Mk 10:35–37). How much self-love lived in them! And there came a time when fear seized one of those who left everything "immediately," and when they asked him: "Are you his disciple?", he answered three times: "I do not know the man" (Mt 26:69–76). And when the Passion of the Lord was approaching, again those who left everything, left Him and slept, "for their eyes were heavy" (Mt

26:43). Their nature had overcome them. They couldn't stand it. And what's more, one of them who left everything—what a terrible thing!—betrayed Him. He put himself and his interest first. The thirty pieces of silver were too great a temptation. The money would obtain who knows how many goods in the world. How strange, to leave everything and then ultimately, because you haven't abandoned yourself, to abandon the One for whom you abandoned everything.

So, my brothers and sisters, it is a constant struggle to respond to God's call. Love is difficult. And the Apostle Paul has these very heavy words about love, when he says that love does not seek its own (1 Cor 13:5). It is as if he is saying that you can love, you can even give your body to be sacrificed, but without the love that "does not seek its own," without the love that has now shifted all the interest and orientation from you to the other, to the One who called you. So love is difficult and responding to God's call is difficult. That's where we all struggle.

God calls us to Him, but He calls us through a person, and, just as the disciples saw a person in front of them when He called them, they had to make the decision to say the declare the resounding "Yes" without it being revealed to them beforehand that they were saying this "Yes" to God. First they said "Yes," and then it was revealed to them that He was God. We turn things around, we want to be sure and we always say:

"Let's wait and see the signs, if he who calls us does miracles, if he has all these characteristics that would show us that this is a person through whom God is calling us."

It is, my brothers and sisters, very difficult to understand what happened to the apostles at that moment. But it is certain that the Lord had not yet revealed His divinity to them. After all, this divinity was not truly revealed until His Resurrection and then with the outpouring of the Holy Spirit at Pentecost. Until then, the apostles had doubts whether it was God or man. There were moments when they saw that it was something divine, that God was present, but in order to understand that God exists they had to surrender themselves to Him first. This is the great mystery. We never understand God unless we surrender ourselves to Him.

So, my brothers and sisters, this passage today has to tell us essential things about our lives and our existence. And it is very important that when we surrender ourselves, when we say "Yes," when we deny everything—all these things on which we base our security—it does not mean that we renounce them—that is, that we destroy them, that they do not exist . On the contrary, when we give them up for the sake of God, then they are returned to us a hundredfold.

The Lord spoke to his disciples at some point precisely about this mystery, the fact that they left everything and followed him. And they asked him: "Well, we have left everything, what then is there for us? What will happen to us?" And the Lord's answer was: "Whoever forsakes all these things will receive a hundredfold" (Mt 19:27–29). Because all these things, my brothers and sisters, by passing through surrender into the hands of God's love, return to us, true now, cleansed from corruption and death. They also participate in the eternity of our existence. They also acquire their true meaning. And so, my brothers and sisters, the abandonment of everything for the sake of God, in the end, is not abandonment, it is not renunciation, it is a way to find them again, so that they too can now regain their eternal existence.

My brothers and sisters, the calling of the apostles is a mystery. The call of God is a mystery. This whole abandonment of everything for God is a mystery. But this mystery is the heart of our Church. Our Church is founded, my brothers and sisters, on those who left everything, and the closer we get to them, the more we receive the grace and eternity that God offers them. They are the martyrs, the holy ones, they are the saints of the Church, who abandoned everything and themselves and in this way received it back a hundredfold, and now they can intercede for us and be guides in our lives, so that we too can approach this abandonment, which is rewarded a hundredfold. Amen.

July 7, 2002

37.
3rd SUNDAY OF MATTHEW
On the Fall and the Kingdom of God (Mt 6:22–33)

But seek first the kingdom of God and His righteousness,
and all these things shall be added to you.

The Lord's words in today's Gospel passage, my dear brothers and sisters, reveal to us the depths of man's tragedy after Adam's fall and man's separation from God. When man decided to take his fate and the fate of the world into his own hands, the consequences were tragic. The Gospel passage that we have just heard describes some of these tragic consequences, which I would like to explore with you, if you allow me (Mt 6:22–33).

The first consequence is that man lost the simplicity of his gaze, the simplicity of his eye.[1] The Lord says that man's eye can show the simplicity of his soul, or the wickedness of his soul. And simplicity is seeing the world around him as he will see it in the Kingdom of God. Wickedness of the gaze and of the eye is to see the world as an enemy, to see the whole world around us as sinful and to look at how to escape and how to manage to survive within this world. Losing the simplicity of his soul, therefore, which is expressed by the simplicity of his gaze, man, says the Lord, lost his light. And while he thinks he sees, deep down he lives in darkness because he sees everything in a complicated way, he sees everything wickedly, and in this way darkness dominates his life, and the light that is inside him becomes darkness. If therefore the light that is in you is darkness," says the Lord, "how great is that darkness!" If what you see with your eyes is darkness, just think, says the Lord, about the real darkness that you have inside your soul. Man has therefore lost the simplicity with which he sees the world.

[1] The word in Mt 6:22 usually translated as "sound" (RSV) or "good" (NKJV)—ἁπλοῦς—literally means "simple."

Another consequence is that—precisely because man entered into this relationship with the world, in which the world is complicated for him—he also lost his peace. That is, man feels such insecurity that he looks at how he will be able to survive in this world. And because of this, he is seized with anxiety, he is seized with agony as to how he will succeed, and therefore concern for tomorrow enters his life. What will happen tomorrow? Will I be able to survive in this world? So man surrenders himself to a struggle for survival, having lost this simplicity of his thought and soul, and is tormented every day how to make ends meet in this world. He is therefore occupied with the care of how he will live.

The third consequence is that, amid this concern for how to make ends meet, man works for money. He makes money god. He works for mammon, as the Lord says in the passage we heard. Because money promises him security and, to gain this security, he surrenders everything to money. He gives up his soul; he sells his soul for money. He is a slave, therefore, to money.

The fourth consequence is that by working for money, making money a god, man finds himself in contradiction with himself and divided within himself. He wants to believe in God, but at the same time he wants to have the power of money. And so he does not know how to reconcile within himself his faith in God with his faith in mammon. He works for two masters, says the Lord, both God and mammon. He becomes divided within himself and becomes schizophrenic, he becomes unhappy. His life is divided into spiritual and material things, while in reality these are one. God's creation is one, both spiritual and material. They are gifts of God and they form a unity, but after the fall man separates them. Thus begins a struggle within him whether he should follow the spiritual and abandon the material or follow the material and abandon the spiritual.

Great is the unhappiness of the man who cannot unite his body and his spirit, and instead looks to decide which of the two he prefers. So man's condition after the fall is tragic, and the Lord describes it in today's passage as idolatry. He says: "For after all these things the Gentiles seek." This anxiety for tomorrow, this slavery to how we will secure ourselves for the future—this, says the Lord, is idolatry. Because what does it all mean? You don't believe that God directs your life. You don't believe that God can take care of everything. So you do not have complete faith in God and that is why you worship idols, such as the powers of this world, such as money and all that is involved in your concern and your agony for tomorrow.

To this entire tragic situation, my beloved brothers and sisters, the Lord comes in today's Gospel passage to offer healing and redemption, and says that man's problem is his priorities. Man doesn't know what to put first and what to put second. He has reversed the priorities and puts the second first and the first second. Which is the first? It is, he says, the Kingdom of God—"seek first the Kingdom of God"—and all the other things that occupy you, all these concerns will be satisfied. "All this will be added to you," it will be an addition to your request for the Kingdom of God. He is not telling us not to take care of ourselves, not to be interested in how we will live in this world, but simply not to put that first. Because this will come when we put the Kingdom of God first.

Let's stop here for a moment, my beloved brothers and sisters, to think about why. What does the Lord want to say with this? The Kingdom of God is God Himself. Man, as Saint Silouan writes, could never quench the thirst for God from within. He thirsts for God. All of man's searching and struggling in this life is really just his search for God. But he loses God in all this, in the gods he creates in his agony, in his anxiety.

When you love a person, you don't care about anything else. First you want to have a relationship with this person. You don't think about the consequences, you don't think about how you will live, what you will do; you prioritize your relationship with this person. And when you make this a priority, then the other things fall into place themselves. So when we prioritize in our lives our relationship with God, our love for God and God's love for us, which He has shown in so many ways, then we have our priorities straight and in the right hierarchy. We put God first, trusting that He, Who brought us into existence, will not abandon us.

So this is what the Kingdom of God means, first and foremost. It also means that in this way we put all things and our whole life on an eternal basis. Because all the things we are searching for in our agony, how to get them, all these are temporary. And while we accumulate wealth, money, glory—all that will give us the feeling that we are safe—there comes a moment we lose all of this. So where is the security they gave us? We did not set the right priorities. We didn't lay the right foundations. The only firm, eternal foundation for our lives is the Kingdom of God.

The Lord tells us to seek first the Kingdom of God and His righteousness, "and all these things shall be added to you." Let us seek God, God's love and His justice—that is, the implementation of His will. If we have this, he says, everything else will follow. This seems absurd to us, my brothers and sisters, but just think about what our world would be like if God's justice prevailed, if God's will prevailed. Would we have this anxiety? Would we have this agony? This running around, trying to catch up to tomorrow? No, everyone would be friendly to us. Our neighbor would not be our enemy, he would be our brother, why should I be afraid? If I am deprived of something tomorrow, my brother will come and give it to me. When the Kingdom of God and His justice prevail, everything happens without any problems.

Do you want, my beloved brothers and sisters, for me to prove this logically? We need only look at those moments in our lives when love prevails between people. Immediately anxiety goes away, and so does care for tomorrow. This does not mean that we are not interested in how we will live, but we do not struggle. It's one thing to be interested and another to be concerned, to struggle.

My brothers and sisters, our current culture is a culture of anxiety. The word "stress" has now become an everyday word in our lives. Of all the people we meet each day, I doubt if there is anyone who does not talk about stress. Look around you and you will see that man has all the good things of God, and yet he runs around. He runs like a hamster on a wheel. He increases his needs, his desires, his consumption, working for money and mammon. It is as if today's Gospel passage, my brothers and sisters, was written for us, the people of today, and not for the previous generations. Because we, the older generations, lived in times when people did not have so many goods, but they had peace and tranquility, and everyone shared among themselves.

So today the passage we heard is addressed to this world of ours and tells us: Turn your priorities upside down so that the anxiety and stress that torment you go away. Trust God, repent, reorient yourself, and from this effort you yourself will solve all the problems of your life by trusting God and His Kingdom. You will be able to obtain this peace, which has been lost and which is more costly than anything else we have in this world.

In a little while, my brothers and sisters, we will hear the Cherubic Hymn being sung. In this hymn there is a phrase that we must always pay attention to: "lay aside every worldly care." Why? Because we enter the Kingdom of God at that moment. The Eucharist is the Kingdom of God and in order to enter it we must put aside the anxiety of life's concerns. To leave them behind us and to entrust them to God, to surrender to the love of God and to the love of other people, and to share with other people the body of Christ—that is, the love of God, and in this way to be redeemed, to be healed.

Let us praise God, my brothers and sisters, Who has given us His Church, Who has given us the Divine Liturgy, so we can—even if just once a week—escape from the worries of life, from this preoccupation with ourselves, with what we will do and how we will survive. Let us trust God and in this way have a taste of what awaits us in the Kingdom of God, which I pray all of us be accounted worthy to inherit, my beloved brothers and sisters. Amen.

June 20, 2004

38.
4th SUNDAY OF MATTHEW
On faith and miracles (Mt 8:5–13)

As you have believed, so let it be done for you.

Today's Gospel passage, my beloved brothers and sisters, ends with these words. And it poses the question to us: Why is faith a necessary condition for God's grace and love to act and be manifested?

In today's passage, a centurion—a military officer of the Roman army—approaches the Lord and asks him to heal his servant, who is "lying at home paralyzed, dreadfully tormented." The Lord willingly answers him: "I will come to heal him." But the centurion believes that he is not worthy to receive the Lord into his house, so he begs Him to heal the servant from afar, because His word will be enough for the miracle to happen. Then the Lord marvels at the faith of the centurion and says: "Not even in Israel have I found so much faith." In other words, an idolater—because the centurion was certainly an idolater—had more faith than an Israelite, who knew the true God. And not only that, but the Lord goes on to make a terrible prediction: "Those who know God, the true God, will eventually lose the Kingdom of God. The Kingdom of God will be given to those who come from east and west and believe."

It is a paradox, my brothers and sisters: How is it possible that the Lord admires and knows and praises the faith of an idolater, and contrasts it with the faith of those who know the true God and finds that the idolater's faith is superior? It is really paradoxical and we must delve deeper into this question because it concerns us all.

Obviously we have an understanding of faith which is not compatible with what the Lord had in mind when He praised the faith of the centurion. Many times we think that faith is to recognize the existence of God. If a believer is someone who recognizes that God exists, then the most faithful beings in the world would be demons. As Saint James says in his epistle, "even the demons believe—and tremble" (James 2:19). The demons believe so much that God exists that we could, with this logic, rank them among the most faithful, but of course we cannot say that the demons have faith. So faith is not to recognize the existence of God, but to love God.

There are also those who consider that faith is to accept the doctrines of the Church, to believe them. And there are people who fight for these doctrines with a zeal that reminds one exactly of the Israelites of the time of the Lord. And they think that in this way they believe. But then, the Israelites, who really knew the true God, would not, according to the Lord's saying, have less faith in relation to the idolatrous centurion.

There are many who do not believe, my brothers and sisters, because we present to them a God who is tyrannical, a God who deprives them of their freedom, a God who does not love them. We do not express this love of God, we do not manifest it to those people and thus they abandon God, the God whom we present to them in this way. So we are the real unfaithful and not those who consider and call themselves unfaithful many times.

So what is faith? What is this faith that makes the Lord exclaim today that even in Israel he did not find such faith as in the centurion? Let us pay attention to the Gospel passage and we will get an answer to this question. First, faith is humility. It is no coincidence that the centurion impresses the Lord by telling him: "I am not worthy to receive you in my house." What does humility mean? It means to feel that you do not deserve what you are asking from God. You don't deserve it, as whatever you get is a gift; it's not something you deserve. Humility basically mean giving up rights and believing that everything we have and everything we ask to receive is not our right, it is a gift. God's love is a gift, we do not deserve it. This is humility at depth and not a superficial humility, as when we say: "I am a sinner, etc." In reality, however, we demand that they recognize our rights; and many times we also have such a demand of God himself.

So the faith of the centurion is admirable, because he renounces all such claims and believes that he is not worthy to receive the Lord in his house. And by renouncing this claim, he also renounces reason, because he believes that the Lord can do this miracle even from afar. He is not a magician, who needs to approach and touch his servant. In this way he reverses the attitude of Adam, who did the exact opposite and lost faith. Adam's attitude was to break his communion with God, to declare himself a god. Here, then, humility is directly linked to Adam's attitude, to overturn this relationship, and the result was now to rely on his reason, on the created world. Thus, if reason does not admit something, if the natural laws do not allow it, then it is not possible, it is considered absurd and we do not ask for it.

So the centurion renounces his captivity to reason and nature, and overcomes them. Faith is therefore not a renunciation of reason, but the transcendence of reason. Faith is to say that yes, there is human reason, yes, nature and natural laws exist, but there is also the possibility, the freedom to overcome them. In this way we are freed from the bonds of reason and from the bonds of nature, in which the fall of Adam has ensnared us and from which the Lord wants to free us through faith; faith, which is freedom from the bonds of reason and from the bonds of nature. And it is also characteristic, my brothers and sisters, that in the passage we heard the miracle takes place from a distance, and this distance is sought by the believer himself, the centurion.

We do not bring God down to search for Him—to touch Him, to prove that He exists—and then believe in Him. First we believe and then God will be revealed to us. This distance is created many times by God Himself, Who hides and withdraws His grace, and withdraws His presence, and we wonder: "Where is God? Why has He abandoned us?" This distance that separates us from God, this is the opportunity for faith. It is the opportunity we have to say that even when it seems that God withdraws—that He does not exist for us, that He does not love us, that He does not take care of us, that He does not listen to our prayers—even then to say that despite this, He exists. Despite this, He loves us. We believe in Him even when we don't feel close to Him, we can't feel

His presence. In God's so-called "absence," faith in His presence is of great importance. That is true, genuine faith.

One wonders, my brothers and sisters, why God requires our faith as a condition for Him to act miraculously. Can't He do it without our faith? Certain theologians of the West have created this impression that faith is a condition for God to act—as if God could not act otherwise—unless we give Him this condition of our faith. But God can act even without faith. But He wants to act with our faith, because He wants, very much wants, our freedom. He wants to know that we approach Him freely, and not because He is mighty and can perform miracles.

When faith precedes the miracle, the miracle is not guaranteed. When faith precedes the miracle, we are free to believe or not believe that it will happen; it may or may not happen. Therefore, He wants our faith to precede the miracle so that He does not force us, through His miracle, to believe. We often say that it takes a miracle to believe. But what is the value of this? Then you will have to believe. And God Himself does not want this faith. It does not satisfy Him. He wants us to be free. He wants us to surrender freely to His embrace. He wants us to freely take this risk of faith. To fall into the abyss and to believe that His hand will come to catch us. This is faith. Not the one that is ensured by prior proofs of God's power. Faith is this risk, to fall into the abyss, into the embrace of God, and to believe that His hand will hold you. Such is true faith.

And this creates, my brothers and sisters, a question that we must all ask ourselves. We who believe in the true God, who know the true God—may His name be glorified—and as Orthodox believers know that there is no other true God than Him: Do we have the faith of the centurion or do we have the faith of the Israelites, about whom the Lord said that they will be outside the Kingdom, where there will be the "gnashing of teeth"? It will be a very difficult end for those who know the true God but do not have true and genuine faith.

This also means that we who know the true God should not view those who do not know the true God with arrogance, fanaticism, or malice. Who knows? It is possible that they believe like the centurion, while we, who know the true God, find ourselves outside of His Kingdom. Therefore, my brothers and sisters, we need a constant check of our faith to see if it is really our wholehearted surrender to God—whether He seems to be present or absent—with absolute trust in His love; may we have a faith that does not depend on the power of God, but on the love of God. Let us not believe that He can do something for us, but believe in Him even if He does not do what we want and ask. When our faith, my brothers and sisters, is characterized by humility and love, then it becomes true and genuine faith. Then, I hope, the Lord will be able to say about us too: "not even in Israel have I found such faith." Amen.

July 21, 2002

39.
4th SUNDAY OF MATTHEW
Faith makes the impossible possible (Mt 8:5–13)

Assuredly, I say to you, I have not found such great faith, not even in Israel!

With these words, the Lord was referring, my beloved brothers and sisters, to the centurion, an officer of the Roman army, and an idolater. And the reasonable question arises how it is possible for an idolater to have greater faith than an Israelite, an Israelite who has known God and to whom the true God has been revealed?

And yet, the Lord says these strange words: that this Gentile had more faith than the Israelites, to such an extent that he says afterwards that many will come from the East and the West and will sit in the Kingdom of God with the forefathers of Israel, and that many Israelites will be outside the Kingdom of God. How can we explain these words? Why did the Lord say this? What was it that he found in the faith of the pagan, the idolater, that made Him praise the centurion?

The Israelites knew the true God. He revealed Himself to Abraham and especially to Moses, to whom God also gave His Law, but they refused to recognize God in the person of Christ. They believed in God, but they did not believe in Christ. And the Lord says that this is not real faith, because the true God is revealed only in the person of Christ. One cannot say "I believe in God" without believing in Christ. Christ is the only path for our faith in God. Why? Because in the person of Christ, not only was God's Law revealed, as had happened with the Israelites, but God Himself, His hypostasis, and above all His love was revealed. Therefore, when someone wants to know God, to believe in the true God, he will have to go through this road of love, in which

God reveals Himself to us in the person of Christ. Therefore, we do not have better, more genuine, or greater access to God than Christ Himself. Unfortunately, the Israelites did not recognize this, while that Gentile, the sinner, the idolater did recognize it. Therefore, his faith was greater and more important than the faith of the Israelites.

There are yet other characteristics of this faith of the centurion which make the Lord praise it and place it above the faith of the Israelites. Pay attention, my brothers and sisters: when the Lord, having heard the request of the centurion to heal his servant, who was being tortured with paralysis, says to him: "I will come and heal him," what did the centurion say? "No, Lord, I am not worthy for you to come into my home." This humility, this awareness of his own sinfulness, was also the door through which the centurion's great faith passed. Because it is not possible, my beloved brothers and sisters, to come to faith in God without going through humility. The biggest obstacle to faith is selfishness. Because faith presupposes, or rather means, trust and surrender to the other. But how can you accept and trust the other when you consider yourself more important and superior than the other?

It is not by chance, my beloved brothers and sisters, that the atheism and unbelief of modern man come from his selfishness. They stem from his conviction that he knows everything, that he with his logic can investigate and know everything, and that he can even, in his own way, with his own ethics, organize his life perfectly without needing God.

This expulsion of God from our lives, which we observe now in our present age, is precisely due to man's lack of humility. Man fails when he cannot understand two things: first, his limitations, that he is not god, he cannot think of everything and do everything correctly; and secondly, his sinfulness. If he does not accept these two things, then he cannot accept God either.

Faith, then, presupposes and needs humility. We cannot say "I believe in God" and at the same time believe in ourselves more than in God. Humility is the path to true faith, and the centurion showed that he had this humility, and this was what impressed the Lord and caused Him to praise his faith.

There is another characteristic in the attitude of the centurion that made the Lord say these words about his faith. The centurion said: "Lord, I feel unworthy for you to come to my house, but I believe that you can do your miracle even from afar, and with just one word." This faith in the impossible, in something that no human can do, this is the essence and reality of faith, my brothers and sisters.

The Israelites had faith in God, they knew the true God. They did not, however, have the humility to admit that their sinfulness did not allow them many times to apply God's Law, while they also had the selfishness to prevent others, the non-Israelites, from approaching God, and thus they remained outside the true faith. Faith, then, is not knowing God, believing that God exists, because Saint James says something very important in his epistle, that "even the demons believe—and tremble!" (James 2:19), And the demons know that God exists.

Saying that "I believe that God exists" does not mean that you have faith. For if you believe that God exists, while you do not believe that God has the power to do anything He wants, and you doubt, not only with your thoughts but with your whole life, when even your prayer to God has in it a doubt—"But can God do this? This surpasses all power."—and you cannot accept this as a possibility, then, no matter how much you believe that God exists, this is not faith. Faith is, therefore, to accept the humanly impossible as possible. And the centurion showed this faith and made the Lord marvel.

My beloved brothers and sisters, we Orthodox know the true God, as the Israelites knew the true God, and there is no doubt that we know him in the person of Christ, but is our knowledge enough to prove our faith? When we falter in difficult times and do not believe that God can make the impossible possible, where is our faith? When we exclude others because of our selfishness—because many times selfishness develops in us because we, like the Israelites then, have the right faith and all others are condemned—this selfishness can cause us to be deprived of the Kingdom of God. And then those whom we do not expect will find themselves in the Kingdom of God, as the Lord says in the passage today. Because they can repent, show humility, and accept that it is possible for God and Christ to do anything, and we can remain outside.

So let us not close the doors, first of our souls and secondly of our Church, to those who do not belong to our Church. God has many ways to bring them to us, to bring them to His Church, to Him. On the contrary, let us look and ask ourselves: "This God, whom our fathers passed down to us, the true God, do we truly believe that He has the power to do anything, or do we fear that some power—perhaps even a dark or demonic one—can prove to be stronger than God?"

I don't want to be too topical, but I can't help saying something, my brothers and sisters, that is related to this issue. There are many people today who are afraid of a number and consider it a symbol of Satan, and they are so afraid that they forget that God is more powerful than that number, and more powerful than Satan, and that their faith in that God is sufficient to defeat all evil. Many times, therefore, the faith of those who claim to know the true God proves to be sick, and unfortunately it can lead to very bad situations.

True faith, then, my brothers and sisters, is not to know the true God with our thoughts, but to know him with our hearts as the One who can do everything out of love for us. Let us believe that even behind our difficulties—and many times behind His silence to our prayers—His love is hidden. Can we believe in this love of God despite all the difficulties of life? Then we believe in the true God as revealed to us in the person of Christ.

My beloved brothers and sisters, Christ also underwent all the temptations, He also underwent the same abandonment by God, and yet His relationship with the Father was not shaken. This is the true faith, and this faith, my brothers and sisters, we must protect it from every temptation that would attempt to shake it. Life is full of such temptations, but by walking in this faith we too will be able to prove ourselves, like the centurion, to be truly believers and be made worthy to be, together with all those who truly believed, in His Kingdom. Amen.

40.
5th SUNDAY OF MATTHEW
Evil (Mt 8:28–9:1)

What have we to do with You, Jesus, You Son of God? Have You come here to torment us before the time?

The Lord came into the world, my beloved brothers and sisters, to free man from the tyranny of evil. There is no greater and more serious form of evil than that which man cannot control, which comes from outside and from which he cannot be freed. This form of evil is called demonic.

It is the evil that comes to man against his will. Of course, his will leaves room for evil to enter. But man can no longer control evil, demonic evil, and the Lord came precisely to free man from this evil, which he cannot avoid on his own.

Today's Gospel passage that we have just heard tells us how the Lord visited the region of the Gergesenes and there he met two demon-possessed people—two people who were under the influence of evil and could not control it. It had them in bonds, and they were in such a terrible condition, the Gospel says, that they inspired terror in everyone, because they were "exceedingly fierce." And they lived in the cemetery, which is indicative of the fact that demonic evil is directly connected with death. After all, the devil wants the death of people.

It is characteristic, my beloved brothers and sisters, that the Lord opens a dialogue with these two demon-possessed men. We will focus our attention on this dialogue, because it has a lot to reveal to us. As soon as the demon-possessed men see the Lord, they say to him: "What have we do to with you, Jesus? What do we have in common? What do you want here? What do you want with us?" This is a confession that there is never a compromise between evil and our all-good God; there is an enormous distance between the demons and God and, as much as we may try to reconcile these two things—God and Satan—they remain incompatible. But in the demon-possessed men's question is hidden something else. It is as if they are saying to the Lord: "Leave us alone. You have your work and we have our work. Evil has nothing to do with good, so let's separate our areas and let each one do his work where he belongs." Evil cultivates this thought in people in order to divide their existence and life into two different areas. And in this way evil reigns in an area and says to the good "don't meddle in my area."

Many times we organize our lives—our social and, I would say, our political lives as well—in such a way as to say to the Church: "Don't meddle with the world. The world now belongs to Satan. You and God belong in another place." "What have we to do with you?" This is indeed a method invented by the wicked in order to survive and be able to have some influence in the world. And the demon-possessed men add a shocking phrase. They don't just say "What have we to do with you, Jesus?", but they add the title "Son of God," which means that they recognize Him as God.

What Saint James says in his epistle is characteristic—that faith, which we often think we have, is not simply recognizing that God exists. Because, says Saint James, "even the demons believe—and tremble!" (James 2:19). So, even the demons recognize that God exists. We have reached the point of thinking that faith is to admit the existence of God, but this is not faith. And the demons teach us that faith is something else—it is trust in God. It is the trust that God can make the impossible possible and above all it is our love for God, which demons do not have. And while they recognize Him as the Son of God, there is within them hatred against God, and it is not possible to call this faith. So the demons also teach us what faith is not and where we should look for faith.

And the dialogue continues and the demon-possessed men say to the Lord. "Have You come here to torment us before the time?" The demons know that their end is suffering, eternal hell. They know it and recognize it and that is why they want to postpone, as much as possible, the coming of the Kingdom of God.

For the Kingdom of God to come and for good to prevail in the world is the desire of all those who have gotten rid of or are trying to get rid of evil. It is the prayer of all believers, as the Lord Himself handed it down to us, when we say with agony "Thy Kingdom come," in other words, "may your Kingdom come quickly." But when one is overcome by evil, he prays that the Kingdom of God does not come quickly. He wants to delay as much as possible. He postpones the hope and expectation of the coming of the Kingdom of God. This mystery is profound, my brothers and sisters, because evil in history still has power and knows that when history ends it will lose its power. It knows that it will be defeated, and this makes it not want the story to end. It is content to continue as we are.

The first Christians, as the book of Revelation describes them to us, had exactly the opposite attitude. "Come, Lord Jesus!" (Rev. 22:20). Because for Christians, history still contains the power of evil, which they felt, which they lived in their skin, and they wanted to get rid of evil. And the only way for them to be freed is for the Lord to come and bind Satan, to defeat evil.

So the Lord came "before the time" to defeat evil. And He will come one day and defeat it once and for all. But already with His assault on the demon-possessed men, He demonstrated precisely that the power of good and God Himself exist in history. God is not something we expect only in the future, but He exists in our lives; and we may not see Him or we may not want to see Him, but He has already defeated evil. He leaves it for last, for His Second Coming, when He will completely eliminate it. He leaves it so that our freedom can be exercised, so that we can choose between good and evil. But the outcome of the war has already been decided. God is victorious.

And the dialogue, my brothers and sisters, progresses to something shocking. The possessed say to the Lord: "If you are going to cast the demons out of us, command us to go there, to the herd of pigs." Nearby, pigs were grazing, and the Lord granted their request. He ordered the demons to go to the pigs, and the pigs, under the influence of the demons, fall down the precipice and drown in the sea.

Evil, my brothers and sisters, does not only affect mankind, evil is not only a matter of human beings, it affects the entire creation, and it affects it by being transposed from man to creation.

Creation itself does not contain evil; man transmits it. And there is no greater proof of this today, my brothers and sisters, than the terrible ecological problem that torments us. What is the ecological problem? What is the ecological crisis but the transfer of evil from man to innocent creation? And just as the herd of pigs is destroyed because the demons leave the people and go to them, so today the entire creation is being swallowed up, destroyed, because man's passions, his greed, his egocentrism transfer demonic power to creation.

Thus, my brothers and sisters, we learn from today's passage that the evil that exists within us, and to which we give in, is not limited to us. We are responsible for all of creation, because it can be transferred from us to all of creation. And God's creations, which are not responsible for evil, suffer, are tortured, and disappear from their very existence.

My beloved brothers and sisters, the demonic is the most extreme form of evil. But it is not the only form of evil—there are other degrees or steps that lead to this most extreme form of the demonic. And as long as we are not possessed by the demonic in its extreme form, we are complacent and think that everything is fine with us. But let's be careful, because evil can start from more "innocent" forms. Every passion that we cannot control is a form of evil. Eradication of passions, healing from passions is the only way to avoid the demonic, this extreme form of evil. The Lord, by healing the demon-possessed men, came to give us the assurance that in the end evil will be defeated, that, no matter how powerful it appears in history, God has the final say and not evil. Moreover, every direct or indirect partnership we have with evil in history brings us one step closer to the demonic, makes us captives of evil. When we become addicted to evil, when our passions take root, then it is too late, then it is not easy to get rid of evil.

The Church, my brothers and sisters, is called a healing center, and it is. Precisely because it helps us to get rid of our passions, to understand that even a small passion can become gigantic and can make us captives. How many people cannot, for example, quit smoking—it is impossible for them. Isn't this slavery to a power that no one can control? We could enumerate many more passions that man is unable to control. My brothers and sisters, it is absolutely necessary to understand that evil descends in our lives from where we least expect it and that we constantly need not only vigilance but also struggle and effort to cleanse our hearts of passions. Because that's where evil nests, in the heart of man. I hope, my brothers and sisters, that today's Gospel passage will give all of us the opportunity to realize how important it is to free ourselves from passions and to be able to say in this way, in contrast to the demon-possessed men, "Come, Lord, quickly, come to impose good on the world. Thy Kingdom come!" Amen.

July 8, 2001

41.
5th SUNDAY OF MATTHEW
On the demon-possessed (Mt 8:28–9:1)

The Gospel passage that we just heard, my dear brothers and sisters, contains truths that we either overlook, or ignore, or do not want to think about.

The Lord goes to an idolatrous region, the region of the Gergesenes. There he meets two demon-possessed men who come out of the tombs in which they lived and who, every time they appeared on the street, caused fear and terror to the residents, with the result that no one could pass through there. They approach the Lord and say: "What do we have in common? Did you come here, Jesus, Son of God, to torture us before our time? If you want to expel us, then order us to go to this herd of pigs instead of being tortured." The Lord gave the command, the demons went into the herd of pigs, and the herd fell off the cliff into the sea and drowned.

The Lord provoked amazement and fear from all the inhabitants who—especially those who owned the pigs and watched them perish—asked Him to leave their region. The Lord took a boat and left.

The demon-possessed men of today's passage, my brothers and sisters, are representatives of all humanity. We are used to classifying people based on ethics into good and bad, according to medicine into healthy and sick, into madmen and sane, and based on the law into free and imprisoned.

The reality, however, is that all people to some extent participate in the situation of the possessed. They participate because evil is so powerful that it holds people captive. Despite what we think as we classify people in this way, it is not really easy to exempt any person from some degree of participation in the evil that they cannot control—that is, the demonic. The demonic is the evil that we cannot control, the evil that comes from outside. It is stronger than us, stronger than our will.

If we pay attention to some characteristics of these demon-possessed men, we will see, my brothers and sisters, how true this is. The possessed lived in the tombs. They were prisoners of death. But what man is not a prisoner of death, since after all the abode of all men is the tomb. But people have the illusion that the dead are one thing and the living are another. This distinction serves us so that we can spend our lives comfortably, because, as I said at the beginning, the truth is very harsh.

If in reality death begins with our birth, with our conception, we are born mortal and death accompanies us. We therefore need liberation from death. We need victory over death. We need someone to get us out of the tombs. And the Lord came precisely to trample down death by death and to give life to those in the tombs.

The other characteristic of the possessed that we heard today in the passage is that no one could pass by them. This rejection of others, this inability for others to coexist with us is a characteristic that more or less all people have. Look at how people demarcate their cities, their states, their nations, and how no one can pass into the territory of another, and also how we humans cannot forgive, that is, exist in the same space with our brothers and sisters.[1] Therefore, every time we cannot get along—or fit together in the same space—with others, the demonic element rises up, although to a lesser degree. Evil wants people to be separated from each other, each one to have his own space and for the other to not be able to enter his own space.

A third characteristic of the possessed is that they confessed the divinity of the Lord. They called him "Son of God." And what does that mean? It means that you can indeed recognize and confess the divinity of Christ, but in reality you are not exempt from the influence of evil and the demonic. And this is of great importance for all of us, my brothers and sisters—especially for those of us who confess the Lord as God—to make us think that this

[1] The Greek word for "forgive," συν-χωρῶ, literally means to "fit into the same space."

confession does not guarantee us freedom from evil. It is very possible that we confess the Lord as God, that we are Christians, while in reality we are captives of passions, which make us captives of evil.

There is another very shocking, I would say, aspect to today's passage. The possessed ask to be sent into the pigs. They transfer evil to innocent nature. What's wrong with the pigs? Why is the natural environment, which we are destroying, being punished? We transfer our passions, our bondage to evil, to the natural world and thus prove that we are in no way exempt from the influence of evil.

The Lord came, my brothers and sisters, to free us from the demonic, because he wanted to free us from all these things that I mentioned. First of all, from death and then from selfishness, which makes us unable to coexist with others, with the result that we divide people into friends and enemies, and we cannot coexist with our enemies. We divide people into those we like and those we don't like—and we cannot coexist with a certain kind of people.

So the Lord came to free us from self-indulgence, because self-indulgence and death are connected to each other. He came to free his entire creation—not just humans—from destruction and evil. Because all creation participates in mortality, it participates in that which does not allow it to live by itself, to exist. And the Lord's intervention here, this saving intervention—because it does not concern only people but all of God's creation—makes us love all of his creation, all of nature.

So it turns out, my brothers and sisters, that we all need healing. And let no one think that he can be exempted from this rule, because the root of all passions is self-love. To some extent we are all subject to selfishness and it takes a great struggle to get rid of it. Not a moral struggle, but a struggle through love—the more you love, the more you are freed from selfishness. So in a positive way, and not in a negative way, the Lord calls us to be cured of selfishness. In this way we will be able to defeat death and protect and sanctify the material creation that surrounds us—that is, to make it co-exist with us, to take it into our eternal existence. In this way, the Lord's offer of deliverance from the demonic will be the salvation not only of people but also of the entire creation.

These thoughts, my beloved brothers and sisters, I wanted to share with you. Our tradition mentions saints, mainly ascetics, who fought with demons in a very subtle way. And this struggle with demons, which characterizes the saints, such as Saint Anthony and many ascetics, is not an exceptional case nor something that has nothing to do with all people.

The struggle with the demonic concerns all of us and this is what I tried to convey to you today with these humble thoughts of mine. To convey to you the feeling that we need liberation from selfishness, from the passions that make us captives of the demonic. It is only with this liberation—which we cannot achieve but only the Lord can grant to us—that we will be able to live eternally in a relationship of love with others and with all of God's creation. Amen.

July 20, 2003

42.
5th SUNDAY OF MATTHEW
The demonic as denial of existence (Mt 8:28–9:1)

In the Gospel passage that we have just heard, my dear brothers and sisters, there is a detail that deserves special attention. The Lord visits the region of the Gergesenes and there he meets two demon-possessed men. These possessed people, as we heard in the passage, came out of the tombs. And another evangelist who describes the same case mentions that these demon-possessed lived in the tombs.

The words "possessed," "demonic," and "demon" essentially describe evil that we cannot control, evil that exceeds our powers. This evil comes from freedom. If there was no freedom, there would be no evil. If God did not make man free, if He did not create free beings, evil would not exist. So evil came from freedom, but the first free beings that God created were angels and not people.

The Bible tells us that the Evil One tempted the first man into evil. That is, the evil into which man fell did not come entirely from him. It is something that precedes him, something that goes beyond him. And, of course, while man had the freedom to reject this evil, he did not reject it. Certain fathers of the Church, such as Saint Irenaeus and Saint Maximus, see man's situation with compassion and say: "Man was in the state of a little child"—in a way, he was deceived. Therefore, evil entered from another source, beyond man, and this is the demonic. What does this demonic thing consist of?

It consists of a clear and strong "no" to God's will. And this "no" to God's will does not only concern God's commandments, but mainly concerns God's will for the world to exist. Existence is God's will. God wanted the world to be created, and that is why the world exists. Therefore, the highest and ultimate "no" that one can say to God is to deny existence, the world, creation. And this is precisely what the first fallen angels, the demons, did, and they continue to do so, wanting to deny and destroy the existence of the world, because in this way they will offend the will of God. This "no" to existence took various forms and prevailed when man accepted the Evil One's suggestion to say "no" to God.

Death entered. Death would not exist without this "no" to God's will for the world to exist. This "no" to existence is death. And since man said "no" to God and cut off communion with God, it was natural that natural death should enter, and that man could not escape from it. To inherit death from generation to generation. To give birth to mortal children—children who, while living, are dying at the same time. This is man's great condemnation and it arose when he cut off communion with God.

This "no" to God's will for the world to exist took another form. The most extreme form it took is that not only death entered the world, but also murder. And, of course, this sounds, my dear brothers and sisters, very extreme. Few are the ones who kill others, but in reality this killing comes from the rejection of the other. God says that he wants the other to exist and we say: "No, we don't want the other to exist."

The rejection of the other can take various forms. I can take a gun and kill him so he doesn't exist, treat him as if he doesn't exist, not care if he exists. Hating him and wanting his death is extreme, and maybe many of us say "But we are not murderers," but the essence of murder is the rejection of the other. And we constantly commit the rejection of the other.

How many people are there in this world that we don't care about? And in fact, when we reject those who have harmed us—our enemies—when we do not forgive them, when we do not love them and perhaps even want their harm, when we prefer perhaps that they did not exist, then it is murder. It is the demonic that says "no" to God's will for the other to exist.

And this can be extended not only to the fact that the other does not exist but, in the case of an extreme demonic situation, that we ourselves do not want to exist. To want to say "no" to our own existence. To say "no" either in the form of suicide—that's why the Church has never accepted suicide, because it is the demonic "no" to existence—or to use our life, our body, in such as a way as to destroy it; it is a tendency to self-destruction. And it even takes the form of the destruction of nature, because God also created nature, and man comes to say: "I will destroy you."

You saw in today's Gospel passage what the demons asked of Christ—to send them into the herd of pigs. And as soon as they entered there, the herd of pigs was killed. Doesn't this remind us a little of what we are doing today, destroying nature? This creation of God, where, making ourselves god and denying God's will, we treat it as our own property with the result that we destroy it, and this also leads to our own self-destruction. How can we defeat the demonic?

First, we cannot defeat the demonic with our own strength. The greatest holy ascetics who fought with demons face to face, such as Anthony the Great and others, knew this very well. You can't do anything with the demonic. Only God's intervention, only God's grace, can free us from the demonic. That is why it was necessary for the Son of God Himself to come, to become a man and to face the demons, as we heard in today's Gospel passage, who, as soon as they saw him, said: "What have we to do with You, Jesus, You Son of God? Have You come here to torment us before the time?" because they knew that He came to abolish them. One day, at the end of history, they find in front of them the One Who would abolish them, Who would abolish the power of the demonic. And He abolished the power of the demonic with His Resurrection.

With the Resurrection, Christ proved that God wants the world to exist, that death is God's enemy and will be defeated. And since Christ defeated death, the tombs were transformed. It is no longer the place where the demonic resides. What do we sing at Easter? "Christ is risen from the dead, by death trampling down upon death, and to those in the tombs He has granted life." And Saint John the Chrysostom in the catechetical discourse we read at Easter says: "Christ is risen, and not one dead remains in the grave," adding: "Christ is risen, and the demons are fallen."

The Resurrection of Christ, therefore, transformed the tombs, where death reigns, into hope of the Resurrection, into faith in the Resurrection, into victory over death. He expelled the possessed from the tombs and established life there. See, then, how the possessed of today's passage, who lived in the tombs, were afraid when they saw Christ, because they saw their end. They saw that the tombs containing death, which the enemy of God desires, would be transformed into life.

And so what remains for us to do, my beloved brothers and sisters? How can we deal with the demonic? There are two ways, apart from the fact that we must recognize that we cannot face evil alone, that we must humble ourselves and not believe that evil has been defeated by our own virtue and effort, either in our culture or in our spiritual life.

One way is "love." And when we say "love," we mean accepting the other instead of rejecting him, instead of saying "no" to his existence. Let's accept him, whoever he is, whether a sinner or an enemy, because that's the only way the demonic will leave. The demonic cannot stand this attitude of love. And the other thing we can do is what we are doing at this moment—it is the Divine Eucharist. Let us believe with all our hearts that the existence of the world, our existence, the existence of the other, all these are gifts, precious gifts, for which we thank the One Who gave them to us—and then the demonic leaves, because what is demonic is the denial of thanksgiving.

Thus, in today's Divine Liturgy and in all Divine Liturgies, we expel the demonic from our lives. We say "yes" to God. We say "yes" with gratitude that He created the world, that we exist. And this "Let us give thanks to the Lord," which we will hear shortly from the celebrant and to which we will all respond, is the answer that man gives with his own power to the provocation of the demonic.

Let us listen, my beloved brothers and sisters, and let us put these two basic things in our hearts—love and gratitude—and let us be grateful to God above all, because God Himself came and redeemed us from the demonic, with the Incarnation and the Resurrection of the Lord. Amen.

July 24, 2005

43.
5th SUNDAY OF MATTHEW
The miracle of the demon-possessed Gergesenes (Mt 8:28–9:1)

In the Gospel passage we just heard, my beloved brothers and sisters, the Lord comes face to face with the demonic, with the power of the demonic, with demon-possessed people.

What is the demonic? To what is this presence and energy of the demons due? It is due to some angels' disobedience and rebellion against the will of God. These angels tried to annihilate God and His will in order to assume His place. The demonic proceeds from this disobedience to God's will.

The essence of the demonic, therefore, is this disobedience as well as their mania to annihilate God Himself and everything He created. That is why the demonic has this tendency to destroy everything, including the demons themselves (they too are God's creations) and anything created by God because it proceeded from Him. And this is how the demonic leads to its own destruction.

This is the situation behind today's Gospel reading, in which the Lord meets two demon-possessed men while visiting the city of the Gergesenes. And it is interesting to see how the demons reacted when the Lord appeared before them. They said: "What have we to do with You, Jesus, You Son of God? Have You come here to torment us before the time?" They recognized that the purpose of the Lord's coming to earth was to destroy the demons, to liberate man and all creation from the power of the Evil One.

The Gospel passage says "Did you come here to destroy us, to torture us before the time?" Because the time of their destruction is the time of the Lord's Second Coming, when the antichrist and evil will be definitively struck down and the Kingdom of God will reign. But the Lord comes to His life on earth before this time to demonstrate that His purpose is to destroy the demonic and the power of the Evil One. The demons therefore recognize God's existence and power and already know what awaits them, but they are bound and determined in their opposition to God and His will, so much so that they cannot free themselves from this fate.

It is also very significant and instructive, my brethren, that the power of the demonic, the power of the Evil One, is active in the rest of creation outside of man. Of course, the Evil One's aim, the demonic's aim, is to conquer man, who is the crown of creation. But it doesn't stop there; the demonic continues even *within* the rest of creation. As we see in today's Gospel passage, the demons enter a herd of pigs and destroy them.

Whatever the Evil One's power touches, it destroys. It will even touch and destroy innocent creatures, which is the rest of creation. It is not an issue of guilt, of whether the herd of pigs was somehow at fault or not. These are the stark facts: that evil exists in the world and that whatever it touches, it destroys.

We see this, my brethren, particularly in our own time, where it has become clear just how much destruction can be wrought on God's innocent creation, on nature, by the evil that resides in man. Everyone is talking today about the ecological problem, which is nothing but the destruction of creation due to man's demonic tendency. Evil is thus extended into the whole creation, since the Evil One wants to destroy not only man but anything, as I said, that was created by God and even God Himself.

Thus, the Lord today destroys the demons possessing the two unfortunate men, and He rids the city of the Gergesenes of their presence, which had truly terrorized the people of the area, as we heard in the Gospel passage. No one dared to go outside. But, despite all that, what was the residents' reaction? They tell Christ: "Go, get out of here, leave our city. We don't want you here." Why, I wonder? Perhaps it was because He had harmed them economically by destroying the herd of pigs? Perhaps because they were so frightened? In any event, the residents' reaction is revealing, my brethren. It reveals just how much man often times prefers to compromise, to live with the demons rather than to live with Christ and to finally expel evil from their midst. From the time Adam fell, man has had the tendency to compromise with evil, and this compromise with evil leads him to chase Christ out of his life.

Economic interests, the pleasures of life, and so many other things seduce us, since evil offers itself to us in a sweet and appealing package, which it always has. And we prefer to hold on to evil and to chase Christ from our lives. My brethren, it is a continual struggle because the demonic has become so mixed up with God within our existence that we need a knife to cut out and clean up this condition.

44.
6th SUNDAY OF MATTHEW
The restoration of man's communion with God (Mt 9:1–8)

The Gospel passage that we just heard, my dear brothers and sisters, describes the healing of a paralytic by the Lord. It is one of the many miracles that the Lord performed during His time on earth. This particular miracle has certain characteristics that we should pay attention to.

First, it is striking that, while the paralytic comes to be healed, the Lord instead says to him: "Your sins are forgiven you." But he didn't come to have his sins forgiven; he came to be made well. So how do we explain the Lord's response?

One explanation is that the Lord didn't just want to cure the symptom; He wanted to cure the cause, just as a good doctor will not simply look to cure the symptom, but will seek to find the cause in order to cure it. And in this case, the cause of the paralytic's illness was sin. But this begs the question: in what sense was sin the cause of the paralytic's illness? Was it in the sense that the paralytic had committed many sins in his life and was therefore punished? That his illness was due to misuse of his body or various sins? The human mind immediately goes there. But there is another explanation: the sins of the paralytic were not his personal sins. The cause of his illness had nothing to do with his personal sins, but with the sin and sinfulness of man in general. And here we have to pay some attention.

Many times, when we see something bad happening, we look for the cause in someone else's fault, in the one where the evil exists. In another case, when the disciples saw the man blind from birth approaching the Lord to heal him, the first thing they asked the Lord was: "Who sinned, this man or his parents, that he was born blind?" (John 9:2), in other words, "Whose fault is it that he became blind? Was it because of his own sins or his parents' sins?" They immediately sought to find responsibility for this man who suffered. And the Lord, of course, answers them: "Neither this man nor his parents sinned" (John 9:3). Personal sins were not the cause.

Many times, my beloved brothers and sisters, sickness is not given by God only to those who have sinned, but even to the saints. Let us remember the Apostle Paul, who says: "a thorn in the flesh was given to me, a messenger of Satan to buffet me" (2 Cor 12:7). He had a very serious illness and about this he says: "I pleaded with the Lord three times that it might depart from me" (2 Cor 12:8), and He answered: "My grace is sufficient for you" (2 Cor 12:9).

Illness or any calamity in human life is often granted not because of our personal sinfulness, but because of God's love for us. For reasons that we cannot always understand and explain. Therefore, if there is any connection between the illness of the paralytic and the sins which the Lord forgives, it is because He wants to show that the cause of every illness and every evil, even death itself, is that man has cut off his communion with God—and this is the source of all sin.

So, when man cut off communion with God, all these troubles entered his life. Therefore, in order to heal evil at its root, the deepest cause of evil, our relationship with God must be restored. Communion with God must be restored, and that is why it is so important that the Lord forgave the sins of the paralytic. But the Lord also does it, as we can tell from the Gospel passage, for another reason.

We see that when the Lord said to the paralytic "Your sins are forgiven you," the scribes who were among the crowd became indignant. The scribes—i.e., those who knew the Law, the Jewish religious leaders of the time—were indignant and said: "This man is blaspheming, only God can forgive sins." And as soon as the Lord understood their thoughts, he answered: "Why do you think evil in your hearts?" And then He immediately performed the miracle to show them that He had this power to forgive sins, even though He was a man.

When the paralytic got up to go to his house, those who were nearby, according to today's Gospel passage, "glorified God, who had given such power to men." A power that belongs only to God, Who gives it to people.

The Lord, therefore, wanted in this way to show us that the forgiveness of sins, which belongs to God alone, comes to us through man. And this is the basis on which the Church rests. Because, when the Lord rose, He said to His disciples: "I give you the power to bind and to loose, and whatever you forgive on earth will be forgiven in heaven" (cf. Mt 18:18). The Lord, in the Gospel passage we heard, exercised this power as a man, showing us that we cannot go directly to God for forgiveness. Man is the way through which we reach God.

It is very easy to say "I will pray in front of the icon or I will ask God to forgive me," and to overlook and marginalize the people whom the Church, God, has designated as those who bring us the forgiveness of sins. Moreover, my beloved brothers and sisters, the forgiveness of our sins is connected with us forgiving the sins of others, as well as others forgiving our own sins.

Therefore, the restoration of our relationship with God, which is the forgiveness of sins, passes through this channel of people. The forgiveness of sins has no other purpose than to bring us into communion with God and with other people—to restore our wounded communion, this wounded existence of ours since the fall of man. That is why today's passage shows us the path that one must follow in order to reach this restoration of his relationship with God and with other people. It is the way of forgiveness of sins: "forgive us our trespasses as we forgive those who trespass against us."

It is extremely important, my brothers and sisters, to restore our relationship with God and with other people—much more important, I would say, than the restoration of our physical health, because this is the root of the whole problem of our physical illness.

My beloved brothers and sisters, the Lord came into the world for one purpose only. He came to once again unite man—and through him all creation—with God, because the purpose of his creation was this *union*. However, man, with the freedom that God Himself gave him, severed this relationship and thus this communion must be restored. The Lord performed various healings and miracles only to show that the evil that resulted from the interruption of this communion is not final, that it will be overcome, and communion with God will be restored. This is the purpose for which the Lord came.

But in order to show how this goal of reconnecting society with God will be achieved, He took upon Himself the sins of others and, on the Cross, He showed us that the way to restore our relationships with God and others is to forgive others to the point of taking their sins upon us, and making them our sins.

And then came the moment of the Resurrection. Evil was defeated. Evil cannot be defeated with evil, as the Apostle Paul reminds us in today's Epistle reading, but it can only be defeated if we do good to those who do us harm. The Apostle says: "Bless those who persecute you" (Rom 12:14), "Do good to those who persecute you and do you harm." This is the most difficult and absurd thing in the world! And yet it is the only way to defeat evil.

This, then, is the path to the forgiveness of sins and restoration of communion with God. And we know that evil will be defeated at the end, that diseases will be eliminated, that death will be overcome, and that the Kingdom of God will prevail. Amen.

July 31, 2005

45.
6th SUNDAY OF MATTHEW
The variety of gifts (Rom 12:6–14)

In the Epistle reading we heard, my beloved brothers and sisters, the Apostle Paul speaks about the gifts that exist in the Church. The Apostle Paul often refers to this great mystery called the "Church" and likens it to a body, the human body, which has many members, and each member has a special gift, a "charisma," a special offering. Likewise, in the body of the Church there are many gifts, which the Holy Spirit gives. On these gifts, my beloved brothers and sisters, we will focus our attention today.

What is a "charisma" a "gift"? The word "charisma" indicates that it is something that we do not have, but is given to us. And what's more, it's something we don't deserve. The gifts of the Holy Spirit are not given because we deserve them, but they are given to us because God, through the Holy Spirit, freely wants to give them to people in His love. And that is why we cannot receive the gifts of the Holy Spirit by our own efforts and virtues.

Certainly, when God sees our effort, He gives His grace, but it is not our effort and our virtues that bring about the Lord's grace. It is the love of God Himself, Who wants to give us His grace, and, through this grace, His very self. That is, He gives the Holy Spirit, Who is one of the Persons of the Holy Trinity. Therefore, He does not give virtues with the gifts, He gives His love with the gifts, which he expresses in various ways through the gifts.

That is why the gifts of the Church, my beloved brothers and sisters, are not meant to be kept for oneself; they are not individual property. When the Holy Spirit breathes and gives His gifts, He gives them not so that he who receives them will keep them, but so that he too can give himself and his love to others, just as he himself received God's love through His gifts.

The gifts are God's love for man, which calls him to give his love to other people, and in this way to circulate God's love, true love, within the body of the Church—and through the Church to the whole world. Whoever, therefore, does not have love, does not have God's gifts, even if he has many virtues. Because sometimes, a person can show special abilities which, however, are not gifts of the Holy Spirit. The Holy Spirit is the love of God that circulates in people.

Therefore, the gifts of the Holy Spirit are a gift of love to be offered. That is why the Apostle Paul constantly emphasizes that whatever gifts one has, if one does not build up the Church, that is, if one does not add a bond of love so that the body of the Church is built up, these are not gifts of the Holy Spirit.

And we see something else, my beloved brothers and sisters, in the way in which the Apostle Paul speaks about gifts in the Epistle reading we heard. "Having then gifts differing according to the grace that is given to us"—the gifts of the Holy Spirit are many and various. Performing miracles is not the only impressive gift of the Holy Spirit. Miracles impress us and we think that there are the gifts of the Holy Spirit. However, if we pay attention to the Epistle reading we heard, the Apostle Paul talks about other, simple gifts. He says, of course, that it is a gift to prophesy in proportion to one's faith, but it is also a gift to lead, to manage the Church. It is a gift to minister to others and to offer hospitality to others. They are simple things that we consider not important and yet they are gifts of the Holy Spirit.

And for this reason the gifts are not only many and simple, but they are also given to ordinary people whom we do not suspect. You will have heard the story in the *Gerontikon*[1] about Saint Anthony, the great elder of the desert, who wanted to know who the holiest man in Alexandria was. And God sent him to meet a cobbler, a shoemaker, who himself had no idea that he was a saint, that he had the grace of God. God revealed to Saint Anthony in this way that those whom we consider simple, those we think are without any special gift, can have the Spirit and the grace of God in them.

[1] Cf. *The Sayings of the Desert Fathers.*

The gifts, therefore, are scattered within the Church. And many times they are not visible because the simplicity of the people who have them hides them, or even because they themselves do not want to reveal them. Real saints never show off their gifts. It is not like magicians who want to impress, to pull off something that impresses the world. The real saints, even if they perform a miracle, will not attach much importance to it and will not promote it, nor will they become marketers of their gifts and themselves. On the contrary, they will hide their gifts as much as they can, because the greatest gift is love, which, however, also means humility.

Whoever prides himself on his gift loses it, because it is no longer a gift. It is as if he is saying: "I am entitled to it, I own it." The gifts of the Holy Spirit, therefore, are given to the humble in order to exercise their love with these gifts. So that the communion of the body of the Church can be built up in this way.

That is why, in the passage we heard, the Apostle Paul mentions things that are simple, and yet he considers them gifts of the Holy Spirit. When, he says, we are "given to hospitality," we must consider it a gift of the Holy Spirit. When we endure sorrow, it is also a gift of the Holy Spirit. And when we let the other person be honored before us, "in honor giving preference to one another."

And we find another gift of the Holy Spirit. The Apostle Paul mentions many things and ends up with the most important and the most difficult of all: "Bless those who persecute you," meaning love our enemies. The greatest gift is to love your enemy. And this is not in our nature. We cannot say that this is something we have, if it is not a gift, if God's grace does not give it to us. Therefore, with God's grace, we can love others and especially our enemies.

Thus, my beloved brothers and sisters, in the Church we can all acquire the gifts of the Holy Spirit and we do not need to have special positions. We need only open our hearts with humility, to ask God for His grace, and to give ourselves to others. Non-clergy, such as monks and lay people, who do not have special positions in the Church, nevertheless have gifts. That is why, my beloved brothers and sisters, we should not despise those who appear externally to have no gift, because they are sinners. We do not know what a sinner can hide inside him, and how much grace he can receive from God.

There is no need to do what is done in the Western Churches, especially today, where they try to do justice, as they say, to the gifts of the Church. They say that women should become priests, because they too should share in the gift of the priesthood. But the gifts, as we said, are varied, and one will have the gift of priesthood, while another will have other gifts. We know that women are treated fairly because a woman can have so many gifts that she does not need to have the gift of priesthood.

So within the Church the gifts are scattered and this is the greatness of the Church, because the Holy Spirit leaves no one outside. It embraces us all and wants to give Its gifts to everyone. The only thing that prevents the Holy Spirit from giving Its gifts is our selfishness, our self-love; many times we want to receive a gift but not to give it. When we do not recognize that everything we are and everything we have is a gift from God, the grace of the Holy Spirit cannot come.

My beloved brothers and sisters, in people's lives there are what we call natural gifts, but there are also gifts that are not natural. A natural gift, for example, is a mother's love for her child. Nature contains a maternal connection. But to love another's child as her own, this is not a gift of nature; it is a gift of the Holy Spirit.

In the Church, the Holy Spirit gives us gifts that our nature does not give us. The fact that I have a gift, let's say that I am smart, does not mean that it is a gift of the Holy Spirit. But when I use my intelligence to contribute to the building up of the Church and not to glorify myself, then this natural gift turns into a gift of the Holy Spirit.

There are, therefore, in our lives the natural gifts, but there are also the gifts of the Holy Spirit. The Church offers us the gifts of the Holy Spirit, precisely because it gives us the great gift of love for God in the person of Jesus Christ, in Christ's sacrifice for us, with the gift of the Holy Spirit, another Person of the Holy Trinity—the One that creates communion, and opens the boundaries of ourselves to embrace others with our love, with God's love.

I pray, my beloved brothers and sisters, that these gifts of the Holy Spirit will be abundantly given to all who seek them, and that with these gifts the body of the Church will be built up and that God will be glorified. Amen.

July 23, 2006

46.
6th SUNDAY OF MATTHEW
"Bless those who persecute you" (Rom 12:6–14)

The Epistle reading we heard today, my beloved brothers and sisters, concludes with these words. These are words that the Apostle Paul addresses to the Christians of Rome, but they are also words that he addresses to us, to the Christians of all ages and the entire world. Let's go a little deeper into these words because they concern us all. What is a blessing? And why does the apostle tell us to bless our enemies, those who persecute us?

A blessing, as the word indicates in Greek, is to say good words about someone else—εὖ λέγειν. The basic meaning of the Greek word for "blessing" is to speak a good word about another. One can understand someone saying a good word about someone who has benefited them or a friend, but saying a good word about an enemy and persecutor goes beyond human logic, human justice.

What good can we say about someone who hurt us? How can we find good words for this person? And yet the Apostle Paul calls us to bless—that is, to say good words—about those who persecute us.

There are, my beloved brothers and sisters, three ways to deal with a persecutor, an enemy. The first is to take revenge on him, to repay him for the harm he did to us. The other is not to speak against him. And this is already a very big step, because it is not easy not to speak against someone who has harmed you. But the Apostle Paul calls us to go even further—that is, not only not to speak against our enemies, not only not to complain and not to criticize, but also to say good words about them, to bless them. And it is not enough just to say good words about the other, but to wish and pray for the good of the other.

But blessing our enemies is really a challenge to human reason. It is something similar to what Saint Maximus says about the tolerance we should show to others. Saint Maximus says that showing tolerance for others is not enough, you must go even further than tolerance and care for them more than for yourself. These steps that the Gospel calls us to take are truly transgressions of reason and justice.

"What good can I say about a bad person?" And yet every bad person definitely has a good side that we must find. But even if we still don't find anything good about him, what matters is that this man is a creation of God, this man was loved by God and Christ, Christ shed His blood for this man and we are not entitled to reject him.

According to the Gospel, one would say that it is very reasonable to say good words about bad people. The meaning of the words "good" or "bad," my dear brothers and sisters, can change so much. For who is the good man who does not have something bad in him? Who is sinless? Who can consider himself better than others and say that "I am the good one and the other is the bad one"? If we see it on this basis, we will understand that it is not so unreasonable to bless bad people.

As I said, speaking good about our enemies and all others in general is not just saying it with the mouth, but wishing it and praying for it. And what will that do? Let us desire and wish for the good of the other, not only in the sense that we want to make him good ourselves, but we want the good of the other to be even more than what we ourselves can offer him. If I cannot cure someone and he is my enemy, it is not enough to simply want to make him well, and since I cannot, I resign. No, I definitely want something to happen, even a miracle, to make him well.

So, therefore, the blessing goes from the stage of good words to the good wishes we have for the other person, and even reaches those wishes that we cannot fulfill, so then we turn to God. And then the blessing becomes a prayer—this is very important. And we say to God: "since we cannot bring about this good that we ask for the other, we beg You, Lord, to bring it about." Therefore, the concept of blessing now includes the blessing of God. Without God's blessing there is no true blessing. Even if we want the good of others, we cannot achieve it without God's blessing.

Thus, my beloved brothers and sisters, the concept of blessing now passes from the level of men and reaches the level of God. A blessing is, in the final analysis, what God bestows on people and because God is the source of all blessings, man blesses God, the source of blessings. Therefore, the blessing moves in two directions: from God to man come the blessings of God, but also from man to God comes the blessing of God. That is why we constantly say in the Church: "Blessed is our God," "Blessed is the Kingdom of the Father." Nothing in the Church can be done without a blessing. Because, in this movement between God's blessing to the world and God's blessing from the world, move all the gifts of God by which the world, the universe lives. I would even say that if this up and down movement ceases—that is, the blessing from heaven to earth and from earth to heaven—the world will collapse. God's blessing sustains the world.

The Church, my beloved brothers and sisters, is the space in which this movement from heaven to earth, and from earth to heaven, takes place continuously. Since the Lord was taken up, He left as a legacy, one might say, His blessing. In the description of the Lord's Ascension in the Gospel, the Evangelist says that, when the Lord ascended into the heavens, "He blessed them..."—that is, He blessed the apostles in particular, who were present, leaving the blessing as a commandment and a legacy to be passed down through the centuries to all people.

Thus, in the Church, the blessing of the Ascension is perpetuated, the blessing left by Christ, who did not bless only with words. He blessed with His own sacrifice, with the words He said on the Cross when He forgave his persecutors and executioners and commended them to the mercy and love of God the Father: "Father, forgive them, for they do not know what they do" (Lk 23:34).

The Lord, therefore, bestowed this blessing on the Church after His Ascension. The Lord gave His blessing first to those entrusted to be His icons, to represent Him in the Church, especially in the Divine Liturgy, but also in general in the whole life of the Church. That is why in the Divine Liturgy, the celebrant constantly repeats this movement of blessing, which is none other than the movement that the Lord made when He was taken up into heaven. We, the clergy, have taken this as a commandment from the Lord to transfer and transmit through the centuries to the whole world. That is why faithful Christians also ask for the blessing of the clergy, the blessing of the bishop and the priest, who exactly perpetuate in the Church the blessing of the Ascended Christ.

So, my beloved brothers and sisters, we humbly ask for the blessing of the other and we all ask for the blessing of Christ, which is the blessing of the Father of Lights, and we walk in this world conveying this blessing to one another with the good words that we say about everyone and even about our enemies, with our prayer for the good of the other—let nothing happen to the other, Lord, even if he is our enemy. In this way, the blessing of Christ's Ascension becomes an experience and a reality in the world, in a world that is tearing itself apart and which the best it hopes for and can give is justice, a justice that says: Let us return the same to the other—you did me harm, so I will hurt you.

Based on society's ethics, taking revenge on someone is not bad. However, to benefit your enemy is something that goes beyond all ethics and logic in our society. This transcendence of ethics and logic is what the Apostle Paul calls us to do today. Not only those who love us, but also those who persecute us, let us bless them, in a double sense: to wish the best for them, but, even further, to place them in the blessing of God, because only He can give them the good that we wish for them.

So, my beloved brothers and sisters, something that is so simple and we say it every day—"Blessed is our God," "Blessed is the Kingdom of God," asking a bishop or priest for "your blessing"—has such a deep meaning that on this blessing rests the existence of the Church, the existence of the whole world and the existence of all of us. Let us, then, from our hearts bless God first, Who is the source of all blessings, and all those we have around us, whether they are our friends and loved ones or even our enemies. Amen.

July 8, 2007

47.
6th SUNDAY OF MATTHEW
Illness, forgiveness of sins, repentance, confession (Mt 9:1–8)

They marveled and glorified God,
who had given such power to men.

The Gospel passage we just heard, my beloved brothers and sisters, concludes with these words. These are the words of those who were present when the Lord healed the paralytic, and at the same time announced to him that all his sins had been forgiven. These words have a special meaning, my brothers and sisters, and I would like to understand their meaning more deeply.

The Lord heals a paralytic and as he usually does in these cases before healing him, he says: "Your sins are forgiven." And He does this for two main reasons.

First, because bodily illness is intertwined with illness in our soul, with sin. This particular person's sins are not necessarily related to his illness. In another case, the healing of a man blind from birth, the Lord emphasized that his infirmity was not due to the sinfulness of a specific person, but rather that his physical illness was connected with decay and death. These were introduced with the fall of man, with man's rebellion against the will of God, that is, with the entry of sin into the world. The entrance of sin into the world brought physical decay and death. That is why physical disease cannot be radically cured, if the sin is not cured first.

The second reason why the Lord, before healing the paralytic, forgives his sins is because in life it is much more important to forgive a person's sins than to give him bodily health. Bodily health is temporary, while the forgiveness of sins ensures eternal life. Despite this, the Lord gives both of these to the paralytic.

The fact that He forgives his sins provokes the reaction of the Scribes who were present and who knew the Jewish Law. And they said: "This man is blaspheming." This is blasphemy because only God can forgive sins. Precisely as a response to this reaction of the Scribes, the crowd comes at the end of the miracle to exclaim: "Glory to God who gave men such power." That is, power even to forgive sins.

This really, my beloved brothers and sisters, needs deeper examination. The only one who can forgive sins is indeed God, no one else. Because man sins against God, and if God does not forgive his sins then they remain in his life. But God provides the forgiveness of our sins in full only through the person of Christ. Why? Because as the Apostle Paul says: Christ was the one who abolished the handwriting of our sins, restored our relationship with God which the first Adam had broken, and—by restoring that relationship with God—united human nature with the divine nature, man with God. This is what brought about man's reconciliation with God. And this provided the basis on which people's sins are forgiven. Outside of Christ, therefore, we cannot speak of the complete forgiveness of sins.

But Christ, my beloved brothers and sisters, is not only God; He is also man. When He forgives the sins of the paralytic, He does so not only as God but also as a man. That is, the forgiveness of sins that comes from God passes through the human nature of Christ. In other words, it passes through man and thus forgiveness and the remission of sins comes to us through men.

The Pharisees and the Scribes are scandalized because they have not yet accepted this great mystery of the Divine Incarnation—that is, that God became a man and dwelt among them. They did not recognize Christ as God. They could not accept that God could become a man. And this is precisely what the Lord wants to emphasize with the miracle He performs and with the proclamation of the remission of the sins of the paralytic: because now the remission of sins passes through man, through human nature.

According to the Lord's teaching, my beloved brothers and sisters, we can never obtain the forgiveness of our sins if we do not forgive the sins of our brother. This interconnected relationship between God's forgiveness of our sins, and our mutual forgiveness with our brothers and sisters, is particularly emphasized in the Lord's Prayer, in which we often pray: "Forgive us our trespasses, as we forgive those who trespass against us." And so it becomes a circle. God forgives our sins, after we forgive the sins of our brother. In other words, the forgiveness of our sins passes through our brothers and sisters.

This is very clear, my dear brothers and sisters, in the great mystery called the Church. Because what is the Church? The Church is the extension of Christ's body throughout the ages. Christ's human nature after the Ascension is extended within the Church, and with the grace of the Holy Spirit to the apostles. So the Lord, after His Resurrection, gave this authority "to remit sins" to the apostles, and the apostles transferred it to the bishops and the bishops to the priests who are spiritual fathers. And so the forgiveness of sins comes to us through man.

This is the great mystery of repentance and confession that our holy Church has. One could bypass this and say: "Since only God forgives sins, then I turn to God, and I ask Him to forgive my sins." However, our Church rejects this. You cannot go directly to God to get forgiveness. You need to go through people. Just as you must go through your brothers and sisters in order to forgive them and they forgive you, so you need to go through a spiritual father, who will not give his own forgiveness but God's. The spiritual father does not forgive on his own; God forgives through the spiritual father. This authority, this function, was given by God to people. Thus, my brothers and sisters, forgiveness of sins and reconciliation with God come to us through men.

My beloved brothers and sisters, this means that the road to the forgiveness of our sins needs to go through two paths: Humility and love. If I do not humble myself before the priest, if I do not humble myself before my brother, if I do not reconcile with my brother and if I do not love him, I do not receive forgiveness of my sins. Thus, through these paths of humility and love comes true forgiveness of our sins. Let us praise, my beloved brothers and sisters, the God who gave us this great gift. It may be very difficult for our selfishness to humble ourselves or even to forgive our brother, but it is a great hope and consolation that we have the opportunity to have our sins forgiven not through God who is not physically present in our lives, but through people. Now we have the certainty that if we observe humility and love, we will receive the forgiveness of our sins from God.

This is the great gift, my beloved brothers and sisters, that amazed the crowd in today's Gospel passage, and caused them to "glorify God Who gave this power to men."

July 27, 2008

48.
7th SUNDAY OF MATTHEW
Receive one another (Romans 15:7)

> *Wherefore receive one another, just as Christ also received us, to the glory of God* (Rom 15:7).[1]

These words of Saint Paul, the Apostle, which we hear in the Church, my brethren, are so deep in their meaning that it is worthwhile to pay attention to them, so we can see what meaning they have for our own life. Saint Paul addressed these words to *the members of the Church*, so they are meant for us to guide us in life (Rom 15:1–7). He starts the reading with an exhortation towards all the members of the Church, towards the faithful and mainly towards those who are stronger in faith and in the spiritual life, and he tells them: "*We then that are strong ought to bear the infirmities of the weak.*" You that feel stronger in the spiritual life, you should bear the infirmities of the weak. You must take upon yourselves the weaknesses of the weak. "And not to please ourselves." Do not please yourselves, do not be self-regarding or self-satisfied that you, yourselves, have progressed in the spiritual life. Other people must seek you and you must satisfy more the needs of your brothers "for even Christ pleased not Himself."

From there he carries on to a really moving reference from a scriptural passage of the prophets, where the prophet addresses God and says: '*The reproaches of them that reproached You fell on me.*' The insults of all of those who insulted you have fallen on me. And Christ takes it upon Himself and Saint Paul understands that the Prophet's words refer to Christ. With this way he wants to show a dimension, which we often forget in the spiritual life, the dimension of our neighbor. We are interested in having good

[1] This homily was translated by the Holy Monastery of Saint John the Baptist, Essex, England. Minor edits have been made for the sake of uniformity.

relations with God, as individuals, but we forget our brother, or even worse, we look at the other person in order to judge him, to criticize him, to examine him. There are Christians who devote all their life to (judgmentally) examining other people. And Saint Paul does not simply say that we must not judge or criticize or examine but he goes on one step further that we should bear other people's sins. It is so hard! Why should I bear the sins of others? Why should I regard myself as equal as or more sinful than others?

The reasons, my brethren, are many but I shall mention only three:

One, is the Lord Himself did exactly that. Not only did He simply bear man's infirmities but also He took on the responsibility for all these. He took the responsibility on the Cross exactly because He was the one who was paying for the sins of others. He did not simply bear the infirmities of others but *He paid for them*. And, what is valid for Christ is valid for all of us, my brethren. This isn't what the Protestants, our fellow Christians, maintain, which is that Christ paid for us and we have nothing else to do but to praise God for this; for them, there is nothing else left but the recognition of Christ's offering. For us, the Orthodox, what Christ did—also apply to us; and we must do exactly what He, Himself did. That is why the spiritual life is difficult because we must take on Christ's Cross. It is this cross that Saint Paul recommends to us, when he presents Christ as the prototype, because He takes on the infirmities and the sins of others.

One other reason is that the Saints of the Church and especially the Fathers of the desert did nothing else but take upon themselves the sins of others. They did this *not with words*, but with all their being they blamed themselves. What we forget is that instead of reproaching our neighbor, we too must take on this responsibility, as Christ did, and as the Saints do for their sins, and accept the way of the Cross.

And a third reason is that we think that we are strong. We forget that once we were weak. But what do I say? We are always weak however much we have progressed in relation to others; in the spiritual life we are vulnerable to falling again. We are not as strong as we think. Even, when we see others as weak and ourselves strong, we must not forget this truth.

And Saint Paul continues, my brethren, even further. He does not simply say that you must not judge and criticize your brother but take on his sins, as it is mentioned at the end of the reading, but to receive your brother. '*Receive one another.*' What does it mean to receive our brother? Simply to tolerate him? Because this is the point where many times we stop. We tolerate him. This is not the meaning of 'receiving.'

Receiving means I receive him within me and I become one with him. Like receiving food and what happens when we receive food? One element of the nature becomes part of our body. It is assimilated by our body, transformed and becomes one body with us.

This is the deeper and bigger mystery that happens in the case of the Church. The members of the Church receive one another, because Christ received them and made them part of his Body. The faithful can no longer exist without Christ, neither Christ without the faithful. He is the Head of the Body and the body cannot exist without a head, but neither head without body. And so Christ having received all the people and especially those with their willingness, who want to be received, the faithful, by receiving them He makes them one body, His own Body.

That is how the reception takes place, as Saint Paul says, for edification. *Edification* is a word that is misunderstood many times, as though it meant progress in the spiritual life of every man. Edification is an image, which Saint Paul borrows from the building of a house. It is not about the progress of one person, it is about the building, the House of God, the House of the Holy Spirit that is the Church. And, therefore, by receiving each other, all together we construct the body of Christ, the Church, and it is only in this way that we can be saved. We can only be saved within the Church. But this happens only when we receive each other and become united in one body. Only thus we shall be saved.

My brethren, we are called by Christ Himself to receive Holy Communion, His body and blood. I wonder if we are conscious of what this means? Perhaps we are conscious of what it means regarding our relationship with God? Perhaps we approach with fear. Perhaps we are approaching prepared—with fasting and perhaps with confession. Perhaps with all that one needs to approach this great mystery. But I wonder are we conscious at that moment that we are not only united with God but also with our brothers? Are we conscious that at that moment Christ receives us and we receive Him, but simultaneously He receives our brothers and we too receive our brothers? It is a view, a dimension of this big mystery of the Holy Communion, which we many times forget.

St. Paul comes to emphasize exactly this. '*Receive one another as Christ receives us.*' And he adds to the Glory of God, because the Glory of God is exactly the reception of all the people in the body of Christ, and in this manner, with this reception, with this body of Christ, God is glorified in the world. He is not glorified with our mere words; He is not glorified even with our individual virtue. He is glorified with the body of Christ that is the Church. And there exactly Saint Paul places today the emphasis by telling all of us: '*Receive one another as Christ received us to the glory of God.*'

Whatever, my brethren, takes place during the Divine Liturgy, it must not stop within the Divine Liturgy, it must continue into our daily life. And it is truly difficult. Spiritual life is not easy. It is a struggle. It is difficult for anybody to accept and receive his brother or sister, to receive him or her and take on his/her sins.

We live in an age of individualism.

Everyone thinks only of himself, and he is not alone in this, in the surroundings of our so-called civilization, but this attitude is also present among Christians.

Individualism has crept in and each one of us tries to be reconciled with God by himself, on his own. He forgets his brother or looks at him as a subject for his criticism and blame and forgets that the meaning of the spiritual life, the fulfillment of our salvation, exists in this receiving of our brother.

When you step outside the vicinity of the Church today, what are some ways you think you could better receive your brother or sister?

My brethren, let this be the criterion for our daily life, for our actions, for our behavior and so the mercy of the Lord will strengthen all of us, so that whatever seems impossible for us may become possible for us through God.

July 22, 2001

49.
7th SUNDAY OF MATTHEW
Bearing the sins of others (Rom 15:1–7)

We who are strong ought to bear with the failings of the weak, and not to please ourselves.

These words, my beloved brothers and sisters, mark the beginning of the Epistle reading we just heard. The Apostle Paul addressed these words to the Christians of Rome, but he also addresses every Christian, every member of the Church, of every age. The strong must bear with the failings of the weak. What do the Apostle Paul's words here mean?

In the Church, as in life in general, there are people who are stronger and people who are weaker—physically stronger, but also spiritually stronger or weaker. The physically weak cannot perform functions that healthy people perform. And the Christian, the strong, is called to do what the physically weak cannot do. But the same applies, my brothers and sisters, to people's faith.

There are people who cannot believe—people who are completely faithless, people of little faith, people whose faith is shaken by every difficulty in life. And believers, the strong, are called to believe for them. Let them take upon themselves the unbelief or lack of faith of others. We think that this is not possible, but it is. Is it possible for us to believe for the sake of others?

In the ancient Church, as it is still today, when we baptize small children, infants, the Protestants accuse us and say: "But infants have no faith, how can you baptize them?" Or when they receive communion: "Why do you give communion to infants, who do not yet have the ability to believe?" All this happens with Baptism and Holy Communion because we who love them believe. When someone loves someone, they can substitute their own faith for the defective or non-existent faith of the other. And God accepts this too. He accepts it because He sees the love that leads us to bring to Him people who are not strong enough to believe on their own.

The same, my brothers and sisters, applies to love. Not all people can love. Not all people can love, above all, as God wants—to love even our enemies. Therefore, those of us who can love, let us replace their lack of love with ours. And many other examples could be given which demonstrate that we are not, as we think, individuals who each take their fate upon themselves—that each one has his own faith, his own love, his own strengths. No, what the Apostle Paul wants to say in the reading today is that we are so bound together, in one body, that each one can take upon himself the weaknesses of the other. And how does one take on the weaknesses of the other?

First of all, by showing understanding and mercy to the other's weakness. We are so willing and so ready to criticize others, those who for some reason do not succeed; we consider anything that scandalizes us to be reprehensible, and we look down on these people. We must, however, be able to show understanding and mercy to others' weakness, especially to those who cannot follow what we, by God's grace, can do.

However, the Apostle Paul does not simply tell us to be merciful and tolerant toward others' weaknesses, but he actually calls us to something much more, almost unimaginable—to personally bear the weaknesses of others. Here, my brothers and sisters, we need to exercise a little caution. In the lives of the fathers of the desert, there are shocking narratives that describe precisely what the Apostle Paul is saying in this sentence that we are trying to analyze.

There are, we read in the lives of these saints, brothers who, when a brother sins against them, cover him and say that they have sinned. There are brothers in the desert who pay for the sins of their brothers, as if they had committed them. There are brothers, these stories say, that when one brother is under the influence of the demon, they beg God to take the demon from their brother and bring it to them, and indeed God allows this.

Saint Barsanouphius, that great ascetic of the desert, says that when one can take on himself half the sins of another, he is on the right path. When, however, he can take upon himself all the sins of the other, then he is perfect.

My beloved brothers and sisters, this is the heart of the Gospel, it is the essence of the Gospel, of our faith. What does this mean? What is it that the Gospel describes? It describes Christ—completely innocent, God—taking upon Himself the sins of others. We say of Christ that he is "The Lamb of God who takes away the sin of the world" (John 1:29), but how easily this escapes us. Because to take upon yourself the sins of others is to become Christ and then you imitate Christ. Then you participate in Christ when you can reach the point of taking upon yourself the sins of others. This, therefore, is demanded by our faith in Christ.

But love also demands this. There is no true love when this does not happen. When we wall ourselves in, and don't want to bear the sins of others, then we don't love. Real love forces us to take upon ourselves the responsibilities for the sins of the other—that is, to take upon ourselves the same weakness of the other as our own weakness.

My beloved brothers and sisters, the Gospel is not easy. It is not easy, especially for all of us who have the tendency to please, as the Apostle Paul says, first ourselves and then others—to consider ourselves first. In the reading we heard from the Apostle Paul about Christ, he refers to this terrible phrase from the Old Testament: "The reproaches of those who reproached You fell on Me" (Ps 68:10 LXX). Can you take the insults of others upon yourself?

We all try, if we are accused, to prove that we are right. Many times we also take our opponents to court because they defamed us, because they wronged us. And the Apostle Paul says on another occasion to the Corinthians: "Why don't you prefer to be wronged, rather than to be justified? You are right, but it is better to accept to be wronged for the sake of your brother" (cf. 1Cor 6:7).

How will we overcome, my beloved brothers and sisters, this wall that we have built around ourselves? That wall that makes us, many times, not see our own sins and see only the sins of others, to criticize others and not to show any sympathy for them?

We should strive instead to reach the point of taking upon ourselves the sins of others.

Let's heed these words of the Apostle Paul: It is the only way, my dear brothers and sisters, for there to be true love and true unity within the Church and among people. It is not love, as I said before, that everyone claims their rights. True love is denying one's rights. How, then, in today's society, in today's culture, which constantly talks about the rights of the individual, how is it possible to apply the Gospel? The Gospel cannot be applied throughout history, by all society, by all people. It is futile to pursue this. The Gospel is in this life something to which we must strive, as much as we can, and not something that we will conquer and implement perfectly.

The Lord, however, gave us the measure to measure our lives and let's keep this measure high, let's keep the bar high, and when we can't reach this height, then let's ask for God's mercy and not try to justify ourselves. We all need God's mercy. Amen.

July 30, 2006

50.
8th SUNDAY OF MATTHEW

Blessing of the loaves, Anaphora, Holy Eucharist (Mt 14:14–22)

The miracle in Gospel passage we just heard, my dear brothers and sisters, is well known, but its deeper meaning deserves our attention.

The Lord withdraws to a deserted place with His disciples, but the crowd discovers that He is there and runs to meet Him. There, the Lord, moved by compassion, heals the sick who had been brought to Him, and when night approaches, the disciples say to Him: "Tell the people to go to the villages to buy food, because it is getting dark and there is nothing to eat." And the Lord answers them: "You give them something to eat." The disciples answer that they have only five loaves and two fish. Then the Lord says to them: "This is enough, bring them here." He blesses them and they multiply, so that they are enough for the whole crowd, which exceeded five thousand people; and not only are there enough, but twelve baskets are left over.

The question that comes to my mind, my beloved brothers and sisters, is why did the Lord bless the loaves and not just order them to multiply? He could have simply given a command, as He did many times, and the miracle would happen. It is characteristic, however, that He blesses the loaves. The fact that He blesses them means two things: that He offers them to God His Father and that a blessing comes from the Father onto the loaves. In other words, the blessing is a double movement. A movement from us to God and from God to us. And does anyone wonder why this blessing was needed for the loaves?

Bread, my brothers and sisters, is the source of our life. From there we extract the material needed to be metabolized and become our life. Bread is simply a symbol of all the food we take from the world around us and which we assimilate to give us energy and strength to live. We forget, however, that this is a gift; it is not something that we ourselves create. And since it is a gift, we must bless the Giver—that is, offer it back to the One Who gave it to us. Let's thank Him for this gift. Thus, when we offer this blessing back to God, it is our thanksgiving for the gifts we receive. It is a confession, that nothing of what we have and of what we receive—even our very life, our very existence and the world that surrounds us—nothing is self-evident, everything has a giver. And our whole life, my brothers and sisters—everything we have—comes from others, and ultimately comes from God.

This is something so true and at the same time neglected by all of us. We take for granted what we receive, as if we deserve it. But we are not entitled to anything; everything is a gift. They are gifts from God. They are given to us through other people, as we saw in today's passage. The Lord gave the bread to the multitudes through His disciples. He "gave the loaves to the disciples; and the disciples gave to the multitudes." This is how God's gift passes from others and reaches us. God never gives us His gifts directly, He gives them to us through others, so that we have reasons to thank not only God but also others.

The blessing on the bread is also a blessing that comes down from God on the food we eat, because food, my dear brothers and sisters, sustains us but in a paradoxical way it also contributes to our decay and death. The food we get is a double-edged sword. It can be a cause and a means for us to wear out and eventually die. And if our food does not have God's blessing, it can move from a source of life to a source of death. So, this great event of human life, so fundamental to our daily life and yet so neglected—namely, the intake of food—if it is not blessed by God, it is not a source of life. Blessing the bread, the Lord recognized that it was a gift from God and brought God's blessing upon it. That's why the bread multiplied and that's why it was not only enough but more than enough. However, when there is no blessing of God, even if the goods we have are many, they are not enough for us. But little becomes much when there is God's blessing.

And I think, my brothers and sisters, that they did not multiply only because they were blessed by God; they also multiplied for another reason, because they were shared. Food, my beloved brothers and sisters, is not only, as I said, a means to sustain ourselves, but it is, pay attention to this, also a means to commune with others. People have never wanted to eat alone. It is a great blessing from God to have company when you eat. Don't eat alone. It is in the very nature of food to share it with others, and this is precisely what is depicted in the miracle we just heard. The Lord took the loaves and broke them into pieces, gave them to His disciples and the disciples "to the multitude," and they all ate and were satisfied. They all ate together. They shared the little, and the little became a lot. They shared the loaves, and the bread became not just food for the body but a means of communion and love between people.

So these are the two sides of the miracle that took place, my brothers and sisters, which we heard in the passage today, that we should focus our attention on. Our food is a gift from God, it is a blessing from God. If it is not blessed by God and is not offered back to God, it will not be enough and may even be harmful. Secondly, food is a means of communion with others. Food exists to be shared and not to be stored, not to be possessed, not to be made ours, our individual property. If it is not shared, our food is not blessed. And if it is not blessed, it is not a source and means of life, and it will not be enough.

The fathers of the Church say that the Lord's miracle today is a "type" of the Divine Eucharist. This is exactly what we do in the Divine Liturgy. What is the Divine Liturgy? We take bread, we take this food, our daily food, and we bring it to God and call it "gifts"—the Holy Gifts. Because these are not self-evident, they come from someone. And this Someone, from Whom they come, we offer these gifts back to Him and say: "Your own of Your own we offer unto You." In other words, "We give You Your own. We give You Your own and we thank You for it and for everything." "On behalf of all, and for all." And this "anaphora," as we call it, the Holy Anaphora, is the central point of the Divine Liturgy. That which we offer back to God, He returns to us blessed. He returns it to us as the Body of His Son, and He makes it "the medicine of immortality," as Saint Ignatius says. The source of eternal life. And this is how the Divine Eucharist becomes food, spiritual food for the whole world. And these gifts of God do not come to us directly from God. As I said, the Lord did not directly give the bread "to the multitude"; He gave it to His disciples, and His disciples gave it "to the multitude." In the same way, God gives us the bread of life in the Eucharist through the successors of the disciples, through the ministers of the Church. This is why the Divine Eucharist is celebrated by the ministers of the Church. It cannot be performed by the laity, because God wants His blessing and the gift of eternal food to pass through His disciples, and the disciples of His disciples. What's more, what happened in the miracle today is what happens also in the Eucharist. The Lord and those who represent Him in the Eucharist break the bread into pieces and give it to the people to share. And in the Eucharist we share the bread of eternal life. Each of us does not take it separately, we all take it together, that is why we cannot celebrate the Eucharist if we are not all gathered together. No one can perform the Divine Eucharist alone in the Orthodox Church. Among other Christians, this happens. But for us Orthodox, the Eucharist presupposes a meeting. We must come together, because we must share the eternal food together.

So, my brothers and sisters, the miracle we heard today is a miracle that is repeated every day, every time we celebrate the Divine Liturgy. It is the miracle on which the Church is based. If you take away this miracle, the Church has no meaning. The Church exists precisely to give back to God, to thank God for the world He gave us, and to receive this blessing from God, and in turn give it to the world to be shared by people among themselves, so that we unite to become one body.

My brothers and sisters, the passage we heard says that the Lord did this miracle in a deserted place. Isn't the place we live in also a wilderness? Doesn't all that I told you sound strange to man today? Isn't it true that the things that are so important to us, in our daily lives, don't have the importance they should? Man has taken food into his hands now. And he says to God: "I don't need you. What should I do with your blessing? I have science, technology, the economy, and I produce goods. Many goods. I multiply the loaves; we don't need God to multiply our food. Industry multiplies it."

But, my brothers and sisters, what kind of food is this? It is now starting to become obvious that this food offers us anything but life and health. Food that is manufactured by man is starting to become problematic. And man himself begins to worry and wants to control his food, he wants to control what they give him as food. Today, they say, they have multiplied food so much that no one should be hungry. But the hungry have also multiplied. Perhaps never before has there been so many hungry people as today. Because, not having the blessing of God, this food is not distributed according to God's will, and each one takes for himself. And thus food increases, it increases for a few, but many remain hungry.

In the past, people were not deprived. Some of us, of the older generation, lived through periods of real poverty; a plate of food was not a given. What's more, our mother and grandmother used to send us to deliver this plate of food to the neighbor who didn't have any, and it made "a lot." And from this little many were filled, many lived. And we lived in a healthier way than today, when man has so much.

This miracle that we heard today, my brothers and sisters, is so important for life that we could say that it expresses the entire Gospel. The whole world, modern man, must understand that God's blessing is necessary for our lives and that God's goods are for us to share. And so maybe we can find, my brothers and sisters, a way out of the impasse we have reached. Perhaps we can see what true happiness is in our lives, and that it depends on God's blessing, on our love and on the sharing of God's goods among us. This is our hope, my brothers and sisters; this will characterize the Kingdom of God when He establishes it in the world. Because the Kingdom of God is likened in the Gospels to a banquet, it is likened to communion, participation in goods. The Church depicts the Kingdom of God in the Eucharist, and I pray, my brothers and sisters, that we all be accounted to become participants and sharers in this Kingdom. Amen.

July 29, 2001

51.
8th SUNDAY OF MATTHEW
The multiplication of the five loaves (Mt 14:14–22)

The Gospel passage we just heard contains one of the Lord's well-known miracles, the miracle of the multiplication of the loaves, in which only five loaves and two fish fed "about five thousand men, besides women and children"—i.e., a large number of people. We remember this miracle of the Lord especially when we celebrate the service of artoklasia. And the service of artoklasia has precisely the meaning of being a repetition, in a way, of this miracle performed by the Lord. But both the fathers of the Church and the expositors of the Gospel primarily connect this miracle of the Lord with the Holy Eucharist. By performing this miracle, the Lord wanted to demonstrate the great mystery of the Holy Eucharist. And this is of particular importance, as we will see shortly. This passage, therefore, is full of meaning, which we are called to think about today for the salvation of our souls and to really know the word of God and what it wants to convey to us.

The first basic meaning is that the Lord is not indifferent to the material needs of people, to food, material food. He felt sorry for the crowd, it says, and He did not let them go hungry. He gave them material food, because the human body needs material food and it is not something we can or should despise. But He gave this material food, these material goods, to people with two actions, two conditions, which are very important.

Pay attention, my brothers and sisters: the Lord did not simply say "distribute the loaves and fishes," and the disciples distributed to everyone so that they would be satisfied. But He took them into His hands and did two things, two very important actions. One was to raise His eyes to heaven, to the Father, and to bless the bread. And the other was to break the loaves and distribute them to everyone; to distribute them indirectly via His disciples. Let us pay attention to these details, my beloved brothers and sisters.

Why didn't the Lord simply give the loaves and fishes, so that the hungry could be filled? Why did He make this move to bless the bread? The blessing of the goods that we have in this life, my dear brothers and sisters, is what is most important—not the goods as such, but the blessing of the goods that we have. And the blessing means that all these goods must first pass through the hands of God, and must be given to us by God Himself; we must not take them, we must not seize them, because they do not belong to us. Only when they become God's gifts to us, when they are blessed by God, only then do they become a source of life and true nourishment. Otherwise, it is food unto death, because let's not forget that material food satisfies us for a period of time, but we are still hungry. It can support us physically, but again this support it gives us is temporary. Because food itself brings death. And if this food remains as it is, natural, then it becomes not only a carrier of life for us, but also a carrier of death. That is why these material goods must pass through the hands of God, be blessed by God.

God's blessing is the greatest, most important gift to the world—a gift of God that is brought to the world by the Church of God. The Church and its ministers when they bless people—and you see how often we do this in the Divine Liturgy but also outside the Divine Liturgy—they are doing nothing else than conveying the Lord's blessing during His Ascension. Observe, my brothers and sisters, how the great event of the Lord's Ascension includes the blessing to the disciples. He was taken up and blessed them. And this blessing, which we always have in the icons—the Lord is never represented without blessing—is borne into the world by the Church through its priests. You will tell me, this is simply a type and for many people, it means nothing. However, its meaning is very deep, because it means that any good material that does not have God's blessing is, as I said, a carrier of death and is not a carrier of true life. And this blessing also means recognition that these material goods do not belong to us, they are not ours, that they are gifts from God and that we simply distribute God's gifts to people. Tell me, does this matter? Yes, my brothers and sisters. It is of great importance, because it is very different to see the goods we have as gifts from God than to see them as our own property. When we see them as gifts from God, then we always live first of all with gratitude for what we have, and secondly, we do not manage them for our own benefit, but we manage them so that God's love for the world is manifested through them.

It is of great importance, my brothers and sisters, to wake up in the morning and to thank God for giving us the gift of existence for one more day, and it is of great importance to wake up in the morning and to enjoy so many good things, as we do today in this world, and recognize the need to say "thank you" to someone. How much the world changes, my brothers and sisters, if we see it as a gift and don't just take it as a random event, as something that just happens. No, our existence, the whole world, and material goods are not just something random, they have a personal source of love and they also have a personal destination; we must recognize that material goods are means to unite with God. God does not give us material goods simply to satisfy our hunger. He wants through all that He gives us to bring us close to Him, to unite with Him. And for this reason, by blessing material goods, we recognize that their purpose and destination does not stop at the material goods themselves; it goes further, it touches on our relationship with God but also our relationship with our brother, our neighbor. And for this reason, in addition to blessing the goods, the Lord also does something else: He distributes the goods, breaks the bread, and gives it to the disciples to distribute so that everyone will be filled.

Thus, passing through God's blessing, we arrive at love for other people. When we recognize that the goods we have are not ours, but are God's gifts, then the way opens to share them with others. It is no coincidence, my brothers and sisters, that in all cases where an attempt was made to distribute goods equally, through various sociological systems, great corruption prevailed. That is, those who distributed them to others, essentially, kept the largest portion for themselves. When these goods are not considered God's blessing for the whole world, then man uses them, is tempted to use them, for himself. And that is why today, my beloved brothers and sisters, while the world has many goods, the goods are not enough, they are not enough for everyone. Meanwhile, five loaves and two fish fed thousands of people. Today, goods are in excess and yet they are not enough, there are people who are hungry, because if we do not pass these goods through God's blessing and if we do not recognize that they are not ours, then our selfishness enters and we use the goods for ourselves.

The blessing of goods is, therefore, of great importance, my brothers and sisters, and it is no coincidence that in our Church at least every sentence of its prayers and every liturgical movement include the blessing of God, they refer to blessing. We begin the Divine Liturgy with "Blessed is the Kingdom of God," we begin every service with "Blessed is our God," we end the Divine Liturgy and every act of worship with the priest's blessing, God's blessing on the people. So everything enters into this atmosphere of blessing, so that in this way we declare that all goods and everything we have belong to God and that they have one destination: to transcend matter itself and become means and ways of uniting us with God and our brothers. That is why, my beloved brothers and sisters, this miracle of today's gospel passage essentially refers, as I said, to the Holy Eucharist, to what we are celebrating at this moment. And at this very moment, with the Divine Liturgy, we do nothing else but have the Lord in front of us, present, who takes the material goods in His hands, the bread and the wine, which you, the lay people, brought so that they could be blessed, so that they are not used as something human and ephemeral, but to be eternal, to acquire eternal significance. And the Lord blesses them, because in the Divine Liturgy Christ Himself presides, and by blessing the bread and offering them up to the Father, as we do and will do shortly in the holy Anaphora, the bread is transformed into a source of life, eternal life, for all of us. And it also becomes a means to unite with God and with each other in love, because the Holy Eucharist is not only union with God, says Saint John of Damascus; we do not only make Him part of our own body and blood, but all of us also become one body together. And so, all that we see in today's miracle, which the Gospel passage described, we see taking place in the Divine

Eucharist, in this great mystery, in which the Lord identifies the bread with Himself, so that the world may live nourished by Christ Himself.

My beloved brothers and sisters, the world needs two things: blessing and communion. And unfortunately these two things are absent from people's lives today. And there lies the cause of man's great problems, because if he has a blessing from God and if he has a communion of goods, then—however few these goods may be—they are sufficient and an abundance. And we see this in people's critical moments. We saw it in the past; today, unfortunately, people have lost this experience that we, the older generations, experienced in times of wars and great misery, when we shared the plate of food we had at home with the neighbor who didn't have anything. And it was enough, yes, it was enough and there was more. Today we have all the goods and they are not even enough for ourselves, much less for our neighbors who are hungry. So what the Gospel passage conveys today to the world, my beloved brothers and sisters, and to each of us, is to always live with the blessing of God, offering up all goods to Him in thanksgiving, and to live in communion, sharing the goods together with others and especially with those who do not have.

This is the Church's message, my dear brothers and sisters, to a world plagued by human self-centeredness, and it is a message that cannot be fully applied within history. However, it is a harbinger of what God is preparing for the world in His Kingdom. And, with the Holy Eucharist, He wants to give us a foretaste of His Kingdom, in which everything will be blessed by God, everything will be offered up to God, and people will share everything with love. This Kingdom, my beloved brothers and sisters, cannot become a reality in history. Only when the Lord comes and establishes His Kingdom, then it will become a reality. For this reason, our prayer and our wish is always that the Kingdom of God will come: "Thy kingdom come," we ask in the Lord's prayer. And the Lord advises us: "But seek first the kingdom of God and His righteousness, and all these things shall be added to you" (Mt 6:33). When the Kingdom of God comes, everything will be added to us.

I pray, my beloved brothers and sisters, that the Lord will account us all worthy of this Kingdom of God. And in this fleeting life, may we anticipate this joy of the Kingdom of God with the Divine Eucharist, with the communion of the Lord's body and blood, but also with the communion of our goods with other people. Then, we will be ready to receive the Kingdom of God when He wants to establish it and bring it to the world, and we will become true participants in it. Amen.

In the Holy Monastery of Saint John the Baptist, Essex, England

July 26, 2015

52.
8th SUNDAY OF MATTHEW
The multiplication of the five loaves (Mt 14:14–22)

All the Lord's miracles, my beloved brothers and sisters, contain deep down within them great and important truths for our lives. And today's Gospel passage presents us with one more miracle of the Lord, which we are called to pay attention to and see its deeper meaning for us as well. The Lord was in a deserted place and, by the time He had spoken to the multitudes and healed their sick, night was approaching. His disciples were worried that these crowds would not have time to make it to a city to buy food for their dinner. That is why the disciples turned to the Lord and begged Him to dismiss the crowds, to give them His blessing to leave to go get food. But the Lord answered "No, let them stay here. Bring me whatever there is, so that these multitudes may eat." And the disciples answer that there are only five loaves and two fish.

The Lord takes the food in His hands, raises His eyes to heaven, blesses them and these five loaves and two fish manage to feed the whole crowd, which, according to the evangelist, consisted of five thousand men, not including the women and children. And not only that, but there were so many loaves left over that they filled twelve baskets.

In this miracle of the Lord, some Church fathers as well as modern interpreters of the Holy Bible see symbolism of the Divine Eucharist, the Divine Liturgy, which we are celebrating here at this moment. After the Lord taught the multitudes, He feeds them. He feeds them with bread, which is enough for their whole lives and to feed the whole world. It is the bread of His body, Christ Himself, whom we partake of in the Holy Eucharist, so that we too may be fed, but also so that the whole world may be fed and live.

I would like us to focus our attention, brothers and sisters, on this symbolism. Because what happened is not simply that the Lord fed the multitudes with bread, with His body. Let us pay attention to the way in which He does it. Initially, it is important that He does not simply take the loaves and fish to give them to the people, but first He looks up to heaven and invokes God's blessing, blesses them Himself, and *then* distributes them.

Why? Couldn't He give the food directly without all this ritual preceding it? No, my brothers and sisters, because God's blessing is the necessary condition for anything to happen in our lives. The blessing is the opening of our heart to God, to include Him in it. But it also moves in the opposite direction, from God to us. God blesses us so that He can take us into His grace and into His heart. This is the blessing that the Church uses continually, and which all the faithful seek to receive from the priests, who also offer up to God all the requests of the people and receive from God His grace, which they then give to the people.

We are returning the blessing, then, when we say: "Blessed is our God always." We bless God, but He also blesses us. A connection takes place between us and God. And this is the way in which God gives His love and His grace. This happens, my brothers and sisters, to reveal something extremely important: all that we have—not only food to live but also our very existence—is not self-evident, as we usually think. They are gifts that come from the love of God and we must recognize them as gifts. We must, therefore, place our whole existence within our relationship with God and within God's blessing. "And what do you have that you did not receive?" asks the Apostle Paul (1 Cor 4:7). Is there anything you have that you didn't get from somewhere else? But every day we live, my brothers and sisters, with this impression that we receive nothing, but rather everything belongs to us, it is ours. But the fact of the matter is that nothing is ours. We receive everything, and our very existence is a gift from God. Therefore, there must be this recognition, this confession, that the food we receive and, by extension, our entire existence is a gift from God; it is not something that can be taken for granted. And in the Divine Liturgy we do this, my beloved brothers and sisters. That is why we call the Divine Liturgy "Eucharist." It means "Thanksgiving," because this is the essence of the Divine Liturgy, the recognition that the world we hold in our hands and our very selves are gifts from God, and we must return them to God with thanksgiving. And that is why the Divine Liturgy has all those moving prayers in the Anaphora, which declare precisely this thing. We thank God "for everything, things known and things unknown," since God has provided us with many more gifts than we recognize and know about, and this is why we use this general formulation and say "for that which we know and that which we do not know." And this is why, my dear brothers and sisters, the Lord takes the loaves and the fish and multiplies them in this way.

The other element we observe in the Lord's miracle today is that He gives the bread, this food which He multiplies, to His disciples and the disciples distribute it to the crowds. And so the food is shared by all. Food, my beloved brothers and sisters, was given to us by God for two reasons. First, in order to sustain ourselves; it is a biological need. But second and more important, to share it with others. Don't think this is strange. When one eats alone, one's food is poison. When he eats with others and shares what he eats, then it becomes a blessing. These gifts of God, therefore, are intended to be shared by others, so that others may also participate. And that is precisely why we call the Eucharist "Communion." Communion with God but also communion among us.

Food, therefore, is not an end in itself, nor is it simply a biological need. Food is a means to commune with God and with each other. That is why the Kingdom of God is described in the Gospels as a banquet, as food, to show that even in the Kingdom of God no one lives in isolation. However holy he may be, whatever virtues he may have, if he does not share his life with others, he cannot say that he belongs to the Kingdom of God, to the communion of saints. Here, then, is a great truth that is hidden in the Gospel passage: that our food, like our whole existence, is to be shared, to be a means of communion with others.

These two great truths, my dear brothers and sisters—that our food and our existence is a gift and that it is a gift not for ourselves but to be shared with others—today's man cannot understand; he does not experience them. First of all, it is characteristic of man today, unfortunately—and all of us participate in this to a greater or lesser degree—that we take our food and existence for granted. Every morning when we wake up, we think that nothing happened. But how can nothing have happened?! Is it a given that we will live today? If we consider our very existence a gift from God, then our thoughts should be continually turned toward God, to bless God and invoke His blessing. In this way, our whole life can become a Divine Eucharist, a Liturgy, as we are living it now. But I said that modern man takes all these for granted. And gratitude has been limited to certain social conventions; when someone gives us something and we say "thank you." However, we do not attribute our very existence and whatever we have (and do not have) to God, Who gives them to us. And that is why the world has reached the point of not appreciating these gifts and wanting to have even more. What we have is not enough and we ask for more. Modern man also forgets that everything he has been given should be shared with others. There is a great lack of goods in this society. That is why goods are not enough. But in the miracle we heard about today, they even had leftovers. But if we share the goods we have with people, my beloved brothers and sisters, and do not selfishly keep them for ourselves, we will see that there will be leftovers. It becomes an enormous amount when you share it. This can be observed even in times of crisis. And in earlier times, when people had the fear of God and lived according to the Gospel, in times of war and misery, the little they had was enough for them and for others, because they shared it with everyone. Today, there are goods that are thrown in the trash, and are not enough, because they are not shared.

So, my beloved brothers and sisters, every time we celebrate the Divine Eucharist, we convey a great reminder to all of us and a confession to the whole world, that the world in which we live, our very existence, and all the goods that we have are gifts and we should give thanks for them. "In everything give thanks" (1Thess. 5:18), says the Apostle Paul. But whatever happens to you, and when you have something and when you lack something, gratitude should be permanent, in all circumstances.

In other words, we are called to extend that which we experience in the Divine Liturgy into our daily lives, each one to the extent he can, and we should consider all goods and our existence as gifts from God, which should be shared with others. We should continually seek the blessing of God, so that whatever we have can become the means for uniting with Him, just as in the Divine Liturgy we unite with Christ and experience a foretaste of the Kingdom of God every time we commune of the body and blood of the Lord. This, my dear brothers and sisters, we must extend it to our daily lives, as much as we can. We must acquire this ethos of thanksgiving, and in this way our lives will change and we will be happier, but we will also be effective in the modern world as witnesses, which Christ has tasked us with. He asks all of us who invoke His name to carry this ethos of thanksgiving into the world. And then, my brothers and sisters, we will see that not only our own lives but also the whole world will slowly be transformed by this witness and we will become, from now on, heirs of the Kingdom of God, of which I pray the Lord will account us all worthy. Amen.

In the Holy Monastery of Saint John the Baptist, Essex, England
August 14, 2016

53.
9th SUNDAY OF MATTHEW
About faith, miracles, fear, and love (Mt 14:22–34)

The Gospel passage that we just heard, my dear brothers and sisters, is one of the most striking passages in the New Testament. The Lord, after performing the miracle of the multiplication of the loaves that we heard about last Sunday, withdrew to the mountain to pray in private. Prayer needs calmness. Prayer requires one to get away from the crowd and the cares of life and to focus exclusively on God.

And the Lord prays in this way and thus sets an example for everyone as to what true prayer is and what it needs. It is an example followed throughout the centuries by the monks of our Church, who also withdraw from the world with only one purpose, prayer. Because the greatest and most important work of the monks is prayer, prayer for the whole world and for themselves, of course.

The Lord, after withdrawing, left His disciples at sea alone in the boat. And He left them all night, not appearing to them until around dawn, thus allowing their patience to be tested and their determination to develop, because God often leaves man alone. He leaves us alone to test our faith and our patience.

And then the Lord appears, walking on the sea. The disciples are scared; they think they are seeing a ghost and the Lord tells them not to be afraid and assures them that it is He. At that moment, a scene unfolds which deserves our attention and to which we will devote some thoughts in the sermon today. The Apostle Peter, this enthusiastic disciple, as soon as he sees the Lord walking on the water, asks Him to walk on the water and go to him. And the Lord says to him: "Come."

What makes an impression, my beloved brothers and sisters, is that Peter does not hesitate, does not put logic before him and say: "How can I jump into the water and how can I walk on the water? The laws of nature are relentless. This is madness. How will I commit this insanity? And yes, Christ is able to do it because He is God, but I, as a human being?" Such thoughts do not cross his mind. Immediately, spontaneously, he throws himself into the sea and takes the leap of faith. Because faith, my beloved brothers and sisters, is a leap, a leap into the void. Faith is the biggest paradox and let's not try to justify faith logically. Faith has no justification and logical proof. Faith is falling into the void, believing that one will still be saved. It is faith in the humanly impossible as possible. And this happens to the Apostle Peter: he immediately throws himself into the sea and actually walks on the water.

But what is important, my dear brothers and sisters, and Saint John Chrysostom notes it, is that Peter does not ask for this grace from the Lord simply to see a miracle, to perform a miracle himself, but to be near Him. "Call me to come to You." I want to come to You. It is not this miracle that Peter seeks, says Saint John Chrysostom, it is to be close to Christ. And this is very instructive because, when we ask God for miracles, it is as if we are using God and His power, as if we are asking for His power and not Himself. But Peter wants to go to Christ Himself, to the person of Christ. And when we ask God for something, what we should ask first is God Himself, to be close to Him. And when we ask for the very person of God, then the Grace of God comes and miracles happen.

We must, therefore, reverse the order, as Peter did. Not first the miracle and then God, but first God and then the miracle. First you believe and seek God Himself, and then the miracle will follow. Don't wait for a miracle to reach the person of God. And Peter continues this journey towards Christ, but at some point the wind becomes strong and Peter is afraid, and from the moment Peter began to be afraid, he sinks.

Where did the fear come from? From where it always comes, my beloved brothers and sisters: from our self-love. Peter, while until that moment he was thinking about Christ, that he was going to meet Christ, at some point he thought about his life: "Now I'm drowning!" The person of Christ was replaced by himself and, in this way, he lost the orientation that allowed him to stand on the water and began to sink. Because, when we think about ourselves, then we are gripped by the fear of losing ourselves and this creates insecurity, failure, and inability to make any miracle happen in our life.

In order for a miracle to happen in our lives, we must empty ourselves of our selfishness, turn our hearts towards some other person and then the fear leaves us. Because, as John says in one of his epistles, "perfect love casts out fear." And when the Lord sees Peter being timid, having little faith and sinking, then He intervenes to save him. But how does He intervene?

The Lord could have commanded the winds to stop. He had done this many times. The elements of nature obeyed the Lord. However, He does not choose this way. He gives him His hand and says: "Come, take My hand." It is not about a miracle, it is about a personal relationship; it is about love. And the Lord gives His hand to show him that it is not only a question of saving his life. "What you want at this moment and what you need is to unite with me, to be united."

Valuable conclusions for our own life emerge from this scene unfolding on the sea, my dear brothers and sisters. We live in an age that cultivates self-love so much that we even want miracles to serve our self-love. We want God to do miracles for us to serve our needs and interests. But God is not an instrument for us to use for ourselves. God wants our love, He wants to give us His person, Himself, as He did in the person of His Son, Christ. Christ did not come to give us goods, nor great teachings. Christ came to give us Himself, God Himself, His Father, and to unite us with Him. Let's make that our priority and everything else will follow.

So, my beloved brothers and sisters, from the analysis we made of this passage, we can conclude generally that in order for fear, all fear, to leave us, we need nothing more than to keep the great and first commandment, this two-fold commandment: Love the Lord your God with all your heart and with all your soul and with all your mind and with all your strength, and love your neighbor as yourself (Mk 12:30–31). If we love God and our fellow man, then we are freed from all fear. We do this on rare occasions. When we love someone, we don't calculate the risks. When we stop calculating the risks, we get out of ourselves, out of our selfishness, and then we empty ourselves so that God's grace can come. And when God's grace comes, everything comes, everything happens, everything is given to us. Amen.

July 29, 2007

54.
10th SUNDAY OF MATTHEW
Biological and spiritual fatherhood (1 Cor 4:9–16)

> *For though you might have ten thousand instructors in Christ, yet you do not have many fathers; for in Christ Jesus I have begotten you through the gospel* (1 Cor 4:15).

I am begging you today, my brothers and sisters, to dive as deeply as we can into these words of the Apostle Paul, which concluded the Epistle reading we just heard. All people have a biological paternity. We have our biological parents, who bring us into this world, who make efforts and sacrifices to raise us and to whom we owe gratitude. Gratitude and honor, because, as God Himself commanded, we must honor our father and our mother. These are our natural, biological parents, who gave us the biological life we have. But man is not satisfied only with his biological birth; he needs something more.

And for this reason, in addition to his natural, biological family, man also has teachers and educators, outside his family as well. We send the child to school. There he will increase his knowledge and with this knowledge he will be able to know the world and respond to the needs of life. And in school and with our teachers, we don't only learn simple knowledge, but we also learn ways of behaving, so that outside of our family circle, we can connect and coexist with the wider society, with all people. Man, therefore, apart from his biological birth, needs something more. He needs education, pedagogy.

Therefore, we have many educators, says the Apostle Paul, but we do not have many fathers. Of course, we all have a biological father, but now the Apostle Paul adds another kind of father. He says "I am your father, because I have begotten you in Christ." You do not have many fathers, "for in Christ Jesus I have begotten you through the gospel." So, my beloved brothers and sisters, we have another kind of fatherhood—a new birth, which is neither our biological birth within the family nor the education we receive in school. It is something different.

What is this spiritual fatherhood? It is a great mystery and a great gift of God, and I would ask you to delve into it as much as we can. Why do we need this other fatherhood? Isn't it enough to have our natural parents, to have our teachers? Why do we need this special spiritual fatherhood? Our society has almost rejected it. We now think that the family and school are enough to make good people. However, my beloved brothers and sisters, this other fatherhood, of which the Apostle Paul speaks, is very important. Because our biological fatherhood, the one we got from our parents, from our physical father, has serious problems.

One problem is that this biological life that our parents give us is connected to death. We are born and at the same time we die. Our parents bring mortal beings into the world, people who are condemned from their very birth to die, to decay. Here, then, is where biological fatherhood does not give us life in its original, absolute form. Biological fatherhood also has another disadvantage—it is forced. It gives us a life that we did not choose. That is why we often hear children—in their teenage years, when the desire for freedom from the bonds of the family awakens in them—say: "And who asked me to be brought into the world?" We received life, which is a gift from God, a blessing from God, but it is forced; it does not contain our freedom. And our parents themselves, who gave us this life, gave it based on physical laws, which are impossible to avoid. We have to do, then, with a life which, apart from being mortal, is also forced; it is not free. And this biological fatherhood has one more disadvantage. It puts us in a closed family circle, in which if we remain trapped inside and do not leave it, then we become complacent, selfish, we only look at ourselves and our own and do not take into account that there are other people outside our family, and they all need our love. Therefore, we must overcome the limits of the biological family, and go further. Natural fatherhood traps us within the confines of the family.

We also have the educators, our teachers, to whom we must always be grateful, because they give us the provisions of life, but the knowledge they give us does not fully satisfy our existence. Man is not only mind, not only knowledge. Man wants other things as well. He wants love, he has feelings, he wants to create friendly relationships, loving relationships. School and teachers cannot provide all this. They go beyond the limits of pedagogy. Human life is a very broad thing, which cannot be enclosed within the family nor within the school. Man wants to overcome all these limits, to embrace the whole world. And all these, my beloved brothers and sisters, need a re-birth. We have to be born again, to be born freely now, without anyone forcing us, but to be born into another family, a wider family, in which there is no exclusion and no death. We need a life that does not die.

Thus, my beloved brothers and sisters, we need the fatherhood that the Apostle Paul speaks of—that is, we need spiritual fathers, who are outside our family and outside our school and who introduce us to new life, to this life that does not die, where Christ Himself is. "For in Christ Jesus I have begotten you through the gospel." So, when we are born in Christ and not simply as a biological person, then we have true life, a life that does not die and a life different from the one that the family and the school give us.

And what does this life contain, this life in Christ? To put it simply, it is to live as Christ lived. It is complex and difficult for anyone to cover it all, but I will mention to you only a couple of things that are special in the life of Christ, which we are also called to imitate in our new life.

Christ was born by emptying Himself of His divinity, and this kenosis means that we too, in order to be born again, must empty ourselves of everything that binds us to ourselves, that is, to self-love. The first step, therefore, in order to be able to live like the Lord, is to empty ourselves of our ego, of the ego that the family cultivates in us many times, because from young children we learn to be the center of attention and love. We must, therefore, discard this selfishness, self-centeredness, die to it, and be reborn in this way. And when we are born again, then we will be born like the Lord, to live not for ourselves but for others. Then we become people of love. And this love, while in the physical family it is limited to a certain circle, this love is now the love of Christ Himself, of God Himself for the world, and it is not exclusive, it does not exclude anyone; it embraces everyone. We must reach, therefore, a love that embraces the whole world: everyone, including sinners, our friends, and even our enemies. Then we are born again, we are born in Christ Jesus. Our person, our being, assumes and takes upon itself the whole world, just as Christ's existence assumed; He assumed the whole world and took it upon Himself. The saints achieve this, of course, with a lot of asceticism. And this is the ideal, which spiritual fatherhood gives us and not biological fatherhood. Therefore, our spiritual father, whom we always need, is the one who will guide us so that Christ is formed in us, so that we too become like Christ. To love and embrace the whole world, without any exclusion, and to take upon ourselves the sins of others, as Christ took them. This, my dear brothers and sisters, presupposes that we now enter another family, apart from the biological one. And here, my beloved brothers and sisters, is the great gift that God gave to all of us and which is called the Church.

The Church is the big family in which we overcome the exclusions that the biological family gives us. We are together with others, we coexist with everyone, both with friends and with enemies, and with those who are like us—the same race with the same language—as well as with others who do not have the same language, the same race. The Church makes no distinction. It is a big family, in which we free ourselves from the bonds and exclusions of the biological family.

That is why, my beloved brothers and sisters, God gives us a new life with our baptism, when He includes us in this family called the Church. And here Christ is formed in us; we become, as I said, open and take all people into our heart—the whole world and all of God's creation, including His material creation, everything. To love them, to embrace them.

And the Church teaches us this in two ways. First, with our spiritual fathers, who will direct us to free ourselves from the passions of our selfishness, our self-love, to uproot what is old in us and what is sinful, but also to experience God's great embrace, which embraces all of creation, and this is what the Church gives us with the Divine Liturgy, with the Eucharist.

What is the Divine Liturgy? It is the moment, my beloved brothers and sisters, when we all gather together regardless of our family relationships and we feel like brothers and loved ones—not only family members but also strangers, those we do not know, those standing next to us in the Divine Liturgy. We all become one body and within this body is our union with each other but also with God. And so our whole life, our existence, takes with it the material creation, because in the Divine Liturgy the material world also participates, and together with our brothers and sisters we all become a new body, a new family, which is not dominated by death but life, eternal life.

I pray, my beloved brothers and sisters, that we honor and respect and thank God for our biological parents, for our biological family, for our siblings, for our teachers, but not to limit ourselves there. I pray that we open our heart to the wider world, to learn to love everyone and everything. And only the great family called the Church will teach us this. Let us take care, my beloved brothers and sisters, to be faithful members of the Church, to cultivate within it this new life, this eternal life, which I hope God will grant us and the whole world to enjoy both now and eternally in His Kingdom. Amen.

In the Holy Monastery of Saint John the Baptist, Essex, England
August 17, 2014

55.
11th SUNDAY OF MATTHEW
Forgiveness as co-existence

Should you not also have had compassion on your fellow servant, just as I had pity on you? (Mt 18:23–35)

Today's Gospel passage, my brothers and sisters, contains a very simple but deeply shocking parable. It contains, I would say, the heart of the Gospel, and it concerns us all. It is as if it were written, as if it were said by the Lord, to each of us.

The Lord likened the Kingdom of God to a human kingdom, in which the king at some point comes and asks to settle accounts with his subjects, with his servants, and then a servant of his is presented, who owed him a thousand talents, a huge amount. The king says that he must pay this amount immediately, but he did not have it, and he replies, "Have patience with me," "Give me some time to pay it off," because otherwise the king would force him to sell his house, his wife, his children, everything he had. And the king had patience with him and wrote off the loan. But when this servant went out, he met one of his fellow servants, a brother, who owed him a hundred dinars—that is, a small amount. And then he turns and says to his brother: "You must pay me this immediately." He replies: "I don't have it. Please give me some time." No. You will pay it and, if you don't pay it, you will go to prison." And he put him in prison. The king found out about this and called this servant and said to him: "I wrote off all your debt. Shouldn't you have had mercy on your servant, just as I had mercy on you?" and gave orders to put him in prison with many tortures. And then, concludes the Lord, "This will happen to all of you, if you do not forgive your brothers' sins from your heart."

My beloved brothers and sisters, I said that this parable applies to all of us, because we are all debtors to God. Debtors of "ten thousand talents." It is not possible to calculate how much we owe God. We owe our existence, we owe this world, which He gave us to live in, we owe the fact that he gave us His own Son, to take us with Him into His Kingdom. And He forgave us, He forgave our sins, because if God judged us based on our sins, no one could be saved. The fact is, my dear brothers and sisters, that we are all sinners. We say it many times, we believe it perhaps, but we deny it every time we do not forgive our brother, every time we show hardness of heart towards him, every time we nurture it in our thoughts and ask for revenge, and every time we judge our brother, because we see him as more sinful than us. In all these cases, we deny what we always say, that "I am a sinner, I am the worst sinner of all." We constantly deny this in practice and in life, because we cannot completely forgive our brother. My beloved, the Lord's most difficult commandment is to forgive our brothers. And the Lord has set this commandment as a condition for our own sins to be forgiven. Let us pay attention to this. Even repentance is not enough for our sins to be forgiven if we do not forgive the sins of our brothers. "Forgive us our trespasses, as we forgive those who trespass against us," we say in the Lord's Prayer. This is a prerequisite. No matter how many virtues we have and, I repeat, no matter how much repentance we show, no matter how much we confess and receive the blessing of the Church for the forgiveness of our sins, they will not be forgiven if we do not forgive the sins of our brother.

The Lord is very stern when He imposes such a terrible punishment on this servant for not forgiving the debt of his fellow servant, his brother. And this forgiveness, says the Lord, must come from your hearts. That is, to uproot from our hearts every memory of the evil that our brother did to us, to forget it, to rid our hearts completely of the memory of evil. And not only that. When the Lord says "from your heart," he also means something positive, because the heart is the center of our love. In other words, we must not only not remember the evil that our brother did to us, but we must also put him in our hearts, to love him, to love our enemy. There is no higher commandment and teaching in the entire history of humanity than our Lord's teaching about loving our enemies. Everything else comes second. Here is the great revolution that the Lord brings. Here is the key to all problems, because if we forgive our enemies, there will no longer be evil in the world; it will be eliminated.

Usually, my brothers and sisters, we believe that by returning evil for evil, we strike and destroy evil. Evil never disappears with evil. It disappears only with good, with love, with forgiveness. And this is what it means to forgive your brother "from your heart."

However, one wonders, why is this so important? Of course, one obvious answer comes to mind. Because it is fair, since God forgives our sins, that we also forgive the sins of others. It is, therefore, a matter of justice. But it is something more, because Christ Himself forgave His enemies, His executioners. And we cannot follow Christ's teaching without getting there. It is easy to say that we follow Christ, but then part ways with him at the Cross, where He says: "Father, forgive them, for they do not know what they do" (Lk 23:34).

And forgiving our brother is also necessary for another important reason. Because in the Kingdom of God, in the end, in our future, we will be called to co-exist with our brother. And if we co-exist eternally with someone whom we have not accepted and forgiven, imagine, my beloved brothers and sisters, what suffering! This is hell! Because hell is not something imposed by God who punishes; it is something we create for ourselves, the moment we create the condition to be tortured eternally, because next to us there is someone whom we never wanted to have beside us in this life. The Greek word for forgiveness, my brothers and sisters, means literally to fit together with the other in the same space, to share the same space; unfortunately, all of life and history demonstrates that we don't do it. Geographically, we have divided the world into countries and nations, where we do not let the neighbor enter, to enter our own space. You will have noticed that this is similar to the behavior of dogs. Dogs, as you know, bark when they see another dog passing through their space, because they feel that the space belongs only to them. And that's why wars and conflicts happen, because we can't fit in the same space, on this earth, all together. We divided it and we clash over this division of the land.

But in the Kingdom of God, my brothers and sisters, all this will be abolished. The Kingdom of God will be one, and the world will be one. And we will all be called to stand next to each other—those whom we fought in this life, whom we expelled from our country, whom we sent as refugees. We will have them by our side, and then, my brothers and sisters, if we have not accepted them "from our heart," we will be tormented eternally because we have them by our side. You cannot live, my brothers and sisters, with someone you have not forgiven. It is the greatest torture. That's why we often say: "I forgive my brother, but I don't want to see him. I can't see him, I can't have him by my side." To have your brother next to you, to co-exist, to share your space with him, this means that you forgive. In the Kingdom of God, my brothers and sisters, there will be one place for all, and we will all co-exist; we must therefore begin this co-existence in this life.

My beloved brothers and sisters, we all have an enemy, we have all suffered injustice, we have all suffered slander, we have all been persecuted, we have been embattled. Here, my beloved brothers and sisters, our eternal life, our eternal existence is tested. How will we react to the evil that has befallen us? If we react with evil, we have eternally condemned ourselves. If we choose forgiveness, absolute forgiveness, to the extent that we love our enemy, then, my dear brothers and sisters, we anticipate the Kingdom of God from here and now, and this will follow us eternally.

This is why, my beloved brothers and sisters, I said that forgiving our brothers is the heart of the Gospel. And that is why I will conclude by mentioning what two of the great fathers of the Church say, the great theologian Saint Maximus the Confessor and Saint Anastasios Sinaitis. They lived around the same time, Saint Maximus a bit earlier, but they share the same spirit, the same tradition.

When Saint Maximus was asked in what way sins will be forgiven, which sins can be forgiven, he mentioned various ways and among them he said that if we do not judge our brother, then we will not be judged either, because this is what the Lord said: "Judge not, that you be not judged" (Mt 7:1). And the Lord, he says, does not lie. Just think that this alone is enough to lead us to the Kingdom of God!

And Saint Anastasios of Sinai says the same thing in one of his sermons. Addressing the faithful, he says that "you may say, 'I can't fast, I can't abstain, I can't imitate the great ascetics. What am I going to do; How will I be saved?" He tells them: "I will show you a way. Forgive your brother, and you will be forgiven."

It is no coincidence that the forgiveness of sins is so emphasized in the Gospel, the forgiveness of the sins of our brothers. Let us bear this in mind, my beloved brothers and sisters. It is not easy, especially if we want to reach the point that the Lord asks of us—to love our enemy. But this is the only sure way to our salvation. I pray, my brothers and sisters, that we will not be like the servant who did not forgive his brother, and thus avoid eternal punishment. Let us always keep in mind that God forgives us and it is our duty to forgive our brothers. Amen.

In the Holy Monastery of Saint John the Baptist, Essex, England
August 24, 2014

56.
12th SUNDAY OF MATTHEW
Keeping the commandments and the Kingdom of God (Mt 19:16–26)

The Gospel passage that we just heard, my dear brothers and sisters, describes the path that one must follow in order to reach the Kingdom of God and obtain eternal life.

A young man approaches the Lord and asks him: "What must I do to inherit eternal life?" The Lord gives him two answers, two steps he must follow. One is to keep all the commandments—the commandments of the Law, the commandments of the Old Testament—which the Lord Himself enumerates when the young man asks him: "Which commandments should I follow?" The second step is to sell all his possessions, all his property, give it to the poor and follow Him.

When the young man heard the first step, he said "I have kept all these things my whole life"—that is, all the Law and the commandments. However when he heard the second step, he was deeply troubled, it says, and he departed because he had a large fortune. My beloved brothers and sisters, let's delve as much as we can into the content of this gospel passage.

The first thing we must note is that keeping God's commandments is necessary for our salvation. It is the first step, the beginning, because if one does not keep the commandments of God, one cannot be saved. We cannot skip this step. The second point we must pay attention to is that even if we keep all God's commandments and all the Law, it does not mean that we will be saved. In fact, here we should be all the more careful, since not only are we not automatically saved when we keep God's commandments, but this can actually hinder our salvation. This will seem paradoxical to you. And yet, judging by the Lord's second step to the young man, we can conclude that one can keep God's commandment and yet still possibly lose the Kingdom of God. And this is for two reasons.

One is that it is possible, as was the case with the Pharisees, to keep the law and, by keeping the law, to feel self-sufficient and entitled to the Kingdom of God. This is what the Pharisees believed and that is why they saw themselves as righteous and justified in the Kingdom of God. They were certain that they would be saved and that all sinners, like the Tax Collector of the parable of the Publican and the Pharisee, would be condemned. By keeping the law, they acquired such pride, such self-righteousness, that it blocked their way to salvation. Because when one is sure that he, himself, with his own strength can gain salvation, he has lost salvation, as God is no longer necessary in his life. It may be enough for him that he managed to keep the Law, which is not easy of course, and when he succeeds, he can say that salvation is his own achievement and not the gift and grace of God.

But salvation, my beloved brothers and sisters, without God—salvation that comes from our own successes—is not true salvation and is not the Kingdom of God. See, then, that one can, like the Pharisees, lose eternal life and the Kingdom, if one stops observing God's commandments.

And the second reason is that in order for one to reach the Kingdom of God, it is not enough to keep certain commandments. One must take the same path that the Lord Himself took, that is, to go through the Cross. In order to travel the way of the Cross, one must deny one's own will, like the Lord in Gethsemane. In other words, one must empty oneself completely of all self-confidence—of the self-confidence that keeping the commandments can give—and abandon oneself completely to the mercy and grace of God. This is the way of the Cross.

This is the path that the Lord calls us to, to sacrifice everything we have and don't have, not only property—which is perhaps easy—but our will itself, which is very difficult. To lose our will and our instinct to protect our life and our existence. To be ready to lose our own life. This is the Cross.

If a man is not ready to give up his riches, how will he be ready to take up the Cross of Christ? How will he be ready to pass through the way of the Cross, which is not simply to lose one's possessions, but to lose oneself? Therefore, my beloved brothers and sisters, the path to salvation that the Lord showed the young man is more difficult than this pious Jew, who kept the law of the Old Testament, imagined.

Thus the Lord pronounced today in a very harsh way that the rich will enter the Kingdom of God with difficulty. It is easier for a camel to pass through the eye of a needle than for a rich man to enter the Kingdom of God. And when the Lord says this, we think that he does not mean us, who are not rich, but he says it about those who have too much. We, who do not have much, will enter the Kingdom of God. But the Lord never says something that concerns only a certain portion of people. What he says applies to all of us. "And how do these words of the Lord concern me, who have no wealth?" They concern me because the deepest meaning of these words is what I said before: whatever we have, we must be ready to give it up, to sacrifice it. "And if I have no wealth and have little?" Even these few things I must be ready to give up. "What if I don't have anything?" Well, I have my life, and I must be ready to give it up. So, my beloved brothers and sisters, all of us without exception are judged by these words of the Lord.

In the life of Saint Anthony, we find the story that when Anthony heard this Gospel passage, he was so shocked that he immediately ran and sold all his property, which was considerable, and left for the desert. But the same biography of our saint also says that when he sold everything and went to the desert, making that great struggle against evil, sin, and the demons, and became such a great ascetic, he said: "Everyone will go to heaven except for me."

We now come to the words spoken by the Lord's disciples in the passage. When the Lord told them these harsh words about the rich, and that they should leave everything, the disciples answered: "Who then can be saved?" Since even Anthony the Great cannot be saved by all that he has done, who will be saved? We should pay attention to the Lord's answer. He looks at them and says: "With humans this is impossible." Salvation is impossible to achieve by man himself. "But with God all things are possible." Salvation is possible only through God's intervention.

So, what does all this mean, my beloved brothers and sisters? It means that, one, we must keep the law with God's commandments, and two, that we should not consider what we have as our own, but be ready to give it up, as the saints, martyrs, and the faithful gave up their very lives. But again, let us not believe that without God's mercy and grace we will be saved.

We cannot earn salvation; it is the grace and gift of the Lord. That is why it is called "Grace."[1] It is something that someone gives us; it is not something that we can earn. "But with God all things are possible." Because God's grace and mercy truly can bless our effort, our initiative, and the offering of our very selves with everything we have. God will receive all this with his grace and bless it and accept it, and offer us in turn our salvation, eternal life, and His Kingdom, which I pray the Lord gives to us all. Amen.

September 3, 2006

[1] In Greek, this word χάρις also means *gratis* or free.

57.
16th SUNDAY OF MATTHEW
(Parable of the Talents)
(Mt 25:14–30)

In the Gospel passage that we heard, my dear brothers and sisters, there is a very strange phrase of the Lord: "For to everyone who has, more will be given, and he will have abundance; but from him who does not have," God will take back what He gave him.[1]

God created man to make him His representative on earth. And just as God Himself is a creator, so He also wants man to be a creator. And He gave him the ability to create, to co-create with Him. And the parable we heard in today's gospel passage is based on this truth. God gave talents to people. He gave them from His property,[2] says the parable. He didn't give them something that wasn't His. And He did not give them anything that belonged to them. The talents He gave them are from His property; that is, He gave them to His servants to increase them, to manage them, but not to appropriate them.

Whatever talents, whatever gifts we have as humans, they do not belong to us! They belong to God, from whom they come. Whether these are natural gifts or spiritual gifts, nothing belongs to us! And the terrible phenomenon is that we appropriate these gifts. We brag about our talents and, most importantly, we use them as we see fit and without offering them "with thanksgiving"[3] to the One Who gave them to us.

Here, then, is the first important point in today's parable: God gave us His property and this means that He gave us something of Himself, that whatever we have are gifts, they are energies of God Himself, which He grants us so that we too can become a kind of god on earth.

[1] Cf. Mt 25:29.
[2] τὰ ὑπάρχοντα, lit. "the existing things." Cf. Mt 25:14.
[3] ἐν εὐχαριστίᾳ. Cf. Col 2:7.

The parable also tells us that God gave these talents to everyone. It is not mentioned anywhere that He left some without any talents. He gave them to everyone. Whether he gave us a lot or a little or only one, we have all been loaned these talents. Everyone has received something. At the very least, everyone has received their very existence, the fact that they exist. And this is perhaps the greatest talent, the greatest gift, that God has given us. This existence of ours—this is what God wants us to cultivate, so that it multiplies, becomes greater, and in this way God is glorified through our own existence.

How many talents He gives to each person is His own affair; God is not bound by our presuppositions, nor by some objective evaluation, who deserves more and who deserves less. He decides with His absolute, free will who will get five talents, who will get two, who will get one. Consequently, there is no objective or moral evaluation for the talents, the gifts that God gives. He can give gifts to people who, according to our judgment, are not worthy of them. And it is possible that those people we think should have His particular gifts, do not get them. God's judgment regarding the distribution of gifts is not objective. He is absolutely free; it is His affair. His talents are His, He gives what He wants to whom He wants.

What unfolds in today's Gospel passage is truly shocking. The one who received the five talents, when the Lord comes to ask for an account of what he did—and this is very important and we must keep this in mind, because an account will be asked for the talents we have received. We will not be left unaccountable as to what we did with God's talents. So he would received the five talents multiplied them and presented his master with another five. He who received two multiplied them and presented them to his master. And finally he who received one talent returns it to his master without having multiplied it. And he does this while blaming the Lord: "I did not dare to increase this talent because I know that you are cruel and you ask for an account and you ask to reap where you did not sow and, consequently, I thought that it was better to conserve it, to put it in the ground and to give it back to you as you gave it to me." And then the wrath of the Lord is really shocking. He leaves no room for mercy towards the useless slave. He immediately orders that he be delivered to the fires of hell and punished there eternally. And this is shocking because it means, my dear brothers and sisters, that God attaches great importance to what we do in this life with the talents He has given us. And it is important because the goal in giving us the talents is not to keep them for ourselves; it is not to conserve them. It is to increase them, to give them to others. This is the purpose for which we are given the talents. And, therefore, the Lord is angry when He gives us these talents and we do not take advantage of them. There is no gift, my beloved brothers and sisters, that we are not called to cultivate ourselves. Our own existence, the world around us, and our natural environment—all these were given to us by God to cultivate. Not to conserve them. Conservation is, many times, something we brag about. We say "he is a conservative man." What does that mean? It means he takes the truths of the Gospel and conserves them. But this is not God's will. It is not the conservation of the truths of the Gospel that God is asking for. It is their cultivation and transmission, it is to pass these truths through our very being, to cultivate them, to interpret them, to offer them to the world. Not as they are, but as the world needs them in every era. That is precisely why, in this way, the slave who received the one talent is eternally condemned. Because he conserved it, he put it in the ground, and because he did not cultivate it, he did not increase it.

Thus, we are, my beloved brothers and sisters, accountable to God. And none of us are exempt from this. There is no one who will not have to give an account for what he received from God. Human life is a life of continuous work. The Lord once said "My Father is working until now, and I am working" (John 5:17). Laziness has no place in the life of a Christian; we cannot rest in what we have received and what we have. We must toil, work, and increase what God has given us.

What a glorious mission this is, my brothers and sisters! God calls us to become like Him, creators in His creation, and to increase everything He has given us. God's expectation that we will increase our talents is so important that, as we have seen, our eternal future, our eternal life is judged by it. And if we don't pay attention to it, and if we leave this life fruitless, then all that remains for us is eternal punishment and eternal hell, because conserving God's talents is a self-serving action. It is in fact such a self-serving action and attitude that we don't really have a place in the Kingdom of God.

These are my thoughts on today's Gospel passage, my brothers and sisters. And let us remember that we are called, as I said, not only to share the specific gifts God has given us, but to give away our very selves, our lives, our very existence. Let us give it away so that we can claim it forever. This is man's calling! To be a creator with God and increase the talents given to us by Him.

Let us pay attention and make no excuses and, above all, let us not blame God himself, saying either that He has not given us any talent or that He is so demanding that it is better to conserve the talent that He gave us? In this way, my brothers and sisters, we will really be able to acquire a place in the Kingdom of God, because the Kingdom of God will itself be a continuous offering and giving back, an ever-increasing giving back of the gifts that God has given us. It will be something like the Holy Eucharist that we celebrate every Sunday, every Divine Liturgy, where all we do is give back God's gifts to Him, but only after we first pass them through our hands, through the labor of our hands—after we make the wheat into *prosphora*,[4] after we make the grapes into wine, after we cultivate and offer this whole gift of God. We do not offer God's gifts back to Him the same as He gave them to us. We offer them after they have passed through the work of our own hands. And this is extremely significant, because in the Divine Liturgy what we offer is nothing less than our own effort, our own labor. In this way, we recognize that everything we have belongs to God and we are accountable to Him, and to Him we should offer everything "with thanksgiving."

These are the challenges posed to us today by the Gospel passage. I pray that we pay attention to them and conform our lives according to the dictates of the Gospel.

Church of Saint Dimitrios, Kifissia

[4] The bread of oblation.

58.
17th SUNDAY OF MATTHEW
(Canaanite Woman)
Concerning faith and freedom

O woman, great is your faith! Be it done for you as you desire (Mt 15:21–28)

Today's gospel passage, my beloved brothers and sisters, is truly shocking. The Lord, travelling to the region of Tire and Sidon, crosses outside the borders of Judea and there he meets a Canaanite woman from a region where no Jews lived, and this woman followed him and cried: "Have mercy on me, O Lord, Son of David; my daughter is severely possessed by a demon." The Lord, however, did not pay any attention to her shouting. He moved on as if He did not hear her. And as if this were not enough, the disciples say to the Lord: "Send her away, for she is crying after us." Here, then, are the first two shocking elements of this narrative (Mt 15:21–28).

The Lord, this merciful God, who came to alleviate people's pain and to wipe away their tears, the one who came to save man, appears to be indifferent to this request, to this women's cry of despair. And if that were not enough: the disciples themselves treat her in the same way, and thus the Lord and his disciples appear not only to avoid this woman's request but to treat it with indifference.

However, there is another shocking element in this narrative. When the disciples said to the Lord, "send her away, because she is bothering us," the Lord opens a dialogue with the Canaanite woman and says: "I was sent only to the lost sheep of the house of Israel [...]. It is not good to take the children's bread and throw it to the dogs." "I came only for the Israelites, to save the people of God, and therefore I cannot take the bread from the children and throw it to the dogs." This attitude is surprising and shocking. Not only does he avoid her request, but he also calls her a dog.

The Canaanite woman's reaction is equally shocking. She is not offended. She does not react in a way that shows that she is humiliated by the Lord's words. Rather, she answers: "Yes, Lord, yet even the dogs eat the crumbs that fall from their masters' table." "Therefore, treat me like a dog that licks up the crumbs which fall from the owners' table, and I will be satisfied with that." Then the Lord cries out: "O woman, great is your faith. Let it be unto you as you desire." And, of course, her daughter was then instantly healed.

Do you ever wonder, my beloved brothers and sisters, why the Lord acted this way, and why our faith must go through so many trials in order to be pleasing to God and bear its fruit? Let's delve deeper into this question, because it is very important for all of us and for our lives.

Faith must first pass through humiliation. We have a misunderstood concept of faith. We think that faith is simply admitting that God exists and that, in any case, as many say: "I am not an atheist, I recognize the existence of a higher power." But even the demons, says the Holy Bible, recognize this, and the demons know that there is a God.

Saying that God exists does not mean that you believe. To really believe you have to empty yourself of yourself, of your self-assurance. If you have self-assurance, then why do you need faith? Why should you believe in God, since you believe in yourself, since you believe in your powers? Today's man has already abandoned his faith, even if he confesses it many times in public. He thinks he holds everything in his hands. He will organize life and history as he thinks best.

This is our current culture, which is based on man's power, his self-assurance that he can do everything. So, what do we need faith for? How can there be faith when we have confidence in ourselves? But this is exactly what humility is: to shake our trust in ourselves to the point where we empty ourselves of ourselves so that God can fit inside. See, then, that humility is a necessary condition for faith. You cannot say "I believe" if you do not go through humiliation. This woman, the Canaanite, went through exactly this humiliation. The Lord allowed and caused this test of her humility to show if she really believed.

Another reason why the Lord allowed the Canaanite woman to undergo this trial is that faith needs patience. It is not possible to say that one believes if one's faith does not pass through the furnace of patience. Because we want what we believe and want to happen, to happen when we want it. But patience is the only way to show that we really believe. Even when the things we ask for do not come, we continue to believe that they will come. This is what is called in theological language an "eschatological orientation"—to believe, like the saints of the Old Testament, that the Lord is coming, that the Messiah will come, that the Kingdom of God will come, and even if it is not visible, evil will be defeated, death will be defeated. Patience is necessary for faith.

The third and most important thing, my brothers and sisters, is that true faith must follow the same path that our Lord followed, which means going through Gethsemane and ultimately the Cross, when His Father abandoned Him: "*Eli, Eli, lama sabachthani?* My God, My God, why have You forsaken Me?" (Mt 27:46). This abandonment by God, to feel that God has left you, is the greatest test of faith. And the Lord, despite being abandoned by His Father, remains faithful unto death.

So, paradoxically, when we feel that God has abandoned us and is not hearing us, this is often a sign that His grace is with us. He has not abandoned us. God does not abandon us until the end and then He only abandons us in order to set us free.

When you follow God and you see Him being present and giving you all His gifts, then it is almost necessary to believe, and it would be quite unreasonable not to believe. However, when you continue to believe despite the fact that you do not see any evidence of God's presence—when He has abandoned you—then you truly believe freely, and God wants us to have a free faith, not a faith that He Himself elicits, and this leads Him to the point of abandoning us. However, this abandonment is salvific, if this is how we finally come out as truly faithful believers.

Such is the faith, my brothers and sisters, of today's Canaanite woman. She passed through the furnace—the furnace of humiliation, the furnace of patience, the furnace of abandonment by God. And just look at how she reacts to all this. She does not abandon her request for help, but neither does she demand it as if God owed her what she was asking for. She asks for it as a gift, absolute grace. She does not deserve it. She asks for it even when everything seemed to indicate that she wasn't going to get it. This is the faith of the Canaanite woman that made the Lord exclaim: "O woman, great is your faith!"

All throughout our lives, my brothers and sisters, our faith is being constantly tested. And many times, we seem very weak in our faith. Many times we are shaken. Many times abandonment by God leads us to abandon God ourselves, and this abandonment of God on our part is our final destruction, because God, respecting our freedom, will never oblige us to return to Him again.

So, we have in our hands this great and powerful weapon called freedom. With this we can be saved and with this we can be destroyed. This is how God made man, giving him freedom. God did not think "It is better not to give him freedom because he might destroy himself, so it's better not to put this weapon in his hands", but on the contrary he thought: "Even if man uses this weapon against himself, he deserves to have it, he must have it"—because this is the characteristic of God Himself, absolute freedom.

So we journey through life with this freedom, and our faith will always be tested by it. Blessed are those who will be able to keep the faith freely when it seems that God has abandoned them, when they go through trials and cannot bear them, when everything fades away, when what happened to the Lord happens to them and He cried out on the Cross "Why have you abandoned me?" Blessed are these people, because within them is hidden God and His grace, and if they keep the faith through this trial, then God will show all His love and all His grace to them.

The saints passed along this road, my brothers and sisters. They did not become holy without going through this road, without feeling many times the abandonment of God's grace, without feeling that they themselves have no power, and that God is not with them. And with this furnace of the experience of being abandoned by God they became holy. And in this way they deserved to see God Himself, to receive His grace and to be sure that, whatever happens, God is there for them and for the whole world. God is now the one in whom man believes freely, since his faith has already been tested in difficulty times by his freedom.

So the Canaanite woman, my beloved brothers and sisters, is an example for all of us, an example of faith. Let us keep this example in our hearts. Every time we feel that God does not hear our prayers, that He does not give us what we ask, let our faith not be shaken. Let us be absolutely sure that God always hears us, always loves us, but awaits our free faith. He wants to see if we freely love Him and believe in Him, not because He gives us what we want, but because we really believe in Him and love Him for that alone.

So God wants a free faith that matches the love we have for Him, so that God does not turn into a tool that we use to gratify our desires and needs. For God to remain, let us love Him freely and may He love us freely. Let us take this example with us, my brothers and sisters, because life always has such trials in store for us and it is good that we have the Canaanite woman as our guide in these difficult times. Amen.

February 9, 2003

59.
SUNDAY OF THE HOLY FATHERS OF THE 4th ECUMENICAL COUNCIL
On fatherhood (Mt 5:14–19)

This Sunday, my beloved brothers and sisters, is dedicated to the memory of the fathers who convened the Fourth Ecumenical Council in Chalcedon in 451 AD. They handed down to us the complete "Christological doctrine"— that is, that the Lord is perfect God and perfect man and that the person of the Lord is the Son and Word of God, "One of the Holy Trinity."

On this occasion, we are called to consider what is "fatherhood" within the Church, and why does our Church rely so much on the fathers? Our Orthodox Church in particular relies on the holy fathers, who handed down to us the correct faith, and believes that these fathers do not belong only to the past but continue to emerge throughout the centuries, in every era. Fatherhood is an essential characteristic of the nature of the Orthodox Church and without fatherhood there is no Church, because there is also no salvation.

There are two kinds of fatherhood in our lives: physical or biological fatherhood and spiritual fatherhood. Physical parentage is what brings us into existence biologically. None of us can come into being without fatherhood. We all have our natural fathers. However, natural paternity is not enough for us to be saved, because nature itself has such defects that it cannot secure our salvation. Let us see these defects so that we can understand how necessary spiritual fatherhood is.

Physical, biological paternity is connected with death; it brings mortal beings to life. The psalmist David says in the 50th psalm: "in sins my mother bore me." We are born in sins, not because there is any moral problem in this birth, not because this birth is sinful in itself, but because it does not give true life, it gives false life. It gives life that is doomed to die. Therefore, if we remain only in physical parentage, we cannot secure true life.

Physical paternity is also flawed because it is coercive. We do not come into the world freely, we come under compulsion. And many times teenagers at their critical age say "And who asked me and brought me into the world?", because really it is a forced existence, which is given to us by our biological fathers. Physical paternity is also an exclusive paternity, limited to only a few persons. The physical father cannot include in his paternity all the children of the world or all the people. Enormous spiritual problems arise in physical fatherhood because the physical father is only or primarily interested in his physical child, and neglects or ignores others. We must love not only our own, not only our family, but all people. We must love in order to free ourselves from the limitations of biological fatherhood.

So, my brothers and sisters, we need a different fatherhood, which will give us our existence, and this is the spiritual father. We call it spiritual, not because it is opposed to the biological, but because it is fatherhood in the Holy Spirit, and that is precisely where its meaning lies. What does it mean to be a father in the Holy Spirit? In the Bible, the Holy Spirit is basically associated with three things. One is freedom. The Apostle Paul says: "where the Spirit of the Lord is, there is liberty" (2 Cor 3:17). Therefore, spiritual fatherhood is based on freedom. Many times, spiritual fathers are tempted to exercise some kind of power and coercion on their spiritual children. The role of the spiritual father is to leave his spiritual child free to make the responsible decision whether to follow his advice or not to follow it and which path to take. Of course, there are cases where spiritual children do not feel free under their spiritual fathers. But "where the Spirit of the Lord is, there is liberty." And this is the great thing about having a spiritual father: the spiritual child knows that nothing forces him to follow the path that his spiritual father shows him.

The Holy Spirit is also connected in the Bible with communion. You hear it every time in the Divine Liturgy: "The grace of our Lord Jesus Christ, and the love of God, and the communion of the Holy Spirit." Where the Holy Spirit blows, good Christians are not simply created; holiness is not the individual property of anyone. Holiness belongs to the body of the Church, and where the Holy Spirit blows, it creates members of the Church; it creates people who draw their holiness from the body of the Church, the body of saints headed by the one and only Holy of Holies.

Spiritual fatherhood aims to incorporate us into this communion of the Church. It is not by chance, my brothers and sisters, that our tradition associated this word, this term, "father," with the clergy and indeed, initially, with the bishop, because, as Saint Ignatius says, he sits in the place of God, in the type of the Father, and because he feeds us with the Divine Eucharist of Christ. Subsequently, the term "father" was given also to the priests, who within the Church, as representatives of the bishops, impart life to its members. Every spiritual leader in the Church becomes the father of spiritual children.

Outside the body of the Church, there is no spiritual fatherhood, because through it the Holy Spirit makes us members of the Church. And this begins with baptism; first we are incorporated into the body of the Church and then the love of God provides us with food for eternal life through our spiritual fathers. The Holy Spirit is connected with the end, with the Kingdom of God, with eternity. It brings to life beings who do not die like biological beings. The relationship is eternal and creates children for eternity, which begins with this life and lasts forever. If we remain only in biological parentage, no matter how perfect it is, no matter how successful the family is, one day we will die, we will be lost. We need the other fatherhood and sonship to find salvation and life, for our world to live.

Our culture, especially in these times, is going through a profound crisis, a fatherhood crisis in general. The crisis of spiritual fatherhood also affects physical fatherhood. We have abolished spiritual fatherhood; therefore, the biological one is also collapsing. Our society is a parricidal society. That is, we live in a society that wants to dissolve every bond, every common relationship where someone is recognized as first, some authority. Today we abolish authorities and providers. But someone gives us everything we have. Someone gives us physical or spiritual existence.

Someone gave us life. Why are we disregarding these persons? Why do we ignore them? We owe them deep gratitude.

Modern society has lost the concept of the gift. Everything has been leveled. Equality has become the ideal of the modern era. If society recognizes a superior who provides, it feels lost. This is how the concepts of obedience and submission also disappeared. These are considered a weakness, and society tries to get rid of them.

By the term "patristic Church"—which aptly defines the Orthodox Church—we do not simply mean that the Church is based on the teaching of the fathers, but that it is nourished by spiritual fatherhood, which gives it existence. This fatherhood is a gift from God and does not depend on us; our value is given to us by the One Who loves us infinitely.

Let us properly cultivate this spiritual, paternal relationship and let us freely surrender to it. Amen.

July 14, 2002

60.

SUNDAY OF THE HOLY FATHERS OF THE 4th ECUMENICAL COUNCIL

The applied life of the Gospel

But he who does them and teaches them shall be called great in the kingdom of heaven.

This Sunday, my beloved brothers and sisters, is dedicated to the fathers of the Church who convened the Fourth Ecumenical Council in Chalcedon, near Constantinople, in 451 AD. For this festive occasion, the Church has selected the Gospel passage that we just heard, which is full of profound meaning, which I would like to explore with you.

The Lord addresses His disciples and calls them "the light of the world." Light has many properties, and all these properties apply to the case of the Lord's disciples. Light is that which reveals the truth. When the light shines, the lie is exposed, and the light that shines from Christ through His disciples exposes every lie, every false teaching. Light also has the ability to reveal the secrets of our hearts. When the light shines, we cannot hide anything from ourselves. The Lord says elsewhere that people hate the light, precisely because they want to hide their deeds (cf. John 3:19). But when the light shines, then their hidden and inner selves are fully revealed.

Light also has the property of giving life. Look at the sun, which is light; it is at the same time a source of life and all beings turn to the sun to draw life from it. The light of the sun and the truth of Christ give life; it is not just a theoretical teaching, it is something from which we draw life. This light which emanates from Christ and is emitted by his disciples is identical with the preaching of God's commandments. Whoever, says the Gospel we heard, obeys these commandments will become great in the

Kingdom of God. The truth of the Gospel is not, I repeat, theory; it is action and application of God's commandments.

Another important element, which the passage we heard reminds us, is that this light, when it shines, does not shine for our own glory, but to glorify our Father in heaven. Christ's disciples do not think of their own glory. There is a great temptation, when we preach the Gospel of Christ, to glorify ourselves. But Christ's disciples must reject this temptation. The glory belongs only to God; it is not possible to glorify the one who preaches or the one who transmits the truth of the Gospel. And the genuine disciple of Christ must always proceed with this spirit.

Finally, the passage we heard ends with this ideal combination of action and teaching. And this combination is not for everyone; it is for some. That is why the Lord says that whoever combines these two—that is, whoever experiences in his life the application of God's commandments—will live the Gospel, and at the same time will teach it, and "he shall be called great in the kingdom of heaven." This, brothers and sisters, aptly characterizes the fathers of the Church, whom we celebrate today. The fathers of the Church are great in the Kingdom of God, they are glorious together with the glory of God, because they not only lived the Gospel but also taught it, and they not only taught it but also lived it. And this combination, so difficult and rare, which the grace of God grants to certain people, characterizes the fathers of the Church. The fathers are great teachers, who, however, were not contemplatives and philosophers who sat in their library and came to know the truth through study. They experienced the truth, they experienced God Himself, the relationship between man and God, and thus they enriched their experience. The fathers we honor today, the 630 fathers who gathered at the Fourth Ecumenical Council, revealed to us and taught us the great mystery of Christ. They revealed to us that our Lord is a perfect God but also a perfect man, that in His person human nature and the divine nature are *united without confusion nor change, without division nor separation*. And although this seems quite theoretical, these fathers experienced it and they invite all of us to experience it in the Church, where each one of us is called to unite his own human nature with the nature of God, in Christ—a union which takes place primarily in two ways.

First, by submitting our will to the will of God, which means asceticism and purification. And secondly, by uniting ourselves with Christ—our human nature with God, in Christ—in the mystery of the Eucharist, where our nature is truly united with the divine nature in the person of Christ. The fathers of the Church at Chalcedon, through this experience, were able to formulate this great teaching of the mystery of Christ. So the teaching of the Church fathers, and specifically this teaching of the Fourth Ecumenical Council, not only concerns specialized theologians, dogmatic theologians; it is something that concerns us all, because we are all called to this mystery that is revealed by the mystery of Christ—that is, the union of human and divine nature. We are called to experience this in the way I told you.

My brothers and sisters, we live in a patricidal age. People no longer want fatherhood. And in English there is a word that has a negative connotation, when we say that someone "patronizes" someone else; it is bad to act like a father to someone else. Truly, as Dostoyevsky said, our age is patricidal. In the Christian world, the Protestants killed the fathers, saying: "We will study the Holy Bible directly, we will find the truth there, and we don't need the fathers." As a result, each of them became a Church father; each of them interpreted the Holy Scripture as they wanted, and thus there were many fathers. And I am afraid that even our brothers, the Roman Catholics—who respect the fathers, who study the fathers—when, in the final analysis, they leave it to the head of their Church to decide such matters based on his putative infallibility, then they indirectly abolish the fathers.

Our Orthodox Church, my brothers and sisters, is the Church of the fathers. For us, our guides are the Church fathers—first, those officially recognized as Church fathers, the fathers we honor today who are irreplaceable. No one can replace them and no one can correct them; they are authentic teachers and we are called simply to follow them. But God gives fathers of the Church in every era. Every age has its fathers, except that these fathers are the children of the great fathers, and if they are not faithful children of the great fathers, they are not proper fathers. We are therefore called, my brothers and sisters, to honor and study the fathers of the Church, but also the contemporary fathers whom God gives us in our lives from time to time, as faithful interpreters of the fathers of the Church, to honor and recognize them.

We must learn, my brothers and sisters, to be children. The world is full of fathers today. Everyone is an authority on almost all subjects. We have destroyed this hierarchy of life and society, and in this way we are now starting to level everything in the Church as well; this is a great danger. Our Church, my brothers and sisters, I repeat, is the Church of the fathers and of fatherhood, of spiritual fatherhood.

When we follow this spirit of the humble study of the fathers of the past—as well as the fathers in our contemporary life—then, my brothers and sisters, we will also be able to hope with the grace and mercy of God, not that we will become great in the Kingdom of God, as the Gospel we heard today says about the few chosen fathers, but that we will at least be small in the Kingdom of God. Even being little in the Kingdom of God, but close to the great fathers, is an enormous blessing. This I pray for all of us, my brothers and sisters. Amen.

61.
SUNDAY OF THE HOLY FATHERS OF THE 4th ECUMENICAL COUNCIL
The true light and the life of the world (Mt 5:14–19)

This Sunday, my beloved brothers and sisters, is dedicated to the memory of the holy fathers who convened the Fourth Ecumenical Council in Chalcedon in 451 AD. The Church has chosen the Gospel passage that we just heard to make us think more deeply about a truth that is of great importance for our salvation and for the life of the whole world.

The Lord likens his disciples to light: "You are the light of the world." Why does the Lord choose this metaphor? If we think more deeply about this question, we will see that light is essential for many reasons.

One reason is that the light allows us to know the truth. When there is no light, all beings are dark and this creates confusion as to existence, as to who exists and who does not exist. It creates confusion as to what is true and what is false. And this confusion is pervasive in human life. Too many things are confused. So we need light so that we can distinguish, so that we can know what the truth of things is. The light is not something that has to do with our knowledge; in other words, it does not enlighten our minds to understand the truth of things. It has to do with the things themselves. The light shines on them and then we understand what is true and what is false. Therefore, light is needed not only to illuminate our minds, but to illuminate the whole world, all beings.

But light is not only the way by which we can know the truth of beings, the truth of things; it is also the way by which beings, things exist and live. Light is not only something that reveals to us the truth of beings, but it is also something that gives life to beings; it has vital energy. It is like the sun, which, by shining on the earth, not only helps us to distinguish beings from each other, but also gives the beings life, existence, energy. Consequently, light, when it is limited only to the revelation of truth without giving us life, is not vital, it is not the light we need.

Light also has the property of leaving nothing dark, nothing hidden. Wherever it shines, it clearly manifests the truth. This is very important, because we humans have a tendency to keep dark compartments inside our souls, not to expose them to the light, and for this reason the light is often annoying and unwanted. We try to hide in the dark so that the light does not shine on us and reveal our secret thoughts, our secret desires, many times our secret actions.

However, as the Lord said in today's Gospel passage: "Nor do they light a lamp and put it under a basket, but on a lampstand, and it gives light to all who are in the house." The light cannot be true and yet be hidden and not have the property of revealing everything that is hidden. It is the light, as we heard from the mouth of the Lord, that shines on the whole world. He tells the disciples: "You are the light of the world." The light is not limited to certain individuals; it is not limited to certain peoples; it is not limited to certain races. It is universal. It is independent of our ethnic and racial and linguistic differences and biases. The light of Christ, the light that the disciples are called to emit, refers to all people without distinction. It is universal and whoever limits it to certain individuals, to certain peoples, is not referring to the light of Christ, but to a human light.

However, it is characteristic, my brothers and sisters, that while the Lord calls His disciples "the light of the world," in other cases He spoke of Himself as the light of the world: "I am the light of the world" (John 8:12). And this leads us to the observation that the disciples of the Lord are light, not because they have light within themselves, but because they are united with the light that is Christ. And from this union with Christ, "the true Light which gives light to every man coming into the world"—as we also say in a prayer from the First Hour—we derive the quality of being the "light of the world." The Lord also says in today's Gospel passage that to be "the light of the world" has an ultimate purpose, which is to glorify our Father in heaven. It is not a light for us to project ourselves. And Christ Himself, as the light of the world, glorified His Father. "I have glorified You on the earth" (John 17:4), He says in the high priestly prayer. Finally, all the light that shines on us is directed to the Father, to the glory of God. Because light, my beloved brothers and sisters, if it does not come from God and does not return to God, is a created light, as we say, a natural light, the light of nature.

The light of nature gives me life, it gives truth, but at the same time it also gives shadows. There is no natural light that does not simultaneously produce a shadow. There is, therefore, no true light in creation. If we humans want to illumine the world or shed light either with the progress of science or with our philosophy or even with our theology, then we are not shedding true light; it is a light that has shadows. In secular art, the shadow always plays a big role in a painting. On the contrary, in a Byzantine icon, the light does not leave shadows, because it shines from outside creation, it comes from outside. So the light needs to not be ours, not to be from this world, to be, as we say in the language of theology, an uncreated light.

So when the Lord says to His disciples "You are the light of the world," He means that they have the uncreated light and with this light—not natural light—they illumine the world. In this way, by attributing all the light to God and not to the natural creation, another important lesson is proven: that the more we give in, the more we recede, the more we allow the light to spread.

A very typical example is Saint John the Baptist and Forerunner, about whom the Holy Gospel records these important words: "He was not that Light, but was sent to bear witness of that Light" (John 1:8). He wasn't that light. And his awareness that he was not the light was so deep that he said that he now had to recede because the real light had come. "He must increase, but I must decrease" (John 3:30). And this is precisely what made him a light. So the more we remove ourselves from the spotlight, the more humble we are, the more the light of God comes and illumines us and makes us part of it.

On the contrary, when we shine the spotlight on ourselves, then the light of God recedes. Because the light, my brothers and sisters, by giving life, simultaneously gives and reveals something much more important, love. He who loves does not promote himself but rather the person he loves; he sacrifices his will in order to promote the will of the one he loves. The light of Christ, the light of which the Lord speaks today, is interwoven with humility and love. And so one cannot say that he illumines the world if he promotes himself, if he has not cut off his own will and has not identified it with the will of the One he loves.

The fathers of the Church whom we honor today, my brothers and sisters, never wanted to promote themselves. They were truly genuine successors of the disciples of Christ, because the purpose and all their teaching had to do with the promotion of Christ alone. Indeed, above all the fathers of the Fourth Ecumenical Council, whom we honor today, did not want to teach and promote anything else but the true Christ. Who is the real Christ? The teaching of the Fourth Ecumenical Council is profound and I will not occupy you with all its aspects. I would just like to underline two things that are directly related to our existence and our salvation.

The fathers of the Fourth Ecumenical Council, by teaching us that Christ is perfect God and perfect man, shed light on our existence, and this light reveals to us two great truths: that man can neither exist nor be saved as man unless he unites with God. If man remains autonomous, with only his own human nature, then the concept of man is lost. He is not truly human, but ends up rather with the nature of animals; he is led to death. But when he is united with the nature of God, then he overcomes death, and lives really and truly—then he is a true man.

In the person of Christ, the two natures are united: the divine and the human. And this is not for any other reason, my brothers and sisters, but for our salvation. Because only uniting our nature with the nature of God can make us true people and give us the possibility to overcome the limits of our creation, among which the most tragic is death itself. That is why our Church, my brothers and sisters, constantly offers us this possibility, to unite our nature with the nature of God in the person of Christ. This happens especially in the Eucharist. When we partake of the body and blood of the Lord, we become "partakers of the divine nature" (2 Pet 1:4), our nature is united with the nature of Christ, God, and thus we can live truly and eternally.

The other truth that comes from the teaching of the fathers we honor today is that this union of the two natures, our nature with God's nature, does not create confusion. The two natures are not confused, we do not cease to be human; we are not absorbed by the divine nature. With His union with us, God does not want to absorb us. He leaves us free, He leaves us to distinguish ourselves from him. According to the fathers of the Fourth Ecumenical Council, in the person of Christ the divine and the human nature are united inseparably but "unconfused." Any confusion—as maintained for example by the Monophysites, whom this Council condemned—would mean that man would cease to be man, being absorbed by the nature of God and thus losing his freedom.

Man, my brothers and sisters, wants his freedom, he wants to be a man, but he thinks that he achieves this when he is separated from God, when he opposes God. Then man becomes autonomous and has the impression that he is now free, since he can reject God Himself. This was the great fallacy of the first man, a fallacy that has continued throughout the ages and which often takes the form of professed atheism, but almost always is implied in our actions and lives, every time we project our own our will and want to show that we can exist as free people obeying our own will and not the will of God.

Every time this happens, the fall of man is repeated, that is, the separation between God and man is repeated. This is how man's whole problem is created: cut off from God and autonomous, he can neither overcome death nor overcome nature and creation in a satisfactory way. All of our culture's dead ends are due to man's autonomy.

So, my brothers and sisters, the light shed by the fathers we honor today has a direct relationship with our daily life, with the life of the whole world. These fathers were ecumenical teachers. The truths they taught are important for the life of the world and not just for the knowledge of a few. God does not reveal Himself,

He does not shed His light so that only a few may know it. He shines it so that the world may live, all people of all times, wherever they may be. What the fathers teach is relevant to everyone, in all times, in all aspects of life. I would even say that they have a relationship not only with humans but also with inanimate beings.

The light that the fathers shed, which is the light of God Himself, gives life to all of us. It is enough for us to understand that only when we reflect this light are we real light. And when we have the impression that we can illumine with our own light, then we fail and cease to be light.

These thoughts, my beloved brothers and sisters, I wanted to share with you today on the occasion of this feast. I pray that the fathers, who intercede for us, give us their light continuously. I pray that we are open to the light of the fathers, that we do not project our own light at the expense of the light of the fathers.

Our Orthodox Church has these two characteristics: it is the Church of the fathers, but it is also the Church of light. Our Church is bathed in this light. All our hymnography, all our liturgy, all our temples are or should be bathed in light. So this must be our tradition. This, my brothers and sisters, is what the fathers we honor today teach us, and I pray that it will be a salvation for all of us. Amen.

62.

SUNDAY OF THE HOLY FATHERS OF THE 4th ECUMENICAL COUNCIL

Keeping the commandments and theosis (Mt 5:14–19)

> *Whoever then relaxes one of the least of these commandments and teaches men so, shall be called least in the kingdom of heaven; but he who does them and teaches them shall be called great in the kingdom of heaven.*

With these words, my dear brothers and sisters, the Church today wants to remind us of the feast of the fathers to whom this Sunday is dedicated. It is about the fathers of the Church who met in Chalcedon in 451 at the Fourth Ecumenical Council to leave us the teaching and doctrine of the Church about the person of the Lord. And the Church applies these words of the Lord to the fathers, because these fathers not only taught but also kept the commandments of God. These words are addressed to all of us as well, and invite us to reflect on them: Why are God's commandments and their observance necessary?

Many believe that God gave the commandments to make us better, to improve morally, to become better people. But if this is true, then why did Christ Himself keep the commandments of God? Christ had no need of moral improvement; He had no need to become better. So it is not the purpose of the commandments to make us better people. Still others believe that, with His commandments, God wants to demonstrate His power, His justice, to make us understand that we are obliged to obey Him because He is God, because He is the mighty lawgiver. This perception often provokes a reaction in man; it provokes his freedom. And just as a teenager comes to a time when he no longer wants to take orders from his father, and thus rebels, so man is provoked to rebel by God's commandments.

No, my brothers and sisters, we must look elsewhere to explain why God gave His commandments. The first and most important reason is that with God's commandments, man was able to exercise his freedom. It is no coincidence that, as soon as God created man and placed him in Paradise, He also gave a commandment—the commandment not to eat from a certain tree. This was no accident. It was the only way for man to exercise his freedom, to say that I accept or reject God. God's commandment was God's will—it was God Himself. By rejecting God's commandment, man rejected God Himself. And God wanted man free not only to accept Him but also to reject Him. And this is the great gift of freedom that God gave to man. Freedom can only be exercised on the basis of a commandment. Man rejected this commandment, which he received from God, and thus lost his way. It was his ruin, but he exercised his freedom. He received this great gift of freedom.

The other reason God gave the commandments and seeks that they be observed is that it is the only way to reverse the first man's attitude. In other words, we will again have to travel through this path of commandments to now be able to correct the first man's mistake. Just as the violation of the commandments brought us to ruin, so the observance of the commandments alone will bring us to salvation. Therefore, if the path to our deification and to our salvation goes through our freedom, then it necessarily also goes through the commandments. We cannot reach salvation or deification (that is, participation in the life of God) without going through the commandments, observing the commandments.

And one more reason is that, with the commandments, God shows us our limits, because the commandments of God are difficult and cannot be observed by human means. So, by requiring us to keep the commandments, He brings us closer to Him and causes us seek Him. Because if we could keep God's commandments on our own power, then we would not need God. We could turn our backs on Him and say "We don't need God and His grace." So God's commandments bring us closer to Him in this way.

Finally, my beloved brothers and sisters, what is of particular importance is that, through the commandments, we practice love. Let's dwell a little on this point. I am moved by something the Lord said to His disciples before His Passion. The Evangelist John records it as follows: "If you love Me, keep My commandments, [...] just as I have kept My Father's commandments and abide in His love" (John 14:15–15:10).

If we delve a little deeper, we see that the observance of the commandments also applied to Christ Himself. Christ kept His Father's commandments to the end, even to the point where He obediently accepted the heaviest commandment—that is, to go to the Cross. It was precisely this obedience to the Father—that is, the Incarnate Son's obedience to God the Father—that was tested in the Garden of Gethsemane. Christ thus showed us the way to express our love to God. Christ Himself demonstrated His love for the Father by keeping His every commandment—especially the most difficult one—and thus calls us to imitate Him in keeping the commandments.

And why is keeping the commandments so important for love? Because love in its essence is nothing else but the coming together of wills: what the one who loves wants, the other whom he loves will also want. When the wills are the same, then we are talking about love. If everyone has his own will and says how he loves the other but does what he wants and is the opposite of what the other wants, then he is not telling the truth. We cannot say that we love if our wills are not the same. We cannot say that we love God when our will is different from His.

The Lord demonstrated this in Gethsemane, when for a moment His human will went to separate from the will of God, immediately—without intervening time or doubt—they became identical and He said: "not as I will, but as You will" (Mt 26:39). This is love. We cannot, therefore, say that we love God and not keep His commandments. We cannot say that we love God and that our will is different from His. This is why, my beloved brothers and sisters, all the commandments—and the Lord said this explicitly—all the commandments are condensed into two: "Love the Lord your God with all your heart and with all your soul and with all your mind and love your neighbor as yourself" (Mk 12:30–31). In other words, precisely what we were discussing a moment ago—love means to identify your own will with the will of God, and to cut off your own will in favor of the will of your neighbor, the other.

Our will, therefore, must move in these two directions, and this means that we must uproot our own will, uproot our self-love, and put in its place God and the other—that is what "as yourself" means. Not to love as you love yourself, but to love the other instead of yourself, in place of yourself. That is why the Lord says that all the Law and the Prophets hang on these two commandments of love for God and neighbor. They can be analyzed, they can become individual commandments, but if they do not start from there, do not lead and do not end there, they are not God's commandments.

Finally, my brothers and sisters, God gave the commandments out of love. He didn't give them to frighten us. He did not give them to impose what He wants arbitrarily. He gave them to us so that we can love as He loves, and that is why keeping the commandments is so important.

The world today, my beloved brothers and sisters, does not tolerate commandments. Even parents try not to give their children any commands so as not to hurt them, and even we spiritual fathers hesitate to give commands. Why did man become like this? Simply, because he stopped loving. Because he loves himself. Because self-love is now the gospel of our modern culture. It is the gospel of our rights: How will we satisfy our rights and our will? Therefore, when the other asks us for something, he should ask it in such a way as not to affect our ego.

In times past, people accepted orders with pleasure, but who, my brothers and sisters, would not accept an order from a person whom they love? His commandment would be our desire. This, then, is why, my brothers and sisters, the commandments of God seem difficult to us. They are meaningless because we have stopped loving. We have stopped loving God and we have stopped loving others. We love only ourselves, and every commandment, whether it comes from God or from another, is for us a challenge to our self-love. It is something we push away, reject, and deny.

It is necessary, therefore, my beloved brothers and sisters, by keeping the commandments, to cleanse ourselves of our selfishness, to develop our love, and only then will we be able to keep these commandments with more joy and satisfaction—then the yoke will be light. Then God's grace will come and we will be able to keep His commandments with joy and not with resentment.

Then truly, my brothers and sisters, we will be in the Kingdom of God, because the Kingdom of God is nothing else but the realization of what we say in the Lord's Prayer: Thy will be done on earth as it is in heaven. Just as in heaven, the will of God is gladly obeyed by the saints and angels (and their "Amen" to the will of God is their joy), so also if we do this, what the Lord said about the fathers of the Church in today's Gospel passage will apply to us also: "he shall be called great in the kingdom of heaven." We will be able, therefore, in this way, passing through the observance of the commandments, to reach the Kingdom of God, which we all eagerly expect and for which we all ask God's grace and mercy. Amen.

July 18, 2004

63.
SUNDAY OF THE HOLY FATHERS OF THE 4th ECUMENICAL COUNCIL
"You are the light of the world" (Mt 5:14–19)

The Lord addressed these words that we heard in the Gospel passage to His disciples, and our Church extends them today to the fathers of our Church. This Sunday is dedicated to the memory of the fathers who convened the Fourth Ecumenical Council in Chalcedon, opposite Constantinople, in 451 AD. They handed down to us a very important dogma of the Church, teaching that our Lord, Jesus Christ, is perfect God and perfect man. The Only-Begotten Son of God, the Word of God, took upon himself human nature—that is, all of us—and united us with God, introduced us to the life of God, within the Holy Trinity, offering us what we call "theosis." In other words, He made simple people like us into gods, to participate in God. And we are called today, my dear brothers and sisters, to attend to this great teaching of the Church fathers of the Fourth Ecumenical Council—to draw out as much as possible from it, because the meanings within it are profound and have lessons for our lives as well.

The first great lesson about the person of the Lord that this teaching of the fathers gives us is that man has been so trapped in sin, decay, and death, in an impasse, that he cannot get out of it on his own, he cannot be saved; because in order for man to be saved from this state in which he fell through disobedience and the fall, God Himself must intervene. In the Old Testament, God sent prophets, angels, and so many others to convey the will of God, but humanity could not be saved, man could not be saved with all this. God Himself had to intervene and He intervened no longer by sending an angel or a prophet, but His own Son. And this, my dear brothers and sisters, is the great mystery of God's love. He gives us Himself, His own Son, so that we can be saved.

"God so loved the world," says the Evangelist John, that He gave His Only-begotten Son (John 3:16). He gave us His Son out of His love. And love, therefore, real love, which only God has to perfection, is not giving something of what you have to others; it is giving your whole self. God gave all of Himself for us to be saved. This is the awesome mystery that the teaching of our Church reveals to us about the person of Christ. And it is not only that He gives himself, His own Son, to save us, but He also shows us the way in which we will be able to unite with Him and be saved in His Son. In other words, the manner in which God—in the person of Christ—united us with Him and saved us is also the manner in which we should be included in the same movement, in order to be united with God. And this manner is very important, my dear brothers and sisters; let's pay attention to it.

Our Lord, becoming man, emptied Himself of His glory. He was humiliated. From the height of His divinity, He came down to the wretched state of man. And He didn't just preach, He didn't just show us which path to follow. He took this situation upon Himself. He took upon Himself our decay, death, pain, everything that torments us since we were cut off from communion with God. He took all this upon Himself. And He even went as far as the Cross, as far as death, as far as Hades—He couldn't go any further from God than man had already gone. And only by going down was He able to raise man, who had fallen, toward God. He took upon Himself man's fate, man's situation, and raised it from death to immortality and life. So the only way for man to be saved, to be united with God, is the way that Christ Himself followed. That is, to humble Himself to the point of taking upon Himself the pain, sorrow, and sins of the whole world, and to die voluntarily so that He could defeat death and overcome involuntary death. This is an awesome mystery, my beloved brothers and sisters. Death is involuntary, we don't want it, but we cannot escape death unless we voluntarily take it upon ourselves. This is the great mystery of Christ Himself, who came down, took our death upon Himself—that is, the human nature which He took upon himself He led to death willingly—so that he could thus defeat death: "trampling down death by death."

The other very instructive thing about this teaching of the fathers whom we honor today is that He did not simply take our sins upon Himself, He did not simply give us absolution, He did not simply redeem us from death, but—as if all that were not enough—He united us with Him, united us with God. The fathers of this Council whom we honor today teach us that human nature was united with God, with the Divine Nature, in the person of the Son of God, inseparably, indissolubly, and thus made us sharers in the life of God, in God Himself. Can you imagine a greater gift than that? So it is not only that He sacrificed Himself, humbled Himself, took upon Himself the whole terrible situation in which we find ourselves, but He also gave us this blessing to participate in the life of God. The mystery of Christ, my beloved brothers and sisters, on which our salvation rests, is truly moving.

And this consists precisely in the fact that our salvation is not simply that our sins are forgiven. It is that we become partakers in the life of God. According to the teaching of the fathers we honor today, all this is done, my dear brothers and sisters, in such a way that our participation, our participation in the life of God, does not abolish us as human beings, does not absorb us. This union of the two natures in Christ, say the fathers of this Ecumenical Council, is indivisible but also unconfused. What does this mean? That God uniting us with Him in the person of Christ made us real people. So being a real person can only happen when you are united with God. The more you unite with God, the more human you become.

We usually contrast man with God. But man, if separated from God, is simply an animal. He is nothing more. What makes man stand out from the rest of nature and from animals is that he can unite with God. Therefore, the Lord made us gods, but He also made us real people by taking human nature upon Himself. What an awesome mystery, my beloved brothers and sisters. And, of course, this is formulated in a philosophical way in the doctrine of the Church. However, what I am trying to tell you is that it is not simply a logical construct. It has to do with our very existence, with our very life. So when we say that we must accept the doctrines of the Church and not fall into heresy, but be faithful to the teaching of the fathers, we say it because these doctrines are lived, they can become life. And for this reason, many saints, great saints of our Church, did not have the education to understand the doctrines as formulated by the fathers, but they experienced them. Because, as I tried to show you, these are not for our minds, they are for our lives. So when we turn them into life, then doctrines are for everyone and not just for theologians or some. And this is what our Church does, my dear brothers and sisters, showing us that, as we heard in the Gospel passage, not only the one who teaches but also the one who does is great in the Kingdom of God. So it shows us how we can apply in our lives this great truth that the fathers of the Fourth Council, whom we honor today, handed down to us.

The Church shows us first of all that we should never expect to be saved by our virtues, or by what the world tries to offer us as a way of salvation: through science, knowledge, ethics, or anything that is human—don't expect to be saved by these. "Do not trust in rulers and in the sons of men, in whom there is no salvation," says the psalmist (Ps 145:3 LXX). Our salvation comes only from God. And we must seek it as a grace and gift from God and not as the result of our own efforts, whether these are efforts in society as a whole or individual efforts, even in our spiritual life.

In our spiritual life, no matter how many virtues we develop, no matter how much effort we put in, no matter how much we exercise asceticism, they are not enough to save us. Only God saves. And for this, as I said at the beginning, it was necessary for God Himself to send His Son to save us.

The other great teaching that the Church offers us—and it is not just a teaching, it is the actualization in our lives of this great truth, of the great mystery of Christ—is its saints. The saints of the Church are those who experienced this doctrine of the fathers, applying the very life of Christ to their own lives. Christ came down and emptied Himself of His glory. The saints also completely empty themselves of all glory. They are humbled, they take upon themselves not only their own sins but also the sins of others, they become one with all humanity. And so, after they themselves have "died," after they have killed their will, then they are resurrected and with their prayer for the whole world they draw us close. This is the great mystery of the saints. It is the actualization of the mystery of Christ in history, in reality.

The other great thing that our Church gives us, so that this great mystery of Christ can be actualized, is, my dear brothers and sisters, the Holy Eucharist. It is what we are celebrating at this moment and what leads us to our union with God. This is now the highest gift. Everything else is a way to get there. But when it arrives, then it is the end. And the Church did not leave us, my beloved brothers and sisters, with only one teaching about the mystery of Christ. He gave us the ability to participate in Christ Himself and, with Him and through Him, to be united with God. This is the great mystery of the Holy Eucharist, in which our nature is united with the nature of God in the person of Christ. And this is why, when we celebrate the Holy Eucharist, my beloved brothers and sisters, we say afterwards that we saw the true light, we received the heavenly Spirit. We have nothing more to wait for. So, my beloved brothers and sisters, the fathers of our Church whom we honor today did not simply give us a teaching, a doctrine for the theologians to talk about. They gave us, revealed to us, a mystery. This mystery has so many aspects that my poor words can only cover a few of them. This great mystery, my beloved, is preserved by our Church in the persons of its saints and especially in the Eucharist, which we celebrate in the Divine Liturgy.

Let us praise God, because His love is so great that He not only saves us from our sins, He not only shows us the way to salvation, but also rewards us with a foretaste of this union with Him in the mystery of the Eucharist, in the body of Christ. Therefore, every time we realize that we belong to this blessed Church of the fathers, who saw this great mystery and handed it down to us, let us try to appear worthy of, and consistent with, this teaching, as much as each of us can. Following this difficult path, which the Son of God Himself followed—the path of emptiness, humiliation, and hoping and believing only in God, and not in people, and not in ourselves—let us taste this joy of union with God, of our deification, every time the Church calls us to partake of the body and blood of Christ. In this way we will be seen as worthy disciples of the fathers of the Church, whom today we especially honor and whose intercession and prayers I hope will always be with us.

In the Holy Monastery of Saint John the Baptist, Essex, England
July 13, 2014

64.
THE NATIVITY OF THE MOTHER OF GOD
According honor to the Virgin Mary

My beloved brothers and sisters, today the Lord once again accounted us worthy of honoring the Nativity of the Virgin Mary. Not just the Church, but the whole world celebrates today, as we sing in the Apolytikion hymn today, "Your birth, O Theotokos, brought joy to the whole world, for from you dawned the sun of righteousness, Christ our God. Freeing us from the curse, He gave us His blessings. Abolishing death, He granted us eternal life."[1]

From you, Virgin Mary, came the one who broke the curse, the curse of the first-formed humans Adam and Eve, which expelled the human race from Paradise. This is the same curse that separated us from God, because we, with our own free will, wanted to distance ourselves from Him. This same curse was removed by the birth of the Virgin Mary. Because through the Virgin came the One who defeated death and opened Paradise to us again. He freed us from death and gave us eternal life. This is the great blessing that resulted from the Virgin's birth, and that is why today our Church celebrates this event with dignity.

We, the Orthodox in particular, honor our Virgin Mary not as an individual, but as the one who brought Christ into the world. Just as we represent her in our icons as the one who is always carrying the Christ child, so by honoring her, we are honoring this great mystery of our salvation that was given to us by Christ Himself.

For this reason, when we say that the Virgin Mary is the holiest person in our Church—because truly there is no one holier than the Virgin Mary—we say this not only because she is the purest being that the human race ever produced, but also because

[1] Narthex Press.

she was cleansed by the Holy Spirit Itself on the day of the Annunciation, so that she would be spotless and undefiled from every point of view, and so that she could receive God Himself within her, and that the Son and Word of God would take flesh and blood from her. We say this not only because she is the embodiment of all virtues, but because she was united with the only truly holy one, who is Christ, the Son of God. She is more united with him than all of us, since she shared her human nature with Christ, and held God Himself in her womb.

There is, therefore, no person holier than the Virgin Mary. There is no person who is so inextricably united with God himself, because all holiness comes from God alone. No man is holy either by his virtues or by his works—he is holy only when he is united with God and receives holiness from God's holiness.

The Virgin Mary, therefore, shows us the way to holiness, our own holiness. And this path is the path of humility that she showed us by submitting herself to the will of God, even if it was paradoxical that she would give birth to the Son of God without going through the biological process that occurs at every human birth.

Thus, with her humility and her faith, and the fact that God can do all things—even that which appears impossible to men—the Virgin Mary shows us the path that leads to us participating in God's holiness. This is why the Church has nothing more exalted to offer us for our salvation, for our holiness, than the Holy Eucharist, in which we are united with the most holy God and become, like the Virgin Mary, one body and one blood with Christ Himself.

This, then, is why we so honor the Mother of God and why our Church celebrates today. Because God, in a supernatural way, gave us the person of the ever-Virgin Mother of God, who has become part of human history. With her birth today, the Virgin provided mankind with the opportunity to unite ourselves once again with God, and to attain Paradise and eternal life.

I pray, my beloved brothers and sisters, that the Virgin Mary will always be an intercessor to God for all of us, and that she will be the model for every person—a model of humility, faith, and virtue. May she also be a model of the way in which we will be saved and united with God—that is, through the mystery of the Eucharist, where we become one with the Lord's body and blood. Happy feast day to all, and may the Virgin help us. Amen.

September 8, 2006

65.
EXALTATION OF THE HOLY CROSS
The meaning of the cross (John 19:6–11, 13–20, 25–28, 30)

We worship your cross, Master, and we praise and glorify your holy Resurrection.

Again, my beloved brothers and sisters, our Church raises the Holy Cross, preserving the ancient ethos and sacred tradition that dates back to Byzantine times. And it is raised before us, so that we can place the flowers of our reverence on it, to express our gratitude for the Lord's sacrifice on the Cross, and to draw aid and strength for the struggles of life from the Holy Cross, from which truly originates great grace, power, and strength.

However, my beloved brothers and sisters, the Holy Cross that we raise today is not simply an object of our reverence. It is not simply a sacred object from which we draw grace and strength. But it is also a model and a compass and a guide for our lives. The Lord's Cross is not here only to be venerated, or only to draw the benefits that it provides, but so that we ourselves can lift it up on our shoulders. For, as the Lord said, "If any man would come after me, let him deny himself and take up his cross and follow me." The Lord's Cross must become our cross too. This message is exceptionally difficult to accept because we do not understand the deeper meaning of the Cross.

The Cross of Christ, my beloved brothers and sisters, has two aspects, two characteristics that have a direct relationship with our own lives. One is that this Cross carries all the imposed crosses of our life. It is no coincidence that, on the Cross, the Lord suffered not only pain and death, but also mockery, betrayal, slander, and persecution. These are a combination of the crosses that we all carry daily. We bear this imposed cross, either because some disease has befallen us or ours, or because we have lost a loved one, or because our friends and acquaintances have betrayed us, or because everyone has abandoned us, both friends and even our children. It is a cross of loneliness and abandonment, as was the Cross of the Lord, whom the disciples also abandoned. This is the cross we are called to take up patiently and without complaining, just as the Lord took it up.

The Cross of Christ, therefore, is not simply for us to venerate. It is up to us to lift these imposed crosses in our own lives and not to grumble and say "Why do I have to suffer so much? Why is my cross so large?" The will of God determines the cross that each of us must take up, and we must accept it without complaining. But the cross is never as unbearable as it would be if we carried it alone. The cross we lift is the same Cross of Christ, and He also bears it with us and therefore gives us strength not to surrender, not to succumb under the weight of this cross.

There is, however, another aspect to the Cross of Christ. Christ bore not only imposed crosses, which I mentioned to you before and which we are all called to bear in this life. Rather, he picked up the cross voluntarily—that is, without being obliged to pick it up. It was a cross he could have avoided. That is why his enthusiastic disciple, when Jesus was about to be arrested in the Garden before His crucifixion, suggested to Christ that he should draw his sword to fight back against those who threatened Him. And the Lord answered him: "If I wanted to avoid the cross, I could call twelve legions of angels"—that was equal to the power of the entire Roman Empire—"to protect me." And indeed he could have. He was God Himself! Who could impose on him a cross that he would not willingly accept? But the Lord accepted the cross voluntarily and in this way told us that in our lives we should not only take up imposed crosses, which we cannot avoid, but also take up crosses that we can avoid. Crosses that we take up voluntarily, not because we simply feel a moral obligation, not because we have a natural love or relationship, such as that of a mother and her child or the members of a family. Because we take up these crosses almost out of necessity. To take up crosses that we are not obliged to take up, that are not for our friends or for our acquaintances, but that are rather for people who are not in our immediate environment, crosses for the sake of people who are even our enemies.

If you take up a cross for the sake of your enemy, then it resembles the Cross of Christ. Because Christ did not die for his friends, says the Apostle Paul, nor for good people. "[P]erhaps for a good man someone would even dare to die. But God demonstrates His own love toward us, in that while we were still sinners, Christ died for us." (Rom 5:7–8).

He died for us, for those who had rebelled against God. This is the Cross of Christ—the cross of a righteous person, taken up for the sake of the unrighteous, for the sake of those who deserved and should have borne the cross. Can you take up a cross that is unjustly imposed on you? Can you take responsibility for the sins of others? Can you say "Let me be treated unjustly, it doesn't matter!"? Then the cross you lift is similar to the Cross of Christ.

How important this is in our everyday lives, my beloved brothers and sisters! People do not tolerate being wronged. They revolt. They claim their rights. If Christ had done the same, he certainly would not have been crucified. Because he was crucified unjustly. But if we are not willing also to sacrifice our rights in our relationships with other people, then we do not take up the Cross of Christ.

Then we have conflict between people, which is precisely what we observe so often in our lives. How many families would have avoided divorce and the dissolution of their families if they had just been willing to say to each other: "It doesn't matter. I am in the right, but so be it. It's better for me to be wronged than someone else." How different would our lives be if we took up the voluntary crosses and not just the imposed ones? Voluntary crosses, my beloved brothers and sisters, were taken up by all the saints of the Church—the martyrs, the ascetics, the righteous. They were not obliged to give their lives. They did it willingly, like Christ himself. He willingly gave His life. Therefore, our Church, projecting before us the Cross of Christ, invites us to take up not only our imposed crosses, but to constantly take up voluntary crosses as well, even where we could avoid them. But we must lift them up because love requires us to take up crosses, even unjust ones, so that you can maintain this love. Because love without sacrifice and without a cross cannot be preserved.

My brothers and sisters, we live in an age in which each one of us looks at how to avoid the crosses of life, how to make this life more comfortable, how to assert our rights more, how to project our ego and will, how to live comfortably in this life that is leavened with pain and sorrow without sacrificing anything. This, unfortunately, is also our culture's ideal. It is an idealistic culture, a culture that idealizes comfort, moderate effort, the avoidance of pain and sacrifice with various painkillers and above all by promoting our own individual interest at the expense of the interest of the other, at the expense of the interest of the whole. This is our culture; it is individualistic and idealistic and surrounds us today in a thousand ways. Even in this culture, today the Church raises the Cross and says: "No, it's not like that! The meaning of life is not to avoid the cross. The meaning of life lies in taking up the cross. And let's lift it up and sacrifice both our interest and our will for the sake of others". Thus, my brothers and sisters, by venerating the Holy Cross that the Church raises today, we will not only receive strength and grace from it to lift the crosses of life, but also the example and model for lifting crosses voluntarily for the sake of others. When that happens, we can be sure that the Cross of Christ will indeed sanctify us, and that the Cross He endured will not be wasted. And so we will be able, passing through the Cross, to reach the Resurrection of the Lord, our resurrection, which is the life of love, the life of our eternal coexistence not only with those who do us good, who benefit us, but also with those who harm us and are even our enemies.

I pray that the meaning of today's feast proves to be salvific for us all, my dear brothers and sisters. Amen.

Holy Church of the Archangels (old), Peristeri
September 14, 2005

66.
ON THE FEAST OF SAINT SOPHIA AND HER THREE DAUGHTERS, FAITH, LOVE, AND HOPE, MARTYRS (†137)
(Mt 10:32)

So every one who acknowledges me before men, I also will acknowledge before my Father who is in heaven (Mt 10:32)

The grace of God has brought us together today, my beloved brothers and sisters, to celebrate four martyrs of our Church, to whom this Church is dedicated—Saint Sophia and her three daughters, Faith, Love, and Hope.

Every time we honor martyrs of our Church, the Church calls us not only to ask them for their help, but also calls us to be inspired by their lives and their example and especially by their martyrdom.

Martyrdom, my beloved brothers and sisters, is greatly honored in the Church, even though it is a great paradox. It is a challenge to our logic. God, who gave us everything, including this life, and calls us to take care of this life and to honor it and to thank Him for it, calls us at some point to let it go, to abandon it. And one wonders: why? Isn't this a paradox? Why should there be martyrdom in the Church? Why should there be people who have to sacrifice their lives, this precious good that God gave us?

This mystery, my beloved brothers and sisters, has its answer and its solution in the Cross of the Lord. That Cross, which we raised and venerated a few days ago, is the center of life not only of the Church but also of the whole world. Because, as a great father of our Church, Saint Maximus the Confessor, says, everything, that is, everything that exists, "is in need of the Cross." Everything must be crucified, must pass through the Cross.

What is the Cross, my beloved brothers and sisters, and why must everything pass through it? It is no coincidence that the four martyrs whom we honor today have four names with which the Holy Scriptures, and especially the Apostle Paul, associate the Cross of the Lord. The Apostle Paul says that the Cross of the Lord, while for the Jews it is a scandal and for the Greeks folly, for the faithful it is the wisdom and power of God. Why is the Cross of Christ wisdom? Why is it not, as I said, a scandal rather than wisdom? It is wisdom, because the Cross of Christ reveals to us three great mysteries, which the daughters of Saint Sophia, whom we honor today, capture with their names.

One is the mystery of love. What is love? We usually think of love as a feeling that we have, that we feel for the other. However, as the Cross of Christ reveals to us, love is something much more difficult. It is the intersection of two wills. On the Cross of Christ, two wills crossed, the will of God and the will of man. And this meeting of the two wills created a conflict of wills. And when the wills of God and man collide, then the Cross is experienced, but true love is also revealed. Real love is exactly the point where the two wills meet, God's will with ours and our will with the others. When these two wills cross and there is a conflict between the two wills, then there is no love. On the contrary, love exists only when there is agreement in this intersection of wills, but someone must die, some "will" of both must die. And on the Cross the will of man died, as the Lord demonstrated in Gethsemane, when He asked for this cup of death, which awaited Him on the cross, to pass. But He added "nevertheless, not as I will, but as You will" (Mt 26:39). Every time, my brothers and sisters, that we say "nevertheless, not as I will, but as You will," then we truly love. But then we also take up the cross, and this cross is a martyrdom. And our life, my beloved brothers and sisters, is martyrdom when we love. Only when we turn our face away from love, then everything is rosy. But love, with its martyrdom, rewards us. It rewards us by maintaining a relationship permanently, eternally. It is the Resurrection that follows. So when we sacrifice our will for the sake of the other, that is, when we lift the Cross of Christ above us, then love is realized and at the same time the Resurrection comes; that is, our love survives and lives forever, as well as our relationship with the other.

The Cross of Christ is wisdom, my beloved brothers and sisters, because it reveals love to us. But it also reveals something else to us, which is the name of one of the daughters of Saint Sophia, faith. And what is faith? There, as with love, we have misunderstood things. We think that faith is when we accept the existence of God, but, as the Holy Bible says, even the demons believe and are afraid (James 2:19). This faith has no value, to believe that God exists. Even the demons know that God exists, but this is not faith. Also, we say that faith is when we accept certain doctrines of the Church and certain truths of the Church. Yes, this is important, but this is not faith at its core. Faith is when we accept the humanly impossible as possible. In other words, our faith is tested again on the Cross of Christ.

Because what is happening on the Cross? We are called to believe that this lowly and weak figure is God. And if He is God, he can protect us and give us what we need, which is very difficult to accept when God seems not to answer our prayers and to be absent, to be dead, as on the Cross. Then our faith is tested and then we have to say "yes, God loves me, even if He doesn't answer my prayers." So we must be able to accept God and the time when He is absent from our life and does not seem to exist. Not only when He performs miracles, but also when He does not perform miracles. This is real faith. Believing because a miracle happened, everyone can do that. But to say at the time of your trial that God loves me and the cross that I carry is a cross that God has given me, and He will not leave me, He will not leave me helpless, that is faith. The Cross of Christ gives us this faith and calls us to manifest it in our lives.

And the third daughter of Saint Sophia, Hope, is also embodied in the Cross of Christ. We hope. We hope in the Resurrection of the Lord. We hope that the Cross is not the last word, that the Cross hides God Himself and therefore the Cross will be transcended, and the Resurrection will come. Can we draw this hope from the Cross of the Lord? Then, my beloved brothers and sisters, we have followed the path of the martyrs of the Church, which, as we see in the saints we celebrate today, is hope, firm expectation and certainty of the Lord's Resurrection and His Kingdom.

So these come from the Cross of the Lord, and that is why they make martyrdom and the martyrs of our Church so important and that is why we honor them. Not only because they intercede for us—and indeed they do—but because they guide our lives so that we too can take up our crosses.

There are two kinds of crosses that we are called to lift. These are the imposed crosses, which we don't want, but are put on our shoulders either by others with their malice, or by nature with its decay, or by so many evils that exist in the world. These are the imposed crosses we are called to bear.

However, there is another type of cross, which is the Cross of the Lord and the cross of the martyrs, and that is the voluntary cross. "As One voluntarily lifted up on the Cross,"[1] the Lord did not take up an imposed cross that He could not avoid. In the Garden before He gave himself up to be crucified, the Lord told His enthusiastic disciple who drew his sword to defend Him, "Put your sword back into its place [...]. Or do you think that I cannot now pray to My Father, and He will provide Me with more than twelve legions of angels?"[2]—which was equal to the entire Roman Empire. He could have! He was God! He could have avoided the Cross. But He took it up voluntarily, because it was necessary for love's sake, for our sake.

And therefore He calls us—and this is the difficult thing in our life—to take up voluntary crosses as well. Along with the crosses that are imposed on us, can we take up voluntary ones as well? In that case, my brothers and sisters, we are following in the footsteps of the martyrs of the Church. Because the martyrs were not obliged to take up the cross; they could have denied Christ. They could have found a thousand ways to avoid martyrdom. The martyrs, therefore, take up a voluntary cross and they call us to take up voluntary crosses as well. Can we take up the crosses of others? Can we be ready to suffer ourselves for the sake of others or instead of others? Then, my beloved brothers and sisters, we are following the path of the Lord's Cross and in the footsteps of the martyrs.

[1] Quote from the first line of the Kontakion of the Feast of the Exaltation of the Cross.

[2] Mt 26:52–53.

Our age, my brothers and sisters, has turned its face away from the cross. It is an age that has deified wealth, good times, and pleasure. This age, our current culture, does everything possible to prevent the cross from entering our lives, to have the best possible time. And that is why the feast of the martyrs is a scandal in our culture.

Why does the Church promote the martyrs? Who is ready in today's age to be a martyr, or to even accept that martyrdom is acceptable and right? No one! The martyrs are there only to intercede for us. But to imitate them as martyrs? No. Our age, then, especially this age of affluence, has turned away from the Cross. But the Church, my beloved brothers and sisters, cannot lower the bar any more. This is the Church's yardstick and measure of the value of our lives: the measure of the Cross. It is a difficult measure. Who among us can reach it? But the Church will never lower the bar to make our lives more convenient. This measure of the Cross invites us to approach it as often as we can, to strive to reach it. And when we strive to reach it and don't reach it—this is only natural—then the bar bows down on its own accord. The condescension and mercy of the Crucified One comes and understands us, forgives us, strengthens us. And so this is our path, my beloved brothers and sisters, the path of all the saints of our Church. This is the path we are called to walk in an age, as I said, that hates the cross.

Therefore, following in the footsteps of the martyrs of our Church, through the intercession of the saints celebrated today, of Saint Sophia and her daughters Love, Faith, and Hope, let us walk this path bearing our crosses, the imposed and the voluntary, as best we can. And then, with the help and mediation of the saints, our life will acquire real meaning. Our life will be filled with love, with light, and, bearing our cross, we will already experience a foretaste of the Resurrection of the Lord and His Kingdom, which I hope the Lord will grant us all. Amen!

Holy Church of Saint Sophia, Anthousa, Attica
September 17, 2013

67.
ANNIVERSARY OF THE CONSECRATION OF THE HOLY CHURCH OF SAINT SILOUAN
Concerning the temple

Today, my beloved brothers and sisters, the Lord, with His grace, allows us to celebrate the 20th anniversary of the consecration of this holy church. Twenty years ago, with the blessing of His All-Holiness Patriarch Demetrios, and the concelebration of the ever-memorable Elder Sophrony, this temple was consecrated and dedicated to the worship of the Triune God.[1]

In an age and a world that is moving toward the loss of the meaning and the sense of sacred, the Church is building temples and dedicating them to the glory of God. The Church builds temples not because it isn't true that all of creation is a temple in which God dwells and is praised, nor because humans, especially the baptized and faithful ones, aren't temples in which God and the Holy Spirit dwell, but because man feels the need and the duty to take at least a part of this creation that God entrusted to him and to dedicate it and make it a place for Him to dwell—to be a holy place, sacred, separate from the rest of the world and dedicated to God.

For us Christians, the most important thing is that inside these temples, the Divine Liturgy is celebrated, the Sacrament of the Eucharist is celebrated, which is nothing other than the offering up to God (*anaphora*) of all creation.

We consider the temple to be holy, because it is where the most important and holiest thing is done—the sanctification of the honorable Body and Blood of the Lord. So inside the temple the Divine Eucharist is celebrated, prayers are offered to God and here the grace and glory of God dwell in a special way.

[1] In Greek, an individual church building is called a "temple." I have sometimes kept this word to distinguish it from the Church universal.

The temple is thus an icon of the heavenly Kingdom of God, an example of the fact that the whole world is destined to become a temple of God in which God will be glorified and His glory will dwell. Thus, for us Orthodox, the temple is the same as the Church, and it is no coincidence that our people say "I'm going to church" to mean "I'm going to the temple."[2]

Man, however, now claims this world, and he claims it at the expense of God, against God's will, and this is the fall of man. Man, instead of offering the world up to God, offers it to himself, and we live this fall especially today, in a secularized society, from which man has excluded God and taken the fate of the world into his own hands.

So today we celebrate the anniversary, one would say the birthday of this temple. To be precise, we celebrated the anniversary of the temple's baptism, because, as in the case of man, our true life does not begin with our biological birth. Celebrating a birthday is a somewhat newer custom. Our real life begins with baptism, when we enter true life, which is not subject to death and decay like our biological life.

That is why, when we celebrate the consecration of a church, the service is almost like the baptism service and even includes the anointing. It is no coincidence that when we inaugurate the temple we anoint the Holy Table with holy Myrrh, just as we anoint a person when he is baptized. It is therefore on the day of the consecration, the day of the baptism of the temple, that is becomes holy, just as every person through his baptism becomes holy and set apart. And man must preserve this holiness throughout his life, just as he preserves and respects the holiness of the temple space.

The Apostle Paul says that we are also the "temple of the living God" (2 Cor 6:16), in whom God dwells. That is to say, just as in the temple we cannot allow something unholy to happen, so in our own bodies we must respect and honor it as a temple of God, as a sanctuary in which God dwells.

[2] See footnote above.

That is why, my beloved brothers and sisters, the anniversary of the opening of the temple reminds us that we too are the "temple of the living God." We must consider our body and our existence as sacred and holy, and respect it.

So let's celebrate the anniversary of the consecration of this temple with this thought—of respect for sanctity of our body, our life, and the whole world. And let us pray for this temple, which was erected by this Holy Monastery with the blessing of the ever-memorable Elder Sophrony, that it will always be under the shelter of the Lord, that the Lord will strengthen this temple so that here prayers and praises to God may be offered up for centuries to come, and that the Divine Eucharist may be celebrated and that the saint to whom this church is dedicated may be honored.

During baptism we get a name and, as I mentioned, the same thing occurs at the consecration of a temple. It gets a name, the name of a saint, and this temple has taken the name of Saint Silouan.

I humbly pray that Saint Silouan and the blessing of the ever-memorable Elder Sophrony always accompany this holy temple, that the Lord will strengthen it together with the holy brotherhood and community, and that He will give to all of us, my beloved brothers and sisters, the grace and blessing of the Lord. Amen.

September 18, 2008

68.
TRANSLATION OH THE APOSTLE AND EVANGELIST JOHN THE THEOLOGIAN
The Theologian of Love (John 9:25–27, 21:24–25)

The Lord has accounted us worthy once again to celebrate, with a festal service in this holy church, the holy memory of the great Apostle and Evangelist John the Theologian, the faithful and beloved friend of the Lord, the author of the fourth Gospel and the Catholic Epistles. He was the first in the entire history of the Church to be honored with the title of Theologian, among three and only three to whom this title has been given. Today it is common to talk about theologians, but the tradition of our Church only knows three theologians: John, whose memory we commemorate today, Gregory the Theologian and Simeon the New Theologian.

The Church is sparing with this title, because the deepest meaning of theology has to do with the revelation of the mystery of God, the existence of God, His personal existence. A revelation that God gave to certain people only in the life of the Church. And He gave to them the gift of being able to write and speak about the being of God, about the very existence of God, so that we can participate in and experience this relationship with God, which the saints have done throughout the ages.

John the Theologian is the one who first spoke to us about the divinity of Christ. He said this unique thing, that: "In the beginning was the Word, and the Word was with God, and the Word was God" (Jn 1:1). In other words, Christ was not just a man; He always existed. He was with God the Father before the world was made, ages ago, and thus He revealed to us the divinity of Christ and the mystery of the Holy Trinity. This is why he deserved the title of Theologian!

John the Theologian revealed theology to us in certain forms which are characteristic of his own teaching. These I would like to point out, if you would permit me. John the Theologian is the theologian of love. The key to knowing God, the key to God being revealed to someone is none other than love. Love for God Himself, which, however, as John says, passes through love for people. We cannot love, says John, God, whom we do not see, if we do not love people, whom we see. Therefore, the way to God is love. All this for the simple reason, as we heard in the epistle reading, that God first loved us. And so he opened the way of love to us. The way to love our brothers and through the love of our brothers to reach God himself and to experience his own love. Because God demonstrated His love for man—the fact that God is love, as we heard in the epistle reading—by giving His Son as a sacrifice for us. And so John is not only the theologian of love, but also a theologian of the Cross of Christ. It is very touching that, of all the disciples of the Lord, the only one who remained faithful to the Cross of Christ, next to the Crucified Christ, was John. All had scattered, all had fled in fear, but that beloved disciple remained near Him on the Cross. And so he demonstrated to us that saying we love has no meaning if we do not participate in the cross of the other. We cannot say that we love Christ and not take up His Cross, not participate in His Cross, and instead turn our backs on him. If John had left and abandoned Christ at the time of the Cross, he would not have been able to have this title of beloved, we would not be able to say that he really loved Christ.

And if, as we said, love for God goes through the other, our love for our brothers is manifested and revealed only when we participate in their cross, in their difficulties, in their sufferings. If we can, we should take those crosses upon ourselves as Christ did; then we really love, because it is easy, my dear brothers and sisters, to say that we love. It is a word that has become worn out, like a banknote that has passed through thousands of hands. It no longer has the content that the word "love" had. We easily say to the other "I love you," we easily say "we love the other." What we mean by this is that we don't hate the other! But love is not simply not hating the other. Love is taking on yourself all the crosses of the other willingly. Take upon yourself, say the early fathers of our Church, the sins of others. Because the Cross of Christ was exactly that—Christ taking on the burden of others' sins. We say that we love, but at the same time, if someone accuses us of being sinners, we immediately respond "No, not me, the other is a sinner!"—the other is sinful, we are good. So we are separated, we do not take the other's cross upon us.

But if we think with this spirit of the Cross of Christ, of love as manifested on the Cross of Christ, then we automatically say that "Yes, the sins of others are ours, I must be punished for them." I don't see myself as innocent. In this spirit of the Cross, love takes on a meaning that we do not usually give it in our lives. And this is what John wants to show us by standing next to the Crucified Christ. He defied all danger and shared the Cross of Christ. Thus, John also proved to be a theologian of the Cross of Christ.

Also next to the Cross there was the Virgin Mary. And there, next to John's support for the Crucified Christ, another side of John's theology is revealed to us. The theology of the Virgin Mary, that is, whoever says that he loves Christ but does not love the Virgin Mary, his mother, is not telling the truth! And unfortunately we also have many Christians, Christians in name, within the Protestant milieu, among the heretics, who do not honor the Virgin Mary. And they cut themselves off and say "We honor Christ, we love Christ." How can we love Christ and not love his mother? So John, loving Christ, sharing the Cross of Christ, now takes into his home and cares for the mother of Christ, the Virgin Mary. And so it shows us that true love for Christ goes through love and respect and honor for the Virgin Mary.

Here, then, are some aspects, my beloved brothers and sisters, of this wonderful mystery of theology, as Saint John reveals it to us. And John the Theologian has—especially for us Greeks—one more aspect, which is moving. He is the one who spread Christianity and founded the Church of Christ in the blessed lands of the forgotten homelands of Ionia in Asia Minor. Those places came to know the Gospel of Christ from John. And this connected his name with those places. And so we cannot forget these places, which many of our parents and ancestors came from, and where our Church, our Ecumenical Patriarchate, still maintains its Metropolises, though under occupation, such as the Metropolis of Pergamon. We, then, particularly honor Saint John then Theologian and turn to him today with gratitude. We thank him because it was through his efforts that those places were sanctified with the Gospel—churches were built, saints and martyrs were born. Thanks to the seed that Saint John sowed in those places, they are always watered by the presence of our holy Church, even if they are currently in the hands of people of another religion.

This saint, my beloved brothers and sisters, we honor today. And we ask for his intercessions, so that God may account us worthy, as much as each of us can with our own personal struggle, to follow this path that he showed us. The way of love that goes through the cross, the way of love that includes our Virgin Mary, the way of love that includes the mystery of the Eucharist because John, as the hymns of our Church say, drew all this theology from his personal and physical relationship with Christ.

When John leaned on the Lord's chest, he received theology. He knew the love of Christ, he returned this love with his own love and thus true theology was revealed to him. So the real and true theology also has within it our physical relationship with Christ, which our Church continues to offer us in the form of communion of Christ's body and blood. Because, when we partake of Christ's body and blood, we do nothing other than what John did when he leaned on Christ's chest. We are united with Christ physically and that is perfect, there is nothing greater than that.

Thus, my brothers and sisters, with our gratitude to Saint John and our prayer that he intercede for us, we honor his memory today in this beautiful church, and on this occasion, as a humble hierarch of a church founded by Saint John the Theologian, I convey to you the blessing of our Ecumenical Patriarch and my personal blessing. Many blessed years!

Chapel of Saint John the Theologian, Church of Saint Anna, Kifissia
September 26, 2005

69.
TRANSLATION OF THE APOSTLE AND EVANGELIST JOHN THE THEOLOGIAN

God is Love (1 Jn 4:12–19)

> *God is love, and he who abides in love abides in God, and God in him* (1 John 4:16)

The Lord has accounted us worthy today, my beloved brothers and sisters, to celebrate with him the passing of the beloved disciple John, for whom our Church reserves the great title of Theologian. He is the only disciple of the Lord who earned this title, whose depth and importance can be seen from everything he wrote and said about God Himself, about the very existence of God, the Being of God. Because other disciples were also accounted worthy to speak about God. The Apostle Paul reached the third heaven and heard ineffable words that cannot be spoken by man (2 Cor 12:4), but only John spoke to us about the very Being of God, what God is.

And we heard a little while ago in the first epistle that he wrote that God is love, not that God has love. Pay attention to this detail. Not because He loves, but because He is love itself. That is to say, love constitutes His Being, it is identified with God's Being, and there is no love anywhere that is as real and as true as in God Himself.

What does Saint John want to say with these important words? He wants to say that God is not a person, an entity that has feelings of love, but is the three persons of the Holy Trinity, where one exists together with the other and for the other, and this relationship of these persons is the very existence of God. Thus, we believe that God is Triune, He is the Holy Trinity, He is not one person, He is three persons, which means precisely that He is love. Because love presupposes and declares a relationship between persons. Love is not a feeling, it is a relationship between persons, so deep and so tied, that one cannot exist without the other. Let there not be "I" without "you", nor "you" without "I"; let there not be the Father without the Son and the Holy Spirit, nor the Son without the Father and the Holy Spirit, nor the Holy Spirit without the Son and the Father. And the Fathers of the Church teach that under no circumstances do these persons act alone. They always act together. Where the Father is, there is also the Son and the Holy Spirit, and this applies to every person of the Holy Trinity.

What binds these three persons is love. The one encompasses (*perichoresis*) the other, say the Fathers of the Church, and the one exists to give space and existence to the other. It is not easy, my dear brothers and sisters, to enter the full depth of this mystery of the Holy Trinity. But we can understand this: that none of the persons of the Holy Trinity can exist without the other, and each person of the Holy Trinity makes room for the other to exist. When Saint John says that "God is love," this is exactly what he means. God's existence is love.

Behold, then, what a great revelation John received and how God does, indeed, reveal His mysteries to whomever He wants and whenever He wants, even the mysteries of His existence. And that is why John the Theologian is the real theologian. Today we misuse this term and talk about theologians. Theologians in general, people who have this attribute of the theologian, have nothing to do with someone knowing—having God reveal to him—the very existence of God.

How did Saint John get this great gift? I think, my beloved brothers and sisters, that he received it because of his close relationship with Christ. It is no coincidence that in the Gospels, John is called the disciple whom Jesus loved, the beloved disciple. He had a special bond with Christ. Especially in relation to the other apostles. He is the one who leaned on Christ's breast at the Mystical (Last) Supper, and the one who asked the Lord who is the one who will betray Him when the Lord said that "one of you will betray me." He is the one who dared to ask such a personal question, and he is the one who not only honored the love that the Lord showed him, not only respected it, but also returned it.

He is the only one who remained next to the Cross out of all His disciples. When the others had scattered, when fear had seized them, he was there next to Christ, and he shared the Cross of Christ in his own way.

What does this tell us? That we cannot speak about God or the Holy Trinity if we do not go through Christ. He reveals God's love to us. Saint John told us today in his epistle, "not that we loved" (1 John 4:10), but because "He first loved us" (1 John 4:19). And God is the One who gave us not, as I say, a feeling. He gave us a part of Himself, His Son. And so the love that sustains God in the Holy Trinity, that constitutes His existence, is also transferred to us in the person of Christ. And Christ is the one who was revealed to us not mentally; with His existence, He brings us the love of God, He makes that love alive. And as a person of the Holy Trinity, He brings us God Himself. And John experienced this with his devotion to Christ, until the end.

But be careful. He had to go through the Cross to experience this. We cannot experience God's love, appreciate it or reciprocate it unless we also experience the Cross that the Son of God experienced. The love of God, crucified love, is that alone which reveals to us the very love of God, God himself.

If, therefore, God is love and if, as Saint John says, we cannot know God in any other way than by passing through love, then, my beloved brothers and sisters, we have before us the path which the Lord has laid out for us to walk. The path of love. But be careful, it is not something simple, because we have to go through the cross of the sacrifice of our will, as I said yesterday in the sermon, of the renunciation of ourselves, because that is the cross. And this is what the Lord Himself did when He was crucified. He cut off His own will, He did the will of His Father, and this led him to the painful way of the Cross. This is exactly what we are called to go through to say that we love God, or that we love our brother. He who loves, says John, "abides in God and God in him." There is nothing else that places us in the life of God, in the existence of God, than love, and everything else, if it does not have love, is useless. The Apostle Paul understood this when he said "if I have all faith, so as to remove mountains," "if I speak in the tongues of men and of angels," if I have all the gifts in the world, "but have not love, I am nothing" (1 Cor 13:1–2). Love is God Himself. God Himself, therefore, is what we ask for in order to live. In Him we want to find ourselves, in the communion of the Holy Trinity, in the three persons who love one another, to experience this love ourselves, living it in our daily lives, with our other brothers and sisters. Loving means sacrificing ourselves for the other to exist, for the other to live, and only then do we move, as far as possible, towards what the Fathers call theosis, our participation in the life of God Himself, which is love.

I have tired you, my beloved brothers and sisters, but the day calls for it. It is the day of the Theologian, the theologian *par excellence*, and whatever anyone says is insufficient. It cannot reach the depth of this great mystery which God wanted to reveal to the apostle, whom we honor today. Let us have his intercession, so that we can follow as much as we can this path, the path of love, and may God account us worthy of this love that is Himself, to experience it eternally with Him, through the intercessions of John the Theologian. Amen!

At the Holy Monastery of Saint John the Baptist, Essex, England
September 26, 2016

70.
SYNAXIS OF THE HOLY ARCHANGELS
The Angels of God (Heb 2:2–10)

By His grace, the Lord has allowed us to gather together for this holy synaxis in honor of the Archangels Michael and Gabriel and all the heavenly powers, the entire angelic world. At this feast, our thoughts turn to the holy angels and today I will devote a few thoughts to this great subject of the angelic powers.

What are angels, my brothers and sisters, and why and in what way do they contribute to our salvation? The Apostle Paul calls angels "ministering spirits sent forth to serve, for the sake of those who are to obtain salvation" (Heb. 1:14). So angels are spirits, they are holy, they are incorporeal, although not in the same sense as God is immaterial and incorporeal, because they are God's creations, they are noetic creations, without having a body that all the material creatures of creation have; they were created by God before the material world and they constitute the noetic, invisible world that surrounds us.

We live in an age where people believe only in what they see with their eyes and what they touch with their hands. We are so gullible that we think that what we see and what we touch are the only things that exist. However, in the "Symbol of Faith" we confess that God is the Maker of all visible and invisible beings. The human mind and human senses can never grasp this entire mystery of the world. There is always something beyond our senses. There is something that we cannot control with our senses and with our logic. And this, my brothers and sisters, even the scientists today are ready to accept. No one believes anymore that everything that we perceive with our senses is everything that exists. Every day we discover new worlds, every day we discover unknown things, invisible things. So the invisible world—with noetic powers—surrounds us.

And the angels belong to these noetic powers. They are "ministering" spirits, says the apostle. Their first and most important activity is to glorify God incessantly around His throne, to sing "Holy, holy, holy Lord of hosts," to praise and glorify God, because this is the purpose of creation: to glorify God, and the angels are the ones who constantly glorify God, both with their eternal chanting but also with their way of life. Therefore, the angels are ministers of the Most High and for this reason our Church considers them to participate in its worship; especially at the time of the Divine Eucharist/Liturgy, as we are now, the angels are present, participating in the worship, ministers to the priests. Don't think this is strange. The Church, if you look at Byzantine iconography, always represents the deacons as angels, because the deacons minister to the bishop and the priests and in this way are icons and types of the angels. The angels therefore participate in the Liturgy, this eternal and universal Liturgy which permanently revolves around the throne of God, and of which this Liturgy that we celebrate is an image. So they are our co-ministering angels, liturgical[1] spirits.

They are also spirits that God sends to fulfill His will. God has a plan for the salvation of the world, and He entrusts this plan to the angels to carry it out. So the angels are those free beings who minister and serve the will of God. They are the ones who never say "no" to God, the ones who live precisely for God's will to be carried out in the world. That is why those angels, also free, who chose not to obey God's will fell, and from them were created the demons, who were also angels, but angels who did not obey God's will, who listened to their own will rather than the will of God, and for this they were condemned to eternal death. Angels, however, always remain faithful to God's will and do what God commands them to do. That is why we see them always active and participating in the great events of our salvation. An Angel of the Lord conveys the message to the Virgin Mary that she will conceive the Lord, and that the Son and Word of God will become flesh. An Angel of the Lord participates in the whole

[1] The word in Heb 1:14 translated by "ministering" is literally "liturgical."

life of Christ, especially in difficult times, such as the time of temptations and the time in Gethsemane when the Lord was about to take the great step towards the Cross: an angel of God stands by him. Angels announce the Resurrection of Christ to the Myrrhbearers. Angels always accompany us in our lives and rejoice when we repent, rejoice when we are on God's path and are saddened when we stray from God's path. There is joy in heaven, says the Lord, "over one sinner who repents" (Lk 15:7); all the angels rejoice. And each one of us has our own angel. We are all under the protection of the angels, since the angels are the closest to God because of their immaterial and spiritual nature, but also because of their free obedience to the will of God. They never disappoint God. So the angels are ministers of our salvation.

And finally, the angels are ministers of the mystery of salvation in Christ. Angels are no longer superior to humans, even if their nature is spiritual, because Christ took upon Himself human nature, and by elevating it, sanctifying it, offering it to the Father, He made it surpass even the angels. And this is why the Fathers and the hymn writers of the Church comment on the Ascension of the Lord in a shocking way. When, it says, the angels saw a man, the incarnate Christ, ascending to the throne of God, they stood up, prostrated themselves, and marveled at how it was possible for a man to ascend so high. Yes, brothers and sisters, man who is the link between the immaterial and the material creation, because he participates in both, the very human being whom Christ assumed, now became higher than the angels, and the angels also submitted to Christ. And the angels now need Christ to be saved; they need Christ to live eternally. Everything now revolves around the person of Christ. And the angels minister this mystery of Christ, the mystery of the salvation of the world in Christ.

My brothers and sisters, it is not easy in our time to convey this message of the existence and ministry of angels. However, when the Church gathers, as it does today, to honor the angels and archangels, it wants to convey this message to the world: not to limit ourselves to the material creation, not to limit ourselves to material goods, not to care only for our body, because there is a spiritual and immaterial world and it surrounds us and cares for our salvation. So we are gathered here today to receive this great message, that we are surrounded by angelic powers, that they protect us, and to draw strength and hope from it. Because when angelic forces surround us, demonic forces can never defeat us. God and His will are stronger than Satan, and the angels, when they surround us in our lives and in our journeys, protect us from all harm.

I pray, my brothers and sisters, that the holy Commanders of the heavenly powers Michael and Gabriel and all the incorporeal powers protect all of you, our Church, our people, and the whole world from all evil and lead us to the eternal Kingdom, where praises to God are constantly offered by the angels and the saints.

Church of the Holy Archangels, Peristeri Attica
November 8, 1998

71.
SYNAXIS OF THE HOLY ARCHANGELS
Angels in our lives (Luke 10:16–21)

Once again, my beloved brothers and sisters, the grace of the Lord has allowed us to reverently celebrate in this beautiful temple, which has been erected and adorned by your piety, the synaxis of the Holy Archangels Michael and Gabriel and all the heavenly incorporeal powers, with the blessing of your esteemed shepherd Metropolitan Chrysostomos, whom I also thank for allowing my humility to lead today's holy assembly.

Today is dedicated to the holy angels. We will also devote some thoughts to them, my dear brothers and sisters, because many times while we call on them and ask for their help, we are not fully aware of their importance for our lives.

The Apostle Paul calls angels "ministering spirits sent forth to serve, for the sake of those who are to obtain salvation" (Heb. 1:14). So the angels are spirits. We confess in the "Symbol of Faith" that God did not only create a visible world, but also an invisible one. We believe, we say, "in one God, the Father, Almighty, Maker of heaven and earth, and of all things visible and invisible." So there is also an invisible world, a world that is not controlled by our senses, an intangible, bodiless world. We too often limit ourselves to accepting and believing in the world that falls under our senses, as if it were the only world that exists. But the whole world is a great mystery, and even those things that fall under our senses cannot be known by us in all their importance and true existence. So our senses cannot perceive everything that exists. And angels are precisely invisible spirits, which our senses cannot perceive, but they are nevertheless true and existent. And today's celebration calls us to escape, as much as we can, from being bound to the material world and to think that there is also an invisible and intangible world. And the angels, says the apostle, are "ministering spirits" (λειτουργικὰ πνεύματα), because the angels, as already described in the Old Testament, have as their primary task to circle around the throne of God and to glorify God with the Trisagion hymn, as the Prophet Isaiah saw and heard it, "Holy, holy, holy Lord of hosts," this hymn that we also repeat in the Liturgy. This is the first work of the angels, to praise the glory of God. And being next to the throne of God and glorifying God, they themselves are glorified and become bright and shine and share in the glory of God. And that is why, my dear brothers and sisters, angels participate in every Divine Liturgy. And at this moment when we celebrate the Divine Liturgy, but also in every Divine Liturgy, the world of angels participates. We humans do not serve the Liturgy alone; the angels are also present. And they also minister to the priests and bishops in their work. And for this reason, the Church, in its iconography, even in the Byzantine era, represents the deacons dressed as angels and the angels dressed as deacons. Because the Divine Liturgy that we celebrate here is the same Liturgy that is celebrated in heaven before the throne of God, and for this reason the angels participate in our worship. The visible and the invisible world unite in the Divine Liturgy, we become one, a community of saints, a community that before the throne of God exclaims with the angels "Holy, holy, holy Lord of hosts, heaven and earth are full of your glory. Hosanna in the highest." This hymn that we will sing shortly here is the hymn that the angels constantly sing before the throne of God.

But the angels have another important characteristic. They are the ones who carry out God's commands with absolute obedience. God created other spirits before He created humans. But many of these spirits did not obey God and, while they are angels, because they did not obey God and rebelled against God, they turned into demons. So there are also demon angels, created by God as angels, who rebelled against the will of God. The angels, however, are those who never oppose the will of God, and they carry this will of God as messengers, as we say, to the world.

That is why angels participate in all the great events of the life of the world, and all the events of our salvation. The Archangel Gabriel came and conveyed to the Virgin Mary the message that she will conceive the Son of God; an angel stood with the Lord in the temptations in the desert; an angel stood with the Lord in Gethsemane shortly before his death on the Cross; angels are in the tomb during His Resurrection and announce the fact of the Resurrection to the myrrhbearing women; there are angels everywhere.

God communicates with His world through angels. Thus, my beloved brothers and sisters, the angels exist in the whole of creation, but also in the Church and in our salvation, "ministering spirits sent forth to serve," for the salvation of the world. Thus the angels become protectors of the world, protectors of us all, and our pious people believe that each one of us has his angel, the angel who protects him, the angel who in difficult times gives him his wings and shelters him from all evil.

The presence of angels in our lives, my dear brothers and sisters, is a fact that every believer not only accepts, but experiences, lives, sees in his life.

But the angels, who are in front of us and lead us in every step of our life, watch over our life. They see our movements, they see our works, they see our thoughts and, when these works and these thoughts are in accordance with God's will, they rejoice. But when these works and thoughts are contrary to God's will, the angels are saddened. And that is why we need great care in our lives so as not to sadden the angels, who accompany us and cover us with their grace.

My beloved brothers and sisters, we live in a materialistic world, in a world, in a culture—a so-called culture, at any rate—which deals with nothing but matter. How will we satisfy our material needs, how will we increase our bodily enjoyment, how will we increase our pleasure. Our world today is nothing but a struggle to increase our standard of living, our wealth, a struggle without end, a struggle which subjects us to mental and physical fatigue and makes us lose our faith in a world which is not material. So the angels today, my beloved brothers and sisters, are calling us to leave the earth, to think that our destiny is to be together with the angels close to God, because that is where our happiness lies and not in the material goods of this world. And that is precisely why today's feast is an opportunity that our Church uses to send a message to the world, the message that there is an intangible world, that matter is not everything, that our destiny is to unite with this intangible world and to be close to the glory of God.

Let us, my dears, realize this message, let us put it deep in our hearts, because we cannot say otherwise that we honor the holy angels, unless we take this message into our hearts and pass it on to the following generations. Our ancestors lived with this faith in the angelic world. They believed that angels accompany them in their journeys and that at the end of their lives, angels receive their souls and take them to the throne of God. Let us acquire this simple faith again, my dear brothers and sisters, in this materialistic world in which we live. Let us be a light, a witness, a true witness to the glory of God. Amen!

Holy Church of Taxiarchs (old) Peristeri
November 8, 2005

72.
ST. NEKTARIOS OF PENTAPOLIS
The cup of ill repute

I am the good shepherd; I know my own and my own know me (John 10:14)

We were brought together by the grace of the Lord, my beloved brothers and sisters, to celebrate the memory of one of the most popular and beloved saints of the Church. A saint who sanctified all the places he passed through. His birthplace of Silyvria, the island of Aegina, which justly boasts because it has his holy relics, but also this school, in whose temple we gathered today, to celebrate his memory. Because even here, Saint Nektarios sanctified this place with his long tenure as director of the Rizarios School, with all the wisdom with which he ran the school and the holiness he set as an example to his students and to our society today.

And now this saint is the one who knows us all by name, just as the good shepherd, our Lord, knows us and we know him. Because he is now in all our hearts. And because he hears our prayers, he hears our requests, he knows our pain, he transfers all this to the throne of God and in this way offers us the grace of God and his miraculous intervention.

But today, when we have gathered to honor his memory, we are given the opportunity, my brothers and sisters, to delve a little deeper into this subject of holiness, which is manifest in the person of Saint Nektarios.

Every saint expresses holiness in his own way. Holiness belongs to God. No man is holy. But God's holiness is expressed through people. And it is expressed in various ways, so that the personal characteristics of each saint are not lost.

So today, looking at the cheerful form of Saint Nektarios, we can draw great lessons about holiness. Because holiness, my brothers and sisters, is not only for specific saints. It is for all of us. This is the measure by which we should measure our lives. So what does the saint whom we honor today show us as a special characteristic of holiness?

First, it reveals to us that holiness is not limited to certain times. Holiness always exists and is manifested in every era. And many times, "where sin abounded," as the apostle Paul says, "grace abounded much more" (Rom 5:20).

And so, in an era in which sin truly abounded, the grace of Saint Nektarios comes to remind us that there is no era, there is no time, there is no place that does not manifest holiness, that is not receptive to God's holiness.

And the holiness of Saint Nektarios still reveals to us that holiness is usually hidden from the eyes of people. It is hidden from the saints themselves, who never reveal their holiness. On the contrary, they consider themselves as the most sinful. It is typical of what we know from the life of the ascetic Saint Anthony, who believed and proclaimed that everyone will go to heaven except him.

Holiness is therefore hidden! And when holiness is hidden, then it is true holiness.

So the saint himself hides it, but God Himself hides it many times, so that he can set before us a terrible truth: that our brother, whom we have next to us, can be a saint; he can be a hidden saint and we don't know it. Let us treat all people as if they were holy, "potential saints."

It is a very sad phenomenon to judge our brothers and find them sinful. It is a great mistake, my brothers and sisters. We should find only ourselves sinners and all others around us as saints.

And this is so true in the life of Saint Nektarios that he himself went through a terrible test, precisely because his holiness was hidden and because of people's tendency to judge others, to criticize them and to find them sinners. And this also manifested itself in the life of Saint Nektarios.

This demonstrates another aspect of Saint Nektarios' holiness—that many times holiness passes through not only praise but also from "ill repute," as the apostle Paul says. That is, not only from the good words that people say about us, but also from the accusations against us; and from there holiness can appear.

Therefore, Saint Nektarios passed through this the test of slander, of accusation, of his agony which we usually call "public approval," which comes from anything other than God. Saint Nektarios passed through all this whirlwind of slander because the Apostle Paul's words also applied to him, that we journey through "good repute and ill repute" (2 Cor 6:8).

And one wonders, why does God allow the saints to be tested thus? He allows it, my brothers and sisters, in order to prove, first, that the judgment of men is as a rule erroneous. Because we humans judge by the surface. We judge by what we see. And reality is not always—actually, almost never—what we see with our eyes. It is that which we see with our hearts! And when our heart is not pure, we do not see the life of others as pure. When our heart is pure, then we see everyone around us as pure. So we judge superficially. We do not know the truth that is hidden in the other's life and existence.

The other reason God allows this is that in this way the most important condition of holiness is ensured: humility. Because only when others accuse and criticize us, then we avoid temptation, which is very alive and strong when others praise us. Then the temptation of selfishness and pride is very strong and, as I said, the most important condition of holiness, which is humility, is not cultivated.

Humility is more easily cultivated when others do not praise us but criticize us, even if it is unfair. Because our Lord was also unfairly criticized. And let us not forget that in His life, as the holy Gospels record, there were many people—one might even say the whole society of the time and especially the rulers of that time—who called him a "glutton and drunkard," socializing with publicans and sinners (Mt 11:19). And He ultimately paid not only the price of ill repute but also the ignominious death of the cross itself, which was the most dishonorable form of death.

It is therefore not possible for the saints, who are icons of Jesus Christ, to avoid this cross of dishonor and ill repute. For this reason, God allows, as he allowed Saint Nektarios, this cup of ill repute. And God allows all this because he wants to show us that in reality no one is holy, that only God is holy.

In a little while at the Divine Liturgy, my brothers and sisters, we will hear this shocking phrase—when we raise the lamb inside, the liturgists exclaim: "The holy things for the holy people of God," that is, we say that this holy body of the Lord is now called to be partaken of by the saints, the members of the Church. And then these members of the Church will exclaim with the mouth of the psalmist: "One is holy, one is Lord, Jesus Christ." No one is holy! Only God is holy! And man's holiness is participation in God's holiness. In this way we understand that no matter how many virtues we have, they do not guarantee us a place among the saints of God. What ensures us holiness is consciousness of our sinfulness; it is our repentance. The Church therefore does not know of any moral virtues that ensure holiness. It knows repentance, the awareness of sinfulness as the door to heaven, the door to the Kingdom of God.

Thus, my beloved brothers and sisters, Saint Nektarios comes today to call us all to imitate his life, because "the feast of a saint is imitation of a saint," as Saint John Chrysostom says. Let us imitate a life of humility. A life that patiently endures temptations and persecutions. A life which in this way expresses the life of our Lord Himself.

And by bringing this holiness into modern society, Saint Nektarios teaches us to approach him not only to derive benefits from him, to derive the grace and benefit that his presence and miraculous energy give. But let us also draw from him the ethos of holiness that he himself inspires. And in this way he gives us the measure with which we should measure ourselves, as he measured himself by the holiness of God. And when we do this, we will also find ourselves lacking in holiness. And in this way we will be able to approach with our humility the ideal of holiness expressed by Saint Nektarios.

The saint does not simply bring us a model of holiness, my brothers and sisters. He also brings us something even more important. The very love of God for man. Because the love of God is expressed precisely through the saints. Through those who are all love themselves, they convey God's love to us. And in this way they give us the deepest meaning of the entire Gospel, which is precisely that God does not abandon the world. He loves man and with His grace constantly surrounds him and protects him. And so, when we venerate the saint and ask for his grace, we find that God still loves us, that God does not abandon us. Even in our trials His love is present. Because the prayer of Saint Nektarios is always with us, with all of us, and that is precisely why it is the expression of the very love of God. Let us run, my brothers and sisters, to the grace of Saint Nektarios with faith that this saint conveys to our world the love of God, the love of God made flesh, and in this way he conveys to us life itself. The life which is true and not false, as our biological life is.

Thus, my brothers and sisters, the saint whom we honor today will become our guide, a guide to the true life of God, and the favors we receive from him will not be just temporary favors, but eternal favors, which will open the gate of eternal life to us, and the Kingdom of God. Amen!

Saint George's Chapel, Rizarios Ecclesiastical School
(old building) on Vasilissa Sofia Street
November 9, 2002

73.
ST. NEKTARIOS OF PENTAPOLIS
(John 10:9–16)

I am the door; if any one enters by me, he will be saved (John 10:9)

Today, the Lord has accounted us worthy, my beloved brothers and sisters, to honor the memory of a contemporary saint, Saint Nektarios, the miracle worker, who was glorified by the Lord so much that he had the gift of healing, but also became known throughout the world, so that daily holy temples are built in his honor, all over the world. It is indeed an amazing case of a man being glorified by God.

Just a few moments ago, we read the Church's appointed Gospel passage for his memory, which begins with these words that I told you earlier. The words of the Lord, that He is the door and only whoever passes through this door will be saved. And there is, really, no saint who does not pass through this door. Holiness is embodied in the person of Christ, and He is the Holy One. That is why in the Divine Liturgy, shortly before Holy Communion, when the priest raises the Holy Bread and says: "The holy things for the holy people of God," the people answer: "One is holy, one is Lord, Jesus Christ." No one else is holy; there is only one Who is holy, Christ. Therefore, all the saints must, in some way, identify with Christ in order to be saints. To participate in holiness, it is not enough to be virtuous, to be a good person, to do good works. We must pass through this door, which is Christ, and, as He Himself told us, only by passing through this door will we be saved.

However, the Lord also called this door a narrow gate (Mt 7:13–14). He says that the gate that leads to salvation and life is narrow. And we must pass through this narrow gate to be led to salvation. The passage through the door, which is Christ, therefore, is not so easy, so painless. Because the Lord himself passed through the narrow gate. He is the one who emptied Himself of His glory and took upon Himself human nature, together with all the consequences that the fall of man and sin had for human nature. And so He humbled Himself to the point of hell; he went through this whole path of sorrows and, in this way alone, he reached the glory of the Resurrection. That is why the saints are called to pass through this narrow gate, to live, to experience what the Lord Himself experienced, to identify with Him in this humiliation, in the descent to hell, in order to then be elevated to the glory of God and His Kingdom.

And the saint whom we honor today, my dear brothers and sisters, followed this path. He reached humility, the ultimate humility, so that he could enjoy the glory that the Lord reserved for him.

Humility, my dear brothers and sisters, is often something that a person achieves on his own, on his own initiative. But there are other times when the humiliation comes from other people, who want to humiliate us, who want to weaken us, and then we are faced with the dilemma of how to react. How to react to hostility, to the malice of people, to slander. Saint Nektarios went through exactly this experience. He was slandered a lot, brutally, and his response was to accept this humiliation unflinchingly. He could have defended himself in many ways because he was innocent, but he left vengeance and restoration to God. He took these attacks that people imposed on him as an opportunity for humility and salvation, and thus he imitated Christ, he identified himself with Christ, who was also slandered. In response to all of them, he remained silent, did not answer, did not try to prove the opposite, but rather left it to God his Father to prove his innocence.

This, of course, my beloved brothers and sisters, is very difficult. When we are attacked, then the old man in us, our nature, tries to defend ourselves, and we react either by trying to justify ourselves, to refute the accusations against us, or by hating the enemies who accuse us unjustly. And that is why it is a spiritual achievement to be able to remain silent when one is slandered.

People usually don't do this. They protest and many times attack their slanderers even through judicial means, because the laws of this world protect our reputation; therefore, they ask for the restoration of their character, so that in this way they can be justified before men. This, however, is not the attitude of the saints. As I said, even the Lord Himself was slandered: "When he was reviled, he did not revile in return; when he suffered, he did not threaten," but instead leaves the judgment to the righteous judge (1Peter 2:23). Saint Nektarios also endured this humiliation without complaint, in such a way as to pass through the narrow gate, that is, through Christ Himself, to take upon himself what Christ Himself bore, this cross of humiliation. And only in this way did he reach the glory with which God surrounded him. After his death, however, God revealed that all the accusations against him were lies, and that Nektarios was a saint. And God revealed this by granting him the power to work miracles, after which all the people revered him as a saint. And this is precisely what happened in the case of our Lord. After His death on the cross, the Resurrection revealed that He was the Son of God, God Himself.

This difficult path, my dear brothers and sisters, means completely burying ourselves, to accept being wronged, as the Apostle Paul says: "Why do you not rather accept wrong?" (1 Cor 6:7). The Apostle asked the Corinthians: "Why do you run to the law courts rather than accept being wronged?" This, however, is contrary to modern ethics. Ethics compels us to be fair, and when we are wronged to restore justice.[1] But as the Lord says, if your righteousness does not exceed that of the Pharisees, because the Pharisees were models of righteousness, you cannot enter the Kingdom of God (cf. Mt 5:20). Therefore, you must be wronged. And this injustice has many forms in our lives. In general, the affliction that injustice causes against us is the affliction that identifies us with Christ, the affliction with which we pass into the Kingdom of God. "It is through many tribulations that we must enter the kingdom of God (Acts 14:22)," says the Apostle. No one can

[1] In Greek, this word δικαιοσύνη can be translated variously as justice, justification, or righteousness.

enter into the Kingdom of God by a comfortable road, by the wide and broad road; this broad road leads to perdition, says the Lord. The way that leads to salvation is the narrow gate; that's why he tells us "enter by the narrow gate" (Mt 7:13).

This, my beloved brothers and sisters, is the road taken by all the saints and martyrs, and we are called to endure the same. I don't know how many of you have suffered slander, but I imagine you will have experienced this temptation to one degree or another. How much do we react to protest our innocence, our holiness, our virtues? This is precisely what makes all the slander and injustice an opportunity for our salvation. Because when we submit to them and let God decide our fate, then we pass precisely through the door, which is Christ. Saint Maximus the Confessor writes in his work, On Love, that there is nothing worse and no heavier thing to bear than slander "either against one's faith or one's manner of life." In these case, he says, there is only one path: to leave it to God to justify us, and not to attempt to justify ourselves.

We have to identify with all these accusations, which is not fair, but deep down we carry with us our own sinfulness. Consequently, we are sinners, and when someone accuses us of sinfulness, of sins, then it is natural to answer: "Yes, you are right, deep down I am not a saint." And then, if we believe this and we maintain this attitude, and we do not protest against the accusations, then we too, like the Lord, are brought out of the depths of man's existence—that is, his hell—and resurrected by God and glorified in His Kingdom.

Few are those who entered the Kingdom of God "through many tribulations." Unfortunately, most of us look to avoid the narrow gate and instead pass through the broad way so as not to trouble ourselves. Saint Nektarios carries this spirit to us today with his life. He is a contemporary saint. And this is of great importance, my brothers and sisters. It means that God did not deprive His Church of the gift of holiness. Saints are not only those who lived many centuries ago, at the beginning of the history of the Church. In every age God raises up saints. That is why God gives us the opportunity, through the saints, our contemporary saints, to keep ourselves, as much as possible, close to their example and to pass as much as we can through the narrow gate, the only door that leads to salvation. Many times, the contemporary saints are not visible. God unveils them later. But we also have visible saints whom we have the privilege of having met personally, and for that, may the name of God be glorified, because He does not abandon us, and does not deprive us of holiness.

Through the prayers of the saints, my beloved brothers and sisters, let us march forward, remaining close to them and trying to pass through the narrow gate. Let us beseech God to account us worthy to live in His Kingdom with the saints and to enjoy, as much as God's grace allows, the sight of His face, His glory, and in this way may the Triune God, the Father, the Son and the Holy Spirit be glorified throughout the ages. Amen.

At the Holy Monastery of Saint John the Baptist, Essex, England
November 9, 2016

74.
ST. NEKTARIOS OF PENTAPOLIS
Memorial for Ekaterina Zizioula

I would like to express my gratitude from the bottom of my heart to the holy abbot, the fathers, brothers and sisters of this holy monastery and to all of you, my beloved brothers and sisters, who prayed for the repose of my dear sister Katherine, who visited this monastery and had a special reverence for both the monastery and Elder Sophrony.

Memory is the only antidote we have against death. But human memory is temporary. Only when we commit our loved ones to the memory of the eternal God, then they live forever. Because whatever God "remembers," whatever He has in His memory, takes existence. It lives. There we always commit our dead, our loved ones, when they depart from this life, that is why the Church has the Divine Liturgy, the Divine Eucharist, where the memory of the Lamb is celebrated, in which we also place the memory of our beloved brothers and sisters, living and reposed.

Let us glorify God and Saint Nektarios, through whose prayers we were accounted worthy today to honor his memory and the memory of our loved ones who have departed this life. Let us commit them to the eternal memory of God.

Eternal be their memory!

At the Holy Monastery of Saint John the Baptist, Essex, England
November 9, 2016

75.
THE APOSTLE ANDREW, THE FIRST-CALLED
Return of the holy relics of Sts. Gregory the Theologian and John Chrysostom (1 Cor 4:9–16)

For I became your father in Christ Jesus through the gospel. I urge you, then, be imitators of me (1 Cor 4:15–16).

Our holy Church has selected these words of the Apostle Paul to honor and celebrate, in eucharistic synaxis, the Apostle Andrew who, according to Basil of Seleucia is the "namesake of courage, the first-called of the Master's disciples, and leader of the apostolic choir." These are the apostolic words that our Mother Church powerfully projects from the holy ambo for our pious reflection and spiritual benefit during today's feast in honor of the founder of this apostolic and first throne of the Orthodox Church. Because these words summarize the nature and character of the Church in general, but also of this church in particular, and they are particularly appropriate for today's eucharistic gathering.

Your All-Holiness, reverend hierarchs, venerable representatives of the most holy Orthodox Churches, venerable representatives of Old Rome, devout congregation,

In every Divine Liturgy, space and time lose their divisive nature and become bodies of communion of the living and the reposed, of the near and far, of the local and the universal Church, of history and the eschaton; in today's Divine Liturgy, these things are taking place in a unique way. The past becomes present today thanks to the repatriation here of the holy relics of two of the most prominent and ever-memorable predecessors of this holy throne, Gregory the Theologian and John Chrysostom. Today, this city becomes ecumenical, thanks to the presence of representatives of the local holy Orthodox Churches. And the present today becomes an expectation of the future, a prayer and a wish for the unity of all. Indeed, this day is great and historic and

God-given! Today, the spiritual father of this church, the Apostle Andrew, presiding spiritually at this feast together with Gregory the Theologian and John Chrysostom, rejoices, and through the mouth of Paul, addressing us, reminds and admonishes us: "For I became your father in Christ Jesus through the gospel. I urge you, then, be imitators of me."

But what does it mean that the apostle "became our father in Christ Jesus through the gospel"? Let us, brothers and sisters, dive into the deeper meaning of these words.

First of all, notice that the apostle clearly distinguishes the quality of "pedagogue" from that of "father" and begetter: "For though you have countless guides in Christ, you do not have many fathers" (1 Cor 4:15). The apostle is not just a teacher, and the gospel is not just a revelation of lofty truths. It is mainly a "birth," different from that given by natural and biological fathers. Because, while natural fathers give birth to mortal beings, the Gospel, as the good news of victory over death, gives birth through the apostles to people redeemed from death, resurrected in the risen Christ.

The apostles, consequently, are not content with the preaching of the Gospel, but they establish churches, build altars, so that the Holy Eucharist—the medicine of immortality according to Saint Ignatius of Antioch, through which people taste victory over death—can be celebrated. In addition, they make bishops, presiders at the Eucharist, through whom the apostolic fatherhood and succession continues until the end of the ages as the redemption of time from decay and death.

Likewise through the adventures of history in the Great Church, whose first altar was built by Saint Andrew the First-Called, the mystery of our birth into a life redeemed from death is celebrated. "What is it, then, in the final analysis", asks a blessed hierarch of the Ecumenical Throne, "what is the commemoration of the Apostle Andrew, what is this feast of the Throne [...]?" "It is," he replies, "a witness. A witness that God lives in history and survives history."

Behold, then, what the Throne is celebrating today. It celebrates the paradox of its survival through the vicissitudes of history. It celebrates its uninterrupted continuity through apostolic succession. It celebrates the fact that, by the grace and mercy of the Lord, the Throne not only preserved apostolic succession without interruption, but also faithfully observed the exhortation of the apostle: "I beseech you, then, be imitators of me." But in what way?

First, with the Throne's faithfulness to the Gospel. A guardian of "the faith which was once for all delivered to the saints" (Jude 3), this Throne preserved the authentic Orthodox teaching that was delivered to us by the Ecumenical Councils and the Church Fathers. Throughout the centuries, this Church never stopped hearing the golden mouth of John and the shepherd's pipe of Gregory the Theologian. All the local Orthodox Churches were drawn to her during the hard times throughout the ages, in order to make sure that they remained steadfast in the faith of their fathers.

Second, this Throne became an imitator of the apostles not only because it was born from them but also because it, like them, also gave birth to another Church "in Christ Jesus through the gospel." It is a boast in the Lord for this Throne because it has been the mother of many churches, whose altars it has nurtured, and to which it can humbly but also with boldness say "I became your father." Everyone rejoices—as, indeed, does this Throne—that most of these churches are already grown and have received not only the Gospel and the Orthodox faith, but also the way we worship the true God.

It is doubtless not profitable for the Mother Church to boast, except in its infirmities (cf. 2 Cor 12:1–5). Perhaps the most authentic proof of the apostolicity of the Throne celebrating today is not what I just mentioned. It is rather found in what precedes "I became your father" in today's epistle lesson. This is because of Paul's shocking words to the Corinthians, which we heard a little while ago and we must hear again:

"We [the apostles] are weak, but you [the Corinthians] are strong. You are held in honor, but we in disrepute" (1 Cor 4:10). In spite of this, "when reviled, we bless; when persecuted, we endure; when slandered, we try to conciliate" (1 Cor 4:12). And this because, as the same apostle writes in another letter to the Corinthians, we apostles walk "in honor and dishonor, in ill repute and good repute [...] as dying, and behold we live; as punished, and yet not killed; as sorrowful, yet always rejoicing; as poor, yet making many rich; as having nothing, and yet possessing everything" (2 Cor 6:8–9).

Here, then, is the most convincing proof of the apostolicity of this Throne. So much of the above could be applied to it! So much could this Throne even say today, as well as through the ages! There is apostolic succession in participating in the sufferings of Christ and the apostles. "Come and see" it in the Church of Saint Andrew the First-Called. There is strength, which "is made perfect in weakness" (2 Cor 12:9). But "we have this treasure in earthen vessels" (1 Cor 4:7) so that you can put your finger here and touch the historical flesh of the Throne that is celebrating today.

Your All-Holiness, beloved brothers and sisters,

The return of the holy relics of two of the most famous holy patriarchs of this Throne is a significant historical event. And this, not only because these holy relics are returning the way they left after eight centuries, but also because they carry with them many meaningful messages from the past in the present for the future. Let's listen carefully to what these holy relics have to say to the Church.

When Gregory the Theologian, bowing to the pleading of the people, left the peaceful life he had chosen for himself in Seleucia in Isauria, in order to come to this city,[1] the Orthodox Church here was being squeezed by the Arian emperors so much that it shrunk to a small, disreputable minority nearing extinction. Saint Gregory, unable to liturgize in his cathedral church, turned the humble house of one of his relatives into a temple, and gave it the name *Anastasia* as a symbol of the Resurrection. And indeed a Resurrection came. How? First, with the unwavering apostolic conviction that history is not directed ultimately by man, but by God. And secondly, with the power of theology. Yes, this Church

[1] Constantinople.

survived at that critical turning point in its history only thanks to the famous theological discourses of Gregory in the humble Church of the Resurrection. Theology is the Church's power over all other forces, diplomatic or economic.

Let us turn now to John Chrysostom, physically present among you all again, telling stories and teaching. He once again addresses "those scandalized by the unfortunate events," and speak to us as well. Sorrows and difficulties must not shake our faith in God's love and in the future:

"You have a Master," he writes, "Who is the most loving of fathers and most caring of mothers… For God's providence is inscrutable, His care incomprehensible, his kindness unsearchable, and his charity unfathomable."

The great interpreter of the mystery of the Church comes today to remind us that nothing is as dangerous for her as her division: "Nothing so provokes God's anger as the division of the Church." Those who are complacent and do not strive, nor work for the unity of the Church, will always be condemned by these words of our father Saint John Chrysostom.

Beloved brothers and sisters,

When Chrysostom's devoted disciple Proclus, as archbishop of the Church here, carried out the transfer of the holy relics of this holy father in 438 AD, the Church was deeply divided. One party, the "Johannites," dedicated to Chrysostom, refused to recognize his successors on the throne, while the Church of Rome had broken communion with the Patriarchates of Constantinople, Alexandria, and Antioch, because these latter had deleted Saint John Chrysostom from the Diptychs. While communion between these Patriarchates and the Church of Rome was restored by the re-insertion of Chrysostom's name in the Diptychs, the "Johannite" schism continued. It only stopped, apparently, when the holy relics of Chrysostom were transferred to Constantinople.

If the energizing effect of the transfer of the holy relics of Saint Chrysostom for the unity of the Church was so great and shocking in that era, we are entitled, if nothing else, to pray that today's return of relics to the saint's cathedral will contribute to overcoming the division that has plagued the Church for a millennium. The road is certainly long and difficult, but "hope does not disappoint." This gesture by Elder Rome and its bishop is a desirable step in the right direction.

Your All-Holiness,

The pulpit now turns to you in conclusion. He considers it his duty to express the Church's gratitude for what has been celebrated today before the eyes of history. Your initiative to ask for the return of the holy relics of two of your predecessors to their cathedral church, which was granted by the bishop of Elder Rome, is yet another in a series of actions during your reign designed to bring about peace and reconciliation.

The return of the holy relics of the two great fathers and teachers, not only of the East but also of the West, will always remind us of our common obligation to promote the unity of the Church of Christ in love and truth. Their presence in the city of your cathedral will serve as a source of sanctification, strength, and hope for your flock, but also for all those who will come here to pay their respects to the Church which was founded by Saint Andrew the First-Called, and shepherded with the wisdom of Gregory the Theologian and John Chrysostom.

May the intercessions to God of the first-called of the apostles and these two great hierarchs and teachers protect and support this holy throne for the good of the whole Church and all people. Amen.

76.
THE APOSTLE ANDREW, THE FIRST-CALLED
Spiritual fatherhood in the life of the Church (1 Cor 4:9–16)

> *For though you have countless guides in Christ, you do not have many fathers. For I became your father in Christ Jesus through the gospel* (1 Cor 4:15)

Today our Church, my beloved brothers and sisters, honors the first-called apostle Andrew, the founder of the Church of Constantinople, the one who was martyred by being crucified in the Greek city of Patras, whose name is borne by so many Orthodox believers. And to honor the memory of this great apostle, the Church chose the apostolic reading that we just heard.

This reading describes the way in which the apostles live, a life that goes through unimaginable difficulties, including attacks against them, and it ends in these words that I just read, in which the Apostle Paul lays out a very serious matter, with which I will occupy you for a few minutes, my brothers and sisters.

Paul says that you can have many teachers, but you don't have many fathers. I am your father who gave birth to you.

What is the difference between teachers and fathers? The difference is that teachers work to make people's lives and themselves better, whereas fathers are the ones who give not the good life, but life itself, existence. Without fathers, we would not exist. However, without teachers, we simply would not be good people. And the apostles are fathers, he says in the passage, and not teachers. They are not teachers; they are the ones who give birth to people.

However, a question arises, my brothers and sisters. We know that we are born from natural fathers. How is it possible to be born by the Apostle Paul? Apart from natural birth, there is another birth, which is not the kind that will make us better people—because that is the work of teachers—but which will make us exist, live, be. We must go a little deeper into this question, my brothers and sisters.

Natural fathers, natural paternity, indeed give us our existence, but they give it to us in a very contradictory way. We are born, but we are born mortal. The fact that we die does not happen at the end of our life, as we think. We die from the first moment we are born. This is a truth that is also established by the science of biology. The human cell, the human being, as soon as it is born, contains death, it already begins to die. So fathers, natural fathers, give us a mortal life. An existence that is negated by its very existence because it contains death.

So if we limit ourselves to our natural fathers, then we succumb to death. Our natural fathers give us this natural life, the one we know, and if we reduce ourselves to it, then we make our own the psalmist's words to God "in sins did my mother bear me" (Ps 50:7). This does not refer to an ethical form of sin, because the way we are born is not bad or immoral. But it refers, precisely, to the fact that we are born into death, which is the result of sin. If there were no sin, if man did not fall, we would not die. Therefore, our natural birth is connected with the fall of man, with his sinfulness, and with the mortality of man.

So we need another birth, and this will come not from our natural fathers but from other fathers. And the apostolic passage says today that the apostles are such fathers. Why? Because the apostles give us another existence through another mother. From the womb of the Church. The Church is not called "Mother" by chance and without reason. We often say and hear "the Mother Church." Indeed, the Church is not a place where we become better and improve morally. It is the place in which we are born again, and this happens primarily through baptism. In baptism we are born, we die, and we are born again. How is this manifested in the Church? It manifests itself in the fact that, while the natural family is a space in which we acquire an identity, a forced existence, inasmuch as we are born whether we want to or not, in the Church we get a free identity. No one forces us to exist. We exist because we freely consented to our existence. While within the family we take our identity, our existence, in an exclusive way, excluding others, excluding those who do not belong to our family, in the Church we take an identity that includes everyone else. This is how we all become brothers and sisters, all of us, regardless of the family we belong to, the tribe we belong to, the nation we belong to; we are all brothers and sisters in the Church. So here is a new identity that comes and is manifest with our baptism and which is maintained with the Eucharist, with the Liturgy that we celebrate in the Church.

It is therefore no coincidence that in the Church we use the word "fathers" and we use it not to denote those clergy who teach us the right things or teach us our faith, but those who give us a rebirth in the baptismal font and feed us with the Divine Eucharist. The first time the word "father" is used in the history of the Church is in relation to the bishop, who is an image of the Father, the heavenly Father. The bishop produces new beings, new existences with baptism and the Holy Eucharist. That is why the title "father" was transferred to the priests, who represent the bishop in this function.

This is how another family develops in our lives, another fatherhood, from that which our natural existence creates for us.

Today, my brothers and sisters, the Great Church of Christ, the Ecumenical Patriarchate, is celebrating, because it is the feast day of the Throne, as we say, the day when its founder is honored. And it is not by chance that this Church is our Mother and we call it "Mother Church," while the other Churches are called "daughter Churches."

It is the Mother Church because it gave birth to all the other Churches, and for this reason it has this priority in the life of the Church. And she is a Mother and she proved to be a Mother because in difficult times she covered all the Orthodox peoples under her wings, took them in her arms, and preserved them in the faith and the life of the Church.

Today, my brothers and sisters, the family is admittedly going through a crisis. Fatherhood is also going through a crisis. Natural parents are reduced to simply progenitors. Biological parents cannot really support the family, if the other paternity, the spiritual paternity, does not also pass into the lives of people. And the crisis of the family today is precisely due to the fact that man forgot that natural paternity is not enough in life. When the family is content with itself, closes in on itself, then it loses itself. When there is another relationship in the family, another spiritual relationship, a relationship given by the Church, then the family is supported and saved as well.

This is why the Church is not limited to our natural birth. With the sacrament of marriage, and primarily through the sacraments of baptism and the Eucharist, it is as if the Church is telling us: "Natural fatherhood is of no use to you; you need another fatherhood in your life."

Thus, my brothers and sisters, today the Apostle Andrew has this great message to convey to us, that as an apostle, a founder of the Church, and indeed founder of this Church from which we all took our ecclesial existence, he brought all of us, who were born in a natural way within a family, to another reality, the reality of the Church. It is only if we are rooted in the Church that we will be able to be saved as natural families.

Let's pay attention to this message, because in our time the crisis that natural fatherhood is going through is unfortunately also transmitted to spiritual fatherhood, and so we have a crisis of natural fathers, as well as a crisis of spiritual fathers. Indeed, let us pray that God will support not only natural fatherhood but also spiritual fatherhood. And in this way alone we will overcome mortality, which accompanies us from the moment of our birth, and we will begin a true and eternal life. Amen.

77. ST. ANTHONY THE GREAT

Lessons from the Desert (Heb 13:17–21)

Obey your leaders and submit to them; for they are keeping watch over your souls, as men who will have to give account.

These words, my beloved brothers and sisters, begin today's Epistle passage, which is dedicated to the memory of Saint Anthony, the great ascetic and professor of the desert, as he is called, to whom many of the great fathers of the Church looked with admiration, such as Saint Athanasios the Great, who wrote Saint Anthony's biography.

We are called today, brothers and sisters, to spend a few moments studying this great professor of the desert. What does he have to teach us, who have so many university degrees, who have progressed so far in the sciences that we are even exploring space? To us who know so much about the human being and all the world's creatures? To us, then, what can this professor of the desert say today?

The knowledge and wisdom of monks and ascetics, my dear brothers and sisters, does not look like the knowledge and wisdom of this world. It does not resemble the knowledge of the scientists, because the scientists study others, other beings, to gain knowledge, while the ascetics of the deserts *study themselves.* There, inside, they search to find the truth. There inside, in this world of their own existence, they discover that which no scientist could discover. So what is it that these ascetics discover when they investigate themselves?

The first important thing they discover, my dear brothers and sisters, is that human nature is sick—it needs treatment. And here, most importantly, they discover their own sinfulness. We try to either downplay and disregard our own sinfulness, or we transfer our attention to others and judge their sinfulness. When we look at the sins of others, my beloved brothers and sisters, we cannot discover the truth of our own existence, which is our own sinfulness. And this was the first great lesson that Saint Anthony learned and taught.

Many of us are familiar with the story from Saint Anthony's life, in which the saint prayed to God, asking Him to reveal the measure of holiness to which he should aspire. The Lord answered: "You have not reached the measure of holiness of a certain shoemaker in the city of Alexandria."

The saint then hastened to see who this great saint was, whose holiness he should strive to attain. When he found him, he asked: "What do you do? How do you live?" And the shoemaker responded: "I don't do anything holy. I simply give a third of what I have to the church, a third to the poor, and the final third I keep for myself to live." But Saint Anthony had already surpassed this, since he sold everything he had when he heard the Gospel reading of the Lord urging the young man: "go, sell what you possess and give to the poor, and you will have treasure in heaven; and come, follow me" (Matt 19:21). He quickly gave away his fortune, which was considerable. Thus, he had surpassed this measure. But he persisted in trying to learn what more the Alexandrian shoemaker did.

So Saint Anthony asked him again: "How do you live? What do you do?" And the shoemaker replied: "Here where I work, I keep one thought continually in mind all day, and that is that everyone in the city will be saved except me, who will go to hell." And then Saint Anthony learned the great lesson that he then passed down to us. He also came to believe that everyone else will be saved while he was not worthy of the Kingdom of God.

Brothers and sisters, you can see how easy this may seem, but how difficult—nay, almost impossible, humanly speaking—it is to incorporate into our own lives. It is not at all easy to see your neighbor as a saint and yourself as a sinner. If this attitude were to color our whole existence, then our lives would be completely changed. Saint Anthony, the professor of the desert, has passed this great lesson on to all the saints throughout the centuries, which they then applied to themselves and in this way only were they sanctified.

Another lesson given to us by Saint Anthony is that we must battle against sin and evil. Let us struggle to the same degree as the Great Anthony, where we wonder "where is God, why has He abandoned me?" "Where were you, Lord, when I was battling with the demons?" And he heard the response: "I was next to you, but I left you to be tried and through this furnace of temptation to prove your true faith." This reminds me, my dear brothers and sisters, of the words of a contemporary saint, to whom this church is dedicated,[1] who said "Keep your mind in hell and despair not." The Lord is with us and even when we are abandoned, it is enough to struggle to do His will, since, while it may seem like He has abandoned us, in reality He is next to us.

And this professor of the desert gives us one more lesson, that the ultimate goal of every exercise is love—to be able to cleanse our heart of passions in order to truly love. We cannot, my beloved brothers and sisters, truly love if our heart is full of passions, since all the passions are summed up in one root of all the passions, which is called φιλαυτία or self-love. And it is natural, when there is self-love, even if there is just a trace of it, that we cannot love the other. This is why we must not consider our asceticism as our ultimate goal, and not have the false impression that we love, but rather we must struggle continually against the passions and particularly against the passion of self-love.

These are the lessons, among many others, my dear brothers and sisters, that Saint Anthony, the professor of the desert, has to teach us, along with all the saints who followed in his footsteps. They are teaching them in an era in which man perceives knowledge and truth in a different way. The knowledge that the world seeks today is a knowledge which, as the apostle Paul says, "puffs up," that is, it inflates man's ego (1 Cor 8:1–2). He believes that he knows everything and can now conquer the world with his knowledge. This is precisely the opposite kind of knowledge from that which the ascetic learns when he discovers his own sinfulness and entrusts his whole life to God.

[1] Saint Silouan the Athonite.

In this world, therefore, that seeks and cultivates knowledge that "puffs up," let us pay attention to these lessons that Anthony the Great and all the teachers of the desert give us. And from this school let us draw the real wisdom that the world needs today. Because man today has a lot of knowledge but no wisdom and that's why he goes from dead end to dead end. We therefore need true wisdom, which I hope God will give to us and to the whole world, through the intercessions of Saint Anthony the Great. Amen.

At the Holy Monastery of Saint John the Baptist, Essex, England
January 17, 2010

78.
ST. EFTHIMIOS THE GREAT
Concerning death and cutting off the passions

Death takes place within us, so that life can begin inside you (2 Cor 4:6–15)

In the reading we heard referring to the Apostles, Saint Paul says: "death takes place within us, (the Apostles,) so that life can begin inside you, (the Corinthians and members of the Church)". (2 Cor 4:6–15).

These moving words are part of the apostolic reading that the Church today dedicates in memory of the great ascetic, Saint Efthimios the Great. In these words such a depth of content is concealed that we must, my brothers and sisters, pause a little and think, as far as we can, with the grace and the enlightenment of the Holy Spirit, what is the deepest meaning of this apostolic reading and the words I told you. For life to begin and to become reality, death—at least for some—must precede. Life cannot be gained without passing through death.

Why is this?

Death entered into the existence of the world and despite the resistance of the will of God. God created the world to live forever and placed man as the crown of this creation, so that man might secure this relation, everlasting communication with God, the only Immortal, that people might live forever. But man, with the freedom he was given by God, decided to cut this tie with the everlasting and Immortal God and proclaim himself God; and in this way to lead the whole creation to death. And so death entered into the creation and into the life of the world; this was inevitable because the world is a creation and not God; but he could surpass this inevitability if he were in communication with the everlasting and Immortal God. But from the moment that man cut this communication death became from there on an inevitable reality. And ever since death has tormented and tortured the whole of the creation, for no creature in the world wants to die. All life within creation has a tendency to avoid death, and man is especially the one who bears the consequences because he also, in every way, tries to avoid death, but finally he gives way and succumbs.

So, my brothers and sisters, man is caged in a continuous battle to win life by avoiding death, and he does not succeed. And the more man attaches himself to life, and especially to his personal life, so much more it is confirmed that death is truly inevitable. So there was no salvation from death for man and the creation without God Himself intervening and taking upon Himself the destiny of the world. The Lord, as the incarnated Love of God, did nothing else apart from taking upon Himself our death. The life, that God gives us in Christ, is the life, which passes from the death of Christ Himself; it is not an easy life and cannot be gained without the experience of death. That is why, my brothers and sisters, Saint Paul writes these moving words referring them to the Apostles, and through the Apostles the Church transfers them to her Saints, to her Martyrs and to her Ascetics. Because they, exactly like Christ, took upon themselves the death of others so that the others might live. This is a reality that applies to all, especially those who have the gift of a spiritual father. Spiritual fathers want to give life, life everlasting to others, and they die daily. If they do not die, everlasting life cannot be born in their spiritual children. The Lord says that if the grain of wheat does not fall to the earth and die, it cannot bring fruit. However, when it falls to the earth and dies, then the fruit that it brings is hundredfold.

How since the death of our Lord and the Saints throughout the ages, is life transferred to others? How does one die so that one gives life to others?

The death that gives life to others is the death of our selfishness. The big problem as to why death has conquered us and we are not able to surpass it, is because we try to surpass it by loving ourselves and by putting all our efforts into grasping hold of life, so that we survive by ignoring others. The reverse, then, is that which will give life to others. To efface your selfishness, the love for yourself is a death. It is the death of my self. If I do not die, you will not be able to exist; for the other to exist presupposes the death of ourselves for the other. So the Saints—like the Lord Himself—did not reckon that it was possible for them to exist and live without the others living. For the Lord all this effort was made easy, because from the beginning God had this love towards Him, and so the Lord submitted in self-sacrifice.

But for the Apostles, the Martyrs and the Ascetics their self-sacrifice was the result of a struggle, especially for the Ascetics; in the struggle the passions, which without exception spring from selfishness, are uprooted. So this death of ours, if it stops there, does not fulfill its destiny. But if this death of ours comes from love for the other, then it does fulfill its destiny. Asceticism without love is without meaning. To uproot your passions in order to develop ethically and spiritually gets you nowhere. Saint Maximos says that only love is that which justifies the Asceticism.

How can we by dying transfer life to others?

There are many ways, my brothers and sisters, but that which comes to my mind at this moment is, above all, we take upon ourselves the sins of others. Sin is that which burdens people so that they are unable to live. And when you take on the sin of another and make it your own, you die, but the other lives.

Is not this what the Lord did on the Cross? Did He not take upon Himself our sins? How would we have been able to live in the state of our sins if another had not mortified the body of our death, our sins, on the Cross?

When we are not ready, my brothers and sisters—and we are not usually ready, to take the blame and the sins of all the others—and we say to ourselves: "we are to blame". Unless we do this how is our brother going to live? But if we do this, it means that we take upon ourselves the death of the other. Here then is one way of giving life to others: by not ever judging or criticizing others, by not looking at other people's sins. The righteous Spiritual Father, who dies by giving life to others, sees the sins that people confess to him, as his own. And only then is he able to love the other, and by loving him he transfers life to him. So for the love, which bears the sins of the world, as the Lamb of God took the sins of the world upon Himself, for such a love we die. Every day, as Saint Paul says, we die so that others may live. This aim is very high—like everything in the Gospel. We cannot reach it, we cannot enforce it, but it is there, it exists, and there it must stay; and with this we must measure ourselves, and with this we must examine ourselves. And this measure, which Saint Paul gives us today, we know very well that what he was saying about himself and the Apostles was also valid for the Saints, the Martyrs and the Ascetics this is not valid for us. We are like those who gain life without offering death. There will always exist those who will die for us; there will always exist those who will love us more than we love them, and there will always exist those who will sacrifice themselves for us.

Let us at least make ourselves grateful, at least glorify God, at least acknowledge Him—like the one out of the ten lepers, as we heard in today's Gospel. This is the least, my brothers that we are able to do, to admit that we exist because others sacrifice themselves, as was first the Lord Himself. To admit that whatever true life we have and are able to receive is owed to the death of others! And we ourselves can do, as far as possible, the same for others, by mortifying our selves, our selfishness and all the passions that result from this. By cultivating love inside us, we are ready too, at least to some degree, to die so that others can live. Amen.

January 20, 2002

79. THREE HIERARCHS

Church, Divine Liturgy, theology

Remember your leaders, those who spoke to you the word of God (Heb 13:7)

My beloved brothers and sisters, today is the feast of the Three Great Hierarchs of our Church, Basil the Great, Gregory the Theologian, and John Chrysostom.

For this occasion, the Church chose the words that we just heard in the Epistle reading: "Remember your leaders, those who spoke to you the word of God." Let us see how the Apostle's words are applied to the case of the Three Hierarchs, whom we honor and celebrate today.

The Church, my beloved brothers and sisters, is a body, says the Apostle Paul, something like the human body, which has many members, and these members each have their own gift. The Church, therefore, is a variety of gifts, which the Holy Spirit gives, and this is how the body of Christ, which is the Church, is composed. There is no gift that is superior to the other. We cannot say that a lay person in the Church has no value and is not necessary for the body of the Church, the body of Christ, to exist.

The Apostle Paul says that none of the members of the body can say to the other members "I have no need of you" (1 Cor 12:21). The head cannot tell the feet that it does not need them, nor can any part of the body say that it does not need another part of the body. And we see this, my dear brothers and sisters, especially in the Divine Liturgy, which we cannot celebrate unless everyone is present, including the laity. The laity, with the "Amen" which they say during the Liturgy, assemble and celebrate the Liturgy. We cannot celebrate Divine Liturgy without the "Amen" of the laity.

But within this body with its many gifts, where everything is necessary and one needs the other, there is a hierarchy. There are those who have received from God the responsibility to lead the people of God. And there are essentially three types of leaders in the Church. There are those who lead the Divine Liturgy, who offer the Holy Eucharist on behalf of the people and consequently have a special honor, to be ahead of the others, because this function they perform is the highest function that the Church has—to offer the Divine Eucharist and to pray for others.

There are also the ones who lead by giving spiritual advice to God's people. They are the ones who have a gift from God and the Holy Spirit to give spiritual advice—they are the spiritual fathers. And they are leaders in the Church, that is to say, they precede others. And finally there are also those who transmit the word of God to the people. They teach about God so that the Church stays on the right path and believers follow the path of truth. The Three Hierarchs had all three of these characteristics of leaders in the Church. Let us see how the Three Hierarchs became our leaders, whom we must, as we have just heard, remember with gratitude.

The Three Hierarchs first gave us the Divine Liturgy. The tradition of the Church assigns written liturgies to all three hierarchs. Only two of the liturgies have remained and we use them continuously, that of Basil the Great and that of Saint John Chrysostom, which we celebrate today. So they gave us this greatest good of the Divine Liturgy.

And why is the Divine Liturgy the highest and greatest good? First, because the Liturgy is the word of God that is prayed. When the word of God becomes a prayer, then it finds its true meaning. The word of God is not something addressed to our mind, to our thinking, like philosophical ideas and theories that we experience every day in the world. God's word is what creates a personal relationship with God. And we express this personal relationship with God through prayer. Therefore, when the word of God becomes a prayer, then its meaning is completed, and the word of God in the Divine Liturgy is not just words, it is a prayer to God. And that is why the Divine Liturgy of Saint John Chrysostom and especially of Basil the Great are full of the word of God, which, as I said, is a prayer to God.

Even more importantly, the Divine Liturgy, the word of God, is not simply a prayer to God, it is the person of God Himself, of Christ—the person of the Son and Word of God who became man. This person of Christ is not simply in the Divine Liturgy, where He prays for us—as the mouth that brings our prayers to the throne of God—but He also becomes flesh so that we can not only hear the word of God, but also take it into us, to become part of our existence, part of our body. This word of God in the Divine Liturgy becomes flesh so that we can commune with it, partake of it.

So, the prayer we do in our home, in our room, in our cell, wherever we may happen to be, is very important, because we must pray, but there is no greater and more important prayer than that which is done at the Divine Liturgy. And precisely for this reason, by writing down the Divine Liturgies, the fathers of the Church gave us the most important and greatest thing they could give us.

But the fathers also gave us the word of God in the form of the doctrines of the Church, that is, theology. These fathers struggled mightily to formulate the doctrines of the Church correctly, because at that time some were trying to pervert the truth of the Church. The illumination of the Holy Spirit was needed for the Church to find the right way, the right faith, the way of truth. Therefore, the fathers of the Church formulated the doctrines and handed them down to us as a precious, priceless inheritance.

Why is the Church's dogmatic inheritance so precious and priceless? Well, firstly, because as I told you, man after his fall cannot easily distinguish falsehood from truth. The mind is confused and constantly asks: Where is the truth? Where is the lie? And in our lives falsehood and the truth are often so confused that we cannot distinguish what is true from what is false.

There are also those who deceive us and tell us that a lie is the truth and the truth is a lie. Inside the Church, therefore, the illumination of the Holy Spirit is needed to find the truth, the path of truth. And this illumination of the Holy Spirit belongs to the fathers of the Church who formulated the doctrines, mainly in the form of the Ecumenical Councils, and handed them down to us. However, doctrines are also important for another reason—because they are life, they are our own life.

Let us think a bit, my brothers and sisters, about the significance of the doctrine of the Holy Trinity in our lives—a doctrine that was formulated with the wisdom, inspiration, and teaching of the Three Hierarchs we are celebrating today. God is Triune, not One; He is not an a single individual but three persons. You will say: "What significance does that have in my life?" It is of great significance because, if man is made in the image of God (and he is), if man wants to be like God (and he must because he has been called to His likeness)—if, these things are true, then man must become like God in the way in which God exists (τρόπος ὑπάρξεως). What does this mean?

In our lives, my beloved brothers and sisters, individualism dominates. We think of ourselves as an individual, we isolate ourselves, we look at how to support our individuality in a thousand ways and we forget that man is not an individual, he is a person—that is, he is someone who acquires an entity through communion with other persons. Because, while an individual can be conceived as an isolated entity, a person is always in communion with others.

Thus God—by not being an individual but rather a Holy Trinity, three persons—provides us a model for our lives, that we too must imitate God in this respect. What is the way to imitate God? It is precisely through love, the communion of the three persons of the Holy Trinity, in which one cannot exist without the other. Likewise, man, with love, cannot feel himself as existing if he is not in a relationship with others. The more he is connected with others, the more he loves and the more he resembles God, the Triune God.

So, it does us no good to say that God exists or that He is a Higher Power. What is needed is what the fathers of the Church, and especially the Three Hierarchs, have handed down for us to believe: that God is love, He is the communion of the body of the Church.

You see, my brothers and sisters, that those things that seem so difficult and so irrelevant to our lives, such as the doctrines of the Church, are actually the source of our life. If we do not have this compass in our lives, we cannot walk properly. This is what the fathers of the Church taught us—to turn doctrines into life. And in the Church this is exactly what we are called to do—to live the doctrines of the Church—and then what we heard in the Gospel passage will apply: "but he who does them and teaches them shall be called great in the kingdom of heaven" (Mt 5:19).

When we combine the right teaching with the right action, with the right way of living, and there is no separation between them, then we are on the right path, on the way to the Kingdom of God. What we need is the grace of God and His mercy to account us worthy of this combination of faith and action, doctrine and life, so that we can follow Him faithfully with the help of those who lead in the Church and shepherd us, and whom we must always honor and remember with gratitude.

My beloved brothers and sisters, the Church, throughout the centuries, has always produced fathers and leaders, and all of us have such today in our lives. God has accounted all of us worthy of such spiritual guides. Particularly in our monastery, we were accounted worthy to have the ever-memorable Elder Sophrony as our spiritual guide. These leaders, then, who have spoken the word of God to us, have themselves combined dogma, theology, and way of life and made them one entity. These are the leaders who transmit to us the living word of God in the Divine Liturgy; they are the ones that we should remember continually with gratitude. Through their prayers and aid, may we walk in our lives in such a way as to be accounted worthy of the Kingdom of God. Amen.

January 30, 2005

80.
THE BRIDEGROOM SERVICE
(Orthros of Holy Wednesday)

Lord, the woman who had fallen into many sins
We commemorate the harlot who anointed the Lord's feet with fragrant ointment.

In the Aposticha hymns, the eponymous Hymn of Kassiani is sung, which begins "Lord, when the woman who had fallen into many sins...."

The person we sing about tonight, my beloved brothers and sisters, is not a saint. She is a sinner, a "woman who had fallen into many sins." And it is to her that our Church dedicates tonight the most beautiful hymns. With the culmination of the eponymous hymn of the nun Kassiani, which we will soon hear sung by the elite choirs of this church.

The solemnity of these days makes it unsuitable for me to speak at length. Our souls are equipped with antennae to receive the loftiest messages directly without the mediation of human words. In spite of this, though, I ask you to allow me to offer just a few words exploring the shocking feelings that tonight's hymns evoke, especially the famous hymn that we will hear shortly.

In this troparion hymn, two abysses are confronted: the abyss of man's sin and the abyss of God's love and mercy. The first one is really an abyss! How did the prince of creation, this image of God, fall? How did the eagle fall and reach the point of crawling on this earth, "submerged in sin," as the hymn says? The depth of man's fall is such that our sinfulness has no bottom; it is a true abyss.

When man crawls on the earth, when man forgets his high calling, when man, above all, is held by the state of death, he is truly pitiful. The depth of his sin also brought him to a depth of recognition. And precisely for this reason, the Church tonight chose a harlot, to project her as a symbol of the state of the human race.

This choice, however, has nothing to do with any contempt we may feel for prostitutes who, either by their own choice or through necessity, have become objects of our scorn. The Church does not share the social prejudice of the so-called "respectable" citizens.

If it chooses the harlot tonight as a central figure, the Church does so because only in this way can it show man's condition after his fall. Because from his fall and beyond, man does nothing else but give up his soul and body; he completely sells out, sometimes for money, sometimes for glory, sometimes for pleasures. He gives up everything, turning this state of prostituting himself into a way of life. This is why the Church projects the symbol of the harlot before us tonight. To show us the condition of all humanity, the condition of each one of us.

And on the other side is the abyss of God's love and mercy. Tonight, my brothers and sisters, "deep calls to deep," as the Psalms say, which is literally "abyss calls upon abyss."[1] Perhaps this abyss is even greater than our sin. Saint John Chrysostom says that God, in becoming man, "fell in love with a harlot," indeed with a "manic eros." In fact, He loved us so much that, despite the fallen state in which we find ourselves, He came and embraced us, became one with us, and took upon Himself our fate. This is indeed an abyss, because it is the greatest paradox and perhaps also the greatest absurdity that has ever existed in the world. Because loving a righteous, holy person is very natural. However, to love a sinner, and indeed in the state to which man has descended after his fall, this is truly unthinkable. I would even say that it is scandalous! And this is precisely what God does with the abyss of His mercy.

And tonight we will listen to the hymn of Kassiani ask: "Who can reckon the multitude of my sins, or fathom the depths of Your judgments, O my life-saving Savior?" Who can fathom the abyss of God's mercy? The fact that he accepts a prostitute, forgives her, loves her—this is the essence of the Gospel, my brothers and sisters: God's love for the sinner is a love that it is very difficult for us to live and apply. Because no one loves a sinner. Usu-

[1] Ps 41:8 LXX (42:7).

ally we marginalize him, take him out of our "civilized" society, and then we feel good about our own holiness. However, the Lord, with the abyss of His mercy, embraced the harlot, who is man in his fallen state.

There's another reason, my brothers and sisters, that the Church presents such a person to us tonight. Under the surface of a sinful person is often hidden a sensitivity, that wells forth in tears like those the sinful woman sheds tonight to wash the feet of the Lord.

"What can I do for the pious ones? What can I do for the righteous, when they cannot cry, when they are not aware of their own sinfulness? Bring me the publicans, bring me the harlots, that I may show who will "enter the kingdom of God before you" (Mt 21:31). These are not my words; these are the words of Christ Himself.

The more sinful person repents more easily than the less sinful. The less sinful sees the more sinful and thinks that he himself is not so sinful. The true sinner knows that he has reached the bottom of his fall and that there is no one more sinful than him. And it fills his soul with true repentance and brings tears to his eyes. And then God's mercy comes. And God's mercy comes only to those who reach the point of despair. Those who believe that they can do it themselves do not need God's mercy. The true sinner is the one who needs God's mercy. And that's why he attracts it.

My brothers and sisters, the hymn we will hear shortly, this masterpiece of poetry and music, is not for the indulgence of our artistic senses. It is to show us the way of salvation. It is to show us how we are all sinners! And how we all need tears of repentance. How our neighbor is not more sinful than us. And how sin should not lead us to despair, because God's mercy is an abyss.

Let us carefully understand this hymn and we will all leave filled not only with solemnity but also with many lessons and, above all, with the lesson of repentance, which tonight our Church wants to convey to all of us. Amen!

Holy Metropolitan Church of Saint Demetrius, Kifissia
April 10, 2001

81.
MEMORY OF SAINT JOHN THE THEOLOGIAN

"Brethren, love one another" (1 John 1:1–7)

John the Theologian, apostle and evangelist, Arsenius the Great (†449).

"God is love, and he who abides in love abides in God, and God in him." (1 John 4:16)

Your All-Holiness, respected hierarchs, venerable clergy, honorable representatives of the local authorities, honorable consul of Greece, prefect of neighboring Lesbos, pious and beloved pilgrims, there are moments when time stops in order for eternity to enter in.

There are moments that emerge as unique and unrepeatable events. Moments during which the very presence of God is revealed to us. And then time stops, to make us think more deeply about how God's providence is working in our lives.

We experience such moments every time we celebrate the Divine Liturgy. The Divine Liturgy is eternity's entrance into time. It is the moment when God Himself enters into our lives and makes us completely change our perspective and experience of time.

And today's Divine Liturgy is also one such, which has the special characteristic of being celebrated in this holy place after the lapse of many years, with the blessing of His All-Holiness the Ecumenical Patriarch, our venerable leader, and with the divine approval of the prefect of the region and in general of the authorities of this region, whom we thank from the bottom of our hearts.

Today, in this holy place, we meet to honor the memory of an apostle who spent his whole life precisely in this area, carrying the message of love, the message of God's love for man and the love that the people ought to have for each other. And this saint, to whom this ancient historical church is dedicated, Saint John the Theologian, was aptly called Theologian by the Church.

Contrary to what happens today, where the title of theologian is given broadly to those who have obtained a university degree, in the ancient Church the title of theologian was given to only three people: John, whose memory we commemorate today, Gregory the Theologian Nazianzus and Simeon the New Theologian.

Why this frugality? Because the name and the meaning and the content of the theologian is not simply to convey to us the word of God or the will of God, but to introduce us into the very being of God, into the very existence of God.

Thus, while the Church, and our faith in general, has many, like the Apostle Paul, who were lifted up by the grace of God to the third heaven and heard unspeakable words, there are very few who did not simply convey to us the word and the will of God but they revealed to us what God is, what is in His very nature.

"In the beginning was the Word, and the Word was with God, and the Word was God" (John 1:1). This great revelation was given to John by a rare and unique privilege. And so John is the theologian *par excellence*. But why did John deserve this great honor? Because, my brothers and sisters, to know the being of God presupposes becoming a partaker of the very existence of God and this cannot be done with the knowledge of our mind. No one can know God with the knowledge of the mind.

What is the way to know God? Well, this is exactly what John reveals to us, it is love! "He who does not love does not know God, for God is love" (1 John 4:8). Only he who loves knows God. And not only the one who loves God, but, as John says, the one who first of all loves his fellow man. Because, as he says, if someone says that "I love God but I do not love my brother, whom I see," he is lying, for if he does not love man, whom he sees, how can he love God, whom he does not see? Thus, John opens for us the way to the knowledge of God. And this road is love.

And John recognized this love. He knew it by privilege, and only God knows why it was granted to him. When he leaned on the chest of the Lord and heard the beating of His heart, by privilege this beloved disciple, "who leaned back on Jesus' chest" (Jn 13:25), learned directly from this bodily communion with God, because God is love. And that love is the only way to come into communion with God. And this physical communion between

John and the Lord reveals to us that saying that we love God and our fellow man is not enough if we do not have physical communion with Him.

This bodily communion is offered by the Church every time we celebrate the sacrament of the Eucharist. It brings us all together. We cannot celebrate the Eucharist from a distance, not even through the media. We must gather with physical presence, and something even more important: to unite with God physically, with the body of His Son. And this is how John reveals to us, that what happened to him, when he leaned on the chest of the Lord and united with His body, also happens to us every time we receive communion, when we celebrate the Divine Eucharist. This is the way, my brothers and sisters, to know God.

And we observe one more important characteristic in the life of Saint John. That he is the only one who remained faithful to the Lord at the time of His Crucifixion. We cannot say that we love God or our fellow man if we abandon him in the time of temptation, fear and misfortune. We must stand by him. Next to the cross he takes up. Let's not abandon him.

And for us Orthodox, it is particularly significant that the mother of our Lord, our Panagia,[1] also stood with John at the Cross. John received the Virgin into his home at the Lord's command and he cared for her until the end of her life. And he shows us the way, because in order to approach and know God, we cannot neglect the honor and love we have for our Virgin Mary.

This great saint, my brothers and sisters, whom we honor today, teaches us all these things, which is why whatever words we may offer today will ultimately prove insufficient.

What remains with us, however, and must continue to remain today in our thoughts and in our hearts is what tradition has preserved: that John, who preached precisely in this region of the world and lived here, when he reached a very old age, could neither say nor do anything else, except to say only four words to the people: "Brethren, love one another." It was as if he summed up in these four words everything he had to say in the Gospel, his epistles, and his Revelation—in other words, his whole life.

[1] A term of endearment for the Virgin Mary.

And this is not simply accidental, my brothers and sisters. At this moment, as the Lord allows us by His grace to celebrate the Divine Liturgy, we feel Saint John walking here among us and speaking the same words to us. To address these words first to us, the faithful Christians—and especially the Orthodox. To understand that without love we cannot be faithful to his preaching and message.

St. John addresses this message of love to those both near and far, to the whole world, indeed to all the peoples of the world. Because nothing is more important than love between peoples, especially when in fact these peoples happen to be neighbors.

Your All-Holiness, you have this message of love the goal of your life, the purpose of your high ministry. You carry it wherever you are. And with this message you prove to be a faithful successor of the Apostle John. You prove to be a faithful interpreter of the Orthodox Church and our tradition. And in this way, allow me to say, you also prove to be a prophet. Because love will finally conquer hate! It is stronger than anything!

We have examples! We begin to feel the greatness and miracles of love. The love that you preached, Your All-Holiness, and that you preach wherever you are, provides tangible examples, such as today's Divine Liturgy. Examples that we will see even in the future. Because this is exactly what happens in the Divine Liturgy! Time becomes the future, time does not fix us in the past. It frees us from the past. Hate keeps us in the past. The time of the Divine Liturgy frees us and opens up the future. This is exactly what love does. That is why God Himself is love. Therefore, only by living love will we live and know God Himself.

This message, Your All-Holiness and my beloved brothers and sisters, echoes in our hearts today in this holy place. And, with your blessing, Your All-Holiness, allow me to pray that this message will be solidified, that these historic walls will continue to spread it. And with this message, may all people and peoples unite and may we be found worthy to know the true God by loving one another—ever more, ever deeper! Amen!

Pergamos, Church of Saint John the Theologian
May 8, 2003

82.
MEMORY OF ELDER SOPHRONY
The Resurrection through the descent into Hades (2 Cor 6:1–10)

The words we heard, my dear brothers and sisters, in the Epistle reading today are truly shocking. The Apostle Paul describes to us the way of life of the apostles, which is and must be the way of life of all believers. And he describes it with contrasts that create many questions for us.

The Apostle says that we, first the apostles and then all the faithful Christians, live in this world as if we are at the same time glorious and dishonorable, with infamy and with praise, as if no one knows us and as if everyone knows us, as if we die continually and yet we live, as if we are poor and yet we make all rich, as if we have nothing and yet possess everything. These contrasts are not, my dear brothers and sisters, rhetorical figures, but precisely express the essence of the Christian's existence in the world.

All of us who believe in Christ exist in the world, in these contrasts and antitheses. Why? Why shouldn't our life be only glory, only honor, with everyone recognizing us and praising us? Why should we not be rich, and give our wealth to others? Why do we go through death every day? The answers I can suggest to these questions, my brothers and sisters, are as follows:

First, because the Lord Himself lived like this. The earthly life of Christ is the synthesis of these contrasts, the expression of all these antitheses. He experienced both glory and dishonor, life and death. He trampled death not with His divine power and by commanding it to disappear, but by enduring death Himself.

What the apostle describes about the life of believers is exactly the image of the Lord's life. And one cannot be a disciple and believer of Christ without copying our model, which is Christ. And why would Christ have to go through these contrasts, experience these paradoxical situations? Because this is the reality of man's existence after the fall.

After the fall of man, our existence was poisoned by evil. Evil entered into all aspects of our lives. As Saint Maximus the Confessor says, pleasure and pain have now become inseparable; and we humans often think that we can separate them and choose only what is pleasing to us, only what is positive for us. And there are many religions, many religions that try to assure us that we can find rest and joy and happiness without going through misery. We are promised ascent to heaven without descent to Hades, but this descent is also the ascent (Eph 4:10). If you don't go down to Hades, then you can't go up to heaven. This is now the truth of our existence and that is why the Lord implemented it and embraced it.

There is no expressway, there is no shortcut, to salvation, joy, life, resurrection, the Kingdom of God. The road goes through Hades. There is one more reason these antitheses are so true and so necessary in the life of Christ: it is only in this way that we can truly say we love people.

No one can love if he does not identify with the other; if he does not take upon himself not only the glory of the other but also the dishonor of the other, not only the praise of the other but also his infamy, not only the joy of the other but also the sadness and pain of the other. If he does not make the tears of others his tears, if he does not feel as a spiritual person, but also as a brother, the sins of the other as his own sins—he cannot say that he loves.

Unfortunately, we distinguish ourselves from others and say: "Well, we're not that sinful." We are shaken if someone proves to be a sinner and we say: "Thank God, I am not like him, I did not kill, I did not commit this terrible crime." Every day we hear about crimes in the news and we say to ourselves: "Thank God, I'm not a criminal, I'm not like him." We lock criminals in prison and we on the outside brag about how good we are. But if we do not say that we also share in the responsibility, in the sinfulness of all others—in our own way, in our own measure, to our own degree—if we do not say this, my brothers and sisters, two things happen: one, we are deceived into thinking that this is how really things are and, two, we do not love. It is a lie to say that we love others if we do not identify with them in everything.

The Lord loved man and all sinners, and today we heard in the gospel passage the very shocking words that the Lord said to the Pharisee. When the Pharisee was scandalized because the Lord accepted the cares and expressions of love of a sinful woman, he asked himself: "But if he is a man of God, he should know what kind of woman is touching him, for she is sinner" (cf. Lk 7:39). And what the Lord said shocks us by saying that the one who is forgiven much also loves much. In other words, the more sinful one is, the more one draws God's mercy, His forgiveness, and in response loves more. One, therefore, who is not conscious of his sinfulness and does not shed tears of repentance, considering himself better than others, he cannot love. The sinner who has received the forgiveness of sins, he is the one who loves.

My brothers and sisters, the grace of the Lord has brought us together today to once again honor the memory of our elder, our blessed spiritual father Sophrony, and these words of the Apostle Paul are absolutely applicable in today's case. The blessed elder, whom we all had the blessing to know up close, taught us both with his words and with his life. First, with what he called "hypostatic prayer," to identify ourselves completely with all people. Only if you include all people in your prayer, only then do you pray as the Lord prayed. This identification with other people, with the righteous but also with sinners, this is what truly makes us imitators of the Lord. And with great theological depth, the late elder analyzed this idea of hypostatic prayer.

This passage we heard from the Apostle Paul also brings to mind the commandment that the elder taught us, which he in turn received from his elder, Saint Silouan, and which we all know by now: "Keep your mind in Hades and despair not." It means exactly what I told you before, that we must go through Hades, because that is the only way we will reach the resurrection. And the Lord descended to Hades and the Resurrection is the Lord's descent into Hades. This passage from Hades, which means our identification with all people and especially with sinners, is a movement that leads to resurrection and life and therefore does not bring despair. You can hold on to hope even in Hades, because you know that Christ passed through Hades and left there the hope of resurrection for all of us.

And finally, the late elder, with his life, showed us that these contrasts that the Apostle Paul speaks of are indeed the life of the faithful Christian. Sick unto death, and yet ever alive and ever strong for our sakes. Poor, and yet he spiritually enriched us all. Unknown to some and well known to others. He went through these contrasts described by the Apostle Paul and in this way made himself a model for us to imitate.

May he intercede for us, my brothers and sisters, and may he inspire us with his life and his teaching. Let us praise the Lord, because he left—together with his memory and his prayers—this holy monastery, which will continue his presence and his teaching. Under the umbrella of the Ecumenical Patriarchate of the Church of Constantinople, the monastery preserves also the intercessions of Saint Euphemia, whose holy relics, as you know, are kept in the Patriarchal Church of Constantinople. I do not consider it a coincidence that today, the day of the elder's repose, is a day of celebration in the Patriarchal Church of Constantinople; it is also a day of commemoration of Saint Olga, Equal to the Apostles, who enlightened the Russians. In this way, the elder, in his person, unites the Orthodox. With his origin and ultimately with his spiritual state, he unites all Orthodoxy, regardless of language or race or ethnicity.

Let us, my brothers and sisters, be grateful to God, and may the elder's blessing always be with us.

July 11, 2000

83.
MEMORY OF ELDER SOPHRONY
The kenosis of love (Lk 7:36–50)

Her sins, which are many, are forgiven,
for she loved much.

Today's Gospel passage, my dear brothers and sisters, is one of the most moving in the entire Gospel. A Pharisee invites the Lord to his house to dine together. He accepts the invitation, goes to the Pharisee's house and there a scene unfolds that really shocks us.

A woman, known throughout society as a sinner, appears before the Lord, falls at His feet and kisses them, covers them with her tears, anoints them with precious myrrh, and wipes them with her hair. This provokes the reaction of the Pharisee but also the words of the Lord that we just heard.

I would like, my brothers and sisters, to dwell on two questions. The first is: Why did the Pharisee react this way? How can we explain it? And the second question is: Why was the Lord's attitude so completely different? How can we explain it? The Pharisee, I think, reacts this way for two main reasons: First, he is taught not to associate with sinners. In the society in which he lives, he is seen as the embodiment of virtue. As a virtuous person, he should not be seen with sinners, because this would result in society's loss of esteem for him. Here, the Pharisee reminds us very much of our own attitude towards sinners, towards those who have been characterized by society as unacceptable. We don't want to associate with them because we are afraid of damaging our own reputation. The motive is purely selfish. We look at how to preserve our own reputation; this is what concerns us, and we sacrifice our love for those people, the sinners. It takes a lot of courage to say: "I accept a sinner, I associate with him, even if it costs me my own good reputation."

Unfortunately, a view has developed within our society, including Christian society, that focuses on maintaining our good personal reputation. If someone impinges on it in any way, we react defensively, which resembles the spirit of the Pharisee more than the spirit of the Gospel. The second reason the Pharisee reacts this way, and is unmoved by the scene unfolding before him, is that he believes that he is not a sinner. And there the Lord indirectly gets him to understand that he too is a sinner by saying to him: "Tell me what you think, Simon. If someone forgives a debt of 500 denaria to one person and also forgives a debt of 50 denaria to another person, which of the two will love their benefactor more?" And Simon answers: "Naturally, the one who had the bigger debt." In this way, the Lord indirectly tells the Pharisee that, even if you do not owe 500 denaria, you certainly owe 50. There is no one who does not owe something to God. There is no one who is not a sinner. And sin is not measured, my brothers and sisters, by the amount, by the quantity; even if the sin is small, even if it represents 50 denaria and not 500, it is a sin. The sinner needs repentance and he needs forgiveness from God. Thus the Lord indirectly teaches the Pharisee that he too is a sinner, something that had not even crossed his mind.

And now the question, my brothers and sisters, is: why does the Lord behave in this way towards the sinful woman? There was another time when the Pharisees were scandalized by the Lord doing something similar, and there He replied almost ironically that "What I am doing is very natural, because those who are well do not need a doctor. The sick need a doctor" (cf. Lk 5:31). It is as if He is saying to them "you who think you are not sick, you do not need Me. I came for those who are sick, for sinners." This is one reason the Lord associates with sinners. But there is another reason which I think is even more important. And that is the fact that the love of God, which the Lord brought into the world, which He embodied in the world, is especially directed towards sinners. Because God, through the mouth of the Lord, taught something that He Himself practiced—love for enemies—and a sinner is nothing if not an enemy of God.

Since man sinned and fell, an enmity towards God has developed. That is why the Apostle Paul says that "when we were enemies we were reconciled to God" (Rom 5:10). The Lord reconciled us to God, because we had made ourselves His enemies. The Lord, loving sinners, lives and does what He taught us, which is to love our enemies and those who harm us. When a sinner offends God with his sin and makes himself His enemy, he needs God's love, and God shows this love more abundantly towards these people.

Thus it shows us that God loves people not because they somehow deserve this love. He loves them even though they do not deserve it. This love is magnificent and free; it is not obligatory. This is the greatness of God's love. He loves those who do not deserve love and even more the repentant sinners, because repentance needs a great deal of courage. I would say that repentance is superior to obedience. We saw this, my brothers and sisters, in the parable of the prodigal. An obedient son does not enjoy the respect, tenderness, and love that the father shows to the repentant sinful son. Because taking the step of repentance is very difficult, it is heroic, and God respects it. Man's repentance attracts God's love.

This is even more true when repentance is accompanied, as in the case of the sinful woman, by tears. Tears not only wash away sins, they soften the heart, they refine the heart. He who thinks that he has never sinned, to the point of weeping for his sins, he remains hard, like the Pharisee who is unmoved by what he sees in front of him. But the tears of the sinful woman move the Lord, and it makes him say: "Her sins are many, yes, but her love is also abundant." And when love battles sin, surely love wins. And love won in this case; the sins of the sinful woman were forgiven. And the Lord taught us all these important things, which we usually forget.

Today, my brothers and sisters, the grace of God has brought us together, brought us together in this Divine Liturgy to once again honor the memory of our blessed elder Fr. Sophrony. We are all indebted to him and that's why we came here. We who knew him personally are indebted to him, but also those who did not know him will be indebted to him, because his legacy is rich and will remain for future generations. It is a legacy of real love and a legacy of teaching, which stems from this love. This is not the place to develop the elder's teaching. Very important books have been written about it and others will be written in the future.

Today's Gospel passage brings to mind certain aspects of his teaching, which really deserve to be highlighted. This love of which the Lord speaks today is the central idea of Elder Sophrony's teaching. It is the way in which one becomes a real, true person, becomes a hypostasis, exists as a unique person. The culture in which we live thinks that it makes us persons when it fills us with selfishness and various social virtues. But Elder Sophrony gives us a very different concept of love. It is the emptying of our soul, the kenosis of ourselves to the point where our self does not exist for us. This kenosis is then filled with divine presence, divine grace, and real love. If you do not go through this kenosis, this emptying, you cannot say that you love. This is why repentance is so important, as it is the emptying of ourselves. And this love that Elder Sophrony taught us—handing down and developing the teaching of his own elder, Saint Silouan—culminates in love for enemies. This is exactly what today's Gospel passage presents us.

To love those who harm you and sin by harming you, this is exactly the kind of love that the Lord demonstrated to people, and that God demonstrates to sinners. Even more, the elder emphasized the importance of tears: those tears that the sinful woman today shed so abundantly at the Lord's feet. The elder taught that tears have more value than anything else, including any other virtue. The tears that accompany repentance cleanse the human soul. They manifest precisely the kind of love that the sinful woman demonstrated to the Lord. It is an external form of a deep internal transformation. This teaching always remains important, and we must not forget it.

Our gratitude to the elder makes us today, my brothers and sisters, want to entreat God that we sinners have him in the Land of the Living, among the saints, and that his intercessions and prayers—which were so fervent and continuous and uninterrupted when he lived among us—continue, since the prayers of a holy man do not stop with death. May his prayers accompany us, so that the Lord may account us worthy to pass through the arena of life imitating, as much as we are able, the example that he left us, and that we may meet again in the Kingdom. Amen.

July 11, 2001

84.
MEMORY OF ELDER SOPHRONY
Evil is defeated by love (2 Cor 6:1–10)

Today, my brothers and sisters, the grace of God has gathered us together again to honor the memory of our blessed elder Father Sophrony. Let us entreat the Lord to accept his prayers for us, because his love continues to cover us and his blessings continue to accompany us.

Today's words from the Apostle Paul are most apt: "as dying, and behold we live." How is it possible to die and live at the same time? How is it possible to reconcile death with life, these two opposite things? It is a paradox on which we will try, my brothers and sisters, to shed some light, drawing from the teaching of the blessed elder, and inspired by his theology. The theology of Elder Sophrony was an ascetic theology *par excellence.* And ascetic theology is characterized by the conviction that, if man does not die, he cannot live, he cannot be resurrected. If he does not go through the cross, he cannot reach the resurrection. If he does not kill his own will, he cannot perform God's will.

Elder Sophrony's theology is inspired by the now well-known saying of Saint Silouan: "Keep your mind in Hades and despair not." And it is a theology that Elder Sophrony developed on Christological principles—that is, on the way in which God presents Himself, in the person of Christ, experiencing death and life. It is really striking, and this is a key tenet in the blessed elder's thought—that God emptied Himself in order to save man, to bring him to Him again. He emptied himself of His glory and identified himself with man, the man of the stomach, and, while he could have saved him with His divine power, He does not use power but instead His love, which reaches the point of kenosis, self-emptying, and now identifying God Himself with the ultimate point of man's fall, which is the place of death, Hades. Hades is nothing other than the mark, the indestructible mark, of man's distance from God's love. Moving away from God's love, man reached Hades, death, and there he could no longer redeem himself, he could not get out of there. So God Himself comes to Hades, to resurrect Adam, by participating in Hades and his death.

It is very characteristic that, in our Orthodox iconography at least, the Resurrection of Christ is represented as the descent into Hades. This is the central point of the Resurrection, because in order to raise Adam, to take him from the land of death and darkness, He Himself had to descend there and take upon Himself the death of Adam. In this way he raised Adam up. In order to ascend, then, man must descend. To go up, you have to go down. As the Apostle Paul says—and the blessed elder frequently noted this—Christ is the One Who ascends as well as the One Who descends to the uttermost regions of the earth. He is the one who descends in order to elevate us, and in this way He shows us that no one can ascend unless he descends to the lowest point of humiliation.

One cannot help but wonder, my brothers and sisters, why things are arranged like this, and what practical consequences there are for all of us. Things are arranged this way because love cannot be realized, it cannot exist, if one does not empty oneself of oneself. We say many times that we love, and we use the word very often. But in reality, in order to truly love someone, one must empty oneself of every element of selfishness and individualism and put the other in one's place. This kenosis, this emptying of ourselves from ourselves, this is exactly what the Lord means when he says "Love your neighbor as yourself." He did not say "love both yourself and your neighbor." He said to put your neighbor in your place.

Put the one you love in place of yourself, because that is what love is.

What is needed therefore is love, that which happened to the Lord, a self-emptying. And another thing is necessary: a complete identification with the other we love, to the point that we take upon ourselves his fate, whatever the other may be. And even if we are not responsible for what the other is, we take upon ourselves the consequences of his sins. We make his sins our own, just as the Lord took upon Himself the sins of mankind, being Himself without sin; in the words of the Apostle Paul, "He made Him who knew no sin to be sin for us" (2 Cor 5:21). He took upon Himself the consequences of our sins and thus we cannot say that we love without simultaneously taking upon ourselves the pain and the consequences of the sins of the one we love. To feel those sins as our own, to be ours, to become ours. In this way, and only in this way, can love become a reality.

We distinguish ourselves from others, we say that we cannot be responsible for the sins of others, that we are not as bad as the other sinners and thus it would be unfair to suffer the consequences of others' sins. But this injustice—actually, this *transcendence* of justice—is precisely what love suffers. Love is the transcendence of justice. What is fair is for the one who commits the sin to pay the price for it. But if this is the case, then we can never understand what happened in the case of Christ. It was precisely a transcendence of justice, since love is not dependent on justice; love surpasses justice. And this is why Christ Himself, the Second Person of the Holy Trinity, descends into Hades, and dies to give life to the one He loves; this is the deepest meaning of the Apostle Paul that we heard in the Epistle reading: "We apostles die, in order that you may live, and from your life we ourselves take, and 'behold we live.' Give this voluntary death as life to others, and from the life of others we ourselves live." Thus, what happened to Christ can happen to each of us.

We are not called to model ourselves after Christ only in certain of His virtues; we must take upon ourselves His very life, His way of being, His manner of living. The consequences therefore of this truth are very important, my brothers and sisters, for our life. They are important because they show us the true meaning of what we call "humility." Humility is not a moral virtue; humility is the same as love. It is this emptying of ourselves, so that the one we love can find space inside us; this emptying of ourselves is humility. Humility is not saying "I'm the worst person," etc., but to take upon ourselves the same fate and the same consequences of others' lives.

The real ascetic feels that he himself is responsible for the sins of everyone else, because sinfulness is something that concerns us all, my brothers and sisters. What the Pharisee did today in the Gospel passage is the exact opposite of what the Lord did. The Pharisee distinguished himself from the sinful woman, who expressed her gratitude to the Lord in this moving way. And the Pharisee said that if the Lord had known how sinful this woman was, he would not have let her touch him. And the Lord answered: "I am approaching this woman because she needs My love and because My love is what makes her come to Me and express her feelings." The Lord therefore identifies Himself with the sinful woman, while the Pharisee distinguishes himself from her. And so two different worlds are presented to us. The world represented by the Pharisee, who distinguishes himself from sinners, and the world represented by the Lord, who identifies Himself with sinners.

See then, how humility is this identification with the other. This is what will finally bring us to the point of going down so low to identify with the "least of these my brethren." Thus, my brothers and sisters, an equation is made in which humility equals glory. This is one of the tenets of the elder's teaching—the greater the humility, the greater the glory. There is an absolute symmetry, and there will be no glory if there is no humility, because, I repeat, this humility, this emptying of ourselves, is identical with love, and without love there can be no salvation.

And this path that the elder blazed also shows us that, according to the example of the Lord, evil cannot be defeated by force. As the Lord says shortly before his Crucifixion to his enthusiastic disciple who wanted to defend him with his sword: "I could call twelve legions of angels", which was equal to the entire army of the Roman Empire, "to defend Me." Didn't the Lord have the power to do whatever He wanted, didn't He have the power to defeat evil? Why did He not choose power to defeat evil, but chose rather to take evil and its consequences upon Himself? Because this is the only way to defeat evil, through love.

Of course, many of us think that force will defeat evil, as this is usually what we see happen in the world. Usually the political powers that be think that, either through military or economic power, they can defeat evil, but in reality it turns out that one cannot defeat evil with power. Evil can only be defeated by love.

This is the path that the Lord blazed and this is the path that the blessed elder continues with his ascetic theology. What does this mean? That these humble and weak ascetics are the greatest force against evil that the world possesses. As paradoxical as it may seem, history confirms it. The Apostle Paul says that "My strength is made perfect in weakness" (2 Cor 12:9), and history confirms it, because indeed those who emptied themselves for the sake of others are the ones who, in the end, are the cohesive force of the world. If the world is left to the strong, it will surely fall apart. The world is held together by the weak, those who have emptied themselves of all strength and those who love. Love sustains the world.

These thoughts, my beloved brothers and sisters, I wanted to share with you today, as we gather here to honor the memory of the blessed elder. It is very true what the Apostle Paul says in the phrase I have just cited, true also for the case of the elder. Indeed, throughout his life he lived as if he were dead, the one who revived others. Throughout his life he lived with human weakness, even with natural biological weakness, and every day he discovered with amazement the truth of the Apostle's words, "and behold we live." And so, we live. And this is really the greatness that God gives to man, when he surrenders himself to Him; He makes him live with wonder every day and to wonder how he lives, because the power he has in his weakness cannot be explained humanly.

And the elder spent his whole life like this, and that is why even after his death he remains alive. Alive to bless us, to pray for us, alive so that we can enjoy the fruits of his labors and sacrifices. Alive in the living Lord, in His body, in the body of the saints, in the body of the Church, which today we constitute with the Divine Eucharist. Let his prayers be with us, my brothers and sisters, and the example of his life an example for our own lives as well. Amen.

July 11, 2002

85.
MEMORY OF ELDER SOPHRONY
On true love (Lk 7:36–50)

But to whom little is forgiven,
the same loves little.

The grace of the Lord has brought us together, my beloved brothers and sisters, to celebrate the holy memorial service of our late Elder Sophrony once again this year. Let us beseech the Lord to keep him in the land of the living, in the company of the saints, where the light of His face shines, the uncreated light, about which the elder taught us with his own life and with his enlightened speech. Let us also ask God to accept his prayers for us and for the whole world, for whom the late elder never stopped praying with his hypostatic prayer, which he taught us and experienced. And he continues to pray for us today.

Today's Gospel passage, dedicated to the memory of the holy, glorious, and great martyr Euphimia, is truly shocking and has messages to convey to us that are very reminiscent of the teaching of our late elder.

The Lord is invited to dine at the home of a Pharisee and there comes a woman known throughout the city for her sinfulness. She falls at the feet of the Lord, anoints them with precious myrrh, kisses them, wets them with her tears, and wipes them with her hair. And the Pharisee is scandalized. "Doesn't he, who tells us that he is also a prophet, know how sinful this woman is? If he knew, he wouldn't let her get close to him." A dialogue opens between the Pharisee and the Lord, which, my brothers and sisters, is the deepest, most moving thing the Gospel has to offer us.

The Lord asks the Pharisee: "If someone owes a large amount, 500 denaria, and another owes a smaller amount, 50 denaria, and the lender forgives both of their debts, which of the two will be more grateful?" And who will love more the master who forgave them the debt? The one who owed the most denaria or the one who owed the least? Of course, the natural answer is: the one who owed the most.

Then the Lord turns to the sinful woman and says to the righteous Pharisee, who kept the Law and the Prophets: "When this woman approached me, she anointed my feet with myrrh, kissed them, wet them with her tears, wiped them with her hair, while you did none of these things for me. And I tell you, therefore, that her many sins are forgiven, because she loved much. And to whom fewer sins are forgiven, the same loves less." This shocking teaching of the Lord comes to stir the waters of the entire culture of that time.

For the ancient Greeks, it was unthinkable to love a sinner, someone unworthy of love. Even for the Jews, who knew the commandments to love the Lord your God and love your neighbor as yourself, it was natural to love the righteous and not the sinner. And so, the Lord comes and overturns this whole hierarchy of values that prevailed—and continues to prevail, in my opinion, in our thinking even today. The just, the good deserve love. The sinner does not deserve it. For the first time in history, the Lord reverses this and says that loving the sinner is much more important than loving the just and the good. Why should things be like this? Let us try to delve a little deeper into this teaching of the Lord.

The first reason, as the Lord puts it, is that this is the way in which God Himself loves. It is God's love. And He showed us this in the person of Christ. In the entire Gospel, and especially in the passage we heard, he wants to highlight this shocking truth—that God loves sinners and gave His life for sinners. He gave Himself. God, therefore, loves sinners and the question arises "why?" Why is this the love of God?

One answer to this is that this is the only way to prove that God's love is free. To love the just, to love the one who deserves love, is obligatory, it is logical, it is necessary. To love the one who doesn't deserve it means that you love freely and no logic, no ethics and no justice obliges you, nothing obliges you.

If you are asked why God loves sinners, admittedly you will not be able to give any answer. The only answer is because He simply wants to, freely. Love for sinners, which means love for enemies, our enemies, is the result of a great truth: that true love is not a natural human trait. Man does not love simply because his nature dictates him to love.

Here we must make a great distinction: there is love that is dictated by our nature. The mother who loves the child loves him because she has a natural bond with him, because her maternal instict leads her there. There are other kinds of love that our nature dictates and they are "forced" love; they are not free.

Only when you love your enemy, then indeed what you do is not dictated by nature but by your freedom. And for this reason, love for sinners, love for enemies is a love that should be called "grace"; it is a gift. It is something that no one deserves. It is obligatory for the mother to love the child, but it is not obligatory for anyone to love his enemy. Surely, when one loves his enemy, when he loves the sinner, he gives him something that he does not deserve; such is the love of God. It is grace, it is a gift, we do not deserve it. This is precisely what the Lord wants to show with His attitude towards sinners, that God's love for all of us is something that we do not deserve and therefore this grace and this free love we must give to others as well, the love that has absolutely no justification.

Another reason why love for sinners is so important in the Gospel is that sinfulness is the condition of all people. The Pharisee could not understand this truth. He separated himself from the sinful woman and said, "I am not so sinful," and that was his great mistake. Therefore, God loves sinners because he loves people and because all people are sinners. It does not matter the form or the amount of the sin.

Every sin is enmity towards God. Every sin makes us transgressors of God's will and there is no one who in one way or another does not transgress God's will. Then, God comes, giving His love to sinners, showing His love to all people, and making us think that we cannot see anyone more sinful than ourselves.

A final reason why God loves sinners is because he wants to show us that only through love can the sinner be corrected. We often get used to hoping and expecting that people will become better with punishment. This is the great mistake of our civilization, which has never been able to understand that with repressive measures—the measures of law and justice—people cannot become better. The Apostle Paul says: to really "punish" your enemy, give him food and water (cf. Rom 12:20)—that is, love him. When, as the Apostle Paul says, we pay back with love, when we "punish" with love, then the other person sees in front of him what real love means, what real holiness means, and in this way he himself is transformed.

There are, therefore, many reasons why the Gospel highlights as its central concept, as its central message, love for sinners and love for enemies. And precisely this is one of the main axes of the teaching of Elder Sophrony. We all know this. It is the teaching he received from Saint Silouan, which he developed and which consists in the fact that nothing else proves our participation in the holiness of God than to love our enemies.

Elder Sophrony had so much sensitivity in this matter! He writes that even for demons one must feel love and pity. The demons may be so repulsive, they may be our enemies, our enemies above all, but even they must be loved, because the Lord did not leave anyone outside of love. Because love for all—even for sinners—is what emerges from hypostatic prayer, about which the elder spoke—that is, from the prayer of the Lord in Gethsemane. This prayer leads the Lord to the Cross; it is offered and referred to God the Father on behalf of all people, all sinners. The Lord therefore identifies Himself with all sinners and brings them before God, before His Father. In this way He calls all of us not to leave anyone out of our love and out of our prayer—no one, especially our enemies.

Elder Sophrony likened human existence to a pyramid which the Lord comes to invert. In human existence, as it is experienced after the fall of man, those at the top of the pyramid dominate those at the bottom. The Lord comes to reverse this and to say that whoever wants to be first must minister to all others, that is, the head of the pyramid must go down to the base.

This is exactly what the Lord does with His Cross and that is why the elder's teaching is so in line with the Gospel, as we heard it today. It is the teaching that transfers this spirit of love for sinners and love for enemies to the spiritual life of man. And it makes it, as the elder said, the measure by which we can measure our spiritual existence.

Whoever loves his enemies, whoever loves sinners, loves and applies the second commandment, which is love your neighbor as yourself. What does it mean to love your neighbor as yourself? It means that, just as we love ourselves even though we are sinners, we demonstrate how we really love our neighbor if we love him despite his sinfulness.

My brothers and sisters, true love is a very difficult thing. We are used to saying we love in a very facile way, but true love is the love that has no justification, logic or ethics, such as love for sinners, love for enemies. This is why Saint Silouan says, and our elder develops, this idea that this is the only measure by which we can measure the extent of our likeness to God. We grow into the likeness of God, to the extent that we love our enemies, that we love sinners. And this measure God gave us through His Son, Who gave Himself for sinners. So there is no other way to sanctify someone, to share in God's holiness. And one who has all the virtues of the world but does not have love for enemies, love for sinners, is very far from salvation.

Let this message, my brothers and sisters, be embedded in our thoughts, because it is the message that comes both from the Holy Gospel and from the teaching of our late Elder Sophrony. And let us be sure that with this message we hold in our hands the compass to follow along the path of salvation.

I pray that the blessings of our elder, which continue to be offered for us, will lead us to acquire this love, a love that is not dictated by any need or logic, but rather defined by love of our enemies, of sinners. And may we, in this way, be accounted worthy to be with him in the Kingdom of the Lord, where God's love will reign eternally. Amen.

July 11, 2003

86.
MEMORY OF ELDER SOPHRONY
Concerning the grace of God (2 Cor 6:1–10)

Working together with him, then, we entreat you not to accept the grace of God in vain.

"We beg you," says the Apostle Paul, "that the grace of God which you have received should not fall into the void and should not prove to be in vain." These words, which we heard in the Epistle reading earlier, acquire, my dear brothers and sisters, a special meaning, as we hear them today, as God allows us to celebrate once again the memorial of our blessed Elder Sophrony. So these words come to us not only directly from the Apostle Paul but also through our elder.

Let's try, my beloved brothers and sisters, to delve a little deeper into these very important words of the Apostle Paul. What is the grace of God? How can the grace of God fall into the void, be in vain? How can God's grace depart? How can it be won back? Here are some thoughts that we can draw, my brothers and sisters, from the wisdom of both the Apostle Paul and the Holy Gospel in general, as well as from the teaching of our blessed elder.

What is grace? Grace is a gift that we do not deserve. In our lives, especially with the rationalism cultivated by modern culture, we are used to thinking of everything as our "right." We work, we have the right to a salary. We offer something, we deserve something in return.

We are used to our lives, and this is especially cultivated by our rationalism and our modern culture, to consider all things as our rights. We work, we deserve a salary. We offer something, we deserve something in return. So many battles are fought today for human rights—everything is rights. We deserve everything. We must take everything. Is nothing in this world a gift anymore? Nothing is a gift in this culture of ours, everything is a right?

This is a great mistake, my dear brothers and sisters, because the most important things in our lives are not rights, but gifts. It's grace. The love we receive from people who love us is not our right, it is a gift. When they love us more than we love them, then it is clearly seen that it is grace that we receive. When in fact they love us while we hate them, then it is even more clearly seen that it is a matter of grace.

God's grace is exactly that—a gift. And as a gift, we can never say that we deserve it, that we are entitled to it. The grace of God begins, my dear brothers and sisters, with our very existence, with the very existence of the world. We see this as a simple given, but it is possible that we could not exist, that this world could not exist. The fact that we exist and that this world exists is not something self-evident, it is a gift, it is exclusively an offer by Someone Who loves us and wants us to exist and wants this world to exist. He was not obliged to create the world. God was not obliged to make us, to bring us into existence—it is all a gift, grace.

If we delve further, we will see that the grace of God does not stop at the fact that He brought us into existence; He wants to eliminate with His love all our transgressions and deviations from His grace, all our apostasy, all our sins, and even the hatred we often show towards Him. And He offers us His own Son, that is, the Only Begotten, the One He loves more than anything else. He offers Him as a man, to take upon Himself our sins and to unite us again with God.

Thus God's grace does not stop only at the fact that He created us, it also goes on to the fact that He redeemed us from our sins, from evil, from death, and brought us back into communion with Him. And God goes even further and gives us not only His Son but also His Holy Spirit, so that with the gifts of the Holy Spirit we can also become partakers of God's life, and become like gods ourselves. Think, my beloved brothers and sisters, how far the grace of God reaches. It's limitless. There is no end. It is infinite, just as His love is also infinite.

But the grace of God can, says the Apostle Paul, fall into the void, prove to be in vain. In other words, you can give a gift to someone you love and they can throw it away, let it go to waste.

You give yourself to him and he throws it away, despises it. The grace of God is often thus not accepted by man, my brothers and sisters; it falls into the void. When does God's grace prove to be in vain?

First of all, when we believe that we deserve it. Since we deserve it, it is not grace. So that's where it proves vain. It falls into the void with our pride, when we think we have a right to what we have. It also proves vain when we do not try to respond to this grace. And basically we can respond to this grace in two ways.

One is to identify our own will (what we desire, what we want) with the will of the One Who gave us His very self, Who gave us His grace. In other words, it is what is called in the life of our Church, observance of God's commandments, observance of God's will. This, my dear brothers and sisters, is not a moral commandment that we must follow; it is something that comes naturally. When we find that God loves us, it is very natural to want our own will, what we desire, to be identical with the will of Him Who loves us.

Since this is what happens, the second way we can respond to His grace is by simply expressing our gratitude and thanks. Wherever there is God's grace, there is also gratitude to God. It is no coincidence that the Greek word for "thanksgiving" has the word "grace" contained within it.[1] Gratitude is our confession that we have received grace, that we have received a gift. And it is not a coincidence that we celebrate the Eucharist and we don't just call it a thanksgiving but we also refer to Communion as the "Holy Gifts." Therefore, everything in the Church is a gift, and everything causes thanksgiving. And so, when our soul is filled with gratitude to God, then grace does not prove vain. But when there is no gratitude, then we receive grace in vain. Grace comes, falls into the void, and does not bear any fruit in us.

Many times, however, my beloved brothers and sisters, the saints teach us—including especially our Elder Sophrony—that the grace of God seems to leave us. It is as if God withdraws all His gifts—withdraws His presence, withdraws His spirit, withdraws

[1] Εὐ-*χαρισ*-τία.

His grace. And then we experience the absence of God's grace. This, as the experience of the saints teaches us, happens because God wants each of us in this way to experience that which His Son, the Christ, experienced. Christ was abandoned by His Father. He even reached the point of saying: "My God, My God, why have You forsaken Me?" (Mt 27:46).

Why did this happen? Had the Father stopped loving His Son? But the love of God the Father for His Son, was, is, and will be immovable. But this withdrawal of His presence, this apparent withdrawal of His love was necessary so that man's freedom could be exercised. And Christ as a man had to freely say "yes" or "no" to God, without being a prisoner of His love. Because love often binds us. If the other loves us, we consider it our duty to love him. And what will happen when the other shows that he doesn't love us? Then our freedom will be clearly discernible: Will we continue to love him? "But if you love those who love you," says the Lord in the Sermon on the Mount, "what credit is that to you? For even sinners love those who love them" (Lk 6:32). There is no grace when you love only those who love you. If you can love those who do not love you, when the love of others is not visible and your own love continues, then you love freely.

Therefore, in order for man's freedom to be exercised, for man's freedom to be seen in his relationship with God and with His grace, God's grace is withdrawn many times. And it withdraws even from the saints, from those who enter into more labors. It often withdraws violently, with a disturbing psychological experience. But it is also withdrawn in the daily experience of all of us humans. When many times our prayers are not answered, we say: "But where is God now that I call on Him and want Him and need Him?" Then, my brothers and sisters, it appears as if God's grace has been withdrawn. But let us never think that God's love is withdrawn, because precisely with this apparent withdrawal of His love, the withdrawal of His grace, God wants to bring us freely to Him, to make us free—because nothing is worth more, my brothers and sisters, than love freely given.

When love is obligatory, when love is driven by instinct and nature, we cannot say that there is grace in these forms of love.

Just as, for example, a mother can love her child out of necessity because of the natural relationship, so all forms of love based on nature are forced. However, true grace exists when there is freedom—absolute freedom—to accept or reject the love of another.

My beloved brothers and sisters, I will not burden you any longer because the church today is packed and many of you are standing. I would just like to finish these few thoughts of mine to emphasize that the Church is the locus of God's grace, the place in which God offers us His grace, with His mysteries, with His blessing—especially with the Divine Eucharist, which gives us His body and blood, Himself. It is also the place of repentance, by which He forgives us our sins. In short, every blessing He gives us in our life He gives through the Church. The Church, we say in theology, is the treasury of God's grace. This is because it is precisely through the Church and its mysteries that God Himself is given completely to us and to the world, so that we can preserve the grace of God and not prove it vain.

In order to preserve the grace which we received first of all with baptism and which God gives us continuously in the life of the Church, in order to preserve it and not prove it vain, we must be living members of the Church and participate in its mysteries. And when we receive the mysteries, we must thank God for it. And in this way the grace will not prove vain.

On the occasion of today's commemoration of our elder, let us especially emphasize that the grace of God that we received through our elder will be kept by being faithful to the Church and its mysteries. And let us be grateful to God and to the elder's memory, because through his hands, through his lips, through his prayers we received the grace of God. God showed us through our elder that He loves us, that He didn't just create us, that He didn't just redeem us from our sins, but that He wants to endow us with the gifts of the Holy Spirit and make us partakers of the very life of God Himself.

In his life, the elder received grace, and grace withdrew from him. And then he received the grace again, a grace that he gave to everyone—to those who were close to him, to those who study his writings, and those who honor his memory. I pray, my dear brothers and sisters, that we preserve this grace that our elder gave us, and not let it prove vain. And with gratitude to God and the elder's memory, let us feel that this love and this grace follow us. And let us know that the elder prays for us continually not only so that this grace may not prove vain, but that it bear fruit, so that we too may experience this grace by bringing it to perfection exactly as God wants it, and so that we made be made worthy to find ourselves in His Kingdom, when everything will be the grace of God. Amen

July 11, 2004

87. MEMORY OF ELDER SOPHRONY

Concerning the grace of God (2 Cor 6:1–10)

Working together with him, then, we entreat you not to accept the grace of God in vain.

My beloved brothers and sisters, once again the Lord has accounted us worthy to celebrate the holy memorial service of our blessed Elder Sophrony. In this Divine Liturgy dedicated to his holy memory, the Epistle reading exhorts us with the voice of the Apostle Paul, which is also the voice of our blessed elder, with these words that I said to you: "Brothers and sisters, we beg you to not let the grace of God that you received be in vain."

But what is the grace of God? How can the grace of God be in vain? And how can the grace of God be recovered? We will devote some thoughts to these questions, my dear brothers and sisters, because they are questions that concern our life, our existence, our eternal life.

Grace is a central theme in the theology of the Apostle Paul. Perhaps no one else in the New Testament refers so often to the grace of God as the Apostle Paul. Why? The answer comes from the Apostle Paul's experience, his personal experience. Let us remember that he was a persecutor of the Church and of Christ Himself. He could never conceive with his mind, he could never explain and understand how he, as a persecutor, "the chief of sinners," as he calls himself (1 Tim 1:15), received this call—to ascend to the third heaven and to see mysteries that human language cannot describe, and finally to become an apostle of Christ.

This experience, this realization that despite his sinfulness he received all this favor and love of God, possessed the Apostle Paul deeply throughout his life. And for this reason, he constantly talks about grace and says that everything is grace. What does this mean? It means that everything we have, everything we are, is a gift. Grace means gift—a gift that no one owes us, a gift that cannot be explained. It is the love of God, grace, because we cannot explain why God loves us. It is one of the most inexplicable mysteries. One writer says that if the devil asked God "Why do you love people?", it would put Him in a difficult position. But this is the only way it proves that God's love is free, because if it was due to some reason it would not be free.

How is this grace of God manifested, this gift that is due only to God's freedom? It has many manifestations, my beloved brothers and sisters, but I will mention only a few of its primary manifestations. Our very existence is the first manifestation. Really, who thinks about why we exist? We sleep, we wake up, we work, we spend our whole lives and never think: "Where did I find this good thing called existence—because I could not even exist?" Did it come by itself? Didn't someone give it to us? Isn't it a gift?"

As we say in dogmatic theology, the entire creation of the world, which is a creation ex nihilo, is the grace of God. And as if it were not enough that God gave us our existence, He gives us—think about it—Himself. He gives us His Son. That is, He calls us to participate in His very existence. He did not simply create the world; He willed for this world to become a partaker of His life, His glory, and His bliss. And the human mind cannot grasp this.

Therefore, the purpose of our creation, the purpose of our existence is to participate in the life of God Himself. This is what the fathers of our Church call theosis. And this deification is offered to us by God as grace, the supreme grace *par excellence*. But we do not accept this, just as the first man did not accept it, who did not want to participate in God's life and wanted to live his own life, who turned his back on God and said: "I am God, I will control my own life and there I will find my happiness, away from you." And what happened then? Again the grace of God pursued man, did not leave him and visited him in a thousand ways through the prophets and the laws of the Old Testament, but above all with the incarnation of His Son, with our Christ.

And when this grace of God embraced man, man struggled against it, he did not want it, and then this grace came to be crucified. This was the culmination of God's love—grace. And on the Cross, Christ becomes a source of grace for the whole world, because it is the point where God now embraces not just creation and man in general, but sinful man. Thus, throughout His life, the Lord shows special love to sinners.

We heard in the Gospel passage today how Simon the Pharisee was scandalized that Christ accepted care and love from a sinful woman, a notorious sinner, and the Lord responded: "But it is exactly on the sinner that God gifts more grace." And the word "to gift" in Greek (χαρίζω) is derived from the word for "grace" (χάρις). He, therefore, Who gives absolution, Who forgives the debt, is God Himself, in the person of Christ, Who embraces and loves the sinner especially. Why? Because the righteous, like the Pharisees, do not see God›s love as grace. As long as the Pharisee keeps the law and is righteous, God is obliged to love him. And Christ comes to overturn this, as "God resists the proud, but gives grace to the humble" (James 4:6). Let us remember the publican, that is, the truly sinful one, who attracts God's grace because he does not believe that he is worthy of His grace.

Therefore, God comes in the person of Christ and gives grace —that is, His love—freely to sinners, and dies for sinners. He does not die for the righteous, says the Apostle Paul: "perhaps for a good man someone would even dare to die" (Rom 5:7). Of course, for a good person, one can die, but to die for sinners is outrageous. This is how God's grace is manifested—an absolute gift.

And God continues to offer His grace through the descent of the Holy Spirit, after the Lord's Ascension and Pentecost, as well as through His Church and its mysteries, and through His saints. All these are gifts of God's grace, which we do not deserve. And neither do we earn them either with our virtue or our effort. We must realize that they are gifts. Otherwise, this grace can prove vain, as the Apostle Paul says. How can it prove vain?

First, with our self-righteousness. If I believe that what God gives is my right, because I worked, I labored, I have virtues, then it is not grace—"rights" are not grace. So, when we justify ourselves, when we don't understand that we don't deserve God's grace, when we don't reach this depth of humiliation, then grace proves vain. Where should it go? Into which heart should it fall? Into the heart that does not believe that what is given to it is grace? The grace of God can also prove vain when we do not confess it, when we do not thank God for this grace.

My brothers and sisters, it is not by chance that the most important moment in the life of the Church and in the life of all of us is this Divine Liturgy that we celebrate, and it is not by chance that we call it "Eucharist" or "thanksgiving." The word "Eucharist" (εὐ-*χαρισ*-τία) contains the word "grace" (χάρις) and is a confession that we received grace, that we received something that was not owed to us. If, therefore, you do not confess the grace of God in thanksgiving, if you do not participate in this mystery of the Eucharist, then the grace of God proves vain. And it also proves vain when we do not offer it others. When we refuse to love those who have hurt us, then how can we have grace?

Therefore, God's grace proves vain in these cases. But the grace of God is recovered after much struggle by the one who will reverse this whole situation. And reversal means first cutting off the passions that come from selfishness, because selfishness gives birth to all passions, says Saint Maximus. That is, we must uproot our self-righteousness from within, and this opens the door for grace to return, which is now seen in our lives through our participation in the life of the Church, in the sacraments and especially in the Eucharist, which is a confession of this grace.

It is primarily through love for enemies, it seems, that we give love as a gift. Because when you love your friend, when a mother loves her child, when we love our relatives, we cannot call it grace; it is obligatory. But when you love your enemy, then you prove that you are like God, you are like Christ, Who loves freely, without being obligated, and thus grace returns.

On this subject of grace, the blessed Elder Sophrony has taught us all a lot, which completely accords with the teaching of the Apostle Paul. He also considers grace to be a call. The call of grace is the first step. It is a great mystery; why did God call the world into existence, why does He call each of us into existence, why does He call us, who are not worthy of the call, into a relationship with Him, a relationship of love, a relationship that reveals to us the very existence of God, His hypostasis, His Light. This call, then, is the first step. However, a characteristic of Elder Sophrony's teaching is that this grace can be withdrawn and is withdrawn. It is withdrawn to the point where we now experience what Christ Himself experienced on the Cross, when He cried out to His Father: "Why have you forsaken me?" (Mt 27:46).

This withdrawal of God's love is a mystery that we cannot explain except again with reference to God's grace. It is the grace of the withdrawal of grace. God does not abandon us by withdrawing His grace; this is the way in which He wants to give it to us. Why? Because in this way we will understand within our very existence that this is grace, that it is not ours, it is not our possession. And in this way we can experience, as Elder Sophrony says, even death, which is the form of the perfect absence of God's grace and love.

When there is death, it is like saying that God has abandoned us. This experience of death, this experience of the absence of God, is called "grace" by Elder Sophrony. Because the purpose of this absence of grace is to make us feel the need for Him Who loves us, and not to take His presence and grace as something given and as our possession. And this grace we now channel to others, with love even toward our enemies, according to the teaching of the elder, which is based on the teaching of Saint Silouan.

My beloved brothers and sisters, we celebrate at this moment the mystery of Grace, the mystery *par excellence* of the Divine Eucharist, which includes especially what the liturgist will call us to do in a little while: "Let us give thanks unto the Lord." This is our thanksgiving also for our blessed Elder Sophrony, since he himself was a gift, an inexplicable gift of God's grace to all of us.

All this, my beloved brothers and sisters, surpasses the logic of man, and those who live in this world according to logic cannot explain it. Those who walk with love and grace may not be able to explain what is happening in their lives, but they know and are certain that something important is happening and it is worth living.

Let us, therefore, include our blessed Elder Sophrony, this great gift of God's grace to all of us, in our "Let us give thanks to the Lord" and let us entreat the Lord to give him a place among the saints and to accept his prayers for us, because love is not interrupted by death. And it is not interrupted because there is this eternal and unending Divine Eucharist. May the prayers of Elder Sophrony be with us so that the grace of God that we received from him does not prove vain. Amen.

July 11, 2005

88.
MEMORY OF ELDER SOPHRONY
Theology of Kenosis (2 Cor 6:1–10)

As having nothing, and yet possessing all things.

These words, my beloved brothers and sisters, conclude today's Epistle reading, which we just heard. It is the culmination of a series of descriptions that characterize the life of the apostles and of all the saints. "We have nothing and yet we have everything." How is it possible to have everything when you have nothing? This is the paradox, my brothers and sisters, to which we will devote a few thoughts today, trying to delve, as much as we can, into the truth of these words of the apostle.

Ever since man abandoned his communion with God and proclaimed himself god, he entered a state of insecurity. He relied on himself and took care, as much as he could, to fill himself and his life with things that were around him, thinking that in this way he would secure himself from all the dangers inherent in his life apart from God, and above all thinking that he will overcome the great problem that his separation from God created for him—namely, the problem of death.

In an attempt to escape death and find security, man developed this tendency to own as many things as possible—to be rich. And so, my dear brothers and sisters, a whole series of passions and problems entered our lives. Self-love came in. That is, to love ourselves so much that we want to protect it in every way and not to be concerned with anything else but ourselves. And from self-love, says Saint Maximus the Confessor, came all our other passions.

This is how our effort to acquire many possessions entered our lives, and not only to acquire these things for ourselves, but also for other people in our lives. War also entered our lives. Every effort was made to become the conquerors of as many people and lands as possible. And this caused a disturbance not only in society at large but also in people's souls. People, trying to possess as much as possible, became slaves to these many possessions and lost their peace of mind. And this is how this paradox occurred: that people become unhappy precisely because they have a lot, with the result that the more they own, the more unhappy they become.

My beloved brothers and sisters, we have only to take a look at our lives today. We have much, much more than previous generations had. But are we happy? Do we have peace? Are we satisfied? Is, perhaps, the fact that we have a lot the very reason that we are unhappy? Maybe if we didn't have so much, we'd be happier? Here are some thoughts that come to mind, my brothers and sisters, as we try to get to the bottom of the Apostle Paul's words.

To have a lot does not necessarily mean you possess a lot. The many things possess us, and we become slaves to these things, to the point that we lose our happiness. We lose our orientation. We don't know why we are in this world and why we exist. Therefore, in order for man to be healed and for mankind to be saved from this predicament in which it found itself after the fall of Adam, who proclaimed himself a god, man's attitude had to be reversed. And this reversal was accomplished by God Himself by sending His Only Begotten Son to become a man and empty Himself of everything.

In the language of theology, we speak of the "kenosis of God," God's self-emptying. This is based on the Apostle Paul's words to the Philippians, in which he says that when the Lord, the Son of God, became man, He "emptied himself, taking the form of a servant" (Phil 2:7). Even though he was God, He emptied himself of everything and in this way He led man on the reverse path from the one blazed by the first man, Adam.

Therefore, when we empty ourselves, we fill it. We fill it because we become free. We are freed from the agony and effort of trying to keep what we have and increase it. We become even richer, because we share the little we have with others. And when we share things, they grow, they increase. But when we keep them to ourselves, they dwindle, they're never enough. And if people today, my brothers and sisters, are not happy, it is because they keep for themselves what they have, whereas, if they gave and shared it with others, they would be richer. So, we become richer in freedom, richer in love, richer in mental peace. And this is everything, this is the key to our happiness.

Our blessed Elder Sophrony, whose holy memorial we have been accounted worthy to celebrate again today, developed this truth in depth with his teaching and with his own life. The truth, that is, that in order to possess everything you must lose everything. You must empty yourself of yourself and reach nothingness, so that the grace of God can enter the void you leave, God Himself can enter, because God does not enter when the self is full of ourselves. There is no space.

In order for God and His grace to enter, we must empty ourselves, expand ourselves. And so this emptiness of ours becomes that nothingness, says Elder Sophrony, from which God made the world. God made the world out of nothing. When we bring ourselves to the state of nothingness, then we give God the material from which He will recreate us. And so, with this emptying of ourselves, the grace of God enters us.

Therefore, the emptying of ourselves has a positive side and a negative side. The negative side is that I empty myself of my own will. I cut off my own will and have nothing but the will of the other. As the Lord Himself in Gethsemane sacrificed His own will and said to His Father: "If this is your will, let it be done." This sacrifice in Gethsemane was made by the human nature that the Lord took upon Himself, "the first kenosis"—the emptying of human self-love. Man was emptied of his selfishness, he cut off his own will. And the Lord opens this way for us, so that we too can follow exactly this path of kenosis, which is man's repentance.

Repentance is this emptying of our will, so that the will of God and the will of our brother become more than our will. So when we empty ourselves of our will and put in the place of our own will the will of God and the will of our brother, then we are filled, we possess everything.

The positive side of this emptying is that God Himself enters our life, into our existence, and the words of the Apostle Paul are fulfilled: "it is no longer I who live, but Christ lives in me" (Gal 2:20). Emptying himself of his own will, the Apostle made a place, he made room, so that Christ Himself could enter into him, that God could enter with his grace. And in this way he became the owner of everything. For what is greater, my beloved brothers and sisters, than possessing God Himself, the Creator of all things? So, everything is at our disposal. We will lack nothing, even when we have nothing. Let us be without not only goods, but also our own will, and even our own self.

We are called, my beloved brothers and sisters to follow throughout our lives this teaching of our blessed Elder Sophrony, which is an interpretation and an allusion to the words of the Apostle Paul that I quoted before. And this is the most important teaching that the elder handed down to us as a legacy. And he left it first of all to this monastery, which follows exactly the path he blazed, and to all of us, to those of us who were blessed to know him personally or through his words.

May his intercession and his prayer to the Lord always be with us, my beloved brothers and sisters, so that the Lord may grant us to follow this difficult path of emptying ourselves, so that God and His grace can enter into us. Amen.

July 11, 2006

89.
MEMORY OF ELDER SOPHRONY

Love, tears of repentance, continual repentance (Lk 7:36–50)

The Gospel passage that we have just heard, my dear brothers and sisters, is one of the most shocking passages of the Gospel. The scene unfolding in the house of the Pharisee, who invited the Lord to dine with him, is so moving that it is difficult to remember, analyze and describe it properly. I will limit myself to only a few observations, to only three points, which deserve our attention.

The first refers to the attitude of this sinful woman. She was a notorious sinner, whom the whole society knew and abhorred. A woman who had indeed committed many sins, as the Lord Himself confesses: "her sins are many." Despite all this, her repentance is enough to erase all her sins. And this reveals to us a great truth, a very comforting and hopeful truth for all of us—that no matter how great the sins we commit, there is always salvation through repentance. There is no sin that repentance, sincere repentance, does not remove.

There is no sin and no sinner that the Church does not accept with love. There are sacred rules of the Church that severely punish those clergy who do not forgive sins for which someone repents. Repentance therefore erases even the greatest sins and consequently there is no dead end in human life, there is no despair, there is no hopelessness. Within the Church, despair and hopelessness are unknown things. Out in the world, one sees people desperate, hopeless, but the Church is the place where all despair and hopelessness are eliminated, because there is repentance.

The second point on which I would like to dwell are this sinful woman's tears of repentance. Tears of repentance are different from tears of despair. The tears shed by this sinful woman are blessed and the Fathers of the Church consider tears to be the most important means for attaining salvation. Our Elder Sophrony, whose memorial service we are celebrating today, has written and said a lot about the importance of tears.

It is not easy to analyze the meaning of tears. I simply point out that they are first of all *cathartic*—they cleanse the human soul and body. It is as if they wash the human soul. They are what detoxify the soul, just as the body expels toxins so it can live and breathe. Thus, the soul with its tears expels the toxins of passions and the toxins of despair. Tears are what soften the human heart and attract God's mercy, because tears empty the human soul, man empties himself. It is as if he is removing from himself all his egoism, all his existence.

And so, what happens with tears is what we call "man's kenosis." He empties himself so that the grace of God and His mercy can come into him. And we all know how hard it is not to like a person who is crying in front of us. We all know how much a person's tears move and shock us. How much more the mercy and love of God, Who is moved by human tears! Also, these tears of repentance bring into man's soul the Holy Spirit—the spirit of meekness, the spirit of kindness, the spirit of love. Here, then, are just some of the reasons why this sinful woman's tears are valued so much by the Lord that He recognizes them and highlights them as something important.

These tears and repentance, however, do not seem to move the Pharisee, and this is the third point on which I would like us to dwell. There are people who are so cruel that they are unmoved, not only by the tears of others, but also their repentance. And the Pharisee of the passage we heard today remains hard and unmoved before the sight of this woman, who repents with tears. To what is this cruelty due?

Unfortunately, we have to admit that it is due to his self-confidence in his own observance of the Law and his belief that every sinner who does not keep God's Law should be punished. This attitude, unfortunately, was typical of the Pharisees during the time of Christ. That is why Christ criticized them and seemed to be quite cruel toward them—because they kept the Law and despised sinners. And the tragic thing is that repentance could not fit into their lives and their piety, because repentance is man's liberation from his past. The Pharisee says in today's passage that if the Lord were truly a prophet, He would know how sinful this woman is. However, the Lord did know that she was sinful, but He did not believe that sinfulness was something that had to remain forever with a person. The Pharisee had trapped the sinful woman in her past. And when we trap man in his past and do not give him a future, then there is no repentance.

Repentance is the door that closes on—and erases—the past and opens to the future. And the Pharisee could not take this step from the past into the future. The Lord, however, with His response to the Pharisee, gives us an image of how exactly God Himself sees sinful people. He sees them with love, with perhaps more sympathy than for the righteous, because no sinner ceases to be a child of God, no sinner is outside of God's love. And the love of God is what abounds in cases where sin abounds, as the Apostle Paul says: "But where sin abounded, grace abounded much more" (Rom 5:20). God's love is directed here in a special way, and that is why the Lord says that the person who owes more when his debt is forgiven certainly has more gratitude toward—and is more attached to—his benefactor than the person who owes less. This then is God's love for sinners who repent.

Today, my beloved brothers and sisters, the Lord calls upon us once more to honor the memory of our venerable Elder Sophrony, on this day of his departure from this world. And it is timely to reflect on Elder Sophrony's teaching on the subject of repentance. His teaching is so rich that it is not possible to include it in a short sermon. I would just like to underline certain points of what the elder taught us about repentance. One of these points is that for the late elder, repentance is the only way to salvation. There is no other way. No one can bypass this road.

The second point is that man's repentance never stops in his life. No one can say that he has now reached a point of holiness and perfection where repentance is not needed, because repentance is the result of our sinfulness. And our sinfulness accompanies us throughout our lives. The more holy one is, the more one feels his sinfulness.

Usually, those who do not realize their sinfulness and, consequently, do not repent are those who are far from God. Because the saint approaches God and sees God's holiness and immediately compares himself. And as virtuous as he is, he understands that his virtues are rags before the holiness of God. When one moves away from God, then he thinks that he is something himself. A saint never thinks he is a saint. Therefore, man needs repentance throughout his life. And this repentance opens the way to salvation.

The late elder went even a step further and spoke not only about the repentance that concerns our personal sins but also about the repentance of the saints, who weep and mourn for the sins of others and for the sins of the whole world. They have "whole Adam" repentance, as the elder would say, repentance that embraces the whole human race. They are thus identified with Adam, who, coming out of Paradise, wept; and he did not weep as an individual, because Adam was a representative of all humanity.

To reach the repentance of the saints, one must love people so much that one is even willing to take on the sins of those who do not repent and to add them to his own repentance. Then he will have truly reached the repentance of the saints, who take upon themselves—through their prayers and their spiritual struggle—all of our sins. That is why we can and do turn to the saints, in order to find, in a certain way, the mercy of God through their prayers.

In this world, the elder left to us—those who knew him personally—the memory of a man who not only knew his own repentance, but also took upon himself the repentance of those who came to him. Therefore, may we have his blessing. I am sure that, even where he is, his love covers all of us and the whole world, and he prays for us so that our repentance is lasting, sincere, deep, and that, by following this path, we can be made worthy of the Kingdom of God. Amen.

July 11, 2007

90.
MEMORY OF ELDER SOPHRONY
On love and sin (Lk 7:36–50)

Her sins, which are many,
are forgiven, for she loved much.

Today's well-known Gospel passage, my dear brothers and sisters, features three main figures: a notorious sinner, a righteous Pharisee, and our Lord, Who opens a dialogue with the Pharisee. The dialogue is prompted when the sinful woman approaches the Lord, anoints His feet with myrrh, wets them with her tears, and wipes them with her hair. This scandalizes the Pharisee, who believes that because this woman is so sinful—and her sinfulness is well known—that the Lord should not let her approach Him.

And then a dialogue opens between the Lord and the Pharisee, and in this dialogue these words that I quoted to you at the beginning are heard: "Her sins, which are many, are forgiven, for she loved much." What connection, my beloved brothers and sisters, does love have with the forgiveness of sins? This is a question that we are called to delve into, as much as we can, during today's commentary on the Gospel passage.

Love is a word well known to all of us, but very, very much misunderstood. We consider love as an emotion, what we feel for the other person. But real love is not what we feel for the other, it is something much deeper; it is the way we relate to the other. And even deeper, it is the way we exist. Because it is the way in which God Himself exists. When John says that God is love (1 John 4:16), he is referring precisely to God's way of being, to His Triune way of existence [τρόπος ὑπάρξεως]. Of what does this way consist?

It consists in the fact that each person derives his identity from his relationship with the other person. Each person empties himself to accommodate the other person inside him. And each person surrenders his existence to the other, and the relationship with the other is what defines love. So love is this emptying, this emptying of ourselves so that the other can fit inside. And what is sin? Exactly the opposite.

How did sin begin? It began precisely with the fact that the first man refused to empty himself so that the other, the supremely Other, God and His will, could find room. Man refused God's request to recognize Him and allow God Himself to dwell in him. And since he refused it, he began to turn towards himself. And this turning towards himself—and not the emptying of his self so that the other can fit in—is self-love, says Saint Maximus, which is also the source of sin. Every sin stems from this self-love.

You see then, my beloved brothers and sisters, that in order for sins to be truly forgiven, we need this emptying of ourselves. We need this movement toward love. And the sinful woman demonstrates this movement today in the Gospel passage we heard. The Pharisee refuses to make this move, but it was precisely because the woman loved much—because she emptied herself to recognize that her existence is filled only by the existence of the other, in this case Christ—that the Lord forgave her sins.

Thus, my beloved brothers and sisters, love gives birth to repentance. And there is no such thing as true love without repentance, simply because this emptying of ourselves is never complete. We always turn to ourselves more than to the other. Therefore, our love is always lacking and therefore we always need repentance. The Pharisee did not believe that repentance was needed. But he who loves knows that he must repent, because he cannot love perfectly.

And at this point comes the measure of real love, which is the love of God, to make us all understand how much we fall short of love and how much we need repentance. True love, then, gives birth to repentance and forgiveness. Because even this forgiveness, my brothers and sisters, is a misunderstood word. We think that forgiveness is not feeling something against the other. No, forgiveness is like love, something positive. It is not that I do not feel hatred for the other, but that the other fits inside me. To join in the same space, to share the same space of existence, the existence of each other. And for this to happen, we must, I repeat, empty ourselves.

So, my beloved brothers and sisters, love gives birth to repentance and forgiveness, and brings remission of our sins. So it is not without reason that the Lord connected love with the forgiveness of sins. It is precisely, my beloved brothers and sisters, what God Himself did to man. When man closed himself off so that God could not fit inside, God emptied Himself. The Son of God emptied Himself so that man could fit inside Him. And He Himself took the form of a man, became a perfect man; and when He became man, he loved sinners most of all.

God's love for sinners, my beloved brothers and sisters, remains the standard and measure of love. It is a love that is very difficult for man to achieve. But it is also the only way for him to truly be freed from his own sins, and to find a place in the life of God, in the Triune life of God, which is love.

The Lord has accounted us worthy again today, my beloved brothers and sisters, to celebrate the holy memorial service of our Elder Sophrony. And as we hear this passage and think these simple thoughts, the teaching of our elder comes to mind, which has love as its axis and center. And love especially for enemies, because love for enemies is like God's love for sinners. As the Apostle Paul also says, we became enemies of God when we sinned.

God then comes and shows His love to sinners, thus showing us the way: if we want perfect love, we will only find it in love towards our enemies. And I don't need to remind you how much the blessed elder emphasized this. It is a teaching that he received from his elder, Saint Silouan, that he then developed himself, and he developed it precisely in this spirit of emptying ourselves. By emptying ourselves, the other comes and dwells, and in this way God Himself finally comes and dwells.

Christ dwells in the hearts of the people He loves, because He wants an empty place to dwell. When the space of our heart is full of ourselves, when the other does not fit inside, how will God dwell? How will Christ dwell? But, I repeat, our emptying is never perfect if our enemy does not also fit inside us.

Let us remember, my beloved brothers and sisters, once more these words of the Gospel, words that the blessed elder lived and taught us. And in this way we will truly and genuinely express our gratitude to the Lord Who blessed us with such a spiritual father, Who showed us the right path, the path that leads us, through love and the forgiveness of our sins, to our union with God and ultimately to His Kingdom. Amen.

July 11, 2008

91.

MEMORY OF ELDER SOPHRONY

The kenosis of the self and the Kingdom of God

As having nothing, and yet possessing all things
(2 Cor 6:1–10)

In the Epistle reading that we just heard, my beloved brothers and sisters, the Apostle Paul, referring to the life of the apostles and by extension of the saints, but also of every Christian, concludes with the paradox: "We live as if we have nothing and yet we have everything." How can we accept this paradox in our lives? How is it possible to have nothing and yet have everything?

These are questions, my beloved brothers and sisters, which the Epistle reading calls upon us to consider today. Ever since man, with his freedom, decided to distance himself from God and to declare himself god, he found himself in a hostile world, not knowing where to find security in life. And the world was hostile because, with man's withdrawal from God, death entered the life of the world and dominated. Death brings fear and insecurity, and man—no longer having anything to rely upon outside himself—began to grab and try to possess whatever he found in front of him as a way to survive.

Thus, the mania for possessions entered man's life. The verb "to have" became synonymous with "to exist," synonymous with human happiness. The more one has, the more secure one feels and the happier one feels. Therefore, the temptation to possess things, to be the possessor of things, came into man's life. And it is paradoxical that the Lord and the Apostle both say that "Christians should have nothing." The reasons are very serious, my dear brothers and sisters, because owning things has serious consequences.

The first and great consequence is that you lose your mental peace because of the anxiety attached to owning things. Since the ideal of life has been reduced to having and possessing things, and since in this life no one can possess everything, an anxiety develops, a double anxiety. First, we are anxious not to lose what we have, because we discover that what we have can be lost. And secondly, we are anxious over how to increase what we have, so that we feel more secure.

Therefore, man suffered this double anxiety, this double agony, and this agony has now marked his life. In today's era, man runs around and tries to increase what he has, but by increasing what he has, he does not feel happy; he feels the need to increase it even more. He thus enters a vicious cycle and cannot escape from this misery. And let's not forget that there were times when people had less and yet were happier. But our era today is such that people have much more, but they are very unhappy. This anxiety, therefore, now eats away at man's health, eats at his happiness.

The second serious consequence of trying to have and possess goods is that we lose our freedom. Yes, it seems paradoxical, but, while we think that acquiring goods gives us more freedom, in fact, in order to acquire these goods, one must work hard and turn even the work blessed by God into a kind of slavery. Work, therefore, became slavery.[1] How did this come about? It came from the fact that man, trying to acquire things, becomes a slave, a slave to others, a slave to the goods themselves.

And the third serious consequence is that we live in an illusion, in the illusion that these goods can ensure us not only our peace and freedom but also our very existence. This illusion has dominated our life; and it is an illusion because all goods pass away, and nothing can give man his real happiness. From this illusion, from this slavery, the Lord came to free man. And in order to free him, he had to reverse this whole mentality that had entered with the fall of man. He had to overturn it, radically. And what was this radical cure? Kenosis, the emptying of everything we have.

[1] In Greek, the words for "work" and "slavery" are the same except for a difference in the accent.

And the Lord comes empties Himself first. It is what we call in theological language "kenosis." He empties Himself of His glory, the divine glory. He abandons what He had as God and takes on, as the Apostle Paul says, the "form of a servant" (Phil 2:7). He becomes a man, and as a man, instead of increasing His goods, He deprives Himself of them. And this deprivation, this divesting of goods, even means that He "has nowhere to lay his head" (Lk 9:58). He is the greatest homeless person in history. Because He had to empty man, the human nature He took upon Himself, empty it of the illusion that the purpose of life is to possess things.

And He not only empties man of goods, my dear brothers and sisters, but also something more important—He empties man of his will. Notice what happened in Gethsemane when the Lord conversed with His Father: His human nature reacts to His imminent death and does not want to go to the Cross, but it is the Father's will for Him to go to the Cross. So the Lord continues: "Nevertheless, not as I will, but as You will" (Mt 26:39)—He empties Himself of His own will.

Kenosis, therefore, man's liberation of man from possessiveness, extends to our very will, and this is the most important thing. Because, when we empty ourselves of our own will, it is very easy to empty it of goods. And this emptying of our own will extends to the cross—that is, up to the denial of our own self. The apostles and the saints also walked along this path blazed by the Lord, which, of course, involved a difficult struggle to try to empty their own will and to come to the point that they could deny their very lives.

Thus, when the Apostle Paul writes "as having nothing," he means not simply having no possessions, but also not having our own will, our very lives. That's why he writes elsewhere "we are killed all day long" (Rom 8:36), we die daily. Can man reach the point of being ready to give his very life? Then, my beloved brothers and sisters, he can say "as having nothing." But after the Lord empties Himself of everything, and after He goes to the Cross, He goes even further: the Resurrection takes place and now the Lord—Who had nothing, Who had given up everything including Himself and His very life—becomes as One "possessing all things."

Man possesses, first of all, the peace of his soul. He possesses certainty. He possesses the truth that goods cannot give him life and happiness. In this way, then, he takes possession of the peace of his soul, possession of the truth, and he learns to live without depending on goods and, to a large extent, also on those who provide him with these goods. He learns to consider these goods as a blessing from God, to accept them, but to be always ready to lose them and not be afraid that by losing them he is also losing himself.

The Apostle Paul says: "I know how to be abased, and I know how to abound. Everywhere and in all things I have learned both to be full and to be hungry" (Phil 4:12). Man becomes truly free. He becomes master of things, because with this divesture of all goods he has emptied himself, not so that nothing can enter, but so that God can enter. Let the One Who gives meaning enter, and, for His sake, also let the "other" enter.

Thus, when we are deprived, we do not empty ourselves so that it remains empty; we empty it so that the other can enter. Our life is filled by the presence of the other, the presence of love, and then, my brothers and sisters, there is no non-existence, then we truly exist. So it is that we possess everything when we renounce everything. As paradoxical as it may seem at first glance, it is true.

Today, my beloved brothers and sisters, the Lord has accounted us worthy to once again honor the memory of our blessed Elder Sophrony and I cannot help but think about everything that he offered us, especially his teaching. The elder's teaching includes exactly what the Apostle Paul says in today's passage. Of course, the elder adapted it to the realities of his life—that is, the life and experience of a monk. And there the elder pinpoints exactly what the Apostle Paul means when he says "as having nothing, and yet possessing all things." He finds three virtues that the monk must have, or rather the three vows that the monk makes: virginity, obedience, and poverty.

Poverty, "as having nothing," cannot exist without the other two and above all without obedience, because obedience, according to the elder, is what empties ourselves of our own will, and in this way poverty becomes easy. For the elder, all this—virginity, obedience, poverty—is simply the path followed by Christ Himself. Therefore, what the elder asks of the monk is to follow the footsteps of Christ—the path of kenosis, of emptying ourselves, so that the monk too can become an icon of Christ in life.

And so, by following along this path, he is freed from the illusions that the world has. And this liberation, of course, is not easy to understand, not only for the monk himself, but especially for the world. Because the world, my brothers and sisters, firmly believes in having, in owning, in the power of possessing things, that is why it believes neither in virginity, nor in obedience, nor in poverty. Therefore, when a person renounces all these, an earthquake occurs in the world, the values of the world are shaken, and the monk is the one who shakes the values of the world.

The elder, therefore, explains these in depth but ultimately it comes down to what the Lord said: "But seek first the kingdom of God and His righteousness, and all these things shall be added to you (Mt 6:33). It is not that we deny the goods, it is that we give them their proper place, after the Kingdom of God. Let us be ready to sacrifice them for the sake of the Kingdom of God. And if these blessings of material goods come back to us, after we have already placed the Kingdom of God at the top of the pyramid of our values, then they take on another meaning, they are welcome. They do not create anxiety in case they are lost, because, even if they are lost, the Kingdom of God exists for us, God exists. This is how a man comes to possess all things.

This teaching of our elder, which is the faithful teaching of the Apostle Paul and the experience of all the saints throughout history, my dear brothers and sisters, is the supreme measure by which we are called to measure ourselves. We cannot reach this measure. This should make us constantly feel our failure, and become humble. And when this measure reaches to the marrow of our bones, to our own will, then you come to understand that we all fail. That is why even the saints are always aware of their sinfulness. Because, when Christ is your measure, how can you reach this measure?

We, therefore, who live in the world, my brothers and sisters, know very well how difficult it is to apply this measure, but let us not despair. God is merciful; it is enough for us to not only respect this measure but also to try to apply it, and, when we do, then God's grace comes, which makes up for what is lacking.

And in this way, following the example of the saints and the example of our Elder Sophrony, let us also proceed with our priorities straight, putting as the first and greatest good the Kingdom of God, the love that empties ourselves to be filled by the presence of the other. This is how the grace of the Lord will come to support us, to strengthen us, so that finally, by God's mercy, we may be accounted worthy of the priority of His Kingdom and live it with Him. Amen.

July 11, 2011

92.

MEMORY OF ELDER SOPHRONY

Joyful sorrow as the experience of the saints

As sorrowful, yet always rejoicing (2 Cor 6:1–10)

In the Epistle reading that we have just heard, my dear brothers and sisters, the Apostle Paul describes the life of the apostles and, by extension, of all the saints, with many paradoxes and contrasts. The apostles, he says, live "by honor and dishonor, by evil report and good report; as deceivers, and yet true; as unknown, and yet well known; as dying, and behold we live." And to this catalog of paradoxes and contradictions the Apostle Paul adds the contrast and the paradox "as sorrowful, yet always rejoicing."

Let us, my beloved brothers and sisters, focus our thoughts on this paradox described by the Apostle Paul, because it is something which the blessed Elder Sophrony, whose holy memory we celebrate today, has much to tell us.

How is it possible to be sad and happy at the same time? How can this great paradox fit in our minds? And why should anyone feel sorry, and not simply rejoice? These are some questions, my dear brothers and sisters, which I would like us to consider, again with the help of the teaching of our blessed elder.

There are, says the Apostle Paul, two kinds of sorrow—godly sorrow and worldly sorrow. And on these types of sorrow the blessed Elder Sophrony has developed a valuable and important teaching for all of us.

Godly sorrow is the sorrow that has two causes and takes two different forms. One cause of our sorrow is—and should be—consciousness of our sinfulness. This is the sorrow that causes repentance, when we feel deeply how much we have offended the love of God, when we do not keep His commandments and constantly discover that we cannot reach this height of the saints.

This awareness of our sinfulness leads us to sorrow, even to tears. And all the fathers of the Church emphasize how important tears it is to shed tears for our sinfulness. Tears wash our heart, wash it of our sins. They cause us sorrow, but this sorrow has a sweetness because it softens our heart. And all the great saints had the gift of tears, because when we are sincerely sorry for our sins, then God gives this gift to wash our soul, to cleanse and purify our heart, so that we can feel accepted by and at home with God.

However, there is another form of sorrow, which is experienced mainly by the saints, those who have progressed in the spiritual life. And it is not sorrow for our own sins, but it is a feeling of sorrow for the sins of the whole world, of all people. The saints take upon themselves the sins of all others. They think that they are to blame for everything. They don't criticize sinners; they don't criticize anyone. They blame themselves as if they themselves are to blame for there being so many sinners in the world, for the will of God not prevailing. They take upon themselves all this burden of the world's sin, and this makes them share in the sorrow caused by the recognition and the realization that evil and sin prevail in the world and that so many people do not want to follow the will of God. This taking on of the sinfulness of all people is precisely what the Lord Himself did, when He took upon Himself the sins of all people. And thus the saints, on this point, are simply imitating the Lord. Therefore, they take up the cross, the cross of others, the one that others should have taken up. They take it upon themselves and this causes them sadness and many times even tears.

An episode is mentioned in the *Life* of Saint Silouan that is very instructive here. Saint Silouan confessed to his spiritual father that he prayed with tears every day for the dead, primarily for those who are in Hades. And his priest told him that this is a gift from God, but another brother, another monk, when Saint Silouan told him this, made him reconsider. He said to him: "It is better to pray and cry for your own sins and not for the sins of the dead." And when Saint Silouan accepted this and stopped weeping for the sins of the dead and wept only for his own sins, then, he says, he completely lost the gift of tears for himself as well.

This is very instructive. When we do not pray and feel sorrow for others, we lose the grace of God also for ourselves. We cannot be saved, my brothers and sisters, without others. We are all united, not in a human nature merely, but in a family. We are children of God. We are all saved together and we are all called to salvation together, and therefore the saint cannot separate himself from others even in his prayer. This explains why the saints are sorrowful not only for their own sins but also for the sins of the whole world. Just as our Lord Himself was, in the prayer in Gethsemane, when He took upon himself all the pain of the world and made it His own. And in this way He united with all people "hypostatically," as our blessed elder would say, and thus he brought all humanity to salvation.

And from this sorrow, the sorrow that comes from the awareness of our sinfulness and at the same time from our participation in the pain and evil that exists in the whole world for all people—from there, my beloved brothers and sisters, comes joy. The joy of the saints comes from their love for the whole world. There is no greater source of joy than love, just as there is nothing else that drives joy out of the world and from our lives like hatred, the disruption of our relationships with other people. This is the real cause of our misery. It is not economic hardship nor any of the things that people try to treat as problems today. Man's great problem is the lack of love, because when there is love, then there is also joy. And it is true joy, it is not fake. This is why, my brothers and sisters, they are "sorrowful, yet always rejoicing." Joy radiates from their faces. There is no malice, there is no hatred. The saint's face exudes joy. It is the joy that the Apostle Paul, writing to the Galatians, calls a "fruit of the Spirit" (Gal 5:22). Among the gifts, the gifts of the Holy Spirit, the Apostle Paul mentions joy second. But it is a joy that, as I said, does not ignore the tragic reality of sin, pain, and death—everything that torments man.

My beloved brothers and sisters, the world especially today wants joy without sorrow. It wants a resurrection without a cross. The world today has "happiness" as its ideal, how a person will enjoy a good time. And he closes his eyes to the tragedy of sin and evil. And so there is a false joy: a joy that evaporates at the moment man comes face to face with the evil in the world. And for this reason, this false joy, which today we try to demonstrate to other people, at some point deflates and then we are in despair. And it is not by chance that in today's era, when we have declared "happiness" a god, we also have the greatest disappointments of man and especially of our young people, disappointments that even lead to suicide.

A false joy, my beloved brothers and sisters, is a source of unhappiness, not a source of happiness. The world considers monks delusional because they do not enjoy "the good life." The world would like them to live as the world itself lives, in this frenzy of joy that does not account for sin, sorrow, pain, or death, which dominates all people. And that is why he cannot understand the Apostle Paul's paradox of being both sorrowful and joyful. That human can combine sorrow and joy, what the tradition of the Church terms "joyful sorrow."[1] This is the experience of the saints, it is the experience of those who have chosen the path of asceticism and monasticism, which the world cannot understand, but which is a great truth. The monks and ascetics do not preach this truth with words, they preach it with their lives, with their experience—as sorrowful, but rejoicing. The world, which cannot lift the crosses of others, should let the monks lift their own cross and the crosses of others. And instead of scorning them, the world should take them as role models, because only in this way will the world be able to find the true path to happiness.

My beloved brothers and sisters, God accounted us worthy to see, to know personally in our lives, such a person in our blessed Elder Sophrony. He is the one who taught true joy, who lived it, and took upon himself all that the contradictions that Apostle Paul mentions to characterize the lives of the apostles and the saints. That is why we turn to him, as to all the saints, to receive his prayers for us through his great love. Because the saints, out of love for the whole world, pray for the whole world. And this is the greatest gift that the saints give to the world: their constant prayer.

[1] Χαρμολύπη is the subject of Step 7 in *The Ladder of Divine Ascent.*

Let us, therefore, ask our blessed Elder Sophrony for his prayer, so that we too may walk on the path that he laid out, to the degree and measure that we are able, and let us pray that the Lord will have mercy on us for our sins, but also for all people, and that we may love sinners with our whole heart, considering ourselves more sinful than all others. By following this path, my beloved brothers and sisters, we will find true joy, through this path of sorrow.

I pray that God will grant us this path to follow through the prayers of our blessed Father Sophrony. Amen.

At the Holy Monastery of Saint John the Baptist, Essex, England
July 11, 2014

93. MEMORY OF ELDER SOPHRONY

"In much patience" (2 Cor 6:1–10)

In the catalog of the Apostle Paul's exhortations to the Corinthians, which we heard in the Epistle reading, my dear brothers and sisters, his exhortation to the faithful to live "in much patience" occupies a prime position.

Allow me today to devote a few thoughts to this exhortation from the Apostle Paul on this great subject, which is of enormous importance for our spiritual life, and for our life in general.

What is patience and why is patience so important for our spiritual life? Our Lord singles out patience in many ways and on many occasions: when He says "he who endures [lit., has patience] to the end will be saved" (Mt 10:22) or when he says "by your patience you will save your souls" (Lk 21:19). The apostles do the same when they exhort us to continue the spiritual struggle of life with patience and when they attribute patience to Christ Himself, speaking of "the patience of Christ" (2 Thess 3:5), or when the Apostle Paul speaks of the "God of patience" (Rom 15:5). All this shows us, my dear brothers and sisters, how important patience is for the life of the believer.

But what is patience? Patience means two things: One is that I endure, I endure temptations, sorrows, pains, trials, the wickedness of people, slander, sickness, and even death. And the other meaning is that I wait, I expect, I look forward to the future. Both of these meanings, my beloved brothers and sisters, are united in one in the persons of our saints. All our saints experienced patience. Patience as endurance of the sorrows, trials, and wickedness of people, which in many cases extended even to martyrdom, and patience as an expectation of the visitation of God's mercy in their lives, as an act of absolute trust in God's love. Our saints drew this patience from the Lord Himself, Who gave us the example of patience in His earthly life.

But why is patience so important? It is important, my dear brothers and sisters, because it accompanies and expresses faith. Many times people say that they believe in God and think that faith is to subscribe to certain teachings and certain doctrines of the Church. Of course, it is also that. But faith is an experience and is manifest at the time of trial. Faith is manifest when God is absent from our lives, when He hides and does not show us His presence, when He seems to abandon us; then our faith is tested. Will we continue to have confidence in God that, despite His absence and this abandonment, He loves us? This great teaching about our abandonment by God was developed extensively by our blessed Elder Sophrony. This is the same experience that our Lord experienced in Gethsemane, or even on the Cross, when it seemed for a moment that His Father had abandoned Him. So there our faith is tested and at the same time our patience. Can we maintain our faith in our sorrows? Can we, when everything is against us, believe that God is with us and that nothing, nothing can remove God's love from our lives? This will give us patience to face all the difficulties of life.

And patience, my dear brothers and sisters, also accompanies love. The Apostle Paul says that love "endures[1] all things" (1 Cor 13:7). When we love, we endure everything for the sake of the person we love, and we do not consider his faults or his feelings towards us, whether they are as we would like them to be or not. Real love is the one that endures everything for the sake of that person we love. And so patience, my dear brothers and sisters, also accompanies our prayer. Ah, yes, prayer without patience has no meaning. "I waited patiently for the Lord, and He heeded me; and He heard my supplication" (Ps 39:2 LXX), says the prophet. Prayer needs patience, because God does not answer our prayers immediately. God knows when He will give us what we need and what we ask for, and He expects us to be patient, until He speaks and He answers. A prayer that insists on its result coming immediately is not a genuine prayer. Real prayer is complete surrender to the will of God. We ask, but when He wants, when He decides,

[1] ὑπομένει: This again is the verbal form of "patience."

He will answer. And then we who pray must have patience. Let us wait on the Lord and He will listen to us.

Patience, my brothers and sisters, has a deeper meaning, because it is a blessing within the great gift that God gave us—and that is time. Yes, our life flows through time. Nothing happens automatically. And time is the context in which our patience is exercised. If we abolish patience, we abolish time. And time is a gift from God and should not be abolished. God gave us the time precisely so that we can exercise our patience in it. And this leads us, my brothers and sisters, to the most important meaning of patience. And this is in the expectation of the Kingdom of God, in the coming of the Lord again. Yes. Christ promised His disciples that He would return immediately and the first Christians waited for His return immediately, and prayed "maranatha"—"the Lord is near, He is coming." But time passed and He did not come. And then impatience seized the Christians. When will the Lord come? When will He come to establish His Kingdom, to wipe away every tear from the earth, to defeat death, to bring justice and love to the world? This made the souls of the first Christians burn with expectation and this expectation was translated into patience, because as the Lord Himself said to His disciples, "It is not for you to know times or seasons which the Father has put in His own authority" (Acts 1:7). It is not for you to know when the Lord will come again to establish His Kingdom. You have to be patient. Wait for the coming of the Lord and do not live without this patience and without this expectation, but wait for Him at every moment, because He can come "like a thief in the night" (1Thess. 5:2), when you do not expect Him. Look forward to the coming of the Kingdom of God with patience, enduring in the meantime all the trials and everything else that afflicts the human race in this life, after the fall of man.

The Apostle Paul calls us to cultivate this patience, my brothers and sisters, and his message is very timely today. Because, my brothers and sisters, our age is hostile to patience. Our age is an age of haste. We want to get everything quickly. We want to quickly obtain information, and technology helps us in this. You see, people no longer wait to read the next day's paper to see what happened today. They want to know what is happening at this moment. And speed has become the ideal of our culture, which abolishes time. Nothing is left to mature over time. This prevails in human relations today as well. People want to quickly establish a relationship which may need time to develop—a time of patience—but man is not patient today. There are many examples we could point to that demonstrate that patience has disappeared from our lives. Look at the way we deal with nature. We do not leave nature's fruits to ripen. We are in a hurry, we cut it before it is ripe because we want to quickly acquire either the food that nourishes us or a financial benefit, and thus our culture is constantly a culture of haste, without patience. So we lose expectation, we lose patience, and that is why we also lose patience with people. We don't tolerate them. If someone is unpleasant to us, we reject him, we don't want to exercise patience to live with him, to endure. How many families are broken up today precisely because there is no patience. Because we want to be happy immediately, to get what we think is good. By banishing patience, we banish the very meaning of our lives. We chase away our happiness.

My beloved brothers and sisters, today the grace of the Lord has accounted us worthy to once again honor the sacred memory of our blessed Elder Sophrony, and we praise God for this. We praise God for this opportunity to honor his memory, but we also praise Him for what the elder has meant for all our lives, and for what he will mean for future generations. Because Elder Sophrony is and will remain a spiritual beacon for the next generations as well. We have lived with him, we have received blessings from his hands, but our elder also left a lot for the future generations. And among this treasury is his teaching on patience. The elder's whole life was a life of patience, patience in sorrows, in illnesses, in many trials, patience in the work he did, because in his case the seed he sowed bore fruit "with patience" (Lk 8:15), as the Lord says in the Parable of the Sower. The seed of the Gospel, the word of God, needs patience to bear fruit. It does not bear fruit immediately. And the elder dedicated his whole life to patiently creating this presence of God's grace here, in this blessed monastery—through great, great patience. And so, my beloved brothers and sisters, he became the teacher of patience who fulfilled the word of the Apostle Paul to the Corinthians, that we should live "in much patience."

I pray, my brothers and sisters, that God may grant us this virtue of patience—which, as I said, is so difficult to acquire today—through His grace, so that we may, like the saints throughout the ages, walk in patience, enduring the trials of life, but also waiting for the coming of the Lord, His Kingdom, which will bring love and peace and justice to this world, and also abolish death.

I pray that the Lord will grant us all this Kingdom of God, my beloved brothers and sisters, through the intercessions of our Elder Sophrony. Amen.

At the Holy Monastery of Saint John the Baptist, Essex, England
July 11, 2015

94.
MEMORY OF ELDER SOPHRONY
Love as the forgiveness of sins (Lk 7:36–50)

But he who is forgiven little, loves little.

The greatest upheaval that the Gospel brought to the world, my dear brothers and sisters, is love for sinners. The ancient Greek world, which had reached the height of civilization, detested sinners. It had developed a great appreciation for the good, the beautiful, the just, but also a great aversion to everything ugly and evil. Judaism developed the same attitude during the Lord's years on earth, especially with the Pharisees, who despised every sinner and exalted their own holiness.

And this is precisely what happened in the case described by today's Gospel passage, which we just heard. A Pharisee invited the Lord to eat with him at his house. And there something very shocking happened. A woman, a notorious sinner, approached the Lord, fell at his feet, wet them with her tears, kissed them, washed them with myrrh, and then the Pharisee said to himself: "If Christ were a prophet, he would know what kind of woman is approaching him and therefore he would not allow her to touch him." It was precisely this expression of hatred towards the sinner. And this gives the Lord the opportunity to demonstrate the exact opposite, to overturn things, as I said at the beginning, because for Him sinners have priority in His heart. He loves them in a special way, more than any other.

And one wonders, my beloved brothers and sisters, why did Christ have this love for sinners? We cannot explain it with human logic. Human logic leads us to the perception that the Pharisee also had: if someone is sinful, he does not deserve our love. We must definitely give priority in our hearts to the good, to those who deserve our love. And our common sense tells us again and again this man is "lovable." I love him because he deserves to be loved. Loving someone who doesn't deserve to be loved is absurd. Our common sense cannot accept this. And the Lord comes and overturns common sense and tells us that the one who deserves our love the most is the sinner—he who, in our opinion, does not deserve it. This is truly a scandal for the logic of man, and the Lord comes today to present this scandal as the essence of His Gospel. And one wonders: Why? How can Christ's love for sinners be explained? The answer, my beloved brothers and sisters, as I said, cannot be found in the logic of man, but is found *in the mystery of God's love.*

God's love is different from what we call "love." And the big difference is that when we say love we mean a feeling towards others, maybe even a relationship with others, but God's love, which is hidden within the very mystery of the Holy Trinity, is something much deeper and very shocking: one person empties himself so that the other can enter. This emptying of ourselves so that the other can enter is the essence of love. And for this reason the love of God is expressed in its fullness only by Christ, because He "emptied Himself, taking the form of a servant" (Phil 2:7). He emptied Himself completely and became a man so that in this way He could assume man in the entirety of his fallen state—that is, in his sinfulness. That is why Christ, the late elder teaches us, whose memory we commemorate today, overturned the pyramid. After the fall, people built a pyramid, where they put the strong—I would even say the righteous— at the top, and they dominated all the lower ones. And a situation was created that we are all used to and in which we live every day. But the Lord comes and overturns the pyramid and puts at the top those who are at the bottom in our daily life. He comes to empty Himself and serve man.

This emptying of Himself, the kenosis of Christ, is also why He addresses himself especially to sinners and loves them. Because this emptying, this kenosis, which God Himself undertook in the person of Christ, meets the kenosis, the emptying that the sinner feels when he realizes his sinfulness and has nothing to justify himself before God. While the Pharisee, in the well-known parable, presented arguments why he deserves God's love (because he does this and that, all that the law requires), the sinner has nothing to justify himself, and the more he is sunk in sin, the more he sees that he has nothing to say to God. "God, look at this thing that I have and show your mercy on it." The sinner, then, like the woman described in today's Gospel passage, is completely empty of himself, and this meets the emptying of Christ, Who now finds there fertile soil to give him grace, to be united and unite man with God.

This great mystery, my beloved brothers and sisters, shows us that love cannot exist if there is no humility at the same time, if there is no repentance at the same time, because then there is no such emptying of ourselves. And since we have not emptied ourselves of our own selves—to the point, the elder would say, of self-hatred—since there is no such humility, no such kenosis and emptying of the self, then there is no love. Because there is no room for the other to enter and dwell inside us. And so, we have misunderstood the concept of love; what man must do when he really wants to develop love is to empty himself as much as possible of himself, of his self-confidence, and even of his virtues. Let him consider them refuse, nothing, so that in this way the other can dwell inside, both Christ and our brother.

And that is why it is so difficult, my dear brothers and sisters, for us in the world to love, because we want to love the other and at the same time not to empty ourselves of our personal interests, of what we like and what we want. If you don't cut off your own will, you can't say you love. And to cut off your own will is not an easy matter; it takes practice, it takes effort. And precisely for this reason our holy Church presents its saints as models, who emptied themselves either by their martyrdom or by their asceticism and in this way they were able and allowed God but also their brother to dwell inside them.

So, my beloved brothers and sisters, this whole matter of God's love for sinners is deep. God loves sinners when they themselves feel their sinfulness. When the sinner does not feel his sinfulness and is full of his selfishness, he cannot attract the grace and love of God. But when he empties himself and believes precisely because of his sinfulness that he does not deserve God's love, then

God's love comes and dwells within him. This, my dear brothers and sisters, is the great mystery of Christ. Christ is precisely this love of God Incarnate, Who emptied Himself and took all of us within Himself and even reached us at our very bottom after the fall, in Hades. And it is there that He finds sinners who are aware of their own sinfulness.

My beloved brothers and sisters, the Pharisee lurks in our lives, and we should pay attention. Every moment when we judge others as sinners and justify ourselves, the Pharisee comes out of us, which distances us from the spirit of Christ. On the contrary, when we think about our sins and find them greater and more than all other people, then Christ comes and dwells. The Pharisee, therefore, we must constantly watch out for, because many times he stealthily, without us realizing it, sneaks into our lives. Criticism is the greatest proof that we do not understand our own sinfulness and that instead we find others sinful. Let us stay far away from criticism, far away from thinking that others are more sinful than we are. Far from this hierarchy of sinfulness, which human morality brings us: "Yes, I am a sinner, but not like the other: I did not kill, I did not commit adultery, I did not do this, I did not do that…" This was precisely the spirit of the Pharisee. There is no hierarchy of sinfulness. We are all sinners and we are all the worst sinners.

Let us embrace this spirit, my beloved brothers and sisters, and then what the Lord said today to the Pharisee, when he was scandalized by the Lord accepting the sinful woman kissing his feet, will happen: "Her sins, which are many, are forgiven, for she loved much." Love creates forgiveness. But on the condition that love is this kenosis, this emptying of ourselves, this conviction that all others, as Anthony the Great said, will be saved except us. This spirit, my beloved brothers and sisters, gives birth to the forgiveness of our sins, it cleanses us, and this is the presupposition for our salvation.

So, my beloved brothers and sisters, let us embrace this spirit and let us try—to the extent that each of us can with our own personal asceticism—to empty ourselves daily of everything that we supposedly have and to let the "other," our brother and of course the Only-Holy God, become our priority, since it is only through His grace that we can be saved from our sins. Amen.

In the Holy Monastery of Saint John the Baptist, Essex, England
July 11, 2016

95.
MEMORY OF ELDER SOPHRONY
The remembrance of death as a gift (2 Cor 6:1–10)

As dying, and behold we live.

There is a paradox in the words we heard today from the Apostle Paul in the Epistle reading. How is it possible to die and live at the same time? I feel called to offer a few thoughts, my dear brothers and sisters, on this paradox, because it defines the way and essence of the Christian's life.

Christians are distinguished from other people precisely because they live this paradox of being dead and simultaneously alive. Man was created by God to live forever. Death is not the will of God; it was not the will of the Creator. Death is the opposite of what God wanted when He created us. That is why the Apostle Paul calls it the "last enemy" (1 Cor 15:26). This enemy will be defeated in the end. The last enemy that will fall under the feet of Christ, the resurrected Christ, is death. Therefore, death is not good, it is not accepted, and it is not in accordance with God's will.

Only God is immortal, by His nature. Because only God had no beginning. We as creatures came into being out of nothing. Death is a threat inherent to the nature of man and every creature. But, when God says that He desires man to be eternal and immortal, He means that He wants to give him His own immortality and eternalness. That's why man acquires immortality when he unites with the immortal God. But when he cuts off his relationship with God, then death reigns. And this is what happened with the first man, our forefather Adam, who decided to cut off his relationship with God and to declare himself god. Thus he cut the thread by which he could have had immortality—that is, his relationship with the immortal God. And consequently, death thenceforth entered our existence; we cannot avoid it, because it has become part of our nature and is transmitted from generation to generation. We are born mortal and we try in various ways to avoid death, because within us the desire for immortality has never disappeared. But the ways in which we try to avoid death lead us towards more death.

Man, since he cut off his communion with God, tries by his own power to avoid death. He develops ways for his person, his ego, to survive. And here lies the big problem. The more the individual, our self, survives, the more death enters our existence. The holy fathers say that self-love is what cultivates death in our existence. We try to save our ego in ways that ultimately lead to death. There is, however, only one way to avoid death: to kill our will, to kill our selfishness. And that's why the road to immortality now goes through death. We cannot have eternal life if we do not taste death. And this is why, when we celebrate the Lord's Resurrection, we sing of this paradox: "by death, trampling down upon death." Death has been defeated by death.

How is this experienced? It is experienced by the saints of our Church, whom we all—each according to his ability—are called to follow down this road. The first and most important thing is, as I said, to eradicate selfishness, self-love. And this is very difficult. All the saints gave themselves over to this great struggle to cut off their own will and allow the will of the other. How painful and difficult this is! But the Lord Himself lived it and modeled it for us first. He experienced it in Gethsemane. This was what led Him to the following words: "If it is possible, let this cup pass from Me," He said to His Father, "nevertheless, not as I will, but as You will" (Mt 26:39). We want to avoid our own death, but we should be willing and ready to sacrifice our will, for the sake of the other's will, and above all for the sake of God's will.

There is, therefore, in the life of the saints a struggle to overcome our own will, to cut it off. This is a death. And this death then leads to life. We die and behold we live. By cutting off our own will, we live truly, but, I repeat, it is a real death, which is not easy to go through. And the path to holiness passes precisely through this narrow gate, through the death of our ego, so that the other can find room and live within us. This is the essence of love, without which we cannot truly live and be saved. Love is not an emotion we feel for the other. Love means to empty ourselves, as the Lord did, Who "emptied Himself, taking the form of a servant" (Phil 2:7)—to empty ourselves so that the other may enter. And of course, the Other *par excellence* is God Himself.

Thus, my beloved brothers and sisters, the saints pass through the road of death to reach life; they live as dead and die alive. This is the mystery which is a reality for the saints. And some saints reached the point of denying their own existence with their martyrdom. They denied life and lived, and continue to live, precisely through this sacrifice of their very life. The martyrs, therefore, the saints, and all those who fought to defeat their selfishness, all of them experienced this paradox: "as dying, and behold we live."

And because today we honor the memory of our Elder Sophrony, it is good to listen to his voice, which repeatedly emphasized in his writings precisely this mystery of Gethsemane, where the Lord cut off His own will so that God's will could be done. He then took within Himself the hypostasis of the whole world. However, the elder presents this subject to us in another way, with what he calls and is called in the ascetic tradition of the Church the "remembrance of death." To remember death, to live with its memory, is a gift from God. It is not easy, it is not simple, but one could say that each of us can remember death and live without even believing in God. And there are many people who live their whole lives with the remembrance of death, with the principle that certain ancient philosophers used to say: let us eat and drink, for tomorrow we die (see also 1 Cor 15:32). So, since we are going to die, let's have a good time in this life and be thankful, because "tomorrow we will die." It is a common philosophy in the world. However, it is not the remembrance of death that Elder Sophrony talks about and that characterizes the saints and ascetics. From the remembrance of death comes the realization of the futility of this world, which, however, leads to more thirst for life. We understand that this world with its mortality cannot give us true life. He who lives with the remembrance of death, with the gift of the memory of death, is not led to despise life, as the thirst for life actually increases more. And with this thirst for life, he makes progress and is led to resurrection, to true life. This remembrance of death that leads to life frees us from many things that make us want to live in this world as "I," with our self, with our self-love. With the remembrance of death, we are henceforth indifferent to the consequences brought about by anything that harms our self and our egoism. We are indifferent to the accusations, the slanders that may be launched against us. We are indifferent to the praises we may hear about ourselves. All these become relative and no longer define our existence. And in the same passage we heard today, the Apostle Paul mentions that we Christians live "in ill repute and good repute." We are indifferent to the accusations they may make against us. If they are true, of course, we must repent. If they are slanders, we will accept them too, because, when we have died to our egoism, neither slanders nor praises mean anything.

The saint, therefore, who has the remembrance of death, is indifferent both to the praises and to the slanders against him. And something more important: He now participates compassionately in the death of all other people.

He takes upon himself not only his own death but also the death of all creation. And for this reason, if he sees even a bird that has died, that has been killed, he will feel sadness inside; he will feel that this sting of death is incompatible with our existence. But in order to feel this, he must experience this remembrance of death. Then, he becomes compassionate towards all mortal beings, and towards his fellow humans, who are mortal, and thus acquires a very delicate, very sensitive soul. Saints are the most sensitive beings in this world. This kindness and delicacy, the sensitivity of the soul, which characterizes them, is precisely due to the fact that they pass through the road of death, the death of their selves, and through the road of the remembrance of death, which always accompanies them.

Today, as we celebrate the memory of our blessed Elder Sophrony, I wanted to highlight these teachings, which of course, he presented with greater wisdom and depth. We should never come to terms with death, but we should also never consider that death is the last word in our lives. It is the road through which we pass to reach the true life.

Through the prayers of our elder, may each one of us follow to the degree we are able this difficult road, which is traveled by those who struggle in this life in the footsteps of our saints, in order to reach eternal life, the Kingdom of God, where death no longer has the last word, where life reigns supreme and where God's will for our immortality is a reality. I pray, through the intercessions of our elder, that all of us along this road will reach that blessed end of the Kingdom of God. Amen.

In the Holy Monastery of Saint John the Baptist, Essex, England
July 11, 2018

96.
DORMITION OF SAINT ANNA
(Gal 4:22–27)

For the desolate has many more children than she who has a husband.

Today is the feast of the Dormition of Saint Anna, mother of our Virgin Mary, and for this feast the Church has appointed a reading from the Apostle Paul's Epistle to the Galatians. In this epistle, which we just heard, the apostle speaks of two kinds of births: natural birth and supernatural birth. One birth is the biological one, from which we all come, and it is truly a blessing from God, but it is a birth necessitated by the laws of nature, and it includes death.

Death is not just an element of our existence at the end of our life, as we usually think, but from the first moment of our conception. We are born mortal. Death accompanies our existence from our birth, and this biological birth of ours has within it the problem of death. That is why it is not easy for man to be freed from death, since he is born that way. And he has been born this way from the moment when the first man, Adam, decided to cut off communion with God, Who is the only source of true and eternal life, and to declare himself god. In this way death entered the world, and all the descendants of Adam are born in this death.

The Apostle Paul exclaims in another of his epistles: "O wretched man that I am! Who will deliver me from this body of death?" (Rom 7:24). Who can deliver me from the death within my own body, within my biological birth, within the laws of nature under which I was born? In order to redeem us from this death, God chose another way of birth. He gave us signs that there is another way of birth, which is not subject to the laws of nature.

From the forefather of our faith, Abraham, we have the first example of a supernatural birth. Sarah, Abraham's wife, is barren and despite this she gives birth to a son. The same happens with Saint Anna, whose memory we honor today. Both she and her husband Joachim were beyond the age of childbearing, making it impossible according to the laws of nature to give birth, and despite this they gave birth to our Virgin Mary, the Mother of God.

This continues and culminates in the birth of Christ Himself, our Lord, who is born of a virgin woman. He is born beyond the laws of nature and biology. And the Lord does this, as I mentioned in the previous cases, not to demonstrate His power, as many want to interpret this fact, since God has no need for such a thing. Even when God demonstrates His power, He never does it for any other reason than to save us and to find a way to demonstrate His charity and His love. The reason the Lord is born beyond the laws of nature in this supernatural way is because only in this way could he avoid the necessary death that each one of us is obliged to undergo. Because if our Savior Himself were subject to the necessity of death, He could not be our real Savior from death. That is why He is born in a supernatural way—that is, in a way that transcends the laws of nature. And this supernatural way of birth continues in the Church with our baptism.

Our baptism is nothing but the death of the old man—that is, the man we inherited from our biological birth—and our rebirth into a new man, who is not subject to the necessity of nature and who is free from death. In the life of the Church, therefore, baptism gives us a new life, a new identity, eternal life, which does not depend on the necessity of our nature.

It is not by chance that the Apostle Paul uses this expression today referring to desolation—to the desolate woman who gives birth without the mediation of a man: "For the desolate has many more children than she who has a husband." The Apostle Paul here alludes to the fact that even the desolate desert—where there is no life, where it is not possible according to the laws of nature for anything to bloom—can also be filled with life!

And this, my dear brothers and sisters, brings to mind what happened in the life of our Church, especially in the desert, when the first monastic communities settled there, and then the desert really blossomed. The desert, which cannot give birth to anything, gave birth to ascetics, hermits, and saints, those who were no longer born according to the laws of nature, but by the spiritual rebirth of their repentance, which was a restoration of their baptism.

The children of the desert therefore become the saints and the faithful monastics of our Church, who really inhabit the desert and fill it with life, true life, life that never dies. So, how can we understand these words of the Apostle Paul which we heard and which the Church connects today with the miraculous birth of our Virgin Mary by Saint Anna? All things are possible with God, but above all what God wants, as I said, is to redeem us from the laws of nature, in which we are trapped.

Therefore, my beloved brothers and sisters, every birth of a child is, as I said, a blessing from God, but this is not enough for a person to have true life, to escape from the laws of death. That is why we also need a new birth, this birth which we receive in baptism, and which is given to us again by our repentance—the constant, sincere, and deep repentance, which makes us free from anything connected with death in our life and gives us true and eternal life.

This repentance that the Fathers of the desert introduced to us, my beloved brothers and sisters, is the only way for us to be born again, to be born into true life. And as the Lord said: "Truly, I say to you, there are some standing here who will not taste death" (Mt 16:28), such as the saints, the faithful, who are truly born again. This is how we are also called, apart from our biological life, for which we must be grateful, to move on to true life, to the life that repentance gives us.

Today the world celebrates a person's birthday with joy, but personally I believe that this is a rather new tradition for our Orthodoxy, although we have saints' birthdays. However, what we should really celebrate is not our biological birth, but our rebirth through baptism within the body of the Church. And this baptism, which we all received, is our entrance to new life, but we must renew it constantly in our lives with our repentance, and in this way live eternally in the Kingdom of God together with the communion of His saints, which I wish, my beloved brothers and sisters, for all of us. Amen.

July 25, 2010

97.
THE TRANSFIGURATION OF THE LORD
(Mt 17:1–9)

The grace of the Lord has brought us together again, my dear brothers and sisters, to celebrate one of the most important feasts of our Church. A feast which, with its deepest content, invites us to reflect and to dedicate a few thoughts during this celebration.

What is the purpose of the Transfiguration of the Lord? Why was the Lord transfigured? Did He transfigure to demonstrate His power? But He has no need to demonstrate His power, and it would not contribute to our salvation. And everything that the Lord did, He did for our salvation. And His Transfiguration on Mount Tabor, this too has something to say about our salvation.

Man was called by God for a supreme destiny, so high that it could be described—as it is indeed described in the Holy Bible and in the fathers of the Church—as the deification of man, his becoming a god. In the ancient Greek world, man's attempt to become a god was considered hubris. Man can never ask to become a god. But in our faith it is not hubris, it is a mission that God Himself assigned to man. To strive to becomes a god. And this corresponds to man's deepest pursuits.

Man, unlike animals and other creatures of creation, is not satisfied with what is in nature. Man wants to overcome the limits of nature. He wants to overcome even death. He has this desire for immortality. All this God gave him, because he destined him to become a sharer of the same glory of God, of the same immortality of God. He destined him for eternal life, as we say, true life, which is not subject to death, to liberate him from corruption. And this desire was put into man by God Himself with the creation of man.

But man made a tragic mistake. He wanted to become a god without God. He proclaimed himself a god and cut off communion with the true God. This is the tragedy of man! This is what we call in the language of the Church "the fall of man."

The first man, Adam, therefore said to himself: "Why should there be a God? Let me make myself a god! Everything and everyone will turn to me, all the honors that belong to God will be given to me. And in this way—that is, by my own power—I will become a god." And trying to achieve this, he entered a dead end. Because by nature he was not a god. He was a creation of God. And so all his weaknesses became manifest, all his inability to become a god by his own strength.

And so, from the moment man decided to become a god without God, he set foot on a misadventure from which he still cannot get out. And he can't get out alone. He thought that he would gain life and avoid corruption by following his natural powers. And he developed biological powers. He thought that by perpetuating his species, by reproducing his species, he would ensure eternity. And this was a great tragedy. Because the reproduction of the species does not avoid death. Mortal beings are born! And all the beings that come into the world bring with them the stamp of death. Thus man became involved in the laws of nature and then wanted to free himself; he intervenes in nature, and by intervening in the laws of nature he creates new dead ends for himself.

So he tries to become a god with the powers of his logic. He tries to become a god with science, with knowledge! And what is the result? The result is known and can be felt every day: science and knowledge create as many problems as they solve. And it is really an illusion for man to believe that through science he will progress to immortality, that he will avoid death! This intervention in nature results from man's discovery that nature cannot give him the immortality he desires. And this intervention becomes the source of enormous problems, which we are experiencing today in the form of the ecological problem, which worries us all.

Man's intervention into his own nature—this enthusiasm we see for man's intervention into his genetics—oh, how many calamities are in store! It is not possible for man to be deified through his own powers. Man must understand that. Yes, he is called by

God to become a god, but he cannot become a god without the true God.

Thus, the Lord's Transfiguration comes to show us that, indeed, man's destiny is deification. His destiny is to become a god, to be transfigured, to be freed from corruption—for his power to shine, for his very body to become light, to become life, to become incorrupt and eternal. And this is what happens on Mount Tabor. The Lord brings before us the image of our own destiny. He does not reveal to us His divinity; He reveals to us the destiny of humanity. The human body is transformed and in this way it shows us the destiny of our own bodies. Our bodies, which we submit either for scientific experiments—supposedly to be able to secure immortality—or for hedonistic purposes—supposedly to enjoy pleasure and happiness—these same bodies are destined to shine, like the body of our Lord on Mount Tabor. And this is the great message of today's feast. We are called to be transfigured and to become like the Lord Himself, "gods."

But what does the Gospel passage we heard include? It includes a voice from heaven, heard by His disciples who were present. It says: "This is my beloved son, in whom I am well pleased; listen to Him." There is no other way to become a god than to obey the Son of God, Christ. To reverse the course of humanity. The only way one can truly become god is by obeying the will of God, as it is expressed through His Son, Jesus Christ.

And it also shows us that, in order for man to be truly transfigured and become a god, we must be enveloped in light, like the Lord's body on Tabor. Our interior must be illumined, our whole body must shine with light. We mustn't fear the dark, we mustn't hide anything in order to have nothing to fear, in order to free ourselves from the darkness, from that which often holds us captive, because we always have something to hide. So the light, the abundant light, is what deifies us, what brings us closer to God, what really makes us gods. In this way, today's feast, my brothers and sisters, bears a message for the modern world.

We find ourselves in a dilemma in our culture: either we become animals and adapt to our nature or we go against our nature in our effort to become gods. And we have this dilemma every day. We say today that we have abandoned the natural way of life and must return to nature. But that's what animals do too. Animals adapt to nature. Is it the destiny of man to adapt to nature? Definitely not! Our destination is to overcome nature, to transcend nature. Because nature contains mortality and decay. But then the problem arises: if we overcome nature—as our civilization tries to do today—by interfering with nature, it reaps all the consequences that we reap today. And so we are at an impasse.

The Transfiguration of the Lord reveals that there is a path, a right path, to overcome nature by obeying the will of God and living with God in Christ. We must let the light of Christ shine in our hearts, understanding that the whole world is God's creation and that we, as the crown of creation, were created to transform it, not by our own interventions into the laws of nature, but by offering it, as His creation, back to God Himself in thanksgiving.

When we respect the world as God's creation, as God's gift, and understand our responsibility for this gift that God gave us, then we will escape from this dilemma, which on the one hand calls us to intervene in nature and to destroy it and on the other hand to conform to nature and obey its laws, as if there is nothing higher and nothing supernatural. In this way, my brothers and sisters, today's feast sends a message to our culture, it sends a message to all of us.

Of course, it is not easy to reverse the flow of history. And, unfortunately, we have now taken a road that seems to be a road of no return. But the Church never gives up hope, it never gives up its effort to convey this message. And those who embrace it and those who understand it and make it their life's experience, they will now be the little yeast that transfigures the world. Because the world is not transfigured, my brothers and sisters, either by violence, or by political systems, or by economic programs. The world is always transfigured by the few, by the saints. Look at history and you will see. All the great things that happened in history were always done by a few. And the few are the ones who essentially directed history. So, let the little yeast be our Church, let it be all of us, those who honor this great feast and those who have gathered today in this holy temple, in a celebration which, truly, is exemplary, thanks to the care of your presiding priest, his assistant priest, and all his co-workers. Thanks also to the work of the mayor of this city all the local authorities, the members of the parish council, all those who, since last night, have made this city into a truly celebratory city, in proper conformity with our tradition.

I pray that the transfigured Lord will support and bless this parish and this city and transform our hearts with His Holy Spirit, so that we too can become the little yeast that will first transform ourselves and then our society and the whole world. Amen!

Holy Church of the Transfiguration of the Lord, Kefalari, Kifissia
August 6, 2002

98.
FEAST OF THE DORMITION OF THE MOST HOLY THEOTOKOS
(Lk 10:38–42, 11:27–28)

The grace of the Lord, my beloved brothers and sisters, has gathered us together again in our beloved birthplace; in this place, which our pious ancestors watered with their sweat, and many times with their blood; in this place, which bears in its soil their sacred relics; in this place, where honor has always been shown to the Virgin Mary, both in the magnificent temple before the fire—due to sins known only to God—but also in the temple reconstructed and decorated through the piety of the refugees. In this church today, therefore, the Virgin Mary has gathered us to honor her memory.

There is no sweeter name on the lips of the faithful Orthodox than the name of the Virgin Mary. One might even say that people invoke the Virgin Mary more than Christ Himself. The love, the tender love, that our Orthodox people have for the Virgin Mary is so deeply rooted, that it obliges us, my brothers and sisters, to think a little: Why this extraordinary honor to the Virgin Mary? Why has the person of the Virgin Mary been so exalted in the Church and in the consciences of the faithful, so that it has a central place in our hymnography, in our prayers, and above all in our hearts?

There are many reasons, my dear brothers and sisters, why the Virgin has this exceptional position. I will highlight only a few of these reasons. The first and most important is that the Virgin Mary is the person in whom all of God's love was revealed, and in whom the salvation of the world took place. Ever since man distanced himself from God and proclaimed himself a god, the path that humanity took was a path to destruction and death. Man now turned to the state of the animals. Man turned to the state of death and destruction. And there was no other way for him to be saved than for God Himself to intervene. But God did not want to intervene in a way that would abolish man's freedom. He wanted to intervene to save the world using human freedom, respecting human freedom. And this is why He sent His Son to become a man and save the world *through man's freedom.*

And how did man manifest his freedom? In the person of the Virgin Mary! The Virgin Mary was the one among all people who freely said "yes" to God; who reversed what Eve, the first woman, had done, by commanding Adam, the first man, to say "no" to God. And now comes another woman, the Virgin Mary, to freely say "yes" to God, so that God can with this "yes"—man's freedom—intervene and save man.

Not only does God intervene thanks to the "yes" of the Virgin Mary, but through her He gives His Son human flesh and blood. Therefore, God takes human flesh and human blood from the Virgin Mary and thus becomes a human being. Thus, there is no person, no human being in the whole world, in the whole creation, who is so closely united with God as is the Virgin Mary. This is the main reason why we honor the Virgin Mary so much. She is the one who gave herself, not only the free "yes" she said to God, but also her own flesh, so that the Son of God could become a man.

But there are other reasons, my brothers and sisters, why we honor the Virgin Mary so much. She revealed to us in her person what a mother means, what motherhood means. The mother is a holy person. Perhaps there is no holier person for man, because she gave her body so that man could be born and gave her whole soul and heart so that man could grow, be nourished, become a man. But human motherhood suffers from something, it has a big flaw. It is exclusive. A mother loves only her own children. There she puts all her weight, all of herself.

Of course, she can also love other children. But first and foremost, and often exclusively, she loves her children and doesn't care if the neighbor's children are unhappy or hungry or in need. First she will take care of her own child: this is her motherly instinct. However, the Virgin Mary shows us a different kind of motherhood. The Virgin Mary became the mother not only of her child, Christ, but also of the whole world. The mother of all people. She transcended the exclusivity that all mothers have. And there was only one way for her to do this: by taking in her heart all the pain of the Cross of her Son. She took upon herself this difficult fate, to give her child as a sacrifice so that the world could be saved. And thus she showed us a way that mothers should always keep in mind, as much as they can: to go beyond the exclusive love of their own children and to love as many children of the world and people outside of their own family as possible. The Virgin Mary is an example of a mother not only because she gave life and protection and upbringing to Christ, but also because she overcame this exclusive love for her child and reached the point where her love covered the whole world, becoming the mother of us all.

One more very important reason we honor the Virgin Mary is because she showed us what real faith means. "Faith" is a word we use very often, and we like to think that we are faithful. But, as the life of the Virgin Mary proves, faith means admitting that the humanly impossible is possible with God. To admit that God can do everything! And this is exactly what happened in the case of Panagia.[1] When the angel told her that she would give birth to the Son of God while she was a virgin, it would have been very logical for her to question this word of God, to consider it absurd and not to accept it. But the exact opposite happened! She says in response to the angel's proclamation: "Behold the maidservant of the Lord! Let it be to me according to your word" (Lk 1:38). This is true faith: to accept the humanly impossible as possible with God. There are times when nothing can convince us that God can change things, when we walk—according to our human powers—with certainty in one direction. Faith is that which leads us to say that, in defiance of all logic, in defiance of all human predictions, God can change everything. My dear brothers and sisters, our ancestors had this faith.

Those of us who were born in this place and spent some years here well remember that, if they hadn't had this faith—this faith that God can do what is humanly impossible—they wouldn't have

[1] A term of endearment for the Virgin Mary. Lit., "the most holy one."

been able to survive, let alone create the magnificent culture they created here, with their churches and schools, and especially the ethos that characterized them. This faith, which is exactly the kind of faith that Panagia displayed, led our ancestors to this place. And that is why, my brothers and sisters, as we gather here today surrounded by the grace of Panagia, there is perhaps nothing more important for us to think about than how we can imitate this faith of our ancestors. We live in a very rational age. People have now taken history into their own hands, they have taken their fate into their own hands, and they think that God is unnecessary. But we see the dead-ends in our civilization, modern man's dead ends, and we know that we need this faith more than ever.

My prayer for us all today, my brothers and sisters, is to imitate and continue the faith of our ancestors in this blessed place, and this faith will work its miracle so that this place will come alive again, and become a place of worship of God, like it used to be. Let us contribute as much as we can to modern man acquiring an ethos similar to that which our forefathers had.

I pray that the Virgin Mary will cover all of you and especially this blessed place, and that she will always account us worthy of honoring her and celebrating her memory. Amen!

Holy Church of the Dormition of the Virgin Mary, Katafygio, Kozani
August 15, 2003

99. FEAST OF THE DORMITION OF THE MOST HOLY THEOTOKOS

(Lk 10:38–42, 11:27–28)

*Blessed is the womb that bore You,
and the breasts which nursed You!*

Once again, my beloved brothers and sisters, the Lord has accounted us worthy to celebrate this great feast of our Orthodox faith, which is dedicated to the Dormition of our Panagia. There is no corner of the earth, where there are Orthodox believers, where there is not a temple dedicated to our Panagia. And in our place here, our forefathers, as their first concern, when they settled, had to build a temple in honor of our Panagia. It is this temple, which today brought us together. This temple suffered the fire and wrath of history, and was destroyed, but it was raised again due to the piety of the faithful citizens of Katafygio.

Thus, we have been accounted worthy once again today, in this temple, to honor our Panagia, to seek out her grace and, above all, to admire and worship the great mystery of our Most-Holy Theotokos. In one of the troparia hymns from Vespers last night, the hymnist uses the phrase «Oh! So impressive are your mysteries!» He stands ecstatic in front of the mystery of the Virgin and wonders and marvels, and he finds no way to explain it logically. For this reason, he reverently bows down and venerates the mystery.

The mysteries,[1] my beloved brothers and sisters, cannot be explained by logic; they are approached only by our reverence, respect, and veneration. We are used to explaining everything with logic, but this is the most irrational thing, because our entire existence is a mystery. The whole world is a mystery. And no matter how much man tries with science to explain this mystery, he

[1] Or "sacraments."

only manages to understand a few things. Most of it remains unexplained and mysterious. Why do we exist? Why does this world exist?

We live, my beloved brothers and sisters, in a mystery, and this is why man, from his first appearance on earth, found himself before this mystery and sought his Creator and worshiped Him. And our Panagia is a great mystery, inexplicable by human logic. Because she is the one who contained God Himself in her body, in this limited human body.

How is it possible for the uncontainable God to fit inside the womb of the Panagia—a woman, a human being? This great mystery is expressed by our Panagia. It is a mystery that is not explained by God's power, but by His love. Because, if this mystery takes place, and the uncontainable God fits inside a person, it is due to God's love. God doesn't want to show His power; He wants to show us His love. He wants to show us that He desires, really desires and seeks, to unite with us, for us to unite with Him, for what we call in the language of theology "deification" to take place—for us to become partakers of God's life and of His glory. And that is why He chose Panagia—to accomplish this great mystery and to unite God with man. This union of God with man is expressed by the mystery of the Panagia.

But this mystery, my dear brothers and sisters, could not be happen if man himself did not freely accept it. God does not want to impose this union with Him on man. Therefore, man, who in the persons of the first-created Adam and Eve denied union with God, now had to freely consent to it. And the path that the man had taken was anything but such a consent. It was a path that denied God and proclaimed man to be God; the union of God and man could thus never happen freely, if from within humanity itself some human being did not say "yes" to this union.

Humanity found such a human being in the person of the Virgin Mary. And so Panagia, my beloved brothers and sisters, represents us all: she is the representative of humanity who said "yes" to God's plan for the salvation of the world, who said "yes" to man's union with God. That is why we honor our Panagia, my beloved brothers and sisters.

We are accustomed to extolling her many admirable virtues and moral qualities. But if we call her more than simply a saint, it is not due to her moral qualities. It is due to the fact that, in her humility, she freely said "yes" to God's plan to unite man with God. Thus she opened the way to salvation. Here, then, is the great mystery of the Virgin Mary. It is she who makes possible the union of man with God freely, without impinging on man's freedom. And in this way our Panagia also becomes a mystery. We would call it the mystery of faith. Because faith is also a mystery. How is it possible for things to happen that are humanly impossible?

When the Virgin Mary faced the angel's invitation to accept the word that she would give birth to the Son of God, she faced something humanly impossible. And with her logic she should have said "But that's not possible, it's out of the question!" However, faith, which is precisely the acceptance of the humanly impossible, makes the Virgin Mary bow her head and say "Let it be as you said, as God said and wills it."

This is how the Virgin Mary, my beloved brothers and sisters, opens the way of faith to us. She is the first person who said that what is humanly impossible can become possible because of God. And if we follow in the footsteps of the Virgin Mary, we are called to have such faith that we do not consider anything impossible for God. The Virgin Mary, therefore, also opens this mystery of faith to us.

Another mystery is also revealed to us, my beloved brothers and sisters: the mystery of virginity. Her apolytikion hymn declares: "You gave birth yet preserved your virginity." This is also a mystery, a miraculous event, that the Virgin Mary conceived and gave birth to Christ while a virgin. "The laws of nature are overcome in you, O immaculate Virgin," our Church sings. The laws of nature are transcended, demonstrating, first, that God—Who made the laws as the Lawgiver—is capable of overcoming those same laws, of violating them. But more importantly, Panagia's virginity shows us that, in order for man to overcome death, to truly be saved and redeemed, he must overcome the laws of nature.

Our Church has always valued virginity as a great mystery. Not so much because it requires great sacrifices from man, but because the Virgin Mary demonstrated that this is the only way to overcome decay and death, since the way in which man is born includes decay and death from the beginning. We are born mortal and the way in which people are conceived and born inevitably leads to death. That is why the Lord is not born in this way; He is born of a virgin, to show that the way of true life, the way of transcending corruption and death, passes through this supernatural birth of man, the one that the Church gives us in our baptism, which causes us to be born again and which is the exact imitation of the birth of Christ.

Here, then, is where the Panagia becomes a symbol of virginity as well. That is why our monasteries—for example on Mt. Athos, which is the pinnacle of monastic life of our Orthodox faith—is under the shelter of Panagia. Panagia rules this place, because she is the symbol of virginity, of another way of life, a life that does not lead to death but to true life, to eternal life.

We could, my beloved brothers and sisters, mention many more aspects of the mystery of the Virgin Mary. But I don't want to tire you more.

It is quite a paradox, but the Virgin Mary and the mystery of virginity also reveal to us the mystery of motherhood, who is the true mother. The Virgin Mary is the one who kept in her heart, passed through her heart the dagger of great sorrow that awaited her in her life, because of the Passion and the Cross of her Son. She was a mother who experienced not only the joy of life but also the sadness and grief that motherhood can cause.

And something else, very important, our Virgin Mary reveals to us, as a mother now, that true motherhood is not only loving one's own child, but also being ready to sacrifice it for the sake of others. The true mother is the one who can become the mother of all children, just as the Virgin Mary became the mother of the whole world, accepting the pain of her Son's Passion to pass through her heart.

The Church honors, my beloved brothers and sisters, in the person of the Virgin Mary, this greatness of virginity combined with motherhood—this true virginity which combines absolute faith and surrender to the will of God, absolute faith in the physically impossible. And it honors her like nothing else.

She is the first by her Son and is always shown holding the Christ child, demonstrating in this way that her holiness is due to her deep relationship with Christ. And she is the one who covers all of us and intercedes for us in difficult times, she is the one who prays for all of us, and she is the one whom we all spontaneously invoke as soon as something unpleasant or dangerous happens to us. "My Panagia!" we all say. Panagia covers the whole world, my beloved brothers and sisters, without distinction, but especially covers those who honor her, such as our nation. She is the mother of our nation. She is the one who in difficulties encourages us to take up the cross, she is the one who never lets us get lost in the end. That is why temples have been built for her everywhere, but our Church in particular, our Orthodoxy, has erected temples to her in those places in which our nation—due to sins known only to God—had to go through difficulties and dangers to the point of annihilation.

One such place is our Pontus, from which so many Orthodox Greeks come who were forced to flee in the catastrophe of 1922 and to disperse to various parts of the earth, primarily here, in our Greece. At this moment, my dear brothers and sisters, after 88 years, the Divine Liturgy is being celebrated, as you will all know from the news. And the Ecumenical Patriarch is celebrating it for the first time in history. And one wonders, how did this happen? How was such a miracle possible? Certainly not without the intervention of the Virgin Mary. Look, the Virgin Mary let us believe for 88 years that it was all over. And she comes today and tells us: O you of little faith! Why did you doubt?

The end of history is in the hands of God, not in the hands of men. Never say that "it's all over!" Let us never put the power of the mighty of the earth above the power of God. This faith, my dear brothers and sisters, let us keep it in our hearts. This is true faith! Let's believe that nothing is over, nothing is impossible! And let us be sure that God will constantly give signs corresponding to our faith that indeed everything is possible.

So the Divine Liturgy at Panagia Soumela is possible today. Tomorrow, perhaps, in Pergamon. I have been humbled to celebrate the Liturgy there—again in a miraculous way—already for four or five years. We cannot attribute all this, my brothers and sisters, to simple circumstances. All this shows that above our head is the shelter of the Virgin Mary. And her grace does not leave us as a nation and as humanity. Panagia is the one who will be able to save humanity from all the ills that man heaps on himself.

Let us put all our hope in the Virgin Mary, my beloved brothers and sisters. Let us, the citizens of Katafygio, march ahead with this faith of our forefathers, passing it down to our children, to the newer generations, and let us be certain that our Panagia will always be with us. I pray for this from the bottom of my heart and I wish you all the grace, protection, and blessing of God.

Holy Church of the Dormition of the Virgin Mary, Katafygio, Kozani
August 15, 2010

100.
FEAST OF THE DORMITION OF THE MOST HOLY THEOTOKOS
(Lk 10:38–42, 11:27–28)

Blessed is the womb that bore You, and the breasts which nursed You!

Today, my beloved brothers and sisters, our holy Church honors the memory of the Dormition of the Most Holy Theotokos and Ever-Virgin Mary, our Panagia, in a solemn way throughout the world. There is no sweeter name on the lips of Orthodox believers than that of the Virgin Mary. We always call on her in the difficulties of our lives. Our Church honors her, commemorating her constantly in all its services and in the Divine Liturgy. Our Church depicts her with her holy icons next to the Lord. There is no other person who is honored by our Church among people as much as our Virgin Mary. And one wonders: why so much honor to the Virgin Mary?

Allow me, my beloved brothers and sisters, to offer a few thoughts on this question, because the Virgin Mary is not only an intercessor before our Lord, she who always rushes to help us in our difficulties, but she is also a guide in our spiritual life. It is she who shows us the way of salvation. The Virgin Mary, my beloved brothers and sisters, is a great mystery; a mystery comparable to that of the incarnation of the Son and Word of God; a great mystery which has so many sides that we could not exhaust them all in a simple sermon. We will highlight only some of these aspects of this great mystery called Panagia.

The Virgin Mary is, my beloved brothers and sisters, *the revelation of the great mystery of God's love for the world*. There is no greater mystery than that God created the world, without needing its existence, and He loves it so much that He wants to take it into His own life, to make it a sharer of His life and blessedness. This great mystery was called, by the Providence of God, to be accomplished by our Virgin Mary. This mystery meant that God would take man into His life, into His very existence. And not only that, but He took within Himself all of creation together with man, who is the crown of creation. In order to do this, God chose this humble daughter, the Virgin Mary, who was called to give flesh and blood to the Son of God, so that the Son of God Himself could be born from her and thus God could unite man with Him and all creation with Him. How are we to conceive of this mystery, my brothers and sisters? It surpasses human thought. "The laws of nature are overcome in you, O immaculate Virgin," sings the Church today. How can man grasp this mystery? Not only because it is a great miracle, but because it shows, as I said, the infinite love of God. No one can conceive, my brothers and sisters, the magnitude of God's love for us. Looking at our Panagia, she understands how God loves us. This is one aspect of the great mystery called Panagia. She is the one who performed, on behalf of all of us, for the whole world, the mystery of God's love. She became the link to unite God with man and the world.

And in this way, another great mystery is revealed to us by the person of the Virgin Mary: *the mystery of holiness*. It is no coincidence that the Virgin Mary was called Panagia by the faithful. The word "saint" was not enough. A bigger word had to be found. Something that surpasses even the word "holiness." And the word "Panagia" was found. That is, "all holiness," concentrated in her person. Why is this? What is it that makes Panagia to be the concentration of all holiness? It is, my brothers and sisters, first of all, as I told you, that the Virgin Mary shows us the path to holiness. And this path was her humility and her obedience to God's will. The path of holiness goes through humility and obedience to God's will, through the observance of God's commandments. This obedience is demonstrated by the Virgin Mary's response to says to the Archangel, "Behold the maidservant of the Lord! Let it be to me according to your word" (Lk 1:38). When we say "may the will of God be done," then the path to holiness opens.

All the saints of the Church followed and are following this path. From humility, from obedience to His will, one starts to reach God. However, it is not enough to start down this path to holiness if one does not reach holiness. And no one can reach holiness as a human being. Holiness is an attribute of God alone. "One is holy, One is Lord."

There is no one holy by nature, except God alone. Therefore, in order to reach holiness, one must unite with God. To surrender yourself to God and let the grace of God come upon you. Then, when man is united with the Holy God, he too acquires holiness. Holiness does not come either with our good deeds or with our efforts or with our practice. It only comes as a gift from God when we unite with him. And the Virgin Mary, my beloved brothers and sisters, united with God more than any other human being, because, as I told you, she lent her human nature, her flesh, her blood, so that God could become man. This is why all holiness is concentrated in her person. There is no one among human beings who embodies holiness like the Virgin Mary.

And the Virgin Mary reveals another mystery to us: *the mystery of faith*. Yes, my brothers and sisters, faith is a mystery. Because faith, at its core, is to accept the humanly impossible as possible. Faith calls us to accept as possible what is completely humanly impossible, what logically no one can accept. And who else experienced this more than Panagia? The Archangel comes and tells her that she will become the mother of God. How is it possible to believe this? That is the great moment of faith, which the Virgin Mary expresses by saying "How is this possible?" Of course, she marvels at this, but she says, if God so wills, it can happen. "For where God so wills, the order of nature is overcome," our Church sings. Can we, my beloved brothers and sisters, imitate our Virgin Mary in this great mystery called faith? Can we, when everything indicates that something cannot be done—that it is humanly impossible to do it—believe that God can make it possible? Then, my beloved, we have faith. Faith is tested in these difficulties of life, in which there is no human hope. But we are called to believe, despite this, that it is possible to make the humanly impossible a reality. So, then, the Virgin Mary reveals to us what faith is.

And she also reveals to us, my beloved brothers and sisters, another mystery: *the mystery of freedom*. Yes, my brothers and sisters, freedom is a concept that man has misunderstood, ever since the first man decided to express his freedom by saying "no" to God. Free, then, is he who can say "yes" or "no" to God. But the result of the freedom of "no" is death; it is destruction. The Virgin Mary reveals to us that the one who is truly free is the one who says "yes" to God. We think that obedience, "yes", is a deprivation of freedom. No. Obedience, the "yes", when it comes freely from within us, and no one forces us to say it, is freedom in all its glory. So in Panagia, we see what it means to be free. Free is he who freely surrenders himself to obedience to God and he who, instead of saying "no," prefers to say "yes." The world cannot comprehend this great mystery of freedom, my brothers and sisters, but it is precisely what our Virgin Mary reveals to us.

And finally, our Virgin Mary reveals to us another great mystery: *the mystery of virginity and motherhood*. Yes, the Virgin Mary is both Virgin and Mother. She is a Virgin because she brings the Son of God into the world as a man, in a way that does not go through the path that leads to decay and death—that is, the path by which the human race reproduces itself after the fall. This path includes life and death together. We are thus born mortal. We live, and from the moment we are born we die at the same time. So this is not the path that leads to real life; it is a road that God allowed after the fall of man. But the real path is that of virginity, which only a few can follow; the Virgin Mary, through her grace, leads the way down a difficult and nearly impassable path. That is why the Virgin Mary is also the guardian of the monks, those who struggle to live this life of virginity. But, paradoxically, the Virgin Mary is at the same time the model of the mother, of motherhood, because she shows us that motherhood also needs some healing after the fall of man. What about motherhood? The mother loves her child exclusively, often at the expense of other children. She cannot go beyond the love for her child and love equally all other children and the whole world. This is a weakness of natural motherhood. The Virgin Mary comes to show us that real motherhood can overcome this exclusivity and bring the mother to such a state that she sees all the children of the world as her own. The Virgin Mary saw in the person of her Son the one who took upon Himself the whole fate of the world, of all people, and thus she became the Mother of the whole world. And that is why she covers us with her love, she covers the whole world. This transcendence of the exclusivity of the family is the path that our Virgin Mary blazes. It is also a difficult road, but it is the only one that will lead us to our salvation.

My beloved brothers and sisters, who can describe this great mystery called Panagia? I have touched on only a few aspects. All we can do is venerate this mystery. To venerate our Virgin Mary, to accept her protection and to believe that because she loved her Son, who loved the whole world, she loves us all and covers us all with her grace. She is the Theotokos, "ever vigilant in intercession."[1] She is the one who does not sleep, who never interrupts her prayer for us. Let us, therefore, my brothers and sisters, take refuge in her grace, with confidence. She understands us, because she is human. She knows what human pain means, since she experienced it. And so our Virgin Mary can be close to us and take our prayers to God.

Today, my dear brothers and sisters, we are called to honor this great mystery with all our hearts. And with all our willingness to follow the path that she blazed, so that we too, as far as possible, can participate in the holiness that she has manifested to an absolute degree. May the Virgin Mary be the intercessor and protector of everyone and the whole world, brothers and sisters. Amen.

In the Holy Monastery of Saint John the Baptist, Essex, England
August 15, 2014

[1] Kontakion of the feast.

101.

FEAST OF THE DORMITION OF THE MOST HOLY THEOTOKOS

(Lk 10:38–42, 11:27–28)

Blessed is the womb that bore You,
and the breasts which nursed You!

The Lord has accounted us worthy, my beloved brothers and sisters, to celebrate the memory of His Most Holy Mother, our Panagia, and to honor her to the best of our abilities. Panagia, who is "higher than the heavens and much purer than the radiance of the sun,"[1] is situated next to the Lord and enjoys His Glory. We are called today to glorify and honor her, despite our weakness, and despite our lack of holiness. In spite of that, God has accounted us worthy today to honor and celebrate her. At the same time, let's ask her to intercede for us to the Lord, because she knows full well our human weakness and human problems. Being next to Christ constantly, she is our greatest intercessor. But at the same time, my beloved brothers and sisters, the Virgin Mary also reveals to us great truths, which deserve our attention, and to which I now turn.

The Virgin Mary first reveals to us the great *mystery of holiness*. What is holiness? The Virgin Mary is full of virtues, she is as pure as the sun, she is holy in this sense more than all other people, because she was cleansed by the Holy Spirit when he visited her on the day of the Annunciation, to prepare her to become a vessel for the coming into the world of the Son and Word of God. Therefore, our Virgin Mary is holy, because she has all the virtues that man can imagine. But we can find many virtues in people who have nothing to do with Christ. And if holiness is simply our virtues, then something is not right. Holiness is not

[1] Megalynarion of the Dormition.

simply the totality of our virtues. It is something more. Because, quite literally, only God is holy. He is the only Holy One. Consequently, perfect holiness cannot be found in people. But people's holiness appears when the person is as close as possible to God, the only Holy One. Thus holiness, which is an attribute of God alone, also becomes our attribute through this communion with God. We draw holiness from this communion and that is why people's holiness always lags behind the holiness of God. However, our Virgin Mary did not simply derive her holiness from God, but took it within herself, within her own existence and in her own body, with the Incarnation of the Son and Word of God. She therefore became a sharer of God's holiness, to the fullest extent that man can share. And she shows us the way, because the closer we are to God, the more power we draw from God's holiness. Holiness is not something we can achieve ourselves. It is something that God gives us by His grace, and that is why holiness requires sanctification, that is, being united with God. That is why, my beloved brothers and sisters, our Church offers us the possibility not only to cultivate the virtues, as many as we can, but also to be sanctified, to unite with Christ, especially through the Eucharist, when we receive the body and the blood of Christ. Then, my beloved brothers and sisters, sanctification makes us also partakers of God's holiness. When in the Divine Liturgy we say "the holy things for holy people of God" shortly before communion, we are saying that we humans can participate and share in the holiness of God, by partaking of the body and blood of Christ. However, the response that the people give when the priest says "the holy things for holy people of God" is very important. The response is: "One is Holy, one is Lord, Jesus Christ." That is where we draw holiness from. And the Virgin Mary is most holy, in a superlative degree holy, precisely because she is in the closest relationship with the only Holy One, who is God and Christ.

So, the Virgin Mary reveals holiness to us, but she also reveals other important things, such as *faith*. What is faith, my beloved brothers and sisters? We often think that faith is knowing the doctrines of the Church, our faith, confessing it, etc. But faith, as we see it in the person of the Virgin Mary, is something different. It is to accept that the humanly impossible is possible with God. When the Virgin received the visit from the Archangel, and he told her that she would give birth to the Son of God, she was faced with an invitation to believe and accept the humanly impossible. How is it possible for a human to give birth to the Son of God? She bowed her head, however, and accepted it and believed it, because God assured it.

Our life, my dear brothers and sisters, is full of trials, to the point where we often wonder: "Where is God? Why did He leave us?" It is precisely in those moments that our faith is tested. To believe that God is present, even in His absence, and that He is present in our trials, and that He can, with His power and grace, allow us to overcome every trial and difficulty. Faith, then, in the person of the Virgin Mary, acquires its true meaning.

However, the Virgin Mary reveals something else to us. She reveals to us what *freedom* means. This freedom is something that we use very often to show and express our will. We are free to do what we want. And when we do what we want, we say that we exercise our freedom. The Virgin Mary herself said: "Behold the maidservant of the Lord! Let it be to me according to your word" (Lk 1:38), may God's will be done. So, when we free ourselves from our own will, then we are truly free. This freedom is revealed to us by the Virgin Mary. And for this reason, real freedom is found in humility, not in persevering and doing our own will. Rather we must say like the Lord Himself in Gethsemane: "not as I will, but as You will" (Mt 26:39)—we must surrender our will to the will of God and also often to the will of our fellow human beings. And in this way we can truly be free. Man's greatest slavery is to his own will. And when his own will is broken, then he is truly freed.

The Virgin Mary reveals to us, my brothers and sisters, many more things. I won't bore you, I won't mention them all, because there are many more. I will only mention, lastly, the great mystery that the Virgin Mary reveals, the *mystery of motherhood* and, at the same time, of *virginity*. It is a great mystery. Virginity meets motherhood in the person of the Virgin Mary. This is because motherhood, as we live it in our lives, is something that needs healing. Certainly, it is a blessing from God that there is a mother who brings children into the world, and she should be honored for this reason. But let's not forget that the children that motherhood brings into the world are mortal, children who, biologically, will die. And they die, biologically, all the time. We die from the moment we are born. So motherhood needs healing, so that this dimension of death, of mortality, disappears. And this is precisely the cure offered by virginity.

Virginity, therefore, is a way to heal motherhood from its negative side and to turn towards true and eternal motherhood. That is why the Virgin Mary brought Christ into the world as a virgin. Because if she brought Christ into the world in the same way that all mothers bring their children, then He would perpetuate mortality, which comes through our biological birth. And the Virgin Mary, with her virginity, showed us that there is motherhood which is not the bearer of death. And for this reason, it shows us that even biological mothers must always keep in mind that motherhood, which is limited to the children we bring into the world, must be opened up to bring our love to all children, to all people. Panagia, because she is both a virgin and a mother, can be—and is—the mother of the whole world. With virginity, therefore, we do not deny motherhood, but we give it a wider dimension, so that it embraces the whole world. To escape from the exclusivity of our own family, of our own children, and to become a mother that will care for and cover with love the whole world, all the children of the world and all people. That is why our Virgin Mary is a Virgin, but also at the same time the Mother of not just a small family, but of the whole world. Her virginity gave her the ability to embrace all people as a mother. It is not easy, my dear brothers and sisters, to exhaust all that the Virgin Mary, whom we honor today, reveals to us. I am limiting myself to what I told you and I invite you all to pay attention to them as teachings that our Virgin Mary gives us. So let's honor her not only with our veneration but also with our discipleship under her. She is a great teacher, who directs our life on the right path.

I pray, my beloved brothers and sisters, that the Virgin Mary, who intercedes with God for all of us, for the whole world, grants us, by her grace, her protection in our lives, but also teaches us to follow her example and the great truths that she reveals to us, and in this way to become her disciples and disciples of our Lord and God Jesus Christ. Amen.

In the Holy Monastery of Saint John the Baptist, Essex, England
August 15, 2016

Afterword

The publication of *101 Sermons* of the late Metropolitan of Pergamon John (Zizioulas) sheds a whole new light on his character and theology. As St. Gregory the Theologian in his sermons showed all the depth of theology that is confirmed in the holy mysteries, so also Metropolitan John confirmed his theology in his liturgical homilies. In this book we meet a shepherd who, with pastoral sensibility, humility, and attention to the needs of his flock, softens and nourishes their hearts. His *logos* was deprived of rhetorical excursus into non-ecclesial thematics and he always used the sermon with a warning: "The sermon must adapt to the eschatological atmosphere and not transpose us from the Kingdom of God to here on earth." For him, place, time, matter, colors, speech, smell, hearing, etc.—everything in the Liturgy witnesses an iconic symbolism that is not a static tableau but a movement in time, containing the historical time of salvation within it. For this reason, he wanted to see the Church during the Eucharist as bathed in light and adorned with all available splendor.

Although every Liturgy is *prima facie* identical, everybody would be enthused by the Metropolitan's exuded eucharistic ethos and style, his movements, vestments, and his gaze. As Rowan Williams noted, "to see him serving the Divine Liturgy was invariably to see exactly what that main thing was for him: the manifestation in Christ, present and coming, of what we hope for in ourselves, our related and interwoven selves, and in our interwoven world, crying out for reconciliation." For this reason, the members of the community couldn't take their eyes off him. But he, too, would regularly fix the congregants with a curious and communicative look—a mysterious, inexplicable, deep, and unfathomable gaze. After the dismissal and the distribution of the antidoron to the whole congregation, he would enjoy the time with everyone, by saying: "I cannot commune with God 'vertically,' in the absence of people, I only find God through others, I thirst for people, I am a *horizontal* person." Maybe because of this personal "horizontalism," Metropolitan John used to preach to the flock, believing that the pious people, who participate in the Eucharist, are a "royal priesthood" (1 Pet 2:9; cf. Rev 5:10) who faithfully keep and maintain the Tradition. I cite one passage from his essay.

> Certainly there are still people—and many of them—who love the Church's feasts and flock to celebrate them, as well as little old ladies—fortunately, there are still plenty of these too—who kiss priests' hands, touch their vestments to receive grace, kiss the icons and holy relics with a faith that is almost "magical," and generally preserve the traditions with piety. If they do not fall victim to wily clerics, these people are the only leaven, the little leaven available to us to preserve and restore iconic symbolism, purifying it from such magical tendencies as may exist.

Metropolitan John did not treat the liturgical space (the architectural formation and internal organization) as scenery for an individual's search for metaphysical security. To reawaken within the Orthodox a true sense of the Eucharistic offering as something authentic, genuine, and truthful—a chaste fruit of a community experiencing Resurrection—he was deeply interested in seeing liturgical "dramaturgy" as an iconic representation of the Kingdom. To achieve this iconic ideal, he kept reminding the hierarchy of the correct understanding of the liturgical event and all aesthetic expressions embellishing the worship: melody, iconography, hymnography, lighting, reading and chanting, sermon. Liturgical typicon does not aim to captivate the individual with psychological appeals or to subordinate it emotionally. Rather, it seeks to include people in a liberated space-time where they will acquire freedom from individualistic priorities and become acquainted with the resurrected Christ through communion with the Spirit.

The editor and the publisher are grateful to The Artos Zois publishing house in Athens and Mr. Stavros Zoumboulakis for permission to publish an excellent English translation by Fr. Gregory Edwards of Metropolitan John' *101 Sermons*.

Los Angeles, July 2023 — *Bishop Maxim of Western America*

Biographical Note

John D. Zizioulas (1931-2023) was a modern theologian and former Metropolitan of Pergamon, in the Ecumenical Patriarchate of Constantinople. He was born in Greece, January 10, 1931. He began his studies at the University of Thessaloniki, but received his undergraduate degree in theology from the University of Athens in 1955, where he also later received a degree of Doctor of Theology.

Metropolitan John's education included a period of study under the Eastern Orthodox theologian Father Georges Florovsky at Harvard Divinity School. He received his M.T.S. at Harvard in 1956 and was a Fellow at Dumbarton Oaks Center for Byzantine Studies. He received a doctorate in theology from the University of Athens in 1965. His doctoral thesis on the bishop in the early Church was recently published in English as *Eucharist, Bishop, Church: The Unity of the Church in the Divine Eucharist and the Bishop During the First Three Centuries* (Brookline, MA: Holy Cross Orthodox Press, 2001). Somewhat later, he taught theology at the University of Edinburgh for a period, before becoming Professor of Systematic Theology at the University of Glasgow, where he held a personal chair in systematic theology for some fourteen years. In addition, he went on to be Visiting Professor at the University of Geneva, King's College London, and the Gregorian University, Rome. He was also a part-time professor at the University of Thessaloniki.

He was consecrated as a bishop on June 22, 1986, and named Metropolitan of Pergamon. He has represented the Ecumenical Patriarchate on international Church bodies for many years. Metropolitan John was a member of the committees for dialogue with the Roman Catholic Church, and with the Anglican Church, and was Secretary of Faith and Order at the World Council of Churches in Geneva, where he gradually came to be recognized as one of the most influential Orthodox theologians of our times. He departed in peace on February 2, 2023.

His ecumenical involvement has led him to publish a number of articles and studies in various periodicals. Some of his books are *L'Être ecclésial* (Paris: Labor et Fides, 1981), *Being as Communion: Studies in Personhood and the Church* (Crestwood, NY: St. Vladimir's Seminary Press, 1985), *Communion and Otherness* (London: T&T Clark, 2006), *Lectures in Christian Dogmatics* (London: T&T Clark, 2009), *The One and the Many* (Los Angeles: Sebastian Press, 2011), *The Eucharistic Communion and the World* (London: T&T Clark, 2011), *Receive One Another: 101 Sermons* (Los Angeles: Sebastian Press, 2023), *Remembering the Future: Toward an Eschatological Ontology* (Los Angeles: Sebastian Press, 2023).

HERE ENDS THE BOOK, "RECEIVE ONE ANOTHER: 101 SERMONS" BY JOHN D. ZIZIOULAS, METROPOLITAN OF PERGAMON, EDITED BY BISHOP MAXIM VASILJEVIC; THIS EDITION IS LIMITED TO 1000 COPIES, IN THE CONTEMPORARY CHRISTIAN THOUGHT SERIES, NUMBER 82, PRINTED AT THE INTERKLIMA-GRAFIKA PRESS IN VRNJCI, SERBIA, OWNED BY KYR LJUBISA CEPERKOVIC, REALIZED BY SEBASTIAN PRESS IN LOS ANGELES, CA, AND FINISHED ON THE 1TH DAY OF AUGUST IN THE YEAR OF THE LORD 2023.